Documents of
American Democracy

Documents of American Democracy

A Collection of Essential Works

Edited by ROGER L. KEMP

McFarland & Company, Inc., Publishers
Jefferson, North Carolina, and London

LIBRARY OF CONGRESS CATALOGUING-IN-PUBLICATION DATA

Documents of American democracy : a collection of
essential works / edited by Roger L. Kemp.
p.   cm.
Includes bibliographical references and index.

ISBN 978-0-7864-4210-2
softcover: 50# alkaline paper ∞

1. United States — Politics and government.   2. United States —
Politics and government — Sources.   I. Kemp, Roger L.
JK31.D63   2010
973 — dc22   2010005417

British Library cataloguing data are available

Front cover images ©2010 Shutterstock

Manufactured in the United States of America

*McFarland & Company, Inc., Publishers
Box 611, Jefferson, North Carolina 28640
www.mcfarlandpub.com*

To Anika,
the best and the brightest

Acknowledgments

Grateful acknowledgment is made to the following organizations for granting permission, and making the resources available, for the materials contained in this volume.

American Democracy Project
Connecticut Consortium for Law & Citizenship Education, Inc.
Connecticut State Library
The Academy of Political Science
ThinkQuest Education Foundation
U. S. National Archives and Records Administration
United Kingdom Parliamentary Archives
Yale University

Table of Contents

Section IV. Territory

Section V. The Future

Appendices

Preface

American citizens have a lot to be proud of! They live in one of the oldest democratic forms of government in the world, and this form of government has helped create a society in which citizens are free to get involved in the political process. Citizens can vote, run for political office, endorse incumbents, promote new public office seekers, or merely back other people who do so. Also, between elections citizens are free to attend public meetings, many of which are required by law, speak about their policy and program preferences at these meetings, write letters to the editor, and even organize others to get involved in "their" political agenda.

The involvement of citizens in the American political process has changed over the years. For many years, citizens believed in *Jacksonian Democracy*, whereby they would get directly involved in the political process by attending meetings, advocating for pieces of legislation, or trying to change or invalidate legislation that they did not like. This political activism on the part of citizens primarily took place before the era of two income families, before there came to be little time for this type of political involvement. Democracy in America was founded on the principle of active political involvement on the part of its citizens.

Most adult households now have both parents working, and family time is limited to a few hours in the evenings after work. Many citizens nowadays merely elect their political representatives, and hold them accountable at voting time from election to election. This evolving type of democratic involvement on the part of citizens is called *Jeffersonian Democracy*. Many citizens have justified this type of political involvement by acknowledging that elections and voting give the common person a chance to elect the uncommon person to represent them. Under this evolving practice, the typical involvement of many citizens in the political process is merely voting at election time.

The political involvement of many Americans in years past included picketing, protesting, marching, signing petitions, attending public meetings, and publicly debating the issues. Today Americans may wear a political button, display a bumper sticker on their car, or place a candidate's sign in their front yard. Many citizens may also contribute financially to political campaigns. Because of other social and economic commitments, American citizens have evolved throughout history from engaging in very active political involvement to more passive political activities.

Everyone will agree that there is no perfect form of government, and the best form is one that has evolved and changed over time to best serve its citizens. Most citizens today take their form of government for granted. After all, it is the only form of government they have ever known. While history is provided to students in high school and college, little time is spent focusing on how our country's democratic form of government was established and, most importantly, how it has evolved over time to become one of the most respected national governments in the world. Many history classes start with the landing of the Pilgrims, and never cover the background and mind-set of the early settlers from the Kingdom of England. They had a form of government that greatly influenced and impacted the early settlers in the New World.

This volume focuses on the basics of the formation of America's democracy, how the country expanded, and the changes that have taken place over the years through legislation, constitutional amendments, supreme court decisions, and the impact of the evolution of our culture over time on our political processes. Many of the political changes to our democracy, and its form of government, resulted over time in response to changing citizen values-and expectations. As American society evolved, so did many aspects of its democracy. These changes have manifested themselves in every changing political process, new and revised laws and regulations, as well as the magnitude and type of services provided by its governments.

For ease of reference, this volume is divided into five sections. The first section introduces the reader to the subject of American democracy. The second section highlights the foundation of our form of government, which was influenced by King John as well as the Parliament of England. Section three, and the longest, contains the core documents that established our democratic form of government. Section four focuses on the territorial expansion of the United States, from the establishment of the colonies to a country with fifty states. The final section examines the future of democracy, as well as its worldwide implications. Several appendices are also included to provide the reader with a greater understanding of the complex and dynamic field of America's democracy.

Based upon this background information, and the conceptual schema developed to assemble and present this material, the five primary sections of this volume are highlighted and briefly examined below.

Introduction

This chapter provides the reader with an introduction to the field of American democracy. It examines the origins of democracy in the world, the path leading to modern democracy, and democracy in the United States. The concluding portion of the chapter is an overview of theories of government. This chapter will give the reader insight into the origins of the history of democracy, its world-wide implications, and provide the foundation upon which to examine and understand the subsequent sections of this volume.

The Foundation

Our founding fathers, when they landed in the New World, had historical precedent for the requirements of government, as well as the liberties that should be given to citizens. The Pilgrims were from the Kingdom of England, and they had knowledge of several documents that formed the basis of the government in their homeland, as well as the freedoms and rights granted to its citizens. The documents examined in this section, which provide the foundation for America's democracy, are highlighted below.

- The *Magna Carta*, which was sealed by King John of England on June 15, 1215. This document is the first one of its kind in England, as well as the rest of the world, to acknowledge the freedoms and rights of citizens.
- The *Petition of Right*, which was approved by the Parliament of England on May 27, 1628. This was the first document approved by the Parliament of England that set forth and acknowledged the rights and liberties of citizens in the American colonies.

• The English *Bill of Rights*, which was approved by the Parliament of England on December 16, 1689. This document set forth the rights and liberties of citizens, and residents from other countries, and required for the Crown to seek the consent of the Parliament before taking certain actions impacting citizens.

The Core Documents

Various documents helped form America's democratic form of government, starting with those created by the Pilgrims soon after their landing in an unfamiliar part of the world far from their home. The original colonists were loyal to England, and it took a war to emancipate the colonies and their residents, the colonists, from the government of their homeland. During this time colonies emerged, citizens were elected to hold public office, wars were fought, treaties were negotiated, and even amendments were made to the basic documents of government over the years. The documents examined in this section include:

• The *Mayflower Compact*, which was signed by the Pilgrims of the New World on November 21, 1620. The first document in the New World was signed to preserve order and establish rules for self-governance.
• The *Fundamental Orders of Connecticut*, which were approved by the Colony Council on January 14, 1639. This document is considered the first written constitution establishing a formal government in the New World.
• The *Declaration and Resolves of the First Continental Congress*, which were approved by the Continental Congress on October 14, 1774. This document was created to make the King and Parliament of England officially aware of the grievances of the colonies.
• The *Declaration of the Causes and Necessity of Taking Up Arms*, which was approved by the Continental Congress on July 6, 1775. This document was prepared to explain why the Thirteen Colonies had taken up arms against England in a battle that was later called the American Revolution.
• The *Virginia Declaration of Rights*, which was approved by the House of Burgesses on June 12, 1776. This document reflects the first declaration of the rights of citizens by a colony in the New World.
• The *Declaration of Independence*, which was approved by the Continental Congress on July 4, 1776. This document is the product of the early days of the Revolutionary War, and officially declared the independence of the American colonies from Great Britain.
• The *Constitution of Massachusetts*, which was approved by the State Constitutional Convention Representatives on June 15, 1780. This document is the oldest functioning written constitution in continuous use by any government in the world.
• The *Articles of Confederation*, which were approved by the Congress of the Confederation on March 1, 1781. This document is historically recognized as the first constitution of the United States of America.
• The *Constitution of the United States*, which was approved by the Congress of the Confederation on September 17, 1787. The original constitution is known as the supreme law of the United States. It provides the foundation, and source of legal authority, as well as built-in checks-and-balances, for the United States and its federal government.
• The *Bill of Rights*, which was approved by the United States Congress on December 15, 1791. This document reflects the first ten amendments to the United States Constitution. While introduced by James Madison in the First United States Congress in 1789, they were not effective until approved by three-fourths of the states two years later.
• The *Other Amendments to the Constitution*

of the United States, which were approved by the United States Congress between February 7, 1795 and May 7, 1992. The *Constitution of the United States* contains an amendment process. This document includes those amendments made to the Constitution since the passage of the Bill of Rights in 1791.

- The *Civil Rights Act*, which was approved by the United States Congress on July 2, 1964. This document mandated an enforcement process to prevent discrimination in voting, the use of public housing, public education, and federally assisted programs.
- The *Voting Rights Act*, which was approved by the United States Congress on August 6, 1965. This document reflects the most significant statutory change in the relationship between the federal and state governments in the area of voting since the Civil War.

Territory

The nation started with the English Colony of Roanoke, which was established in 1585. This colony ceased to exist as the residents either went their own way to avoid the aboriginal people, and to find suitable farmland to grow food. The Virginia Company of Plymouth, England, was granted rights to land in what became the Colony of Virginia. The people they brought over lived in a settlement subsequently called Jamestown. The first citizens not involved in a private venture such as the Virginia Company were the Pilgrims, who landed in what later became known as the Colony of Massachusetts. The American War of Independence ultimately led to the recognition of the original 13 colonies in the New World. What was Colonial America ultimately became the United States of America, which now consists of 50 states. The documents included within relative to the territorial formation of America are listed below.

- The *Treaty of Paris*, which was approved by the Congress of the Confederation on September 3, 1783. This document led to the recognition of the original 13 colonies in the New World.
- The *Land Ordinance*, which was approved by the Congress of the Confederation on May 20, 1785. This document led to the westward expansion of the original colonies.
- The *Northwest Ordinance*, which was approved by the Congress of the Confederation on July 13, 1787, and led to the ultimate colonization of the land northwest of the Ohio River.
- The *Louisiana Purchase Treaty*, which was approved by the United States Congress on April 30, 1803. This document led to the expansion of the nation to the south and southwest of the original Thirteen Colonies.
- The *Transcontinental Treaty*, approved by the United States Congress on February 22, 1819. This document led to the expansion of the nation in parts of what would later be called the state of Florida.
- The *Resolution for the Annexation of Texas*, which was approved by the United States Congress on March 1, 1845. This document approved the voluntary annexation for the Republic of Texas to become a part of the United States of America.
- The *Oregon Treaty*, which was approved by the United States Congress on June 15, 1846. This document between the United Kingdom of Great Britain and Ireland settled the border dispute for what was then known as Oregon Country, which is located in the northwest section of the United States.
- The *Treaty of Guadalupe Hidalgo*, which was approved by the United States Congress on February 22, 1848. This document gave the United States legal rights to southwestern and western portions of the United States.
- The *Gadsden Purchase Treaty*, which was

approved by the United States Congress on December 30, 1853. This document settled the ongoing border dispute between the United States and Mexico in the territory that now forms the states of Arizona and New Mexico.

- The *Alaska Treaty*, which was approved by the United States Congress on March 30, 1867. This document approved the transfer of the Territory of Alaska from Russia to the United States of America.
- The *Hawaii Resolution*, which was approved by the United States Congress on July 7, 1898. This document approved the annexation of the Hawaiian Islands as a territory, and granted legal possession of this area to the United States of America.

The Future

The final chapter of this volume, *The Future of Democracy*, examines the impact that democracy has had on the United States of America, as well as the goal of its government to advance freedom and democracy throughout the world over the years. The author discusses the history of America's democracy, including past problems and threats, and goes on to examine international threats facing our nation and its citizens, as well as their form of government. The author states that the underlying theme of American history has been the willingness of our government, as influenced by its politicians, to defend our security and our interests in ways that, in the long run, have led to the expansion of democratic values and institutions. He concludes by stating that America, and its form of government, is looked upon as a model to emulate by citizens of other countries throughout the world.

Appendices

Many hours were spent researching the valuable resource materials contained in this volume. Since this volume focuses on docu-

ments, every effort was made to provide background information for the reader to become more familiar with the history of America's democratic form of governance. To this end, some thirteen appendices are included to further examine the formation of the Thirteen Colonies, their colonial expansion, the number of states in the United States, the Presidents of the United States, and formal Declarations of War approved by the U. S. Congress. Other appendices include the number of government units in America, the voting rights history that has evolved in the United States, and major decisions by the Supreme Court throughout our history. Also included is a listing of abbreviations and acronyms, a glossary of terms, and a listing of state libraries. Finally, and of great value, are a listing of important national resources and a bibliography of books and periodicals in this field. The resource materials contained in the appendices are briefly examined below.

- *Original Thirteen British Colonies*—Listed by the name of the colony, the year each was founded, as well as the name of the founder.
- *States and Their Dates of Admission to the Union*— Each state is listed in rank order based on the date of its admission to the United States, along with the date on which each state was admitted to the Union.
- *Presidents of the United States*— Listed by the name of each president, their number of years in office, and their political party affiliation.
- *Formal Declarations of War by the United States*— Listed by the name given to each war, the countries we fought against in each war, who was president at the time that each declaration was approved, and the name and date of the document that concluded each war.
- *Number of Governmental Units in the United States*— Listed categorically for the

federal, state, and local governments. The number of units is shown for 1962 and 2007, along with the changes that have taken place over the years in each category.

- *United States Voting Rights History*— Voting rights, or the expansion of them, are listed by year, the document approved and/or action taken, and the legal impact of the law or court decision that was made to grant or acquire them.
- *Major Cases in Supreme Court History*— Listed by the name of each major court case, the year in which each case was decided, and a summary of the legal impact of the court decision made.
- *Local Government Historical Document*— The first local government in the American colonies to declare its independence from Great Britain was Mecklenburg County, North Carolina, on May 20, 1775. Because of its significance, this document is shown in its entirety.
- *Abbreviations and Acronyms*— Numerous abbreviations and acronyms are listed that relate to American democracy and the federal government.
- *Glossary*— A list of words and terms that relate to American democracy and our federal government.
- *State Library Resource Directory*— The public library for each state is listed in alphabetical order by state. Each library has a wealth of information about the history of the state, as well as our federal government.
- *National Resource Directory*— This directory reflects organizations and associations listed categorically for the public, nonprofit, and educational sectors. The listings in each category are shown in alphabetical order.

- *Bibliography*— Books that relate to America's democracy and form of government and related subjects. A list of periodicals that relate to America's democracy and form of government and related subjects, is included in the bibliography.

I would like to emphasize that many volumes that contain important documents of government and governance do not include the history that led to their preparation, consideration, and approval. In some cases, citizens have been involved in petition signing, protest marches, political demonstrations, and even battles and wars, such as when the colonies were granted their independence. For example, it is common knowledge that the civil rights movement in the early 1960s and the activities that took place throughout the nation during this time led to the adoption of the Civil Rights Act of 1964. For this reason, every document in this volume contains a section titled "The History" that precedes that portion of the chapter titled "The Document." The purpose of this format is to place every document in its proper historical and political context at the time of its approval.

Lastly, I would like to personally thank representatives from several organizations for providing resources and advice during the preparation of this volume. These organizations include civic education associations, professional organizations, nonprofit foundations, national government agencies (in the United States and United Kingdom), as well as educational institutions. All of these organizations, and particularly their staffs, provided valuable input and documents significant and important to this volume. These organizations are listed in the Acknowledgments.

SECTION I: THE INTRODUCTION

CHAPTER 1

American Democracy

Eric Barr, John Baird, *and* Taylor Rankin

*Origins of Democracy**

The word "democracy," as well as the concept it represents, can be traced back to the area surrounding the Mediterranean Sea. The beginnings of democracy can be credited to the Greeks of the sixth century, B.C. The word comes from two Greek words: demos, meaning "the people," and kratein, meaning "to rule." These two words are joined together to form democracy, literally meaning "rule of the people" (Pious). The Greek system of government was perhaps closer to a true democracy or rule by the people than any other in history. The Greeks viewed dictatorship as the worst possible form of government, so their government evolved as the exact opposite. Their civilization was broken down into small city-states (never more than 10,000 citizens), and all the men voted on all issues of government. There were no representatives in the Greek system of government. Instead, they ruled themselves directly; each man was a life long member of the decision making body. This was almost a total democracy except for the fact that women and slaves (over 50 percent of the population) were not considered citizens and were not allowed to vote. Despite this, no other civilization has come as close to democracy as its creators, the Greeks, and many later civilizations have incorporated this Greek idea as part of the foundation of their government (Lee; Lefebvre).

Ideas of democracy similar to that of the Greeks were used by the Romans, though not to the same extent. The Roman Empire (509–27 B.C.) took some of their governmental ideals from the Greeks. Their government was a representative democracy, which had representatives from the nobility in the Senate and representatives from the commoners in the Assembly. Governmental power was divided between these two branches and they voted on various issues. Many Roman political thinkers were fond of democracy. The Roman Statesman Cicero was one. Cicero suggested that all people have certain rights that should be preserved. He and other political philosophers of the time taught that governmental and political power should come from the people (Lefebvre; Lee). After the trend of democracy was started by the Greeks and carried on by the Romans, it has been seen in many later governmental systems throughout history.

Democracy in the Middle Ages

Though democracy was not directly instituted in the Middle Ages, many democratic

---

*Originally published as portions of *A More Perfect Union: An Exploration of American Democracy*, Oracle Education Foundation, Redwood Shores, California, 1999. Reprinted with permission of the publisher.

ideas were prevalent throughout the period. Because Christianity, which taught that men were created equal in the eyes of God, was deeply ingrained into the society of the Middle Ages, the democratic idea of equality was understood by many of the people. The Middle Ages, however, utilized another form of government, which was developed during this period, called feudalism. Feudalism stressed that all people have certain rights and developed a system of courts to defend these rights. From these courts came the modern day judicial branch of the American government along with many of the ideas such as kings councils, assemblies and eventually parliamentary systems (Sanford 20–27).

Democracy in England

In A.D. 1215, the Magna Carta opened the door to a more democratic system in England. Nobles forced King John to sign this "Great Charter" that created the English "Parliament," or law-making body, and stated that the written laws held a higher power than the king, thereby limiting the power of the Royal family and giving some of that power to the people. Later, the Petition of Right (1628) stipulated that the King could no longer tax without parliament's permission and the Bill of Rights (1689) provided freedom of speech and banned cruel or unusual punishment. These strengthened Parliament further and gave the people more right to express themselves. Though these reforms did not make England a true democracy in any sense, they did incorporate democratic ideals, which would later be used to form the government of the United States (Lefebvre; Pious).

The concept of democracy continued to be prevalent in Europe with the philosophies of an English philosopher by the name of John Locke and a French philosopher named Jean Jacques Rousseau. Locke's book, *Two Treatises* (published in 1690), stated that under the "social contract," the government's job was to protect "natural rights," which included "the right to life, liberty, and the ownership of property." Rousseau expanded on this idea with his book, *The Social Contract*, in 1762. In essence, these two philosophers said that the people should have input on how their government is run. This school of thought paved the way for modern day American Democracy (Lefebvre).

The Path of Modern Democracy

The American Revolution is another important event in the history of democracy. The first step, of course, in America's pursuit of democracy was the Declaration of Independence in 1776. In this great document, written by Thomas Jefferson, many ideas are taken from the aforementioned philosophers, Locke and Rousseau. From Locke, Jefferson borrowed the idea that all men are created equal, and he altered the right to life, liberty and property to "the right to life, liberty and the pursuit of happiness." Jefferson borrowed a little from Rousseau as well when he said that all men should have the right to take up arms against the government if it did not respect these rights (Jefferson).

In the French Revolution, a similar cause was espoused. Political thinkers and philosophers such as Montesquieu, Voltaire, and Rousseau inspired the people by building off of American ideas and insisting that freedom comes only after the legislative, judicial and executive branches of the government are separated. The people of France overthrew the king, then set forth the "Declaration of the Rights of Man," which changed Locke's right to life, liberty and property to the right to "liberty, property, security, and resistance to oppression." (The resistance to oppression probably came from Rousseau.) These ideas, like the ones in the American Declaration of Independence, lended themselves to a partially democratic system where the powers of the king are limited and the people have some say in their government (Pious; Lefebvre).

All over the world, revolutions began to spring up against monarchies, and democratic governments began to develop. Before the end of the 19th century, almost all of the Western European monarchies had adopted a constitution allowing the power of the Royal Family and giving some power to the people. Parliamentary type representative legislatures were also developed in many of these countries, giving the people more power to rule (Pious).

With the growing success of democracy in the United States and in other countries throughout the world, democracy became more and more popular. By the 1950's, almost every independent country on the planet had a government that embodied some of the principles and ideals put forth in democracy. The model nation for these principles became the United States (Pious; Sanford 20–27).

Democracy in America

Modern American democracy is in the form of a democratic republic or a representative democracy. A representative democracy came about in the United States because the colonists were tired of taxation without representation and wanted a more fair system where the people had more say in the rule of the country. They did not desire the Athenian form of democracy, however, as they feared it would give the people too much power and would lend control of the government to the uneducated masses. What they came up with was a representative democracy wherein elected representatives rather than direct rule by the people rule the government. These representatives are elected with the idea that they will accurately represent their constituents, but in case some don't, the U.S. government is divided into three branches to keep corruption in check. These three branches are the Executive, Legislative, and Judicial branches; no one branch contains absolute power, rather, each branch

is balanced off of the others creating a system of checks and balances to protect the principals of democracy. This system is in no way perfect, and this is why we must pursue a more perfect form of democracy and a more perfect union between our citizens, states and country (Pious; Sanford 20–27).

Theories of Government

A discussion of American democracy presupposes a basic understanding of what government is and what purposes it fulfills. But in reality, as one cannot comprehend what hot means without experiencing cold, one cannot achieve the fullest understanding of American democracy without a basic knowledge of other theories of government.

One method by which governments may be classified is according to distribution of power. In a unitary government, the central government possesses much authority and decision-making power. Local government bodies simply serve as administrative arms of the central government. Great Britain is a familiar example of a unitary government; individual British countries have little of the power commonly exercised by American states. France, with 90 departments grouped in 36 provinces, also has a unitary form of government. It is important, however, to note that unitary governments are not inherently less democratic than other forms (Sanford 10).

Power is distributed completely opposite of a unitary government in a confederate government. Local governments protect and preserve their own authority by forming a weak central government. The United States has briefly employed confederate systems of government, in the Articles of Confederation, whose weaknesses led to the current federal system, and in the southern states' attempts to form the Confederate States of America (Sanford 10).

In a federal government, power is split between a central government authority and its constituent states. Usually, an overriding law of the land, known as a constitution, allocates duties, rights, and privileges to each level of government. The constitution usually defines how power is shared between national, state, and local governments; the power to amend this constitution is usually granted to the citizens or their governmental representatives (Sanford 10–11).

A second way by which governments may be classified is according to decision-making power. There are two basic categories in which governments are classified. In a totalitarian government, the power of rulers is not limited by outside forces, such as elections or public opinion. Totalitarian systems also restrict personal freedom in most cases.

Principles and Models

To better understand the problems democracy faces, we must first understand the principles of democracy. "Democracy is a system of rule that permits citizens to play a significant part in the governmental process," according to *American Government* by Theodore Lowi and Benjamin Ginsberg (A32). There are various interpretations of this definition and consequently many models of democracy. These models can be separated into two categories, direct and indirect. In direct democracies, all citizens are actively involved in making decisions, while in indirect democracies, citizens elect representatives to make laws and administer governmental affairs (Green 27).

REFERENCES

Ginsberg, Benjamin and Theodore J. Lowi. *American Government: Freedom and Power*. New York: W.W. Norton and Company, 1996.

Green, Carl R. and William R. Sanford. *Basic Principles of American Government*. New York: Amsco School Publications, 1977.

Jefferson, Thomas. "The Declaration of Independence." Indiana School of Law — Bloomington. http://www.law.indiana.edu/uslawdocs/declaration.html. 14 March 1999.

Lee, John, Emily Wichman, and Robert Herman. "A Quick History of Democracy." *The Future of Democracy*. http://tqd.advanced.org/3154/info/history.html. 5 March 1999.

Lefebvre, Eliot. *The World History of Democracy*. http://www.geocities.com/Area51/Cavern/6381/history2.html. 5 March 1999.

Pious, Richard M. "Democracy." *Microsoft Encarta 98 Encyclopedia*. Microsoft Corporation, 1997.

NOTE

For additional information about the democratic form of government, including comments by leading sociologists, please refer to *A More Perfect Union: An Exploration of American Democracy* <http://library.thinkquest.org/26466/>. This website was designed for educational use by both adults and children.

At the time this was written, John Baird, Eric Barr and Taylor Rankin were members of the ThinkQuest Team Project, Oracle Education Foundation, Redwood Shores, California.

SECTION II: THE FOUNDATION

CHAPTER 2

Magna Carta (June 15, 1215)

King John of England

The History

Magna Carta and Its American Legacy*

Before penning the Declaration of Independence — the first of the American Charters of Freedom — in 1776, the Founding Fathers searched for a historical precedent for asserting their rightful liberties from King George III and the English Parliament. They found it in a gathering that took place 561 years earlier on the plains of Runnymede, not far from where Windsor Castle stands today. There, on June 15, 1215, an assembly of barons confronted a despotic and cash-strapped King John and demanded that traditional rights be recognized, written down, confirmed with the royal seal, and sent to each of the counties to be read to all freemen. The result was Magna Carta — a momentous achievement for the English barons and, nearly six centuries later, an inspiration for angry American colonists.

Magna Carta was the result of the Angevin king's disastrous foreign policy and overzealous financial administration. John

had suffered a staggering blow the previous year, having lost an important battle to King Philip II at Bouvines and with it all hope of regaining the French lands he had inherited. When the defeated John returned from the Continent, he attempted to rebuild his coffers by demanding scutage (a fee paid in lieu of military service) from the barons who had not joined his war with Philip. The barons in question, predominantly lords of northern estates, protested, condemning John's policies and insisting on a reconfirmation of Henry I's Coronation Oath (1100), which would, in theory, limit the king's ability to obtain funds. (As even Henry ignored the provisions of this charter, however, a reconfirmation would not necessarily guarantee fewer taxes.) But John refused to withdraw his demands, and by spring most baronial families began to take sides. The rebelling barons soon faltered before John's superior resources, but with the unexpected capture of London, they earned a substantial bargaining chip. John agreed to grant a charter.

The document conceded by John and set with his seal in 1215, however, was not what we know today as Magna Carta but

*Originally published as "Magna Carta and Its American Legacy," *Featured Documents*, U.S. National Archives and Records Administration, Washington, DC, 2008. For additional information see "Magna Carta and Its American Legacy," *Featured Documents*, U.S. National Archives and Records Administration, College Park, Maryland, 2008. This agency is listed in the *National Resource Directory* section of this volume.

rather a set of baronial stipulations, now lost, known as the "Articles of the barons." After John and his barons agreed on the final provisions and additional wording changes, they issued a formal version on June 19, and it is this document that came to be known as Magna Carta. Of great significance to future generations was a minor wording change, the replacement of the term "any baron" with "any freeman" in stipulating to whom the provisions applied. Over time, it would help justify the application of the Charter's provisions to a greater part of the population. While freemen were a minority in 13th-century England, this term would eventually include all English, just as "We the People" would come to apply to all Americans in this century.

While Magna Carta would one day become a basic document of the British Constitution, democracy and universal protection of ancient liberties were not among the barons' goals. The Charter was a feudal document and meant to protect the rights and properties of the few powerful families that topped the rigidly structured feudal system. In fact, the majority of the population, the thousands of unfree laborers, is only mentioned once, in a clause concerning the use of court-set fines to punish minor offenses. Magna Carta's primary purpose was restorative: to force King John to recognize the supremacy of ancient liberties, to limit his ability to raise funds, and to reassert the principle of "due process." Only a final clause, which created an enforcement council of tenants-in-chief and clergymen, would have severely limited the king's power and introduced something new to English law: the principle of "majority rule." But majority rule was an idea whose time had not yet come; in September, at John's urging, Pope Innocent II annulled the "shameful and demeaning agreement, forced upon the king by violence and fear." The civil war that followed ended only with John's death in October 1216.

On indefinite loan from the Perot Foundation, a 1297 version of Magna Carta shares space with the Charters of Freedom in the National Archives Rotunda.

To gain support for the new monarch — John's 9-year-old son, Henry III — the young king's regents reissued the charter in 1217. Neither this version nor that issued by Henry when he assumed personal control of the throne in 1225 were exact duplicates of John's charter; both lacked some provisions, including that providing for the enforcement council, found in the original. With the 1225 issuance, however, the evolution of the document ended. While English monarchs, including Henry, confirmed Magna Carta several times after this, each subsequent issue followed the form of this "final" version. With each confirmation, copies of the document were made and sent to the counties so that everyone would know their rights and obligations. Of these original issues of Magna Carta, 17 survive: 4 from the reign of John; 8 from that of Henry III; and 5 from Edward I, including the version now on display at the National Archives.

Although tradition and interpretation would one day make Magna Carta a document of great importance to both England and the American colonies, it originally granted concessions to few but the powerful baronial families. It did include concessions to the Church, merchants, townsmen, and the lower aristocracy for their aid in the rebellion, but the majority of the English population would remain without an active voice in government for another 700 years.

Despite its historical significance, however, Magna Carta may have remained legally inconsequential had it not been resurrected and reinterpreted by Sir Edward Coke in the early 17th century. Coke, Attorney General for Elizabeth, Chief Justice during the reign of James, and a leader in Parliament in opposition to Charles I, used Magna Carta as a weapon against the oppressive tactics of the Stuart kings. Coke argued that even kings must comply to common law. As he proclaimed to Parliament in 1628, "Magna Carta ... will have no sovereign."

Lord Coke's view of the law was particularly relevant to the American experience for it was during this period that the charters for the colonies were written. Each included the guarantee that those sailing for the New World and their heirs would have "all the rights and immunities of free and natural subjects." As our forefathers developed legal codes for the colonies, many incorporated liberties guaranteed by Magna Carta and the 1689 English Bill of Rights directly into their own statutes. Although few colonists could afford legal training in England, they remained remarkably familiar with English common law. During one parliamentary debate in the late 18th century, Edmund Burke observed, "In no country, perhaps in the world, is law so general a study." Through Coke, whose four-volume Institutes of the Laws of England was widely read by American law students, young colonists such as John Adams, Thomas Jefferson, and James Madison learned of the spirit of the charter and the common law — or at least Coke's interpretation of them. Later, Jefferson would write to Madison of Coke: "a sounder whig never wrote, not of profounder learning in the orthodox doctrines of the British constitution, or in what were called English liberties." It is no wonder then that as the colonists prepared for war they would look to Coke and Magna Carta for justification.

By the 1760s the colonists had come to believe that in America they were creating a place that adopted the best of the English system but adapted it to new circumstances; a place where a person could rise by merit, not birth; a place where men could voice their opinions and actively share in self-government. But these beliefs were soon tested. Following the costly Seven Years' War, Great Britain was burdened with substantial debts and the continuing expense of keeping troops on American soil. Parliament thought the colonies should finance much of their own defense and levied the first direct tax, the Stamp Act, in 1765. As a result, virtually every document — newspapers, licenses, insurance policies, legal writs, even playing cards — would have to carry a stamp showing that required taxes had been paid. The colonists rebelled against such control over their daily affairs. Their own elected legislative bodies had not been asked to consent to the Stamp Act. The colonists argued that without either this local consent or direct representation in Parliament, the act was "taxation without representation." They also objected to the law's provision that those who disobeyed could be tried in admiralty courts without a jury of their peers. Coke's influence on Americans showed clearly when the Massachusetts Assembly reacted by declaring the Stamp Act "against the Magna Carta and the natural rights of Englishmen, and therefore, according to Lord Coke, null and void."

But regardless of whether the charter forbade taxation without representation or if this was merely implied by the "spirit," the colonists used this "misinterpretation" to condemn the Stamp Act. To defend their objections, they turned to a 1609 or 1610 defense argument used by Coke: superiority of the common law over acts of Parliament. Coke claimed "When an act of parliament is against common right or reason, or repugnant, or impossible to be performed, the common law will control it and adjudge such an act void. Because the Stamp Act seemed to tread on the concept of consensual taxation, the colonists believed it, "according to Lord Coke," invalid.

The colonists were enraged. Benjamin Franklin and others in England eloquently argued the American case, and Parliament quickly rescinded the bill. But the damage was done; the political climate was changing. As John Adams later wrote to Thomas Jefferson, "The Revolution was in the minds of the people, and this was effected, from 1760 to 1775, in the course of 15 years before a drop of blood was shed at Lexington."

Relations between Great Britain and the colonies continued to deteriorate. The more Parliament tried to raise revenue and suppress the growing unrest, the more the colonists demanded the charter rights they had brought with them a century and a half earlier. At the height of the Stamp Act crisis, William Pitt proclaimed in Parliament, "The Americans are the sons not the bastards of England." Parliament and the Crown, however, appeared to believe otherwise. But the Americans would have their rights, and they would fight for them. The seal adopted by Massachusetts on the eve of the Revolution summed up the mood—a militiaman with sword in one hand and Magna Carta in the other.

Armed resistance broke out in April 1775. Fifteen months later, the final break was made with the immortal words of the Declaration of Independence: "We hold these truths to be self-evident, that all Men are created equal, that they are endowed by their Creator with certain unalienable Rights, that among these are Life, Liberty and the Pursuit of Happiness." Although the colonies had finally and irrevocably articulated their goal, Independence did not come swiftly. Not until the surrender of British forces at Yorktown in 1781 was the military struggle won. The constitutional battle, however, was just beginning.

In the war's aftermath, many Americans recognized that the rather loose confederation of States would have to be strengthened if the new nation were to survive. James Madison expressed these concerns in a call for a convention at Philadelphia in 1787 to revise the Articles of Confederation: "The good people of America are to decide the solemn question, whether they will by wise and magnanimous efforts reap the just fruits of that Independence which they so gloriously acquired ... or whether by giving way to unmanly jealousies and prejudices, or to partial and transitory interests, they will renounce the auspicious blessings prepared for them by the Revolution." The representatives of the states lis-

tened to Madison and drew heavily from his ideas. Instead of revising the Articles, they created a new form of government, embodied in the Constitution of the United States. Authority emanated directly from the people, not from any governmental body. And the Constitution would be "the supreme Law of the Land"—just as Magna Carta had been deemed superior to other statutes.

In 1215, when King John confirmed Magna Carta with his seal, he was acknowledging the now firmly embedded concept that no man — not even the king — is above the law. That was a milestone in constitutional thought for the 13th century and for centuries to come. In 1779 John Adams expressed it this way: "A government of laws, and not of men." Further, the charter established important individual rights that have a direct legacy in the America Bill of Rights. And during the United States' history, these rights have been expanded. The U.S. Constitution is not a static document. Like Magna Carta, it has been interpreted and reinterpreted throughout the years. This has allowed the Constitution to become the longest-lasting constitution in the world and a model for those penned by other nations. Through judicial review and amendment, it has evolved so that today Americans — regardless of gender, race, or creed — can enjoy the liberties and protection it guarantees. Just as Magna Carta stood as a bulwark against tyranny in England, the U.S. Constitution and Bill of Rights today serve similar roles, protecting the individual freedoms of all Americans against arbitrary and capricious rule.

The Document*

Magna Carta

John, by the grace of God, king of England, lord of Ireland, duke of Normandy

*Words and terms included in the glossary that follows the document are marked with a asterisk.

and Aquitaine, and count of Anjou, to the archbishops, bishops, abbots, earls, barons, justiciaries, foresters, sheriffs, stewards, servants, and to all his bailiffs and liege subjects, greetings. Know that, having regard to God and for the salvation of our soul, and those of all our ancestors and heirs, and unto the honor of God and the advancement of his holy Church and for the rectifying of our realm, we have granted as underwritten by advice of our venerable fathers, Stephen, archbishop of Canterbury, primate of all England and cardinal of the holy Roman Church, Henry, archbishop of Dublin, William of London, Peter of Winchester, Jocelyn of Bath and Glastonbury, Hugh of Lincoln, Walter of Worcester, William of Coventry, Benedict of Rochester, bishops; of Master Pandulf, subdeacon and member of the household of our lord the Pope, of brother Aymeric (master of the Knights of the Temple in England), and of the illustrious men William Marshal, earl of Pembroke, William, earl of Salisbury, William, earl of Warenne, William, earl of Arundel, Alan of Galloway (constable of Scotland), Waren Fitz Gerold, Peter Fitz Herbert, Hubert De Burgh (seneschal of Poitou), Hugh de Neville, Matthew Fitz Herbert, Thomas Basset, Alan Basset, Philip d'Aubigny, Robert of Roppesley, John Marshal, John Fitz Hugh, and others, our liegemen.

1. In the first place we have granted to God, and by this our present charter confirmed for us and our heirs forever that the English Church shall be free, and shall have her rights entire, and her liberties inviolate; and we will that it be thus observed; which is apparent from this that the freedom of elections, which is reckoned most important and very essential to the English Church, we, of our pure and unconstrained will, did grant, and did by our charter confirm and did obtain the ratification of the same from our lord, Pope Innocent III, before the quarrel arose between us and our barons; and this we will observe, and our will is that it be ob-

served in good faith by our heirs forever. We have also granted to all freemen of our kingdom, for us and our heirs forever, all the underwritten liberties, to be had and held by them and their heirs, of us and our heirs forever.

2. If any of our earls or barons, or others holding of us in chief by military service shall have died, and at the time of his death his heir shall be full of age and owe "relief," he shall have his inheritance by the old relief, to wit, the heir or heirs of an earl, for the whole barony of an earl by £100; the heir or heirs of a baron, £100 for a whole barony; the heir or heirs of a knight, 100s, at most, and whoever owes less let him give less, according to the ancient custom of fees.

3. If, however, the heir of any one of the aforesaid has been under age and in wardship, let him have his inheritance without relief and without fine when he comes of age.

4. The guardian of the land of an heir who is thus under age, shall take from the land of the heir nothing but reasonable produce, reasonable customs, and reasonable services, and that without destruction or waste of men or goods; and if we have committed the wardship of the lands of any such minor to the sheriff, or to any other who is responsible to us for its issues, and he has made destruction or waste of what he holds in wardship, we will take of him amends, and the land shall be committed to two lawful and discreet men of that fee, who shall be responsible for the issues to us or to him to whom we shall assign them; and if we have given or sold the wardship of any such land to anyone and he has therein made destruction or waste, he shall lose that wardship, and it shall be transferred to two lawful and discreet men of that fief, who shall be responsible to us in like manner as aforesaid.

5. The guardian, moreover, so long as he has the wardship of the land, shall keep up the houses, parks, fishponds, stanks, mills, and other things pertaining to the land, out of the issues of the same land; and he shall

restore to the heir, when he has come to full age, all his land, stocked with ploughs and wainage, according as the season of husbandry shall require, and the issues of the land can reasonable bear.

6. Heirs shall be married without disparagement, yet so that before the marriage takes place the nearest in blood to that heir shall have notice.

7. A widow, after the death of her husband, shall forthwith and without difficulty have her marriage portion and inheritance; nor shall she give anything for her dower, or for her marriage portion, or for the inheritance which her husband and she held on the day of the death of that husband; and she may remain in the house of her husband for forty days after his death, within which time her dower shall be assigned to her.

8. No widow shall be compelled to marry, so long as she prefers to live without a husband; provided always that she gives security not to marry without our consent, if she holds of us, or without the consent of the lord of whom she holds, if she holds of another.

9. Neither we nor our bailiffs will seize any land or rent for any debt, as long as the chattels* of the debtor are sufficient to repay the debt; nor shall the sureties of the debtor be distrained* so long as the principal debtor is able to satisfy the debt; and if the principal debtor shall fail to pay the debt, having nothing wherewith to pay it, then the sureties shall answer for the debt; and let them have the lands and rents of the debtor, if they desire them, until they are indemnified for the debt which they have paid for him, unless the principal debtor can show proof that he is discharged thereof as against the said sureties.

10. If one who has borrowed from the Jews any sum, great or small, die before that loan be repaid, the debt shall not bear interest while the heir is under age, of whomsoever he may hold; and if the debt fall into our hands, we will not take anything except the principal sum contained in the bond.

11. And if anyone die indebted to the Jews, his wife shall have her dower and pay nothing of that debt; and if any children of the deceased are left under age, necessaries shall be provided for them in keeping with the holding of the deceased; and out of the residue the debt shall be paid, reserving, however, service due to feudal lords; in like manner let it be done touching debts due to others than Jews.

12. No scutage* nor aid shall be imposed on our kingdom, unless by common counsel of our kingdom, except for ransoming our person, for making our eldest son a knight, and for once marrying our eldest daughter; and for these there shall not be levied more than a reasonable aid. In like manner it shall be done concerning aids from the city of London.

13. And the city of London shall have all it ancient liberties and free customs, as well by land as by water; furthermore, we decree and grant that all other cities, boroughs, towns, and ports shall have all their liberties and free customs.

14. And for obtaining the common counsel of the kingdom anent the assessing of an aid (except in the three cases aforesaid) or of a scutage, we will cause to be summoned the archbishops, bishops, abbots, earls, and greater barons, severally by our letters; and we will moreover cause to be summoned generally, through our sheriffs and bailiffs, and others who holds of us in chief, for a fixed date, namely, after the expiry of at least forty days, and at a fixed place; and in all letters of such summons we will specify the reason of the summons. And when the summons has thus been made, the business shall proceed on the day appointed, according to the counsel of such as are present, although not all who were summoned have come.

15. We will not for the future grant to anyone license to take an aid from his own free tenants, except to ransom his person, to make his eldest son a knight, and once to marry his eldest daughter; and on each of

these occasions there shall be levied only a reasonable aid.

16. No one shall be distrained for performance of greater service for a knight's fee, or for any other free tenement, than is due therefrom.

17. Common pleas shall not follow our court, but shall be held in some fixed place.

18. Inquests of novel disseisin*, of Mort d'Ancestor*, and of darrein presentment* shall not be held elsewhere than in their own county courts, and that in manner following; We, or, if we should be out of the realm, our chief justiciar, will send two justiciaries through every county four times a year, who shall alone with four knights of the county chosen by the county, hold the said assizes* in the county court, on the day and in the place of meeting of that court.

19. And if any of the said assizes cannot be taken on the day of the county court, let there remain of the knights and freeholders, who were present at the county court on that day, as many as may be required for the efficient making of judgments, according as the business be more or less.

20. A freeman shall not be amerced* for a slight offense, except in accordance with the degree of the offense; and for a grave offense he shall be amerced in accordance with the gravity of the offense, yet saving always his "contentment"; and a merchant in the same way, saving his "merchandise" and a villain shall be amerced in the same way, saving his "wainage" if they have fallen into our mercy; and none of the aforesaid amercements shall be imposed except by the oath of honest men of the neighborhood.

21. Earls and barons shall not be amerced except through their peers, and only in accordance with the degree of the offense.

22. A clerk shall not be amerced in respect of his lay holding except after the manner of the others aforesaid; further, he shall not be amerced in accordance with the extent of his ecclesiastical benefice.

23. No village or individual shall be compelled to make bridges at river banks, except those who from of old were legally bound to do so.

24. No sheriff, constable, coroners, or others of our bailiffs, shall hold pleas of our Crown.

25. All counties, hundred, wapentakes, and trithings (except our demesne manors) shall remain at the old rents, and without any additional payments.

26. If anyone holding of us a lay fief shall die, and our sheriff or bailiff shall exhibit our letters patent of summons for a debt which the deceased owed us, it shall be lawful for our sheriff or bailiff to attach and enroll the chattels of the deceased, found upon the lay fief, to the value of that debt, at the sight of law worthy men, provided always that nothing whatever be thence removed until the debt which is evident shall be fully paid to us; and the residue shall be left to the executors to fulfill the will of the deceased; and if there be nothing due from him to us, all the chattels shall go to the deceased, saving to his wife and children their reasonable shares.

27. If any freeman shall die intestate*, his chattels shall be distributed by the hands of his nearest kinsfolk and friends, under supervision of the Church, saving to every one the debts which the deceased owed to him.

28. No constable or other bailiff of ours shall take corn or other provisions from anyone without immediately tendering money therefor, unless he can have postponement thereof by permission of the seller.

29. No constable shall compel any knight to give money in lieu of castle-guard, when he is willing to perform it in his own person, or (if he himself cannot do it from any reasonable cause) then by another responsible man. Further, if we have led or sent him upon military service, he shall be relieved from guard in proportion to the time during which he has been on service because of us.

30. No sheriff or bailiff of ours, or other person, shall take the horses or carts of any freeman for transport duty, against the will of the said freeman.

31. Neither we nor our bailiffs shall take, for our castles or for any other work of ours, wood which is not ours, against the will of the owner of that wood.

32. We will not retain beyond one year and one day, the lands those who have been convicted of felony, and the lands shall thereafter be handed over to the lords of the fiefs.

33. All kydells for the future shall be removed altogether from Thames and Medway, and throughout all England, except upon the seashore.

34. The writ which is called praecipe* shall not for the future be issued to anyone, regarding any tenement whereby a freeman may lose his court.

35. Let there be one measure of win throughout our whole realm; and one measure of ale; and one measure of corn, to wit, "the London quarter"; and one width of cloth (whether dyed, or russet, or "halberget"), to wit, two ells within the selvedges; of weights also let it be as of measures.

36. Nothing in future shall be given or taken for a writ of inquisition of life or limbs, but freely it shall be granted, and never denied.

37. If anyone holds of us by fee-farm, either by socage* or by burage*, or of any other land by knight's service, we will not (by reason of that fee-farm, socage, or burage), have the wardship of the heir, or of such land of his as if of the fief of that other; nor shall we have wardship of that fee-farm, socage, or burage, unless such fee-farm owes knight's service. We will not by reason of any small serjeancy which anyone may hold of us by the service of rendering to us knives, arrows, or the like, have wardship of his heir or of the land which he holds of another lord of knight's service.

38. No bailiff for the future shall, upon his own unsupported complaint, put anyone to his "law," without credible witnesses brought for this purposes.

39. No freemen shall be taken or imprisoned or disseised* or exiled or in any way destroyed, nor will we go upon him nor send upon him, except by the lawful judgment of his peers or by the law of the land.

40. To no one will we sell, to no one will we refuse or delay, right or justice.

41. All merchants shall have safe and secure exit from England, and entry to England, with the right to tarry there and to move about as well by land as by water, for buying and selling by the ancient and right customs, quit from all evil tolls, except (in time of war) such merchants as are of the land at war with us. And if such are found in our land at the beginning of the war, they shall be detained, without injury to their bodies or goods, until information be received by us, or by our chief justiciar, how the merchants of our land found in the land at war with us are treated; and if our men are safe there, the others shall be safe in our land.

42. It shall be lawful in future for anyone (excepting always those imprisoned or outlawed in accordance with the law of the kingdom, and natives of any country at war with us, and merchants, who shall be treated as if above provided) to leave our kingdom and to return, safe and secure by land and water, except for a short period in time of war, on grounds of public policy — reserving always the allegiance due to us.

43. If anyone holding of some escheat* (such as the honor of Wallingford, Nottingham, Boulogne, Lancaster, or of other escheats which are in our hands and are baronies) shall die, his heir shall give no other relief, and perform no other service to us than he would have done to the baron if that barony had been in the baron's hand; and we shall hold it in the same manner in which the baron held it.

44. Men who dwell without the forest need not henceforth come before our justiciaries of the forest upon a general summons,

unless they are in plea, or sureties of one or more, who are attached to the forest.

45. We will appoint as justices, constables, sheriffs, or bailiffs only such as know the law of the realm and mean to observe it well.

46. All barons who have founded abbeys, concerning which they hold charters from the kings of England, or of which they have long continued possession, shall have the wardship of them, when vacant, as they ought to have.

47. All forests that have been made such in our time shall forthwith be disafforested; and a similar course shall be followed with regard to river banks that have been placed "in defense" by us in our time.

48. All evil customs connected with forests and warrens, foresters and warreners, sheriffs and their officers, river banks and their wardens, shall immediately by inquired into in each county by twelve sworn knights of the same county chosen by the honest men of the same county, and shall within forty days of the said inquest, be utterly abolished, so as never to be restored, provided always that we previously have intimation thereof, or our justiciar, if we should not be in England.

49. We will immediately restore all hostages and charters delivered to us by Englishmen, as sureties of the peace of faithful service.

50. We will entirely remove from their bailiwicks, the relations of Gerard of Athee (so that in future they shall have no bailiwick in England); namely, Engelard of Cigogne, Peter, Guy, and Andrew of Chanceaux, Guy of Cigogne, Geoffrey of Martigny with his brothers, Philip Mark with his brothers and his nephew Geoffrey, and the whole brood of the same.

51. As soon as peace is restored, we will banish from the kingdom all foreign born knights, crossbowmen, serjeants, and mercenary soldiers who have come with horses and arms to the kingdom's hurt.

52. If anyone has been dispossessed or removed by us, without the legal judgment of his peers, from his lands, castles, franchises, or from his right, we will immediately restore them to him; and if a dispute arise over this, then let it be decided by the five and twenty barons of whom mention is made below in the clause for securing the peace. Moreover, for all those possessions, from which anyone has, without the lawful judgment of his peers, been disseised or removed, by our father, King Henry, or by our brother, King Richard, and which we retain in our hand (or which as possessed by others, to whom we are bound to warrant them) we shall have respite until the usual term of crusaders; excepting those things about which a plea has been raised, or an inquest made by our order, before our taking of the cross; but as soon as we return from the expedition, we will immediately grant full justice therein.

53. We shall have, moreover, the same respite and in the same manner in rendering justice concerning the disafforestation or retention of those forests which Henry our father and Richard our brother afforested, and concerning the wardship of lands which are of the fief of another (namely, such wardships as we have hitherto had by reason of a fief which anyone held of us by knight's service), and concerning abbeys founded on other fiefs than our own, in which the lord of the fee claims to have right; and when we have returned, or if we desist from our expedition, we will immediately grant full justice to all who complain of such things.

54. No one shall be arrested or imprisoned upon the appeal of a woman, for the death of any other than her husband.

55. All fines made with us unjustly and against the law of the land, and all amercements, imposed unjustly and against the law of the land, shall be entirely remitted, or else it shall be done concerning them according to the decision of the five and twenty barons whom mention is made below in the clause for securing the pease, or according to the judgment of the majority of the same, along

with the aforesaid Stephen, archbishop of Canterbury, if he can be present, and such others as he may wish to bring with him for this purpose, and if he cannot be present the business shall nevertheless proceed without him, provided always that if any one or more of the aforesaid five and twenty barons are in a similar suit, they shall be removed as far as concerns this particular judgment, others being substituted in their places after having been selected by the rest of the same five and twenty for this purpose only, and after having been sworn.

56. If we have disseised or removed Welshmen from lands or liberties, or other things, without the legal judgment of their peers in England or in Wales, they shall be immediately restored to them; and if a dispute arise over this, then let it be decided in the marches by the judgment of their peers; for the tenements in England according to the laws of England, for tenements in Wales according to the law of Wales, and for tenements in the marches according to the law of the marches. Welshmen shall do the same to us and ours.

57. Further, for all those possessions from which any Welshman has, without the lawful judgment of his peers, been disseised or removed by King Henry our father, or King Richard our brother, and which we retain in our hand (or which are possessed by others, and which we ought to warrant), we will have respite until the usual term of crusaders; excepting those things about which a plea has been raised or an inquest made by our order before we took the cross; but as soon as we return (or if perchance we desist from our expedition), we will immediately grant full justice in accordance with the laws of the Welsh and in relation to the foresaid regions.

58. We will immediately give up the son of Llywelyn and all the hostages of Wales, and the charters delivered to us as security for the peace.

59. We will do towards Alexander, king of Scots, concerning the return of his sisters and his hostages, and concerning his franchises, and his right, in the same manner as we shall do towards our owner barons of England, unless it ought to be otherwise according to the charters which we hold from William his father, formerly king of Scots; and this shall be according to the judgment of his peers in our court.

60. Moreover, all these aforesaid customs and liberties, the observances of which we have granted in our kingdom as far as pertains to us towards our men, shall be observed by all of our kingdom, as well clergy as laymen, as far as pertains to them towards their men.

61. Since, moreover, for God and the amendment of our kingdom and for the better allaying of the quarrel that has arisen between us and our barons, we have granted all these concessions, desirous that they should enjoy them in complete and firm endurance forever, we give and grant to them the underwritten security, namely, that the barons choose five and twenty barons of the kingdom, whomsoever they will, who shall be bound with all their might, to observe and hold, and cause to be observed, the peace and liberties we have granted and confirmed to them by this our present Charter, so that if we, or our justiciar, or our bailiffs or any one of our officers, shall in anything be at fault towards anyone, or shall have broken any one of the articles of this peace or of this security, and the offense be notified to four barons of the foresaid five and twenty, the said four barons shall repair to us (or our justiciar, if we are out of the realm) and, laying the transgression before us, petition to have that transgression redressed without delay. And if we shall not have corrected the transgression (or, in the event of our being out of the realm, if our justiciar shall not have corrected it) within forty days, reckoning from the time it has been intimated to us (or to our justiciar, if we should be out of the realm), the four barons aforesaid shall refer that matter to the

rest of the five and twenty barons, and those five and twenty barons shall, together with the community of the whole realm, distrain and distress us in all possible ways, namely, by seizing our castles, lands, possessions, and in any other way they can, until redress has been obtained as they deem fit, saving harmless our own person, and the persons of our queen and children; and when redress has been obtained, they shall resume their old relations towards us. And let whoever in the country desires it, swear to obey the orders of the said five and twenty barons for the execution of all the aforesaid matters, and along with them, to molest us to the utmost of his power; and we publicly and freely grant leave to everyone who wishes to swear, and we shall never forbid anyone to swear. All those, moreover, in the land who of themselves and of their own accord are unwilling to swear to the twenty five to help them in constraining and molesting us, we shall by our command compel the same to swear to the effect foresaid. And if any one of the five and twenty barons shall have died or departed from the land, or be incapacitated in any other manner which would prevent the foresaid provisions being carried out, those of the said twenty five barons who are left shall choose another in his place according to their own judgment, and he shall be sworn in the same way as the others. Further, in all matters, the execution of which is entrusted to these twenty five barons, if perchance these twenty five are present and disagree about anything, or if some of them, after being summoned, are unwilling or unable to be present, that which the majority of those present ordain or command shall be held as fixed and established, exactly as if the whole twenty five had concurred in this; and the said twenty five shall swear that they will faithfully observe all that is aforesaid, and cause it to be observed with all their might. And we shall procure nothing from anyone, directly or indirectly, whereby any part of these concessions and liberties might be revoked or diminished; and

if any such things has been procured, let it be void and null, and we shall never use it personally or by another.

62. And all the will, hatreds, and bitterness that have arisen between us and our men, clergy and lay, from the date of the quarrel, we have completely remitted and pardoned to everyone. Moreover, all trespasses occasioned by the said quarrel, from Easter in the sixteenth year of our reign till the restoration of peace, we have fully remitted to all, both clergy and laymen, and completely forgiven, as far as pertains to us. And on this head, we have caused to be made for them letters testimonial patent of the lord Stephen, archbishop of Canterbury, of the lord Henry, archbishop of Dublin, of the bishops aforesaid, and of Master Pandulf as touching this security and the concessions aforesaid.

63. Wherefore we will and firmly order that the English Church be free, and that the men in our kingdom have and hold all the aforesaid liberties, rights, and concessions, well and peaceably, freely and quietly, fully and wholly, for themselves and their heirs, of us and our heirs, in all respects and in all places forever, as is aforesaid. An oath, moreover, has been taken, as well on our part as on the part of the barons, that all these conditions aforesaid shall be kept in good faith and without evil intent. Given under our hand — the above named and many others being witnessed — in the meadow which is called Runnymede, between Windsor and Staines, on the fifteenth day of June, in the seventeenth year of our reign.

GLOSSARY

Amerce— To impose a fine. Also to publish by fine or penalty.

Assize— A court, usually but not always consisting of twelve men, summoned together to try a disputed case. They performed the functions of jury, except the verdict was rendered from their own investigation and knowledge and not from upon evidence adduced.

Burage— One of three species of free socage holdings. A tenure where houses and lands formerly the site of houses in an ancient borough are held of some lord by a certain rent.

Chattel— Personal property as opposed to real property. A personal object which can be transported.

Darrein Presentment— Writ of Assize when a man or his ancestors under whom he claimed presented a clerk to a benefice, who was instituted, and afterwards, upon the next avoidance, a stranger presented a clerk and thereby disturbed the real patron.

Distrain— The act of taking as a pledge another's property to be used as an assurance of performance of an obligation. Also a remedy to ensure a court appearance or payment of fees, etc.

Disseise— To dispossess or to deprive.

Escheat— Right of the lord of a fee to re-enter upon the same when it became vacant by the extinction of the blood of the tenant.

Intestate— To die without a will.

Mort d'Ancestor— Real action to recover a person's lands of which he had been deprived on the death of his ancestor by the abatement of intrusion of a stranger.

Novel Disseisin— Writ of Assize for the recovery of lands and tenements.

Praecipe— An original writ drawn up in the alternative commanding the defendant to do the thing required.

Scutage— Tax or contribution raised by someone holding lands by knight's service used to furnish the King's army.

Socage— A species of tenure where the tenant held lands in consideration of certain inferior services of husbandry by him to the lord of the fee.

CHAPTER 3

Petition of Right (May 27, 1628)

Parliament of England

The History*

The Petition of Right is a major English constitutional document, which sets out specific liberties of the subject that the king is prohibited from infringing. The Petition of Right was produced by the English Parliament in the run-up to the English Civil War. It was passed by Parliament in May 1628, and given the royal assent by Charles I in June of that year. The Petition is most notable for its confirmation of the principles that taxes can be levied only by Parliament, that martial law may not be imposed in time of peace, and that prisoners must be able to challenge the legitimacy of their detentions through the writ of habeas corpus. Additionally, the Petition's ban on the billeting of troops is reflected in the Third Amendment of the United States Constitution.

Parliament passed the Petition of Right in 1628 in response to a number of perceived violations of the law by Charles I in the first years of his reign. In 1626, Charles had convened Parliament in an effort to obtain desperately needed funds for the continuation of his unsuccessful war with Spain. Unhappy with the prosecution of the war, however, Parliament swiftly began impeachment proceedings against Charles' favorite and principal counselor, the Duke of Buckingham. In order to protect Buckingham, Charles was forced to dissolve Parliament before it had voted any subsidies.[1] Left without recourse to parliamentary taxation, Charles resorted to two forms of extra-parliamentary taxation to raise the funds he needed — a benevolence and a Forced Loan — that were of doubtful legality at best. He also began to billet soldiers in civilian homes, both as a cost-saving measure and as a means of punishing his political opponents.

Citing the Forced Loan's illegality, a number of gentlemen refused to pay, and many of them were imprisoned as a result. Ultimately, five of the imprisoned gentlemen — the so-called "Five Knights" (since they were all knights) petitioned the Court of King's Bench for writs of habeas corpus to force the government to specify the reason for their imprisonment. Seeking to avoid a direct challenge of the legality of the Loan, Charles refused to charge the prisoners with a specific crime, instead declaring on the re-

*Originally published as "Petition of Right," *Wikipedia*, Wikimedia Foundation, Inc., San Francisco, California, November 2009. For additional information see "The Civil War: Charles I and the Petition of Right," *Living Heritage*, United Kingdom Parliamentary Archives, London, England, 2009. This agency is listed in the *National Resource Directory* section of this volume.

turn to the writs that the knights were detained "*per speciale mandatum domini regis*" ("by special command of our lord the king").[2]

In the resulting hearings before the King's Bench — the famous Five Knights' Case — counsel for the Knights argued that imprisonment by "special command" amounted to a fundamental violation of the principle of due process established by chapter twenty-nine of Magna Carta, which declared that imprisonment could only occur in accordance with the law of the land. The Five Knights' counsel claimed, therefore, that the king, upon receipt of a writ of habeas corpus, must return a specific cause of detention, the legality of which could be assessed by the courts. In contrast, Robert Heath, the Attorney General, claimed that the king had a prerogative right to imprison by royal command for reasons of state, and these detentions could not be challenged by habeas corpus.

Faced with conflicting precedents, and undoubtedly, political pressure, the Court decided to remit the Knights to prison while taking the case under advisement. Although equivocal, this decision was taken as a major victory for the king, and a significant blow to the opponents of his extra-legal policies. It was largely a desire to overturn immediately this ruling that would provide the primary impetus for the House of Commons' decision to create the Petition of Right in the subsequent Parliament.[3]

Elections for a new Parliament occurred in February and early March 1628, and Parliament assembled on March 17th. As Charles made clear in his opening speech, his purpose for calling Parliament was supply, and he urged Parliament not to waste time in "tedious consultations."[4] Initially, Parliament began to consider Charles' request for funds, but very quickly shelved this in favor of discussing grievances related to the Forced Loan and the Five Knights' Case. Sir Edward Coke first proposed legislation to overturn the holding in the Five Knights' Case on March 21st, and from that date until the passage of the Petition

of Right, consideration of grievances dominated the House of Commons' daily schedule.[5] The debates in the House focused on demonstrating that Charles' actions had been contrary to the existing law — the Commons were wary of appearing to innovate, as doing so would likely be viewed by Charles as an assault on his prerogative. On April 3rd, the House passed four resolutions declaring that imprisonment without cause shown and taxation without consent of Parliament were illegal.[6] These resolutions would form the core of the later Petition of Right. Over the course of April, additional grievances concerning billeting of troops and the use of martial law were added to the developing legislation.

On May 6th, the House voted to proceed by way of petition of right rather than by bill, seeing this as the best way to gain a redress of grievances without appearing to overly-threaten the royal prerogative.[7] A draft of the Petition was prepared by the Commons, and sent to the Lords for their approval. The Lords, influenced by letters from Charles opposing the Petition, attempted to insert alterations that would have largely nullified the effect of the Petition. The Commons, however, rejected all but the most insignificant of the Lords' edits.[8] On May 27th, the Petition was finally approved by both Houses of Parliament and presented to Charles for the royal assent.

Initially, Charles tried to avoid assenting to the Petition, and on June 2nd he unsuccessfully attempted to satisfy the Commons with a simple expression of good intentions. On June 7th, however, the king made a surprising *volte-face*, and approved the Petition — though with the simultaneous declaration that the Commons "neither mean nor can hurt my prerogative." Charles' sudden approval of the Petition was almost certainly influenced by secret conferences he had held with the judges of the central courts in May, in which the judges had hinted that the Petition could not prevent Charles from exercising his prerogatives in the future.[9]

Thus, Charles had accepted the Petition without any intention of abiding by it — as would be demonstrated by his conduct during the 1630s.[10]

In enacting the Petition, Parliament sought redress on the following points:

- Taxation without Parliament's consent
- Forced loans
- Arbitrary arrest
- Imprisonment contrary to Magna Carta
- Arbitrary interference with property rights
- Lack of enforcement of *habeas corpus*
- Forced billeting of troops
- Imposition of martial law
- Exemption of officials from due process

The Petition was largely shaped by the common lawyers in the House of Commons, including notably Sir Edward Coke, John Selden, John Pym, and Sir John Eliot. The Petition is retrospective in nature: it claims to merely reconfirm ancient liberties, rather than establish new rights. Thus, it relies heavily on Magna Carta, the *Statutum de tallagio non concedendo* of Edward I's reign, and various statutes from the reign of Edward III relating to due process as precedents. Pym even claimed that the rights demanded predated the Norman conquest and had been confirmed by successive kings. In reality, however, the Petition significantly expanded the recognized rights of Englishmen. The King was under great financial pressure, and agreed to the Petition in June. In practice, however, Charles failed to abide by the limitations of the Petition. The Petition's limitation of military law jurisdiction prevented William III from disciplining rebellious troops during the Glorious Revolution requiring the passage of the Mutiny Act of 1689.

The Document

Petition of Right

The Petition exhibited to his Majesty by the Lords Spiritual and Temporal, and Commons, in this present Parliament assembled, concerning divers Rights and Liberties of the Subjects, with the King's Majesty's royal answer thereunto in full Parliament.

To the King's Most Excellent Majesty,

I. Humbly show unto our Sovereign Lord the King, the Lords Spiritual and Temporal, and Commons in Parliament assembled, that whereas it is declared and enacted by a statute made in the time of the reign of King Edward I, commonly called Stratutum de Tellagio non Concedendo, that no tallage or aid shall be laid or levied by the king or his heirs in this realm, without the good will and assent of the archbishops, bishops, earls, barons, knights, burgesses, and other the freemen of the commonalty of this realm; and by authority of parliament holden in the five-and-twentieth year of the reign of King Edward III, it is declared and enacted, that from thenceforth no person should be compelled to make any loans to the king against his will, because such loans were against reason and the franchise of the land; and by other laws of this realm it provided, that none should be charged by any charge or imposition called a benevolence, nor by such like charge; by which statutes before mentioned, and other the good laws and statutes of this realm, your subjects have inherited this freedom, that they should not be compelled to contribute to any tax, tallage, aid, or other like charge not set by common consent, in parliament.

II. Yet nevertheless of late divers commissions directed to sundry commissioners in several counties, with instructions, have issued; by means whereof your people have been in divers places assembled, and required to lend certain sums of money unto your Majesty, and many of them, upon their refusal so to do, have had an oath administered unto them not warrantable by the laws or statutes of this realm, and have been constrained to become bound and make appearance and give utterance before your Privy

Council and in other places, and others of them have been therefore imprisoned, confined, and sundry other ways molested and disquieted; and divers other charges have been laid and levied upon your people in several counties by lord lieutenants, deputy lieutenants, commissioners for musters, justices of peace and others, by command or direction from your Majesty, or your Privy Council, against the laws and free custom of the realm.

III. And whereas also by the statute called "The Great Charter of the Liberties of England," it is declared and enacted, that no freeman may be taken or imprisoned or be disseized of his freehold or liberties, or his free customs, or be outlawed or exiled, or in any manner destroyed, but by the lawful judgment of his peers, or by the law of the land.

IV. And in the eight-and-twentieth year of the reign of King Edward III, it was declared and enacted by authority of parliament, that no man, of what estate or condition that he be, should be put out of his land or tenements, nor taken, nor imprisoned, nor disinherited nor put to death without being brought to answer by due process by law.

V. Nevertheless, against the tenor of the said statutes, and other the good laws and statutes of your realm to that end provided, divers of your subjects have of late been imprisoned without any cause showed; and when for their deliverance they were brought before your justices by your Majesty's writs of habeas corpus, there to undergo and receive as the court should order, and their keepers commanded to certify the causes of their detainer, no cause was certified, but that they were detained by your Majesty's special command, signified by the lords of your Privy Council, and yet were returned back to several prisons, without being charged with anything to which they might make answer according to the law.

VI. And whereas of late great companies of soldiers and mariners have been dispersed into divers counties of the realm, and the inhabitants against their wills have been compelled to receive them into their houses, and there to suffer them to sojourn against the laws and customs of this realm, and to the great grievance and vexation of the people.

VII. And whereas also by authority of parliament, in the five-and-twentieth year of the reign of King Edward III, it is declared and enacted, that no man shall be forejudged of life or limb against the form of the Great Charter and the law of the land; and by the said Great Charter and other the laws and statutes of this your realm, no man ought to be adjudged to death but by the laws established in this your realm, either by the customs of the same realm, or by acts of parliament; and whereas no offender of what kind soever is exempted from the proceedings to be used, and punishments to be inflicted by the laws and statutes of this your realm; nevertheless of late time divers commissions under your Majesty's great seal have issued forth, by which certain persons have been assigned and appointed commissioners with power and authority to proceed within the land, according to the justice of martial law, against such soldiers or mariners, or other dissolute persons joining with them, as should commit any murder, robbery, felony, mutiny, or other outrage or misdemeanor whatsoever, and by such summary course and order as is agreeable to martial law, and is used in armies in time of war, to proceed to the trial and condemnation of such offenders, and them to cause to be executed and put to death according to the law martial.

VIII. By pretext whereof some of your Majesty's subjects have been by some of the said commissioners put to death, when and where, if by the laws and statutes of the land they had deserved death, by the same laws and statutes also they might, and by no other ought to have been judged and executed.

IX. And also sundry grievous offenders, by color thereof claiming an exemption, have escaped the punishments due to them by the laws and statutes of this your realm, by reason that divers of your officers and ministers of justice have unjustly refused or forborne to proceed against such offenders according to the same laws and statutes, upon pretense that the said offenders were punishable only by martial law, and by authority of such commissions as aforesaid; which commissions, and all other of like nature, are wholly and directly contrary to the said laws and statutes of this your realm.

X. They do therefore humbly pray your most excellent Majesty, that no man hereafter be compelled to make or yield any gift, loan, benevolence, tax, or such like charge, without common consent by act of parliament; and that none be called to make answer, or take such oath, or to give attendance, or be confined, or otherwise molested or disquieted concerning the same or for refusal thereof; and that no freeman, in any such manner as is before mentioned, be imprisoned or detained; and that your Majesty would be pleased to remove the said soldiers and mariners, and that your people may not be so burdened in time to come; and that the aforesaid commissions, for proceeding by martial law, may be revoked and annulled; and that hereafter no commissions of like nature may issue forth to any person or persons whatsoever to be executed as aforesaid, lest by color of them any of your Majesty's subjects be destroyed or put to death contrary to the laws and franchise of the land.

XI. All which they most humbly pray of your most excellent Majesty as their rights and liberties, according to the laws and statutes of this realm; and that your Majesty would also vouchsafe to declare, that the awards, doings, and proceedings, to the prejudice of your people in any of the premises, shall not be drawn hereafter into consequence or example; and that your Majesty would be also graciously pleased, for the further comfort and safety of your people, to declare your royal will and pleasure, that in the things aforesaid all your officers and ministers shall serve you according to the laws and statutes of this realm, as they tender the honor of your Majesty, and the prosperity of this kingdom.

REFERENCES

1. Conrad Russell, *Parliaments and English Politics 1621–1629* (Oxford: Clarendon Press, 1979), 267–322 *passim*.
2. Roger Lockyer, *The Early Stuarts* (New York: Longman, 1989), 220–224.
3. Russell, 334–335.
4. Robert C. Johnson et al., eds., *Commons Debates 1628*, vol. 2 (New Haven: Yale University Press, 1977), 2.
5. Ibid., 45.
6. Ibid., 291.
7. *Commons Debates 1628*, vol. 3, 280.
8. Russell, 371–374.
9. *Commons Debates 1628*, vol. 6, 46.
10. Russell, 383.

CHAPTER 4

Bill of Rights (December 16, 1689)

Parliament of England

The History*

The Bill of Rights (a short title conferred by the Short Titles Act 1896, section 1 and the first schedule) is an act of the Parliament of England, whose title is *An Act Declaring the Rights and Liberties of the Subject and Settling the Succession of the Crown*. It is often called the English Bill of Rights.

The Bill of Rights was passed by Parliament in December 1689 and was a restatement in statutory form of the Declaration of Right, presented by the Convention Parliament to William and Mary in March 1688, inviting them to become joint sovereigns of England. It enumerates certain rights to which subjects and permanent residents of a constitutional monarchy were thought to be entitled in the late 17th century, asserting subjects' right to petition the monarch, as well as to bear arms in defense. It also sets out — or, in the view of its drafters, restates — certain constitutional requirements of the Crown to seek the consent of the people, as represented in Parliament.

Along with the 1701 Act of Settlement

the Bill of Rights remains, today, one of the main constitutional laws governing the succession to not only the throne of the United Kingdom, but, following British colonialism, the resultant doctrine of reception, and independence, also to those of the other Commonwealth realms, whether by willing deference to the act as a British statute or as a patriated part of the particular realm's constitution.[1] Since the implementation of the Statute of Westminster in each of the Commonwealth realms (on successive dates from 1931 onwards) the Bill of Rights cannot be altered in any realm except by that realm's own parliament, and then, by convention, and as it touches on the succession to the shared throne, only with the consent of all the other realms.[2]

In the United Kingdom, the Bill of Rights is further accompanied by the Magna Carta, Habeas Corpus Act of 1679 and Parliament Acts 1911 and 1949 as some of the basic documents of the uncodified British constitution. A separate but similar document, the Claim of Right Act, applies in Scotland. Further, a bill of rights has been

*Originally published as "Bill of Rights 1689," *Wikipedia*, Wikimedia Foundation, Inc., San Francisco, California, November 2009. For additional information see "The Glorious Revolution: The Convention and Bill of Rights," *Living Heritage*, United Kingdom Parliamentary Archives, London, England, 2009. This agency is listed in the *National Resource Directory* section of this volume.

listed, in the Republic of Ireland's Statute Law Revision (Pre-Union), as an English act of Parliament to be retained as part of the country's law.[3] The English Bill of Rights 1689 inspired in large part the United States Bill of Rights.[4][5]

The Bill of Rights laid out certain basic tenets for, at the time, all Englishmen. These rights continue to apply today, not only in England, but in each of the jurisdictions of the Commonwealth realms as well. The people, embodied in the Parliament, are granted immutable civil and political rights through the act, including:

- Freedom from royal interference with the law. Though the sovereign remains the fount of justice, he or she cannot unilaterally establish new courts or act as a judge.
- Freedom from taxation by Royal Prerogative. The agreement of Parliament became necessary for the implementation of any new taxes.
- Freedom to petition the monarch.
- Freedom from the standing army during a time of peace. The agreement of Parliament became necessary before the army could be moved against the populace when not at war.
- Freedom for Protestants to bear arms for their own defense, as suitable to their class and as allowed by law.
- Freedom to elect members of Parliament without interference from the sovereign.
- Freedom of speech and debates; or proceedings in Parliament ought not to be impeached or questioned in any court or place out of Parliament.

Certain acts of James II were also specifically named and declared illegal by the Bill of Rights, while James' flight from England in the wake of the Glorious Revolution was also declared to be an abdication of the throne.

Also, in a prelude to the Act of Settlement to come twelve years later, the Bill of Rights barred Roman Catholics from the throne of England as "it hath been found by experience that it is inconsistent with the safety and welfare of this Protestant kingdom to be governed by a papist prince"; thus William III and Mary II were named as the successors of James VII and II and that the throne would pass from them first to Mary's heirs, then to her sister, Princess Anne of Denmark and her heirs and, further, to any heirs of William by a later marriage. The monarch was further required to swear a coronation oath to main the Protestant religion.

The Bill of Rights was later supplemented by the Act of Settlement of 1701 (while the Claim of Right Act in Scotland was supplemented by the Act of Union, 1707). Both the Bill of Rights and the Claim of Right contributed a great deal to the establishment of the concept of parliamentary sovereignty and the curtailment of the powers of the monarch. Leading, ultimately, to the establishment of constitutional monarchy, while also along with Penal Laws, settled the political and religious turmoil that had convulsed Scotland, England and Ireland in the 17th century.

It was a predecessor of the United States Bill of Rights, the Canadian Charter of Rights and Freedoms, the United Nations Universal Declaration of Human Rights and the European Convention on Human Rights. For example, as with the Bill of Rights, the U.S. constitution requires jury trials and prohibits excessive bail and "cruel and unusual punishments."

Similarly, "cruel, inhuman or degrading punishments" are banned under Article 5 of the Universal Declaration of Human Rights and Article 3 of the European Convention on Human Rights.

The bill continues to be cited in legal proceedings in the Commonwealth realms. For instance, on 21 July 1995 a libel case brought by Neil Hamilton (then a member of Parliament) against *The Guardian* was stopped after Justice May ruled that the Bill of Rights' prohibition on the courts' ability to question parliamentary proceedings would prevent *The Guardian* from obtaining a fair trial. Section 13 of the Defamation Act, 1996, was subsequently enacted to permit an MP to waive his parliamentary privilege.

The Bill of Rights was also invoked in New Zealand in the 1976 case of Fitzgerald v. Muldoon and Others, which centered on the purporting of newly appointed Prime Minister Robert Muldoon that he would advise the Governor-General to abolish a superannuation scheme established by the New Zealand Superannuation Act, 1974, without new legislation. Muldoon felt that the dissolution would be immediate and he would later introduce a new bill in Parliament to retroactively make the abolition legal. This claim was challenged in court and the Chief Justice declared that Muldoon's actions were illegal as they had violated Article 1 of the Bill of Rights, which provides "that the pretended power of suspending laws of the execution of laws by regal authority without consent of parliament is illegal."

Two special designs of the British commemorative two pound coins were issued in the United Kingdom in 1989 to celebrate the tercentenary of the Glorious Revolution. One referred to the Bill of Rights and the other to the Claim of Right. Both depict the Royal Cypher of William and Mary and the mace of the House of Commons; one also shows a representation of the St. Edward's Crown and, another, the Crown of Scotland.

The Document

Bill of Rights

An Act Declaring the Rights and Liberties of the Subject and Settling the Succession of the Crown

Whereas the Lords Spiritual and Temporal and Commons assembled at Westminster, lawfully, fully and freely representing all the estates of the people of this realm, did upon the thirteenth day of February in the year of our Lord one thousand six hundred eighty-eight [old style date] present unto their Majesties, then called and known by the names and style of William and Mary, prince and princess of Orange, being present in their proper persons, a certain declaration in writing made by the said Lords and Commons in the words following, viz.:

- Whereas the late King James the Second, by the assistance of divers evil counsellors, judges and ministers employed by him, did endeavour to subvert and extirpate the Protestant religion and the laws and liberties of this kingdom;
- By assuming and exercising a power of dispensing with and suspending of laws and the execution of laws without consent of Parliament;
- By committing and prosecuting divers worthy prelates for humbly petitioning to be excused from concurring to the said assumed power;
- By issuing and causing to be executed a commission under the great seal for erecting a court called the Court of Commissioners for Ecclesiastical Causes;
- By levying money for and to the use of the Crown by pretence of prerogative for other time and in other manner than the same was granted by Parliament;
- By raising and keeping a standing army within this kingdom in time of peace without consent of Parliament, and quartering soldiers contrary to law;
- By causing several good subjects being Protestants to be disarmed at the same time when papists were both armed and employed contrary to law;
- By violating the freedom of election of members to serve in Parliament;
- By prosecutions in the Court of King's Bench for matters and causes cognizable only in Parliament, and by divers other arbitrary and illegal courses;
- And whereas of late years partial corrupt

and unqualified persons have been returned and served on juries in trials, and particularly divers jurors in trials for high treason which were not freeholders;

- And excessive bail hath been required of persons committed in criminal cases to elude the benefit of the laws made for the liberty of the subjects;
- And excessive fines have been imposed;
- And illegal and cruel punishments inflicted;
- And several grants and promises made of fines and forfeitures before any conviction or judgment against the persons upon whom the same were to be levied;
- All which are utterly and directly contrary to the known laws and statutes and freedom of this realm;

And whereas the said late King James the Second having abdicated the government and the throne being thereby vacant, his Highness the prince of Orange (whom it hath pleased Almighty God to make the glorious instrument of delivering this kingdom from popery and arbitrary power) did (by the advice of the Lords Spiritual and Temporal and divers principal persons of the Commons) cause letters to be written to the Lords Spiritual and Temporal being Protestants, and other letters to the several counties, cities, universities, boroughs and cinque ports, for the choosing of such persons to represent them as were of right to be sent to Parliament, to meet and sit at Westminster upon the two and twentieth day of January in this year one thousand six hundred eighty and eight [old style date], in order to such an establishment as that their religion, laws and liberties might not again be in danger of being subverted, upon which letters elections having been accordingly made;

And thereupon the said Lords Spiritual and Temporal and Commons, pursuant to their respective letters and elections, being now assembled in a full and free representative of this nation, taking into their most se-

rious consideration the best means for attaining the ends aforesaid, do in the first place (as their ancestors in like case have usually done) for the vindicating and asserting their ancient rights and liberties declare

- That the pretended power of suspending the laws or the execution of laws by regal authority without consent of Parliament is illegal;
- That the pretended power of dispensing with laws or the execution of laws by regal authority, as it hath been assumed and exercised of late, is illegal;
- That the commission for erecting the late Court of Commissioners for Ecclesiastical Causes, and all other commissions and courts of like nature, are illegal and pernicious;
- That levying money for or to the use of the Crown by pretence of prerogative, without grant of Parliament, for longer time, or in other manner than the same is or shall be granted, is illegal;
- That it is the right of the subjects to petition the king, and all commitments and prosecutions for such petitioning are illegal;
- That the raising or keeping a standing army within the kingdom in time of peace, unless it be with consent of Parliament, is against law;
- That the subjects which are Protestants may have arms for their defence suitable to their conditions and as allowed by law;
- That election of members of Parliament ought to be free;
- That the freedom of speech and debates or proceedings in Parliament ought not to be impeached or questioned in any court or place out of Parliament;
- That excessive bail ought not to be required, nor excessive fines imposed, nor cruel and unusual punishments inflicted;
- That jurors ought to be duly impanelled and returned, and jurors which pass upon men in trials for high treason ought to be

freeholders;

- That all grants and promises of fines and forfeitures of particular persons before conviction are illegal and void;
- And that for redress of all grievances, and for the amending, strengthening and preserving of the laws, Parliaments ought to be held frequently.

And they do claim, demand and insist upon all and singular the premises as their undoubted rights and liberties, and that no declarations, judgments, doings or proceedings to the prejudice of the people in any of the said premises ought in any wise to be drawn hereafter into consequence or example; to which demand of their rights they are particularly encouraged by the declaration of his Highness the prince of Orange as being the only means for obtaining a full redress and remedy therein.

Having therefore an entire confidence that his said Highness the prince of Orange will perfect the deliverance so far advanced by him, and will still preserve them from the violation of their rights which they have here asserted, and from all other attempts upon their religion, rights and liberties, the said Lords Spiritual and Temporal and Commons assembled at Westminster do resolve that William and Mary, prince and princess of Orange, be and be declared king and queen of England, France and Ireland and the dominions thereunto belonging, to hold the crown and royal dignity of the said kingdoms and dominions to them, the said prince and princess, during their lives and the life of the survivor to them, and that the sole and full exercise of the regal power be only in and executed by the said prince of Orange in the names of the said prince and princess during their joint lives, and after their deceases the said crown and royal dignity of the same kingdoms and dominions to be to the heirs of the body of the said princess, and for default of such issue to the Princess Anne of Denmark and the heirs of her body, and for

default of such issue to the heirs of the body of the said prince of Orange. And the Lords Spiritual and Temporal and Commons do pray the said prince and princess to accept the same accordingly.

And that the oaths hereafter mentioned be taken by all persons of whom the oaths have allegiance and supremacy might be required by law, instead of them; and that the said oaths of allegiance and supremacy be abrogated.

I, A.B., do sincerely promise and swear that I will be faithful and bear true allegiance to their Majesties King William and Queen Mary. So help me God.

I, A.B., do swear that I do from my heart abhor, detest and abjure as impious and heretical this damnable doctrine and position, that princes excommunicated or deprived by the Pope or any authority of the see of Rome may be deposed or murdered by their subjects or any other whatsoever. And I do declare that no foreign prince, person, prelate, state or potentate hath or ought to have any jurisdiction, power, superiority, pre-eminence or authority, ecclesiastical or spiritual, within this realm. So help me God.

Upon which their said Majesties did accept the crown and royal dignity of the kingdoms of England, France and Ireland, and the dominions thereunto belonging, according to the resolution and desire of the said Lords and Commons contained in the said declaration.

And thereupon their Majesties were pleased that the said Lords Spiritual and Temporal and Commons, being the two Houses of Parliament, should continue to sit, and with their Majesties' royal concurrence make effectual provision for the settlement of the religion, laws and liberties of this kingdom, so that the same for the future might not be in danger again of being subverted, to which the said Lords Spiritual and Temporal and Commons did agree, and proceed to act accordingly.

Now in pursuance of the premises the said Lords Spiritual and Temporal and Commons in Parliament assembled, for the ratifying, confirming and establishing the said declaration and the articles, clauses, matters and things therein contained by the force of law made in due form by authority of Parliament, do pray that it may be declared and enacted that all and singular the rights and liberties asserted and claimed in the said declaration are the true, ancient and indubitable rights and liberties of the people of this kingdom, and so shall be esteemed, allowed, adjudged, deemed and taken to be; and that all and every the particulars aforesaid shall be firmly and strictly holden and observed as they are expressed in the said declaration, and all officers and ministers whatsoever shall serve their Majesties and their successors according to the same in all time to come.

And the said Lords Spiritual and Temporal and Commons, seriously considering how it hath pleased Almighty God in his marvellous providence and merciful goodness to this nation to provide and preserve their said Majesties' royal persons most happily to reign over us upon the throne of their ancestors, for which they render unto him from the bottom of their hearts their humblest thanks and praises, do truly, firmly, assuredly and in the sincerity of their hearts think, and do hereby recognize, acknowledge and declare, that King James the Second having abdicated the government, and their Majesties having accepted the crown and royal dignity as aforesaid, their said Majesties did become, were, are and of right ought to be by the laws of this realm our sovereign liege lord and lady, king and queen of England, France and Ireland and the dominions thereunto belonging, in and to whose princely persons the royal state, crown and dignity of the said realms with all honours, styles, titles, regalities, prerogatives, powers, jurisdictions and authorities to the same belonging and appertaining are most fully, rightfully and entirely invested and incorporated, united and annexed. And for preventing all questions and divisions in this realm by reason of any pretended titles to the crown, and for preserving a certainty in the succession thereof, in and upon which the unity, peace, tranquility and safety of this nation doth under God wholly consist and depend, the said Lords Spiritual and Temporal and Commons do beseech their Majesties that it may be enacted, established and declared, that the crown and regal government of the said kingdoms and dominions, with all and singular the premises thereunto belonging and appertaining, shall be and continue to their said Majesties and the survivor of them during their lives and the life of the survivor of them, and that the entire, perfect and full exercise of the regal power and government be only in and executed by his Majesty in the names of both their Majesties during their joint lives; and after their deceases the said crown and premises shall be and remain to the heirs of the body of her Majesty, and for default of such issue to her Royal Highness the Princess Anne of Denmark and the heirs of the body of his said Majesty; and thereunto the said Lords Spiritual and Temporal and Commons do in the name of all the people aforesaid most humbly and faithfully submit themselves, their heirs and posterities for ever, and do faithfully promise that they will stand to, maintain and defend their said Majesties, and also the limitation and succession of the crown herein specified and contained, to the utmost of their powers with their lives and estates against all persons whatsoever that shall attempt anything to the contrary.

And whereas it hath been found by experience that it is inconsistent with the safety and welfare of this Protestant kingdom to be governed by a popish prince, or by any king or queen marrying a papist, the said Lords Spiritual and Temporal and Commons do further pray that it may be enacted, that all and every person and persons that is, are or shall be reconciled to or shall hold communion with the see or Church of Rome, or shall profess the popish religion, or shall marry a papist, shall be excluded and be for ever incapable to inherit, possess or enjoy the crown and government of this realm and Ireland and the dominions thereunto belonging or any part of the same, or to have, use or exercise any regal power, authority or jurisdiction within the same; and in all and every such case or cases the people of these realms shall be and are hereby absolved of their allegiance; and the said crown and government shall from time to time descend to and be enjoyed by such person or persons being Protestants as should have inherited and enjoyed the same in case the said person or persons so reconciled, holding communion or professing or marrying as aforesaid were naturally dead; and that every king and queen of this realm who at any time hereafter shall come to and succeed in the imperial crown of this kingdom shall on the first day of the meeting of the first Parliament next after his or her coming to the crown, sitting in his or her throne in the House of Peers in the presence of the Lords and Commons therein assembled, or at his or her coronation before such person or persons who shall administer the coronation oath to him or her at the time of his or her taking the said oath (which shall first happen), make, subscribe and audibly repeat the declaration mentioned in the statute made in the thirtieth year of the reign of King Charles the Second entitled, *An Act for the more effectual preserving the king's person and government by disabling papists from sitting in either House of Parliament.* But if it shall happen that such king or queen upon his or her succession to the crown of this realm shall be under the age of twelve years, then every such king or queen shall make, subscribe and audibly repeat the same declaration at his or her coronation or the first day of the meeting of the first Parliament as aforesaid which shall first happen after such king or queen shall have attained the said age of twelve years.

I. All which their Majesties are contented and pleased shall be declared, enacted and established by authority of this present Parliament, and shall stand, remain and be the law of this realm for ever; and the same are by their said Majesties, by and with the advice and consent of the Lords Spiritual and Temporal and Commons in Parliament assembled and by the authority of the same, declared, enacted and established accordingly.

II. And be it further declared and enacted by the authority aforesaid, that from and after this present session of Parliament no dispensation by *non obstante* of or to any statute or any part thereof shall be allowed, but that the same shall be held void and of no effect, except a dispensation be allowed of in such statute, and except in such cases as shall be specially provided for by one or more bill or bills to be passed during this present session of Parliament.

III. Provided that no charter or grant or pardon granted before the three and twentieth day of October in the year of our Lord one thousand six hundred eighty-nine [old style date] shall be any ways impeached or invalidated by this Act, but that the same shall be and remain of the same force and effect in law and no other than as if this Act had never been made.

References

1. Toporoski, Richard (Summer, 1996). "*Monarchy Canada: The Invisible Crown.*" http://www.monarchist.ca/mc/invisibl.htm.
2. Statute of Westminster; 1931 c.4 22 and 23 Geo 5.
3. Acts Retained
4. http://www.icons.org.uk/theicons/collection/eccentricity/biography/true-eccentrics.
5. http://www.thegloriousrevolution.org/docs/english%20bill%20of%20rights.htm.

SECTION III: CORE DOCUMENTS

CHAPTER 5

Mayflower Compact (November 21, 1620)

Pilgrims of the New World

The History*

The settlers who came to the New World brought with them a great deal of baggage in the form of ideas and beliefs they had held dear in England. Indeed, many of them, such as the Puritans, came to America so they could live in stricter accord with those beliefs. The Pilgrims, a branch of the Puritans, arrived off the coast of Massachusetts in November 1620, determined to live sacred lives according to biblical commands, and in so doing to build a "city upon a hill" that would be a beacon to the rest of the world.

But aside from their religious enthusiasm, the Pilgrims also knew that the English settlement founded a few years earlier at Jamestown in Virginia had practically foundered because of the lack of a strong government and leadership. They would not make that mistake, and agreed that once a government had been established, they would obey the commands of its leaders.

In making this compact, the Pilgrims drew upon two strong traditions. One was the notion of a social contract, which dated back to biblical times and which would re-

ceive fuller expression in the works of Thomas Hobbes and John Locke later in the century. The other was the belief in covenants. Puritans believed that covenants existed not only between God and man, but also between man and man. The Pilgrims had used covenants in establishing their congregations in the Old World. The Mayflower Compact is such a covenant in that the settlers agreed to form a government and be bound by its rules.

The Compact is often described as America's first constitution, but it is not a constitution in the sense of being a fundamental framework of government. Its importance lies in the belief that government is a form of covenant, and that for government to be legitimate, it must derive from the consent of the governed. The settlers recognized that individually they might not agree with all of the actions of the government they were creating; but they, and succeeding generations, understood that government could be legitimate only if it originated with the consent of those it claimed to govern.

On November 21, 1620, forty-one adult male passengers signed the Mayflower Com-

*Originally published as "The Mayflower Compact (1620)," *Basic Readings in U.S. Democracy*, InfoUSA, Bureau of International Information Programs, U.S. Department of State, Washington, DC, 2009. For additional information see "Pilgrims," *Cape Cod National Seashore History and Culture*, National Park Service, U.S. Department of the Interior, Washington, DC, 2007. This agency is listed in the *National Resource Directory* section of this volume.

pact. The compact served as a device to preserve order and establish rules for self-government. The signers agreed to combine themselves into a "civil Body Politick" that would enact and obey "just and equal laws" that were made for the "general good of the colony." This commitment to justice and equality would be reiterated in many later documents, including the U.S. Constitution.

There were two other colonies in the New World prior to the landing of the Pilgrims in 1620. The first was the Roanoke Colony, which was located on Roanoke Island in the Virginia Colony and financed by Sir Walter Raleigh in the late 16th century. Between 1585 and 1587, several groups attempted to establish this colony, but had abandoned the settlement. The final group of colonists disappeared after three years had elapsed without receiving supplies from the Kingdom of England during the Anglo-Spanish War, leading to the continuing mystery commonly known as "The Lost Colony."

The second settlement was the first successful English settlement in the New World. Named after King James I of England, Jamestown was founded in the Virginia Colony in May of 1607. Jamestown was founded for the purpose of making a profit from gold mining for its investors, while also establishing a permanent foothold in the New World for England. These settlers were given a charter and funded by the Virginia Company, a private corporation. Other successful colonies in North America were in Spanish dominions such as New Spain, New Mexico, and Spanish Florida.

Because the first settlement at Roanoke did not materialize, and the second settlement at Jamestown was a private venture, the Pilgrims are recognized as the first group of emigrants to the New World to draft their own charter, or compact as they called it, and to establish their own civil society with a governmental structure.

The Document

Mayflower Compact

We whose names are underwritten, the loyal subjects of our dread Sovereign Lord King James, by the Grace of God of Great Britain, France and Ireland, King, Defender of the Faith, etc.

Having undertaken, for the Glory of God and advancement of the Christian Faith and Honour of our King and Country, a Voyage to plant the First Colony in the Northern Parts of Virginia, do by these presents solemnly and mutually in the presence of God and one of another, Covenant and Combine ourselves together into a Civil Body Politic, for our better ordering and preservation and furtherance of the end aforesaid; and by virtue hereof to enact, constitute and frame such just and equal Laws, Ordinances, Acts, Constitutions and Offices, from time to time, as shall be thought most meet and convenient for the general good of the Colony, unto which we promise all due submission and obedience. In witness whereof we have hereunder subscribed our names at Cape Cod, the 11th of November, in the year of the reign of our Sovereign Lord King James, of England, France and Ireland the eighteenth, and of Scotland the fifty-fourth. Anno Domini 1620.

— Signed by forty-one (41) adult male passengers.

CHAPTER 6

Fundamental Orders of Connecticut (January 14, 1639)

Colony Council

The History*

The Fundamental Orders were adopted by the Connecticut Colony council on January 14, 1639.[1][2] The orders describe the government set up by the Connecticut River towns, setting its structure and powers.

It has the features of a written constitution, and is considered by some as the first written Constitution in the Western tradition,[3] and thus earned Connecticut its nickname of *The Constitution State*. John Fiske, a Connecticut historian, was the first to claim that the Fundamental Orders were the first written Constitution, a claim disputed by some modern historians.[4] The orders were transcribed into the official colony records by the colony's secretary Thomas Welles. It was a Constitution for the colonial government of Hartford and was similar to the government Massachusetts had set up. However, this Order gave men more voting rights and opened up more men to be able to run for office positions.

In 1635 a group of Massachusetts Puritans and Congregationalists who were dissatisfied with the rate of Anglican reforms, sought to establish an ecclesiastical society subject to their own rules and regulations. The Massachusetts General Court granted them permission to settle the cities of Springfield, Windsor, Wethersfield, and Hartford.[5] Ownership of the land was called into dispute by the English holders of the Warwick Patent of 1631. The Massachusetts General Court established the March Commission to mediate the dispute, and named Roger Ludlow as its head. The Commission named 8 magistrates from the Connecticut towns to implement a legal system. The March commission expired in March 1636, after which time the settlers continued to self-govern. On May 29, 1638 Ludlow wrote to Massachusetts Governor Winthrop that the colonists wanted to "unite ourselves to walk and lie peaceably and lovingly together." Ludlow drafted the Fundamental Orders, which were adopted on January 14, 1639, which established Connecticut as a self-ruled entity.

There is no record of the debates or proceedings of the drafting or enactment of the Fundamental Orders. It is postulated that the farmers wished to remain anonymous to avoid retaliation by the English authorities. According to John Taylor:[6]

*Originally published as "Fundamental Orders of Connecticut," *Wikipedia*, Wikimedia Foundation, Inc., San Francisco, California, December 2008. For additional information see "The First Constitution of Connecticut," *Historical Antecedents*, Secretary of State, State of Connecticut, Hartford, Connecticut, 2008. This agency is listed in the *National Resource Directory* section of this volume.

The men of the three towns were a law unto themselves. It is known that they were in earnest for the establishment of a government on broad lines; and it is certain that the ministers and captains, the magistrates and men of affairs, forceful in the settlements from the beginning, were the men who took the lead, guided the discussions, and found the root of the whole matter in the first written declaration of independence in these historical orders.

The Fundamental Orders of Connecticut is a short document, but it contains some principles that were later applied in creating the United States government. Government is based in the rights of an individual, and the orders spell out some of those rights, as well as how they are ensured by the government. It provides that all free men share in electing their magistrates, and uses secret, paper ballots. It states the powers of the government, and some limits within which that power is exercised.

In one sense, the Fundamental Orders were replaced by a Royal Charter in 1662, but the major outline of the charter was written in Connecticut and embodied the Orders' rights and mechanics. It was carried to England by Governor John Winthrop and basically approved by the British King, Charles II. The colonists generally viewed the charter as a continuation and surety for their Fundamental Orders; the Charter Oak got its name when that charter was supposedly hidden in it, rather than be surrendered to the King's agents.

Today, the individual rights in the Orders, with others added over the years, are still included as a "Declaration of Rights" in the first article of the current Connecticut Constitution, adopted in 1965.

The Document

Fundamental Orders

For as much as it hath pleased Almighty God by the wise disposition of his divine providence so to order and dispose of things that we the Inhabitants and Residents of Windsor, Hartford and Wethersfield are now cohabiting and dwelling in and upon the River of Connectecotte and the lands thereunto adjoining; and well knowing where a people are gathered together the word of God requires that to maintain the peace and union of such a people there should be an orderly and decent Government established according to God, to order and dispose of the affairs of the people at all seasons as occasion shall require; do therefore associate and conjoin ourselves to be as one Public State or Commonwealth; and do for ourselves and our successors and such as shall be adjoined to us at any time hereafter, enter into Combination and Confederation together, to maintain and preserve the liberty and purity of the Gospel of our Lord Jesus which we now profess, as also, the discipline of the Churches, which according to the truth of the said Gospel is now practiced amongst us; as also in our civil affairs to be guided and governed according to such Laws, Rules, Orders and Decrees as shall be made, ordered, and decreed as followeth:

1. It is Ordered, sentenced, and decreed, that there shall be yearly two General Assemblies or Courts, the one the second Thursday in April, the other the second Thursday in September following; the first shall be called the Court of Election, wherein shall be yearly chosen from time to time, so many Magistrates and other public Officers as shall be found requisite: Whereof one to be chosen Governor for the year ensuing and until another be chosen, and no other Magistrate to be chosen for more than one year: provided always there be six chosen besides the Governor, which being chosen and sworn according to an Oath recorded for that purpose, shall have the power to administer justice according to the Laws here established, and for want thereof, according to the Rule of the Word of God; which choice shall be

made by all that are admitted freemen and have taken the Oath of Fidelity, and do co-habit within this Jurisdiction having been admitted Inhabitants by the major part of the Town wherein they live or the major part of such as shall be then present.

2. It is Ordered, sentenced, and decreed, that the election of the aforesaid Magistrates shall be in this manner: every person present and qualified for choice shall bring in (to the person deputed to receive them) one single paper with the name of him written in it whom he desires to have Governor, and that he that hath the greatest number of papers shall be Governor for that year. And the rest of the Magistrates or public officers to be chosen in this manner: the Secretary for the time being shall first read the names of all that are to be put to choice and then shall severally nominate them distinctly, and every one that would have the person nominated to be chosen shall bring in one single paper written upon, and he that would not have him chosen shall bring in a blank; and every one that hath more written papers than blanks shall be a Magistrate for that year; which papers shall be received and told by one or more that shall be then chosen by the court and sworn to be faithful therein; but in case there should not be six chosen as aforesaid, besides the Governor, out of those which are nominated, then he or they which have the most writen papers shall be a Magistrate or Magistrates for the ensuing year, to make up the aforesaid number.

3. It is Ordered, sentenced, and decreed, that the Secretary shall not nominate any person, nor shall any person be chosen newly into the Magistracy which was not propounded in some General Court before, to be nominated the next election; and to that end it shall be lawful for each of the Towns aforesaid by their deputies to nominate any two whom they conceive fit to be put to election; and the Court may add so many more as they judge requisite.

4. It is Ordered, sentenced, and de-

creed, that no person be chosen Governor above once in two years, and that the Governor be always a member of some approved Congregation, and formerly of the Magistracy within this Jurisdiction; and that all the Magistrates, Freemen of this Commonwealth; and that no Magistrate or other public officer shall execute any part of his or their office before they are severally sworn, which shall be done in the face of the court if they be present, and in case of absence by some deputed for that purpose.

5. It is Ordered, sentenced, and decreed, that to the aforesaid Court of Election the several Towns shall send their deputies, and when the Elections are ended they may proceed in any public service as at other Courts. Also the other General Court in September shall be for making of laws, and any other public occasion, which concerns the good of the Commonwealth.

6. It is Ordered, sentenced, and decreed, that the Governor shall, either by himself or by the Secretary, send out summons to the Constables of every Town for the calling of these two standing Courts one month at least before their several times: And also if the Governor and the greatest part of the Magistrates see cause upon any special occasion to call a General Court, they may give order to the Secretary so to do within fourteen days' warning: And if urgent necessity so required, upon a shorter notice, giving sufficient grounds for it to the deputies when they meet, or else be questioned for the same. And if the Governor and major part of Magistrates shall either neglect or refuse to call the two General standing Courts or either of them, as also at other times when the occasions of the Commonwealth require, the Freemen thereof, or the major part of them, shall petition to them so to do; if then it be either denied or neglected, the said Freemen, or the major part of them, shall have the power to give order to the Constables of the several Towns to do the same, and so may meet together, and choose to themselves a

Moderator, and may proceed to do any act of power which any other General Courts may.

7. It is Ordered, sentenced, and decreed, that after there are warrants given out for any of the said General Courts, the Constable or Constables of each Town, shall forthwith give notice distinctly to the inhabitants of the same, in some public assembly or by going or sending from house to house, that at a place and time by him or them limited and set, they meet and assemble themselves together to elect and choose certain deputies to be at the General Court then following to agitate the affairs of the Commonwealth; which said deputies shall be chosen by all that are admitted Inhabitants in the several Towns and have taken the oath of fidelity; provided that none be chosen a Deputy for any General Court which is not a Freeman of this Commonwealth.

The aforesaid deputies shall be chosen in manner following: every person that is present and qualified as before expressed, shall bring the names of such, written in several papers, as they desire to have chosen for that employment, and these three or four, more or less, being the number agreed on to be chosen for that time, that have the greatest number of papers written for them shall be deputies for that Court; whose names shall be endorsed on the back side of the warrant and returned into the Court, with the Constable or Constables' hand unto the same.

8. It is Ordered, sentenced, and decreed, that Windsor, Hartford, and Wethersfield shall have power, each Town, to send four of their Freemen as their deputies to every General Court; and Whatsoever other Town shall be hereafter added to this Jurisdiction, they shall send so many deputies as the Court shall judge meet, a reasonable proportion to the number of Freemen that are in the said Towns being to be attended therein; which deputies shall have the power of the whole Town to give their votes and allowance

to all such laws and orders as may be for the public good, and unto which the said Towns are to be bound.

9. It is Ordered, sentenced, and decreed, that the deputies thus chosen shall have power and liberty to appoint a time and a place of meeting together before any General Court, to advise and consult of all such things as may concern the good of the public, as also to examine their own Elections, whether according to the order, and if they or the greatest part of them find any election to be illegal they may seclude such for present from their meeting, and return the same and their reasons to the Court; and if it be proved true, the Court may fine the party or parties so intruding, and the Town, if they see cause, and give out a warrant to go to a new election in a legal way, either in part or in whole. Also the said deputies shall have power to fine any that shall be disorderly at their meetings, or for not coming in due time or place according to appointment; and they may return the said fines into the Court if it be refused to be paid, and the Treasurer to take notice of it, and to escheat or levy the same as he does other fines.

10. It is Ordered, sentenced, and decreed, that every General Court, except such as through neglect of the Governor and the greatest part of the Magistrates the Freemen themselves do call, shall consist of the Governor, or some one chosen to moderate the Court, and four other Magistrates at least, with the major part of the deputies of the several Towns legally chosen; and in case the Freemen, or major part of them, through neglect or refusal of the Governor and major part of the Magistrates, shall call a Court, it shall consist of the major part of Freemen that are present or their deputiues, with a Moderator chosen by them: In which said General Courts shall consist the supreme power of the Commonwealth, and they only shall have power to make laws or repeal them, to grant levies, to admit of Freemen, dispose of lands undisposed of, to several Towns or

persons, and also shall have power to call either Court or Magistrate or any other person whatsoever into question for any misdemeanor, and may for just causes displace or deal otherwise according to the nature of the offense; and also may deal in any other matter that concerns the good of this Commonwealth, except election of Magistrates, which shall be done by the whole body of Freemen.

In which Court the Governor or Moderator shall have power to order the Court, to give liberty of speech, and silence unseasonable and disorderly speakings, to put all things to vote, and in case the vote be equal to have the casting voice. But none of these Courts shall be adjourned or dissolved without the consent of the major part of the Court.

11. It is Ordered, sentenced, and decreed, that when any General Court upon the occasions of the Commonwealth have agreed upon any sum, or sums of money to be levied upon the several Towns within this Jurisdiction, that a committee be chosen to set out and appoint what shall be the proportion of every Town to pay of the said levy, provided the committee be made up of an equal number out of each Town.

14th January 1639 the 11 Orders above said are voted.

REFERENCES

1. The January 14, 1638 date was in the old style Julian Calendar, before conversion to the modern new style Gregorian Calendar.
2. "Fundamental Orders." *The Columbia Encyclopedia, Sixth Edition.* Columbia University Press. 2005.
3. Lutz, Donald S.; Schechter, Stephen L.; Bernstein, Richard J. (1990). *Roots of the Republic: American founding documents interpreted.* Madison, Wis: Madison House. Pp. 24. ISBN 0-945612-19-2.
4. Secretary of the State of Connecticut (2007). "STATE OF CONNECTICUT Sites Seals Symbols. *The Connecticut State Register and Manual.* State of Connecticut.
5. Horton, Wesley W. (1993-06-30). *The Connecticut State Constitution: A Reference Guide.* Reference guides to the state constitutions of the United States. No. 17. Westport, Connecticut: Greenwood Press. pp. 2.
6. Taylor, John M. *Roger Ludlow: The Colonial Lawmaker.* G.P. Putnam's Sons, New York, NY, 1900.

CHAPTER 7

Declaration and Resolves of the First Continental Congress (October 14, 1774)

Continental Congress

The History*

The first Continental Congress met in Carpenter's Hall in Philadelphia, from September 5, to October 26, 1774. Carpenter's Hall was also the seat of the Pennsylvania Congress. All of the colonies except Georgia sent delegates. These were elected by the people, by the colonial legislatures, or by the committees of correspondence of the respective colonies. The colonies presented there were united in a determination to show a combined authority to Great Britain, but their aims were not uniform at all. Pennsylvania and New York sent delegates with firm instructions to seek a resolution with England. The other colonies' voices were defensive of colonial rights, but pretty evenly divided between those who sought legislative parity, and the more radical members who were prepared for separation. Virginia's delegation was made up of a most even mix of these and, not coincidentally, presented the most eminent group of men in America: Colo. George Washington, Richard Henry Lee, Patrick Henry, Edmund Pendelton, Colo. Benjamin Harrison, Richard Bland, and at the head of them Peyton Randolph — who would immediately be elected president of the convention.

The objectives of the body were not entirely clear but, with such leadership as was found there, a core set of tasks was carried out. It was agreeable to all that the King and Parliament must be made to understand the grievances of the colonies and that the body must do everything possible to communicate the same to the population of America, and to the rest of the world.

The first few weeks were consumed in discussion and debate. The colonies had always, up to this time, acted as independent entities. There was much distrust to overcome. The first matter to be considered by all was A Plan of Union of Great Britain and the Colonies, offered by Joseph Galloway of Pennsylvania. The plan was considered very attractive to most of the members, as it proposed a popularly elected *Grand Council* which would represent the interests of the

*Originally published as "First Continental Congress," *United States History*, Independence Hall Association, Carpenters' Hall, Philadelphia, Pennsylvania, 2008. For additional information see "The American Revolution, 1763–1783: The Colonies Move Toward Open Rebellion, 1773–1774," *American Memory Timeline*, Library of Congress, Washington, DC, 2003. This agency is listed in the *National Resource Directory* section of this volume.

colonies as a whole, and would be a continental equivalent to the English Parliament. Poised against this would be a *President General*, appointed by the crown, to represent the authority of the king in America. Conflict in Boston overcame the effort at conciliation. The arrival of the Suffolk County (Boston) resolves just prior to the vote on the Plan of Union caused it to be discarded by a narrow margin.

On October 14, the Declaration and Resolves established the course of the congress, as a statement of principles common to all of the colonies. Congress voted to meet again the following year if these grievances were not attended to by England.

The Document

Declaration and Resolves of the First Continental Congress

Whereas, since the close of the last war, the British parliament, claiming a power, of right, to bind the people of America by statutes in all cases whatsoever, hath, in some acts, expressly imposed taxes on them, and in others, under various presences, but in fact for the purpose of raising a revenue, hath imposed rates and duties payable in these colonies, established a board of commissioners, with unconstitutional powers, and extended the jurisdiction of courts of admiralty, not only for collecting the said duties, but for the trial of causes merely arising within the body of a county:

And whereas, in consequence of other statutes, judges, who before held only estates at will in their offices, have been made dependant on the crown alone for their salaries, and standing armies kept in times of peace: And whereas it has lately been resolved in parliament, that by force of a statute, made in the thirty-fifth year of the reign of King Henry the Eighth, colonists may be transported to England, and tried there upon ac-

cusations for treasons and misprisions, or concealments of treasons committed in the colonies, and by a late statute, such trials have been directed in cases therein mentioned:

And whereas, in the last session of parliament, three statutes were made; one entitled, "An act to discontinue, in such manner and for such time as are therein mentioned, the landing and discharging, lading, or shipping of goods, wares and merchandise, at the town, and within the harbour of Boston, in the province of Massachusetts-Bay in New England"; another entitled, "An act for the better regulating the government of the province of Massachusetts-Bay in New England;" and another entitled, "An act for the impartial administration of justice, in the cases of persons questioned for any act done by them in the execution of the law, or for the suppression of riots and tumults, in the province of the Massachusetts-Bay in New England;" and another statute was then made, "for making more effectual provision for the government of the province of Quebec, etc." All which statutes are impolitic, unjust, and cruel, as well as unconstitutional, and most dangerous and destructive of American rights:

And whereas, assemblies have been frequently dissolved, contrary to the rights of the people, when they attempted to deliberate on grievances; and their dutiful, humble, loyal, and reasonable petitions to the crown for redress, have been repeatedly treated with contempt, by his Majesty's ministers of state:

The good people of the several colonies of New-Hampshire, Massachusetts-Bay, Rhode Island and Providence Plantations, Connecticut, New-York, New-Jersey, Pennsylvania, Newcastle, Kent, and Sussex on Delaware, Maryland, Virginia, North-Carolina and South-Carolina, justly alarmed at these arbitrary proceedings of parliament and administration, have severally elected, constituted, and appointed deputies to meet, and sit in general Congress, in the city of Philadelphia, in order to obtain such establishment, as that their religion, laws, and liberties, may not be subverted: Whereupon the deputies so appointed being now assembled, in a full and free representation of these colonies, taking into their most serious consideration, the best means of attaining the ends aforesaid, do, in the first place, as Englishmen, their ancestors in like cases have usually done, for asserting and vindicating their rights and liberties, DECLARE,

That the inhabitants of the English colonies in North-America, by the immutable laws of nature, the principles of the English constitution, and the several charters or compacts, have the following RIGHTS:

Resolved, N.C.D. 1. That they are entitled to life, liberty and property: and they have never ceded to any foreign power whatever, a right to dispose of either without their consent.

Resolved, N.C.D. 2. That our ancestors, who first settled these colonies, were at the time of their emigration from the mother country, entitled to all the rights, liberties, and immunities of free and natural-born subjects, within the realm of England.

Resolved, N.C.D. 3. That by such emigration they by no means forfeited, surrendered, or lost any of those rights, but that they were, and their descendants now are, entitled to the exercise and enjoyment of all such of them, as their local and other circumstances enable them to exercise and enjoy.

Resolved, 4. That the foundation of English liberty, and of all free government, is a right in the people to participate in their legislative council: and as the English colonists are not represented, and from their local and other circumstances, cannot properly be represented in the British parliament, they are entitled to a free and exclusive power of legislation in their several provincial legislatures, where their right of representation can alone be preserved, in all cases of taxation and internal polity, subject only to the negative of their sovereign, in such manner as has been

heretofore used and accustomed: But, from the necessity of the case, and a regard to the mutual interest of both countries, we cheerfully consent to the operation of such acts of the British parliament, as are bonfide, restrained to the regulation of our external commerce, for the purpose of securing the commercial advantages of the whole empire to the mother country, and the commercial benefits of its respective members; excluding every idea of taxation internal or external, for raising a revenue on the subjects, in America, without their consent.

Resolved, N.C.D. 5. That the respective colonies are entitled to the common law of England, and more especially to the great and inestimable privilege of being tried by their peers of the vicinage, according to the course of that law.

Resolved, N.C.D. 6. That they are entitled to the benefit of such of the English statutes, as existed at the time of their colonization; and which they have, by experience, respectively found to be applicable to their several local and other circumstances.

Resolved, N.C.D. 7. That these, his Majesty's colonies, are likewise entitled to all the immunities and privileges granted and confirmed to them by royal charters, or secured by their several codes of provincial laws.

Resolved, N.C.D. 8. That they have a right peaceably to assemble, consider of their grievances, and petition the king; and that all prosecutions, prohibitory proclamations, and commitments for the same, are illegal.

Resolved, N.C.D. 9. That the keeping a standing army in these colonies, in times of peace, without the consent of the legislature of that colony, in which such army is kept, is against law.

Resolved, N.C.D. 10. It is indispensably necessary to good government, and rendered essential by the English constitution, that the constituent branches of the legislature be independent of each other; that, therefore, the exercise of legislative power in several colonies, by a council appointed, during pleasure, by the crown, is unconstitutional, dangerous and destructive to the freedom of American legislation.

All and each of which the aforesaid deputies, in behalf of themselves, and their constituents, do claim, demand, and insist on, as their indubitable rights and liberties, which cannot be legally taken from them, altered or abridged by any power whatever, without their own consent, by their representatives in their several provincial legislatures.

In the course of our inquiry, we find many infringements and violations of the foregoing rights, which, from an ardent desire, that harmony and mutual intercourse of affection and interest may be restored, we pass over for the present, and proceed to state such acts and measures as have been adopted since the last war, which demonstrate a system formed to enslave America.

Resolved, N.C.D. That the following acts of parliament are infringements and violations of the rights of the colonists; and that the repeal of them is essentially necessary, in order to restore harmony between Great Britain and the American colonies, viz.

The several acts of Geo. III. ch. 15, and ch. 34.-5 Geo. III. ch.25.-6 Geo. ch. 52.-7 Geo. III. ch. 41 and ch. 46.-8 Geo. III. ch. 22. which impose duties for the purpose of raising a revenue in America, extend the power of the admiralty courts beyond their ancient limits, deprive the American subject of trial by jury, authorize the judges certificate to indemnify the prosecutor from damages, that he might otherwise be liable to, requiring oppressive security from a claimant of ships and goods seized, before he shall be allowed to defend his property, and are subversive of American rights.

Also 12 Geo. III. ch. 24, intituled, "An act for the better securing his majesty's dock-yards, magazines, ships, ammunition, and stores," which declares a new offence in America, and deprives the American subject

of a constitutional trial by jury of the vicinage, by authorizing the trial of any person, charged with the committing any offence described in the said act, out of the realm, to be indicted and tried for the same in any shire or county within the realm.

Also the three acts passed in the last session of parliament, for stopping the port and blocking up the harbour of Boston, for altering the charter and government of Massachusetts-Bay, and that which is entitled, "An act for the better administration of justice, etc."

Also the act passed in the same session for establishing the Roman Catholic religion, in the province of Quebec, abolishing the equitable system of English laws, and erecting a tyranny there, to the great danger (from so total a dissimilarity of religion, law and government) of the neighboring British colonies, by the assistance of whose blood and treasure the said country was conquered from France.

Also the act passed in the same session, for the better providing suitable quarters for officers and soldiers in his majesty's service, in North-America.

Also, that the keeping a standing army in several of these colonies, in time of peace, without the consent of the legislature of that colony, in which such army is kept, is against law.

To these grievous acts and measures, Americans cannot submit, but in hopes their fellow subjects in Great Britain will, on a revision of them, restore us to that state, in which both countries found happiness and prosperity, we have for the present, only resolved to pursue the following peaceable measures: 1. To enter into a non-importation, non-consumption, and non-exportation agreement or association. 2. To prepare an address to the people of Great-Britain, and a memorial to the inhabitants of British America: and 3. To prepare a loyal address to his majesty, agreeable to resolutions already entered into.

CHAPTER 8

Declaration of the Causes and Necessity of Taking Up Arms (July 6, 1775)

Continental Congress

The History*

The Declaration of the Causes and Necessity of Taking Up Arms was a document issued by the Second Continental Congress on July 6, 1775, to explain why the Thirteen Colonies had taken up arms in what had become the American Revolutionary War, and represents an important development in the political thought that went into the American Revolution. The final draft of the Declaration was written by John Dickinson, who incorporated language from an earlier draft by Thomas Jefferson.

The Declaration describes what colonists viewed as the unconstitutional effort by the British Parliament to extend its jurisdiction into the colonies following the Seven Years' War. Objectionable policies listed in the Declaration include taxation without representation, extended use of vice admiralty courts, the several Coercive Acts, and the Declaratory Act. The Declaration describes how the colonists had, for ten years, repeatedly petitioned for the redress of their grievances, only to have their pleas ignored or rejected by the British monarchy and government. Even though British troops have been sent to enforce these unconstitutional acts, the Declaration insists that the colonists do not yet seek independence from the British Empire, only a self-governing place within it. They have taken up arms "in defence of the Freedom that is our Birthright and which we ever enjoyed until the late Violation of it," and will "lay them down when Hostilities shall cease on the part of the Aggressors."

In the 19th century, the authorship of the Declaration was disputed. In a collection of his works first published in 1801, John Dickinson took credit for writing the Declaration. This claim went unchallenged by Thomas Jefferson until many years later, when Jefferson was nearly 80 years old. In his autobiography, Jefferson claimed that he wrote the first draft, but Dickinson objected that it was too radical, and so Congress allowed Dickinson to write a more moderate

*Originally published as "Declaration of the Causes and Necessity of Taking Up Arms," *Wikipedia*, Wikimedia Foundation, Inc., San Francisco, California, October 2009. For additional information see "The American Revolution, 1763–1783: First Shots of War, 1775," *American Memory Timeline*, Library of Congress, Washington, DC, 2003. This agency is listed in the *National Resource Directory* section of this volume.

version, keeping only the last four-and-a-half paragraphs of Jefferson's draft. Jefferson's version of events was accepted by historians for many years. In 1950, Julian P. Boyd, the editor of Jefferson's papers, examined the extant drafts and determined that Jefferson's memory was faulty and that Dickinson claimed too much credit for the final text.

According to Boyd, an initial draft was reportedly written by John Rutledge, a member of a committee of five appointed to create the Declaration. Rutledge's draft was not accepted and does not survive. Jefferson and Dickinson were then added to the committee. Jefferson was appointed to write a draft; how much he drew upon the lost Rutledge draft, if at all, is unknown. Jefferson then apparently submitted his draft to Dickinson, who suggested some changes, which Jefferson, for the most part, decided not to use. The result was that Dickinson rewrote the Declaration, keeping some passages written by Jefferson. Contrary to Jefferson's recollection in his old age, Dickinson's version was not less radical; according to Boyd, in some respects Dickinson's draft was more blunt. The bold statement near the end was written by Dickinson: "Our cause is just. Our union is perfect. Our internal resources are great, and, if necessary, foreign assistance is undoubtedly attainable." The disagreement in 1775 between Dickinson and Jefferson appears to have been primarily a matter of style, not content.

The Document

Declaration of the Causes and Necessity of Taking Up Arms[1]

If it was possible for men, who exercise their reason to believe, that the divine Author of our existence intended a part of the human race to hold an absolute property in, and an unbounded power over others, marked out by his infinite goodness and wisdom, as the objects of a legal domination never rightfully resistible, however severe and oppressive, the inhabitants of these colonies might at least require from the parliament of Great-Britain some evidence, that this dreadful authority over them, has been granted to that body. But a reverance for our Creator, principles of humanity, and the dictates of common sense, must convince all those who reflect upon the subject, that government was instituted to promote the welfare of mankind, and ought to be administered for the attainment of that end. The legislature of Great-Britain, however, stimulated by an inordinate passion for a power not only unjustifiable, but which they know to be peculiarly reprobated by the very constitution of that kingdom, and desparate of success in any mode of contest, where regard should be had to truth, law, or right, have at length, deserting those, attempted to effect their cruel and impolitic purpose of enslaving these colonies by violence, and have thereby rendered it necessary for us to close with their last appeal from reason to arms. — Yet, however blinded that assembly may be, by their intemperate rage for unlimited domination, so to sight justice and the opinion of mankind, we esteem ourselves bound by obligations of respect to the rest of the world, to make known the justice of our cause.

Our forefathers, inhabitants of the island of Great-Britain, left their native land, to seek on these shores a residence for civil and religious freedom. At the expense of their blood, at the hazard of their fortunes, without the least charge to the country from which they removed, by unceasing labour, and an unconquerable spirit, they effected settlements in the distant and unhospitable wilds of America, then filled with numerous and warlike barbarians. — Societies or governments, vested with perfect legislatures, were formed under charters from the crown, and an harmonious intercourse was established between the colonies and the kingdom from which they derived their origin. The mutual benefits of this union became in a short time so extraordinary, as to excite astonishment. It is universally confessed, that the amazing increase of the wealth, strength, and navigation of the realm, arose from this source; and the minister, who so wisely and successfully directed the measures of Great-Britain in the late war, publicly declared, that these colonies enabled her to triumph over her enemies.— Towards the conclusion of that war, it pleased our sovereign to make a change in his counsels.— From that fatal movement, the affairs of the British empire began to fall into confusion, and gradually sliding from the summit of glorious prosperity, to which they had been advanced by the virtues and abilities of one man, are at length distracted by the convulsions, that now shake it to its deepest foundations.— The new ministry finding the brave foes of Britain, though frequently defeated, yet still contending, took up the unfortunate idea of granting them a hasty peace, and then subduing her faithful friends.

These devoted colonies were judged to be in such a state, as to present victories without bloodshed, and all the easy emoluments of statuteable plunder.— The uninterrupted tenor of their peaceable and respectful behaviour from the beginning of colonization, their dutiful, zealous, and useful services during the war, though so recently and amply acknowledged in the most honourable manner by his majesty, by the late king, and by parliament, could not save them from the meditated innovations.— Parliament was influenced to adopt the pernicious project, and assuming a new power over them, have in the course of eleven years, given such decisive specimens of the spirit and consequences attending this power, as to leave no doubt concerning the effects of acquiescence under it. They have undertaken to give and grant our money without our consent, though we have ever exercised an exclusive right to dispose of our own property; statutes have been passed for extending the jurisdiction of

courts of admiralty and vice-admiralty beyond their ancient limits; for depriving us of the accustomed and inestimable privilege of trial by jury, in cases affecting both life and property; for suspending the legislature of one of the colonies; for interdicting all commerce to the capital of another; and for altering fundamentally the form of government established by charter, and secured by acts of its own legislature solemnly confirmed by the crown; for exempting the *"murderers"* of colonists from legal trial, and in effect, from punishment; for erecting in a neighbouring province, acquired by the joint arms of Great-Britain and America, a despotism dangerous to our very existence; and for quartering soldiers upon the colonists in time of profound peace. It has also been resolved in parliament, that colonists charged with committing certain offences, shall be transported to England to be tried.

But why should we enumerate our injuries in detail? By one statute it is declared, that parliament can *"of right make laws to bind us in all cases whatsoever."* What is to defend us against so enormous, so unlimited a power? Not a single man of those who assume it, is chosen by us; or is subject to our control or influence; but, on the contrary, they are all of them exempt from the operation of such laws, and an American revenue, if not diverted from the ostensible purposes for which it is raised, would actually lighten their own burdens in proportion, as they increase ours. We saw the misery to which such despotism would reduce us. We for ten years incessantly and ineffectually besieged the throne as supplicants; we reasoned, we remonstrated with parliament, in the most mild and decent language.

Administration sensible that we should regard these oppressive measures as freemen ought to do, sent over fleets and armies to enforce them. The indignation of the Americans was roused, it is true; but it was the indignation of a virtuous, loyal, and affectionate people. A Congress of delegates from the

United Colonies was assembled at Philadelphia, on the fifth day of last September. We resolved again to offer an humble and dutiful petition to the King, and also addressed our fellow-subjects of Great-Britain. We have pursued every temperate, every respectful measure; we have even proceeded to break off our commercial intercourse with our fellow-subjects, as the last peaceable admonition, that our attachment to no nation upon earth should supplant our attachment to liberty.— This, we flattered ourselves, was the ultimate step of the controversy: but subsequent events have shewn, how vain was this hope of finding moderation in our enemies.

Several threatening expressions against the colonies were inserted in his majesty's speech; our petition, tho' we were told it was a decent one, and that his majesty had been pleased to receive it graciously, and to promise laying it before his parliament, was huddled into both houses among a bundle of American papers, and there neglected. The lords and commons in their address, in the month of February, said, that "*a rebellion at that time actually existed within the province of Massachusetts-Bay; and that those concerned with it, had been countenanced and encouraged by unlawful combinations and engagements, entered into by his majesty's subjects in several of the other colonies; and therefore they besought his majesty, that he would take the most effectual measures to inforce due obediance to the laws and authority of the supreme legislature.* "— Soon after, the commercial intercourse of whole colonies, with foreign countries, and with each other, was cut off by an act of parliament; by another several of them were intirely prohibited from the fisheries in the seas near their coasts, on which they always depended for their sustenance; and large reinforcements of ships and troops were immediately sent over to general Gage.

Fruitless were all the entreaties, arguments, and eloquence of an illustrious band of the most distinguished peers, and com-

moners, who nobly and strenuously asserted the justice of our cause, to stay, or even to mitigate the heedless fury with which these accumulated and unexampled outrages were hurried on. — Equally fruitless was the interference of the city of London, of Bristol, and many other respectable towns in our favor. Parliament adopted an insidious manoeuvre calculated to divide us, to establish a perpetual auction of taxations where colony should bid against colony, all of them uninformed what ransom would redeem their lives; and thus to extort from us, at the point of the bayonet, the unknown sums that should be sufficient to gratify, if possible to gratify, ministerial rapacity, with the miserable indulgence left to us of raising, in our own mode, the prescribed tribute. What terms more rigid and humiliating could have been dictated by remorseless victors to conquered enemies? In our circumstances to accept them, would be to deserve them.

Soon after the intelligence of these proceedings arrived on this continent, general Gage, who in the course of the last year had taken possession of the town of Boston, in the province of Massachusetts-Bay, and still occupied it a garrison, on the 19th day of April, sent out from that place a large detachment of his army, who made an unprovoked assault on the inhabitants of the said province, at the town of Lexington, as appears by the affidavits of a great number of persons, some of whom were officers and soldiers of that detachment, murdered eight of the inhabitants, and wounded many others. From thence the troops proceeded in warlike array to the town of Concord, where they set upon another party of the inhabitants of the same province, killing several and wounding more, until compelled to retreat by the country people suddenly assembled to repel this cruel aggression. Hostilities, thus commenced by the British troops, have been since prosecuted by them without regard to faith or reputation. — The inhabitants of Boston being confined within that town by the general their governor, and having, in order to procure their dismission, entered into a treaty with him, it was stipulated that the said inhabitants having deposited their arms with their own magistrate, should have liberty to depart, taking with them their other effects. They accordingly delivered up their arms, but in open violation of honour, in defiance of the obligation of treaties, which even savage nations esteemed sacred, the governor ordered the arms deposited as aforesaid, that they might be preserved for their owners, to be seized by a body of soldiers; detained the greatest part of the inhabitants in the town, and compelled the few who were permitted to retire, to leave their most valuable effects behind.

By this perfidy wives are separated from their husbands, children from their parents, the aged and the sick from their relations and friends, who wish to attend and comfort them; and those who have been used to live in plenty and even elegance, are reduced to deplorable distress.

The general, further emulating his ministerial masters, by a proclamation bearing date on the 12th day of June, after venting the grossest falsehoods and calumnies against the good people of these colonies, proceeds to "*declare them all, either by name or description, to be rebels and traitors, to supersede the course of the common law, and instead thereof to publish and order the use and exercise of the law martial.*"—His troops have butchered our countrymen, have wantonly burnt Charlestown, besides a considerable number of houses in other places; our ships and vessels are seized; the necessary supplies of provisions are intercepted, and he is exerting his utmost power to spread destruction and devastation around him.

We have received certain intelligence, that general Carelton *[Carleton]*, the governor of Canada, is instigating the people of that province and the Indians to fall upon us; and we have but too much reason to apprehend, that schemes have been formed to excite domestic enemies against us. In brief, a part of these colonies now feel, and all of them are sure of feeling, as far as the vengeance of administration can inflict them, the complicated calamities of fire, sword and famine. We[2] are reduced to the alternative of chusing an unconditional submission to the tyranny of irritated ministers, or resistance by force.—The latter is our choice.—We have counted the cost of this contest, and find nothing so dreadful as voluntary slavery.—Honour, justice, and humanity, forbid us tamely to surrender that freedom which we received from our gallant ancestors, and which our innocent posterity have a right to receive from us. We cannot endure the infamy and guilt of resigning succeeding generations to that wretchedness which inevitably awaits them, if we basely entail hereditary bondage upon them.

Our cause is just. Our union is perfect. Our internal resources are great, and, if necessary, foreign assistance is undoubtedly attainable.—We gratefully acknowledge, as signal instances of the Divine favour towards us, that his Providence would not permit us to be called into this severe controversy, until we were grown up to our present strength, had been previously exercised in warlike operation, and possessed of the means of defending ourselves. With hearts fortified with these animating reflections, we most solemnly, before God and the world, declare, that, exerting the utmost energy of those powers, which our beneficent Creator hath graciously bestowed upon us, the arms we have been compelled by our enemies to assume, we will, in defiance of every hazard, with unabating firmness and perseverence, employ for the preservation of our liberties; being with one mind resolved to die freemen rather than to live slaves.

Lest this declaration should disquiet the minds of our friends and fellow-subjects in any part of the empire, we assure them that we mean not to dissolve that union which has so long and so happily subsisted between us, and which we sincerely wish to see restored. — Necessity has not yet driven us into that desperate measure, or induced us to excite any other nation to war against them. — We have not raised armies with ambitious designs of separating from Great-Britain, and establishing independent states. We fight not for glory or for conquest. We exhibit to mankind the remarkable spectacle of a people attacked by unprovoked enemies, without any imputation or even suspicion of offence. They boast of their privileges and civilization, and yet proffer no milder conditions than servitude or death.

In our own native land, in defence of the freedom that is our birthright, and which we ever enjoyed till the late violation of it — for the protection of our property, acquired solely by the honest industry of our fore-fathers and ourselves, against violence actually offered, we have taken up arms. We shall lay them down when hostilities shall cease on the part of the aggressors, and all danger of their being renewed shall be removed, and not before.

With an humble confidence in the mercies of the supreme and impartial Judge and Ruler of the Universe, we most devoutly implore his divine goodness to protect us happily through this great conflict, to dispose our adversaries to reconciliation on reasonable terms, and thereby to relieve the empire from the calamities of civil war.

REFERENCES

1. Primarily the work of Thomas Jefferson and John Dickinson. p. 168 Morison, Samuel Eliot, Henry Steele Commager, and William E. Leuchtenburg. *The Growth of the American Republic: Volume 1.* Seventh Edition. New York: Oxford University Press; 1980. (Note added by the Avalon Project).
2. From this point the declaration follows Jefferson's draft.

CHAPTER 9

Virginia Declaration of Rights (June 12, 1776)

House of Burgesses

The History*

The Virginia Declaration of Rights is a document drafted in 1776 to proclaim the inherent natural rights of men, including the right to rebel against "inadequate" government. It influenced a number of later documents, including the United States Declaration of Independence (1776), the United States Bill of Rights (1789), and the French Revolution's Declaration of the Rights of Man and of the Citizen (1789). The Declaration was adopted unanimously by the Virginia Convention of Delegates on June 12, 1776 as a separate document from the Constitution of Virginia adopted on June 29, 1776.[1] It was later incorporated within the Virginia State Constitution as Article I, and a slightly updated version may still be seen in Virginia's Constitution, making it legally in effect to this day.

It was initially drafted by George Mason *ca.* May 20–26, 1776, and later amended by Thomas Ludwell Lee and the Convention to add Section 14 on the right to uniform government. Mason based his document on the rights of citizens described in earlier works such as the English Bill of Rights (1689), and the Declaration can be considered the first modern Constitutional protection of individual rights for citizens of North America. It rejected the notion of privileged political classes or hereditary offices such as the members of Parliament and House of Lords described in the English Bill of Rights.

The Declaration consists of sixteen articles on the subject of which rights "pertain to [the people of Virginia] ... as the basis and foundation of Government."[1] In addition to affirming the inherent nature of natural rights to life, liberty, and property, the Declaration both describes a view of Government as the servant of the people, and enumerates various restrictions on governmental power. Thus, the document is unusual in that it not only prescribes legal rights, but it also describes moral principles upon which a government should be run.[2]

The Virginia Declaration of Rights heavily influenced later documents. Thomas Jefferson is thought to have drawn on it when he drafted the United States Declaration of Independence one month later (July 1776).

---

*Originally published as "Virginia Declaration of Rights," *Wikipedia*, Wikimedia Foundation, Inc., San Francisco, California, November 2009. For additional information see "The Virginia Declaration of Rights," *American Treasurers of the Library of Congress*, Library of Congress, Washington, DC, 2002. This agency is listed in the *National Resource Directory* section of this volume.

James Madison was also influenced by the Declaration while drafting the Bill of Rights (completed September 1787, approved 1789), as was the Marquis de Lafayette in voting the French Revolution's Declaration of the Rights of Man and of the Citizen (1789).

The importance of the Virginia Declaration of Rights is that it was the first constitutional protection of individual rights, rather than protecting just members of Parliament or consisting of simple laws that can be changed as easily as passed.

The Document

Virginia Declaration of Rights

I. That all men are by nature equally free and independent, and have certain inherent rights, of which, when they enter into a state of society, they cannot, by any compact, deprive or divest their posterity; namely, the enjoyment of life and liberty, with the means of acquiring and possessing property, and pursuing and obtaining happiness and safety.

II. That all power is vested in, and consequently derived from, the people; that magistrates are their trustees and servants, and at all times amenable to them.

III. That government is, or ought to be, instituted for the common benefit, protection, and security of the people, nation or community; of all the various modes and forms of government that is best, which is capable of producing the greatest degree of happiness and safety and is most effectually secured against the danger of maladministration; and that, whenever any government shall be found inadequate or contrary to these purposes, a majority of the community hath an indubitable, unalienable, and indefeasible right to reform, alter or abolish it, in such manner as shall be judged most conducive to the public weal.

IV. That no man, or set of men, are entitled to exclusive or separate emoluments or privileges from the community, but in consideration of public services; which, not being descendible, neither ought the offices of magistrate, legislator, or judge be hereditary.

V. That the legislative and executive powers of the state should be separate and distinct from the judicative; and, that the members of the two first may be restrained from oppression by feeling and participating the burthens of the people, they should, at fixed periods, be reduced to a private station, return into that body from which they were originally taken, and the vacancies be supplied by frequent, certain, and regular elections in which all, or any part of the former members, to be again eligible, or ineligible, as the laws shall direct.

VI. That elections of members to serve as representatives of the people in assembly ought to be free; and that all men, having sufficient evidence of permanent common interest with, and attachment to, the community have the right of suffrage and cannot be taxed or deprived of their property for public uses without their own consent or that of their representatives so elected, nor bound by any law to which they have not, in like manner, assented, for the public good.

VII. That all power of suspending laws, or the execution of laws, by any authority without consent of the representatives of the people is injurious to their rights and ought not to be exercised.

VIII. That in all capital or criminal prosecutions a man hath a right to demand the cause and nature of his accusation to be confronted with the accusers and witnesses, to call for evidence in his favor, and to a speedy trial by an impartial jury of his vicinage, without whose unanimous consent he cannot be found guilty, nor can he be compelled to give evidence against himself; that no man be deprived of his liberty except by the law of the land or the judgement of his peers.

IX. That excessive bail ought not to be required, nor excessive fines imposed; nor cruel and unusual punishments inflicted.

X. That general warrants, whereby any officer or messenger may be commanded to search suspected places without evidence of a fact committed, or to seize any person or persons not named, or whose offense is not particularly described and supported by evidence, are grievous and oppressive and ought not to be granted.

XI. That in controversies respecting property and in suits between man and man, the ancient trial by jury is preferable to any other and ought to be held sacred.

XII. That the freedom of the press is one of the greatest bulwarks of liberty and can never be restrained but by despotic governments.

XIII. That a well regulated militia, composed of the body of the people, trained to arms, is the proper, natural, and safe defense of a free state; that standing armies, in time of peace, should be avoided as dangerous to liberty; and that, in all cases, the military should be under strict subordination to, and be governed by, the civil power.

XIV. That the people have a right to uniform government; and therefore, that no government separate from, or independent of, the government of Virginia, ought to be erected or established within the limits thereof.

XV. That no free government, or the blessings of liberty, can be preserved to any people but by a firm adherence to justice, moderation, temperance, frugality, and virtue and by frequent recurrence to fundamental principles.

XVI. That religion, or the duty which we owe to our Creator and the manner of discharging it, can be directed by reason and conviction, not by force or violence; and therefore, all men are equally entitled to the free exercise of religion, according to the dictates of conscience; and that it is the mutual duty of all to practice Christian forbearance, love, and charity towards each other.

Adopted unanimously June 12, 1776 Virginia Convention of Delegates drafted by Mr. George Mason.

REFERENCES

1. Preamble, Virginia Declaration of Rights.
2. Lieberman, Jethro (1987). *The Enduring Constitution: A Bicentennial Perspective*. West Publishing Co., p. 28.

CHAPTER 10

Declaration of Independence (July 4, 1776)

Continental Congress

The History*

Since its creation in 1776, the Declaration of Independence has been considered the single most important expression of the ideals of U.S. democracy. As a statement of the fundamental principles of the United States, the Declaration is an enduring reminder of the country's commitment to popular government and equal rights for all.

The Declaration of Independence is a product of the early days of the Revolutionary War. On July 2, 1776, the Second Continental Congress — the legislature of the American colonies — voted for independence from Great Britain. It then appointed a committee of five — John Adams, Benjamin Franklin, Thomas Jefferson, Roger Sherman, and Robert R. Livingston — to draft a formal statement of independence designed to influence public opinion at home and abroad. Because of his reputation as an eloquent and forceful writer, Jefferson was assigned the task of creating the document, and the final product is almost entirely his own work. The Congress did not approve all of Jefferson's original draft, however, rejecting most notably his denunciation of the slave trade. Delegates from South Carolina and Georgia were not yet ready to extend the notion of inalienable rights to African Americans.

On July 4, 1776, the day of birth for the new country, the Continental Congress approved the Declaration of Independence on behalf of the people living in the American colonies. The Declaration served a number of purposes for the newly formed United States. With regard to the power politics of the day, it functioned as a propaganda statement intended to build support for American independence abroad, particularly in France, from which the Americans hoped to have support in their struggle for independence. Similarly, it served as a clear message of intention to the British. Even more important for the later Republic of the United States, it functioned as a statement of governmental ideals.

In keeping with its immediate diplomatic purposes, most of the Declaration consists of a list of 30 grievances against acts of the British monarch George III. Many of these were traditional and legitimate griev-

*Originally published as "Declaration of Independence — Further Readings," *American Law and Legal Encyclopedia*, Net Industries, LLC, Savoy, Illinois, 2009. For additional information see "The History of the Declaration of Independence," *The Charters of Freedom*, U.S. National Archives and Records Administration, College Park, Maryland, 2004. This agency is listed in the *National Resource Directory* section of this volume.

ances under British Constitutional Law. The Declaration firmly announces that British actions had established "an absolute Tyranny over these States." Britain's acts of despotism, according to the Declaration's list, included taxation of Americans without representation in Parliament; imposition of standing armies on American communities; establishment of the military above the civil power; obstruction of the right to trial by jury; interference with the operation of colonial legislatures; and cutting off of trade with the rest of the world. The Declaration ends with the decisive resolution that "these United Colonies are, and of Right ought to be Free and Independent States; that they are Absolved from all Allegiance to the British Crown, and that all political connection between them and the State of Great Britain, is and ought to be totally dissolved."

The first sentences of the document and their statement of political ideals have remained the Declaration's most memorable and influential section.

Ever since their creation, these ideas have guided the development of U.S. government, including the creation of the U.S. Constitution in 1787. The concepts of equal and inalienable rights for all, limited government, popular consent, and freedom to rebel have had a lasting effect on U.S. law and politics.

The Document

Declaration of Independence[1][2]

When in the course of human events, it becomes necessary for one people to dissolve the political bands which have connected them with another, and to assume among the powers of the earth, the separate and equal station to which the laws of nature and of nature's God entitle them, a decent respect to the opinions of mankind requires that they should declare the causes which impel them to the separation.

We hold these truths to be self-evident:

That all men are created equal; that they are endowed by their Creator with certain unalienable rights; that among these are life, liberty, and the pursuit of happiness; that, to secure these rights, governments are instituted among men, deriving their just powers from the consent of the governed; that whenever any form of government becomes destructive of these ends, it is the right of the people to alter or to abolish it, and to institute new government, laying its foundation on such principles, and organizing its powers in such form, as to them shall seem most likely to effect their safety and happiness. Prudence, indeed, will dictate that governments long established should not be changed for light and transient causes; and accordingly all experience hath shown that mankind are more disposed to suffer, while evils are sufferable than to right themselves by abolishing the forms to which they are accustomed. But when a long train of abuses and usurpations, pursuing invariably the same object, evinces a design to reduce them under absolute despotism, it is their right, it is their duty, to throw off such government, and to provide new guards for their future security. Such has been the patient sufferance of these colonies; and such is now the necessity which constrains them to alter their former systems of government. The history of the present King of Great Britain is a history of repeated injuries and usurpations, all having in direct object the establishment of an absolute tyranny over these states. To prove this, let facts be submitted to a candid world.

He has refused his assent to laws, the most wholesome and necessary for the public good.

He has forbidden his governors to pass laws of immediate and pressing importance, unless suspended in their operation till his assent should be obtained; and, when so suspended, he has utterly neglected to attend to them.

He has refused to pass other laws for the

accommodation of large districts of people, unless those people would relinquish the right of representation in the legislature, a right inestimable to them, and formidable to tyrants only.

He has called together legislative bodies at places unusual uncomfortable, and distant from the depository of their public records, for the sole purpose of fatiguing them into compliance with his measures.

He has dissolved representative houses repeatedly, for opposing, with manly firmness, his invasions on the rights of the people.

He has refused for a long time, after such dissolutions, to cause others to be elected; whereby the legislative powers, incapable of annihilation, have returned to the people at large for their exercise; the state remaining, in the mean time, exposed to all the dangers of invasions from without and convulsions within.

He has endeavored to prevent the population of these states; for that purpose obstructing the laws for naturalization of foreigners; refusing to pass others to encourage their migration hither, and raising the conditions of new appropriations of lands.

He has obstructed the administration of justice, by refusing his assent to laws for establishing judiciary powers.

He has made judges dependent on his will alone, for the tenure of their offices, and the amount and payment of their salaries.

He has erected a multitude of new offices, and sent hither swarms of officers to harass our people and eat out their substance.

He has kept among us, in times of peace, standing armies, without the consent of our legislatures.

He has affected to render the military independent of, and superior to, the civil power.

He has combined with others to subject us to a jurisdiction foreign to our Constitution and unacknowledged by our laws, giving his assent to their acts of pretended legislation:

For quartering large bodies of armed troops among us;

For protecting them, by a mock trial, from punishment for any murders which they should commit on the inhabitants of these states;

For cutting off our trade with all parts of the world;

For imposing taxes on us without our consent;

For depriving us, in many cases, of the benefits of trial by jury;

For transporting us beyond seas, to be tried for pretended offenses;

For abolishing the free system of English laws in a neighboring province, establishing therein an arbitrary government, and enlarging its boundaries, so as to render it at once an example and fit instrument for introducing the same absolute rule into these colonies;

For taking away our charters, abolishing our most valuable laws, and altering fundamentally the forms of our governments;

For suspending our own legislatures, and declaring themselves invested with power to legislate for us in all cases whatsoever.

He has abdicated government here, by declaring us out of his protection and waging war against us.

He has plundered our seas, ravaged our coasts, burned our towns, and destroyed the lives of our people.

He is at this time transporting large armies of foreign mercenaries to complete the works of death, desolation, and tyranny already begun with circumstances of cruelty and perfidy scarcely paralleled in the most barbarous ages, and totally unworthy the head of a civilized nation.

He has constrained our fellow-citizens, taken captive on the high seas, to bear arms against their country, to become the executioners of their friends and brethren, or to fall themselves by their hands.

He has excited domestic insurrection

among us, and has endeavored to bring on the inhabitants of our frontiers the merciless Indian savages, whose known rule of warfare is an undistinguished destruction of all ages, sexes, and conditions.

In every stage of these oppressions we have petitioned for redress in the most humble terms; our repeated petitions have been answered only by repeated injury. A prince, whose character is thus marked by every act which may define a tyrant, is unfit to be the ruler of a free people.

Nor have we been wanting in our attentions to our British brethren. We have warned them, from time to time, of attempts by their legislature to extend an unwarrantable jurisdiction over us. We have reminded them of the circumstances of our emigration and settlement here. We have appealed to their native justice and magnanimity; and we have conjured them, by the ties of our common kindred, to disavow these usurpations which would inevitably interrupt our connections and correspondence. They too, have been deaf to the voice of justice and of consanguinity. We must, therefore, acquiesce in the necessity which denounces our separation, and hold them as we hold the rest of mankind, enemies in war, in peace friends.

We, therefore, the representatives of the United States of America, in General Congress assembled, appealing to the Supreme Judge of the world for the rectitude of our intentions, do, in the name and by the authority of the good people of these colonies solemnly publish and declare, That these United Colonies are, and of right ought to be, FREE AND INDEPENDENT STATES; that they are absolved from all allegiance to the British crown and that all political connection between them and the state of Great Britain is, and ought to be, totally dissolved; and that, as free and independent states, they have full power to levy war, conclude peace, contract alliances, establish commerce, and do all other acts and things which independent states may of right do. And for the support of this declaration, with a firm reliance on the protection of Divine Providence, we mutually pledge to each other our lives, our fortunes, and our sacred honor.

—[Signed by] JOHN HANCOCK
[President]

REFERENCES

1. Mr. Ferdinand Jefferson, Keeper of the Rolls in the Department of State, at Washington, says: "The names of the signers are spelt above as in the facsimile of the original, but the punctuation of them is not always the same; neither do the names of the States appear in the facsimile of the original. The names of the signers of each State are grouped together in the facsimile of the original, except the name of Matthew Thornton, which follows that of Oliver Wolcott."— Revised Statutes of the United States, 2d edition, 1878, p. 6.
2. The first local government in the American colonies to declare its independence from Great Britain was Mecklenburg County, North Carolina, on May 20, 1775. The county declared its independence from Great Britain immediately after the Battle of Lexington, in what is now called the Commonwealth of Massachusetts. Additional information concerning the "Mecklenburg Declaration of Independence" can be found on the Library of Congress website, which is listed in the *National Resource Directory* section of this volume. Because of its significance, this document is shown in its entirety in the Appendix of this volume under the heading "Local Government Historical Document."

CHAPTER 11

Constitution of Massachusetts (June 15, 1780)

State Constitutional Convention Representatives

The History*

The Constitution of the Commonwealth of Massachusetts is the fundamental governing document of the Commonwealth of Massachusetts, one of the 50 individual state governments that make up the United States of America. It was drafted by John Adams, Samuel Adams, and James Bowdoin during the Massachusetts Constitutional Convention between September 1 and October 30, 1779. Following approval by town meetings, the Constitution was ratified on June 15, 1780, became effective on October 25, 1780, and remains the oldest functioning written constitution in continuous effect in the world.

The Massachusetts Constitution was the last of the first set of the state constitutions to be written. Consequently, it was more sophisticated than many of the other documents. Among the improvements was the structure of the document itself; instead of just a listing of provisions, it had a structure of chapters, sections, and articles. This structure was replicated by the U.S. Constitution. It also had substantial influence on the sub-

sequent revisions of many of the other state constitutions. The Massachusetts Constitution has four parts: a preamble, a declaration of rights, a description of the framework of government, and articles of amendment.

The constitutional conventional pioneered by Massachusetts became a crucial component of the ratification process through which the United States Constitution was accepted by the states, including Massachusetts, in the 1780s.

The Document

Massachusetts Constitution

PREAMBLE

The end of the institution, maintenance, and administration of government is to secure the existence of the body-politic, to protect it, and to furnish the individuals who compose it with the power of enjoying, in safety and tranquillity, their natural rights and the blessings of life; and whenever these great objects are not obtained the people have

*Originally published as "Massachusetts Constitution," *Wikipedia*, Wikimedia Foundation, Inc., San Francisco, California, November 2009. For additional information see "John Adams and the Massachusetts Constitution," *Education Resource Center Report*, Supreme Judicial Court, Commonwealth of Massachusetts, Boston, Massachusetts, 2007. This agency is listed in the *National Resource Directory* section of this volume.

a right to alter the government, and to take measures necessary for their safety, prosperity, and happiness.

The body politic is formed by a voluntary association of individuals; it is a social compact by which the whole people covenants with each citizen and each citizen with the whole people that all shall be governed by certain laws for the common good. It is the duty of the people, therefore, in framing a constitution of government, to provide for an equitable mode of making laws, as well as for an impartial interpretation and a faithful execution of them; that every man may, at all times, find his security in them.

We, therefore, the people of Massachusetts, acknowledging, with grateful hearts, the goodness of the great Legislator of the universe, in affording us, in the course of His providence, an opportunity, deliberately and peaceably, without fraud, violence, or surprise, of entering into an original, explicit, and solemn compact with each other, and of forming a new constitution of civil government for ourselves and posterity; and devoutly imploring His direction in so interesting a design, do agree upon, ordain, and establish the following declaration of rights and frame of government as the constitution of the commonwealth of Massachusetts.

Part The First

A Declaration of the Rights of the Inhabitants of the Commonwealth of Massachusetts.

Article I. All men are born free and equal, and have certain natural, essential, and unalienable rights; among which may be reckoned the right of enjoying and defending their lives and liberties; that of acquiring, possessing, and protecting property; in fine, that of seeking and obtaining their safety and happiness.

Art. II. It is the right as well as the duty of all men in society, publicly and at stated seasons, to worship the Supreme Being, the great Creator and Preserver of the universe.

And no subject shall be hurt, molested, or restrained, in his person, liberty, or estate, for worshipping God in the manner and season most agreeable to the dictates of his own conscience, or for his religious profession or sentiments, provided he doth not disturb the public peace or obstruct others in their religious worship.

Art. III. As the happiness of a people and the good order and preservation of civil government essentially depend upon piety, religion, and morality, and as these cannot be generally diffused through a community but by the institution of the public worship of God and of the public instructions in piety, religion, and morality: Therefore, To promote their happiness and to secure the good order and preservation of their government, the people of this commonwealth have a right to invest their legislature with power to authorize and require, and the legislature shall, from time to time, authorize and require, the several towns, parishes, precincts, and other bodies-politic or religious societies to make suitable provision, at their own expense, for the institution of the public worship of God and for the support and maintenance of public Protestant teachers of piety, religion, and morality in all cases where such provision shall not be made voluntarily.

And the people of this commonwealth have also a right to, and do, invest their legislature with authority to enjoin upon all the subject an attendance upon the instructions of the public teachers aforesaid, at stated times and seasons, if there be any on whose instructions they can conscientiously and conveniently attend.

Provided, notwithstanding, That the several towns, parishes, precincts, and other bodies-politic, or religious societies, shall at all times have the exclusive right and electing their public teachers and of contracting with them for their support and maintenance.

And all moneys paid by the subject to the support of public worship and of public teachers aforesaid shall, if he require it, be uniformly applied to the support of the public teacher or teachers of his own religious sect or denomination, provided there be any on whose instructions he attends; otherwise it may be paid toward the support of the teacher or teachers of the parish or precinct in which the said moneys are raised.

And every denomination of Christians, demeaning themselves peaceably and as good subjects of the commonwealth, shall be equally under the protection of the law; and no subordination of any sect or denomination to another shall ever be established by law.

Art. IV. The people of this commonwealth have the sole and exclusive right of governing themselves as a free, sovereign, and independent State, and do, and forever hereafter shall, exercise and enjoy every power, jurisdiction, and right which is not, or may not hereafter be, by them expressly delegated to the United States of America in Congress assembled.

Art. V. All power residing originally in the people, and being derived from them, the several magistrates and officers of government vested with authority, whether legislative, executive, or judicial, are the substitutes and agents, and are at all times accountable to them.

Art. VI. No man nor corporation or association of men have any other title to obtain advantages, or particular and exclusive privileges distinct from those of the community, than what rises from the consideration of services rendered to the public, and this title being in nature neither hereditary nor transmissible to children or descendants or relations by blood; the idea of a man born a magistrate, lawgiver, or judge is absurd and unnatural.

Art. VII. Government is instituted for the common good, for the protection, safety, prosperity, and happiness of the people, and not for the profit, honor, or private interest of any one man, family, or class of men; therefore the people alone have an incon-

testable, unalienable, and indefeasible right to institute government, and to reform, alter, or totally change the same when their protection, safety, prosperity, and happiness require it.

Art. VIII. In order to prevent those who are vested with authority from becoming oppressors, the people have a right at such periods and in such manner as they shall establish by their frame of government, to cause their public officers to return to private life; and to fill up vacant places by certain and regular elections and appointments.

Art. IX. All elections ought to be free; and all the inhabitants of this commonwealth, having such qualifications as they shall establish by their frame of government, have an equal right to elect officers, and to be elected, for public employments.

Art. X. Every individual of the society has a right to be protected by it in the enjoyment of his life, liberty, and property, according to standing laws. He is obliged, consequently, to contribute his share to expense of this protection; to give his personal service, or an equivalent, when necessary; but no part of the property of any individual can, with justice, be taken from him, or applied to public uses, without his own consent, or that of the representative body of the people. In fine, the people of this commonwealth are not controllable by any other laws than those to which their constitutional representative body have given their consent. And whenever the public exigencies require that the property of any individual should be appropriated to public uses, he shall receive a reasonable compensation therefor.

Art. XI. Every subject of the commonwealth ought to find a certain remedy, by having recourse to the laws, for all injuries or wrongs which he may receive in his person, property, or character. He ought to obtain right and justice freely, and without being obliged to purchase it; completely, and without any denial; promptly, and without delay, conformably to the laws.

Art. XII. No subject shall be held to answer for any crimes or no offence until the same if fully and plainly, substantially and formally, described to him; or be compelled to accuse, or furnish evidence against himself; and every subject shall have a right to produce all proofs that may be favorable to him; to meet the witnesses against him face to face, and to be fully heard in his defence by himself, or his counsel at his election. And no subject shall be arrested, imprisoned, despoiled, or deprived of his property, immunities, or privileges, put out of the protection of the law, exiled or deprived of his life, liberty, or estate, but by the judgment of his peers, or the law of the land.

And the legislature shall not make any law that shall subject any person to a capital or infamous punishment, excepting for the government of the army and navy, without trial by jury.

Art. XIII. In criminal prosecutions, the verification of facts, in the vicinity where they happen, is one of the greatest securities of the life, liberty, and property of the citizen.

Art. XIV. Every subject has a right to be secure from all unreasonable searches and seizures of his person, his houses, his papers, and all his possessions. All warrants, therefore, are contrary to this right, if the cause or foundation of them be not previously supported by oath or affirmation, and if the order in the warrant to a civil officer, to make search in suspected places, or to arrest one or more suspected persons, or to seize their property, be not accompanied with a special designation of the persons or objects of search, arrest, or seizure; and no warrant ought to be issued but in cases, and with the formalities, prescribed by the laws.

Art. XV. In all controversies concerning property, and in all suits between two or more persons, except in cases in which it has heretofore been otherways used and practised, the parties have a right to a trial by jury; and this method of procedure shall be held sacred, unless, in causes arising on the high seas, and such as relate to mariners' wages, the legislature shall hereafter find it necessary to alter it.

Art. XVI. The liberty of the press is essential to the security of freedom in a State; it ought not, therefore, to be restrained in this commonwealth.

Art. XVII. The people have a right to keep and to bear arms for the common defence. And as, in time of peace, armies are dangerous to liberty, they ought not to be maintained without the consent of the legislature; and the military power shall always be held in an exact subordination to the civil authority and be governed by it.

Art. XVIII. A frequent recurrence to the fundamental principles of the constitution, and a constant adherence to those of piety, justice, moderation, temperance, industry, and frugality, are absolutely necessary to preserve the advantages of liberty and to maintain a free government. The people ought, consequently, to have a particular attention to all those principles, in the choice of their officers and representatives; and they have a right to require of their lawgivers and magistrates an exact and constant observation of them, in the formation and execution of the laws necessary for the good administration of the commonwealth.

Art. XIX. The people have a right, in an orderly and peaceable manner, to assemble to consult upon the common good; give instructions to their representatives, and to request of the legislative body, by the way of addresses, petitions, or remonstrances, redress of the wrongs done them, and of the grievances they suffer.

Art. XX. The power of suspending the laws, or the execution of the laws, ought never to be exercised but by the legislature, or by authority derived from it, to be exercised in such particular cases only as the legislature shall expressly provide for.

Art. XXI. The freedom of deliberation, speech, and debate, in either house of the legislature, is so essential to the rights of the people, that it cannot be the foundation of any accusation or prosecution, action or complaint, in any other court of place whatsoever.

Art. XXII. The legislature ought frequently to assemble for address of grievances, for correcting, strengthening, and confirming the laws, and for making new laws, as the common good may require.

Art. XXIII. No subsidy, charge, tax, impost, or duties, ought to be established, fixed, laid, or levied, under any pretext whatsoever, without the consent of the people, or their representatives in the legislature.

Art. XXIV. Laws made to punish for actions done before the existence of such laws, and which have not been declared crimes by preceding laws, are unjust, oppressive, and inconsistent with the fundamental principles of a free government.

Art. XXV. No subject ought, in any case, or in any time, to be declared guilty of treason or felony by the legislature.

Art. XXVI. No magistrate or court of law shall demand excessive bail or sureties, impose excessive fines, or inflict cruel or unusual punishments.

Art. XXVII. In time of peace, no soldier ought to be quartered in any house without the consent of the owner; and in time of war, such quarters ought not be made but by the civil magistrate, in a manner ordained by the legislature.

Art. XXVIII. No person can in any case be subjected to law-martial, or to any penalties or pains, by virtue of that law, except those employed in the army or navy, and except the militia in actual service, but by authority of the legislature.

Art. XXIX. It is essential to the preservation of the rights of every individual, his life, liberty, property, and character, that there be an impartial interpretation of the laws, and administration of justice. It is the right of every citizen to be tried by judges as free, impartial, and independent as the lot of humanity will admit. It is, therefore, not

only the best policy, but for the security of the rights of the people, and of every citizen, that the judges of the supreme judicial court should hold their offices as long as they behave themselves well, and that they should have honorable salaries ascertained and established by standing laws.

Art. XXX. In the government of this commonwealth, the legislative department shall never exercise the executive and judicial powers, or either of them; the executive shall never exercise the legislative and judicial powers, or either of them; the judicial shall never exercise the legislative and executive powers, or either of them; to the end it may be a government of laws, and not of men.

PART THE SECOND

The Frame of Government

The people inhabiting the territory formerly called the province of Massachusetts Bay do hereby solemnly and mutually agree with each other to form themselves into a free, sovereign, and independent body-politic or State, by the name of the commonwealth of Massachusetts.

CHAPTER I.—THE LEGISLATIVE POWER

Section I.—The General Court

Article I. The department of legislation shall be formed by two branches, a senate and house of representatives; each of which shall have a negative on the other.

The legislative body shall assemble every year on the last Wednesday in May, and at such other times as they shall judge necessary; and shall dissolve and be dissolved on the day next preceding the said last Wednesday in May; and shall be styled the *General Court of Massachusetts.*

Art. II. No bill or resolve of the senate or house of representatives shall become a law, and have force as such, until it shall have been laid before the governor for his revisal; and if he, upon such revision, approve thereof, he shall signify his approbation by signing the same. But if he have any objection to the passing such bill or resolve, he shall return the same, together with his objections thereto, in writing, to the senate or house of representatives, in whichsoever the same shall have originated, who shall enter the objections sent down by the governor, at large, on their records, and proceed to reconsider the said bill or resolve; but if, after such reconsideration, two-thirds of the said senate or house of representatives shall, notwithstanding the said objections, agree to pass the same, it shall, together with the objections, be sent to the other branch of the legislature, where it shall also be reconsidered, and if approved by two-thirds of the members present, shall have the force of law; but in all such cases, the vote of both houses shall be determined by yeas and nays; and the names of the persons voting for or against the said bill or resolve shall be entered upon the public records of the commonwealth.

And in order to prevent unnecessary delays, if any bill or resolve shall not be returned by the governor within five days after it shall have been presented, the same shall have the force of law.

Art. III. The general court shall forever have full power and authority to erect and constitute judicatories and courts of record or other courts, to be held in the name of the commonwealth, for the hearing, trying, and determining of all manner of crimes, offences, pleas, processes, plaints, actions, matters, causes, and things whatsoever, arising or happening within the commonwealth, or between or concerning persons inhabiting or residing, or brought within the same; whether the same be criminal or civil, or whether the said crimes be capital or not capital, and whether the said pleas be real, personal, or mixed; and for the awarding and making out of execution thereupon; to which courts and judicatories are hereby given and granted full power and authority, from time to time, to administer oaths or affirmations, for the better discovery of truth in any mat-

ter in controversy, or depending before them.

Art. IV. And further, full power and authority are hereby given and granted to the said general court from time to time, to make, ordain, and establish all manner of wholesome and reasonable orders, laws, statutes, and ordinances, directions and instructions, either with penalties or without, so as the same be not repugnant or contrary to this constitution, as they shall judge to be for the good and welfare of this commonwealth, and for the government and ordering thereof, and of the subjects of the same, and for the necessary support and defence of the government thereof; and to name and settle annually, or provide by fixed laws, for the naming and settling all civil officers within the said commonwealth, the election, and constitution of whom are not hereafter in this form of government otherwise provided for; and to set forth the several duties, powers, and limits of the several civil and military officers of this commonwealth, and the forms of such oaths or affirmations as shall be respectively administered unto them for the execution of their several offices and places, so as the same be not repugnant or contrary to this constitution; and to impose and levy proportional and reasonable assessments, rates, and taxes, upon all the inhabitants of, and persons resident, and estates lying, within the said commonwealth; and also to impose and levy reasonable duties and excises upon any produce, goods, wares, merchandise, and commodities whatsoever, brought into, produced, manufactured, or being within the same; to be issued and disposed of by warrant, under the hand of the governor of this commonwealth, for the time being, with the advice and consent of the council, for the public service, in the necessary defence and support of the government of the said commonwealth, and the protection and preservation of the subjects thereof, according to such acts as are or shall be in force within the same.

And while the public charges of government, or any part thereof, shall be assessed on polls and estates, in the manner that has hitherto been practised, in order that such assessments may be made with equality, there shall be a valuation of estates within the commonwealth, taken anew once in every ten years at least, and as much oftener as the general court shall order.

CHAPTER I

Section 2.— Senate

Article I. There shall be annually elected, by the freeholders and other inhabitants of this commonwealth, qualified as in this constitution is provided, forty persons to be councillors and senators, for the year ensuing their election; to be chosen by the inhabitants of the districts into which the commonwealth may from time to time be divided by the general court for that purpose; and the general court, in assigning the numbers to be elected by the respective districts, shall govern themselves by the proportion of the public taxes paid by the said districts; and timely make known to the inhabitants of the commonwealth the limits of each district, and the number of councillors and senators to be chosen therein: *Provided*, That the number of such districts shall never be less than thirteen; and that no district be so large as to entitle the same to choose more than six senators.

And the several counties in this commonwealth shall, until the general court shall determine it necessary to alter the said districts, be districts for the choice of councillors and senators, (except that the counties of Dukes County and Nantucket shall form one district for that purpose,) and shall elect the following number for councillors and senators, viz: ... [39 senators].

Art. II. The senate shall be the first branch of the legislature; and the senators shall be chosen in the following manner, viz: There shall be a meeting on the first Monday in April, annually, forever, of the inhabitants of each town in the several counties of this commonwealth, to be called by the selectmen, and warned in due course of law, at least seven days before the first Monday in April, for the purpose of electing persons to be senators and councillors; and at such meetings every male inhabitant of twenty-one year of age and upwards, having a freehold estate of the value of sixty pounds, shall have a right to give in his vote for the senators for the district of which he is an inhabitant. And to remove all doubts concerning the meaning of the word "inhabitant," in this constitution, every person shall be considered as an inhabitant, for the purpose of electing and being elected into any office or place within this State, in that town, district, or plantation where he dwelleth or hath his home.

The selectmen of the several towns shall preside at such meetings impartially, and shall receive the votes of all the inhabitants of such towns, present and qualified to vote for senators, and shall sort and count them in open town meeting, and in presence of the town clerk, who shall make a fair record, in presence of the selectmen, and in open town meeting, of the name of every person voted for, and of the number of votes against his name; and a fair copy of this record shall be attested by the selectmen and the town clerk, and shall be sealed up, directed to the secretary of the commonwealth, for the time being, with a superscription expressing the purport of the contents thereof, and delivered by the town clerk of such towns to the sheriff of the county in which such town lies, thirty days at least before the last Wednesday in May, annually; or it shall be delivered into the secretary's office seventeen days at least before the said last Wednesday in May; and the sheriff of each county shall deliver all such certificates, by him received, into the secretary's office seventeen days before the said last Wednesday in May.

And the inhabitants of the plantations unincorporated, qualified as this constitution provides, who are or shall be empowered and required to assess taxes upon themselves toward the support of government, shall have the same privilege of voting for councillors and senators, in the plantations where they reside, as town inhabitants have in their respective towns; and the plantation meetings for that purpose shall be held annually, on the same first Monday in April, at such place in the plantations, respectively, as the assessors thereof shall direct; which assessors shall have like authority for notifying the electors, collecting and returning the votes, as the selectmen and town clerks have in their several towns by this constitution. And all other persons living in places unincorporated, (qualified as aforesaid,) who shall be assessed to the support of government by assessors of an adjacent town, shall have the privilege of giving in their votes for councillors and senators in the town where they shall be assessed, and be notified of the place of meeting by the selectmen of the town where they shall be assessed, for that purpose, accordingly.

Art. III. And that there may be a due convention of senators, on the last Wednesday in May, annually, the governor, with five of the council, for the time being, shall, as soon as may be, examine the returned copies of such records; and fourteen days before the said day he shall issue his summons to such persons as shall appear to be chosen by a majority of voters to attend on that day, and take their seats accordingly: *Provided, nevertheless,* That for the first year the said returned copies shall be examined by the president and five of the council of the former constitution of government; and the said president shall, in like manner, issue his summons to the persons so elected, that they may take their seats as aforesaid.

Art. IV. The senate shall be the final judge of the elections, returns, and qualifications of their own members, as pointed out in the constitution; and shall, on the said last Wednesday in May, annually, determine and declare who are elected by each

district to be senators by a majority of votes; and in case there shall not be the full number of senators returned, elected by a majority of votes for any district, the deficiency shall be supplied in the following manner, viz: The members of the house of representatives, and such senators as shall be declared elected, shall take the names of such persons as shall be found to have the highest number of votes in such district, and not elected, amounting to twice the number of senators wanting, if there be so many voted for, and out of these shall elect by ballot a number of senators sufficient to fill up the vacancies in such district; and in this manner all such vacancies shall be filled up in every district of the commonwealth; and in like manner all vacancies in the senate, arising by death, removal out of the State or otherwise, shall be supplied as soon as may after such vacancies shall happen.

Art. V. *Provided, nevertheless,* That no person shall be capable of being elected as a senator [who is not seized in his own right of a freehold within this commonwealth, of the value of three hundred pounds at least, or possessed of personal estate to the value of six hundred pounds at least, or of both to the amount of the same sum, and] who has not been an inhabitant of this commonwealth for the space of five years immediately preceding his election, and, at the time of his election, he shall be an inhabitant in the district for which he shall be chosen.

Art. VI. The senate shall have power to adjourn themselves; provided such adjournments do not exceed two days at a time.

Art. VII. The senate shall choose its own president, appoint its own officers, and determine its own rules of proceedings.

Art. VIII. The senate shall be a court, with full authority to hear and determine all impeachments made by the house of representatives, against any officer or officers of the commonwealth, for misconduct and maladminstration in their offices; but, previous to the trial of every impeachment, the members of the senate shall, respectively, be sworn truly and impartially to try and determine the charge in question, according to the evidence. Their judgment, however, shall not extend further than to removal from office, and disqualification to hold or enjoy any place of honor, trust, or profit under this commonwealth; but the part so convicted shall be, nevertheless, liable to indictment, trial, judgment, and punishment, according to the laws of the land.

Art. IX. Not less than sixteen members of the senate shall constitute a quorum for doing business.

Chapter I.

Section 3.— House of Representatives

Article I. There shall be, in the legislature of this commonwealth, a representation of the people, annually elected, and founded upon the principle of equality.

Art. II. And in order to provide for a representation of the citizens of this commonwealth, founded upon the principle of equality, every corporate town containing one hundred and fifty ratable polls, may elect one representative; every corporate town containing three hundred and seventy-five ratable polls, may elect two representatives; every corporate town containing six hundred ratable polls, may elect three representatives; and proceeding in that manner, making two hundred and twenty-five ratable polls the mean increasing number for every additional representative.

Provided, nevertheless, That each town now incorporated, not having one hundred and fifty ratable polls, may elect one representative; but no place shall hereafter be incorporated with the privilege of electing a representative, unless there are within the same one hundred and fifty ratable polls.

And the house of representatives shall have power, from time to time, to impose fines upon such towns as shall neglect to choose and return members of the same, agreeably to this constitution.

The expenses of travelling to the general assembly and returning home, once in every session, and no more, shall be paid by the government out of the public treasury, to every member who shall attend as seasonably as he can, in the judgment of the house, and does not depart without leave.

Art. III. Every member of the house of representatives shall be chosen by written votes; and, for one year at least next preceding his election, shall have been an inhabitant of, and have been seized in his own right of a freehold of the value of one hundred pounds, within the town he shall be chosen to represent, or any ratable estate to the value of two hundred pounds; and he shall cease to represent the said town immediately on his ceasing to be qualified as aforesaid.

Art. IV. Every male person being twenty-one years of age, and resident in any particular town in this commonwealth, for the space of one year next preceding, having a freehold estate within the same town, of the annual income of three pounds, or any estate of the value of sixty pounds, shall have a right to vote in the choice of a representative or representatives for the said town.

Art. V. The members of the house of representatives shall be chosen annually in the month of May, ten days at least before the last Wednesday of that month.

Art. VI. The house of representatives shall be the grand inquest of this commonwealth; and all impeachments made by them shall be heard and tried by the senate.

Art. VII. All money bills shall originate in the house of representatives; but the senate may propose or concur with amendments, as on other bills.

Art. VIII. The house of representatives shall have power to adjourn themselves; provided such adjournments shall not exceed two days at a time.

Art. IX. Not less than sixty members of the house of representatives shall constitute a quorum for doing business.

Art. X. The house of representatives

shall be the judge of the returns, elections, and qualifications of its own members, as point out in the constitution; shall choose their own speaker, appoint their own officers, and settle the rules and order of proceeding in their own house. They shall have authority to punish by imprisonment every person, not a member, who shall be guilty of disrespect to the house, by any disorderly or contemptuous behavior in its presence; or who, in the town where the general court is sitting, and during the time of its sitting, shall threaten harm to the body or estate of any of its members, for anything said or done in the house; or who shall assault any of them therefor; or who shall assault or arrest any witness, or other person, ordered to attend the house, in his way in going or returning; or who shall rescue any person arrested by the order of the house.

And no member of the house of representatives shall be arrested, or held to bail on mesne process, during his going unto, returning from, or his attending the general assembly.

Art. XI. The senate shall have the same powers in the like cases; and the governor and council shall have the same authority to punish in like cases; *Provided*, That no imprisonment, on the warrant or order of the governor, council, senate, or house of representatives, for either of the above-described offences, be for a term exceeding thirty days.

And the senate and house of representatives may try and determine all cases where their rights and privileges are concerned, and which, by the constitution, they have authority to try and determine, by committees of their own members, or in such other way as they may, respectively, think best.

Chapter II. — Executive Power

Section I. — Governor

Article I. There shall be a supreme executive magistrate, who shall be styled "The governor of the commonwealth of Massachu-

setts;" and whose title shall be "His Excellency."

Art. II. The governor shall be chosen annually; and no person shall be eligible to this office, unless, at the time of his election, he shall have been an inhabitant of this commonwealth for seven years next preceding; and unless he shall, at the same time, be seized, in his own right, of a freehold, within the commonwealth, of the value of one thousand pounds; and unless he shall declare himself to be of the Christian religion.

Art. III. Those persons who shall be qualified to vote for senators and representatives, within the several towns of this commonwealth, shall, at a meeting to be called for that purpose, on the first Monday of April, annually, give in their votes for a governor to the selectmen, who shall preside at such meetings; and the town clerk, in the presence and with the assistance of the selectmen, shall, in open town meeting, sort and count the votes, and form a list of the persons voted for, with the number of votes for each person against his name; and shall make a fair record of the same in the town books, and a public declaration thereof in the said meeting; and shall, in the presence of the inhabitants, seal up copies of the said list, attested by him and the selectmen, and transmit the same to the sheriff of the county, thirty days at least before the last Wednesday in May; and the sheriff shall transmit the same to the secretary's office, seventeen days at least before the said last Wednesday in May; or the selectmen may cause returns of the same to be made, to the office of the secretary of the commonwealth, seventeen days at least before the said day; and the secretary shall lay the same before the senate and the house of representatives, on the last Wednesday in May, to be by them examined; and in case of an election by a majority of all the votes returned, the choice shall be by them declared and published; but if no person shall have a majority of votes, the house of representatives shall, by ballot, elect two out of four persons, who had the highest number of votes, if so many shall have been voted for; but, if otherwise, out of the number voted for; and make return to the senate of the two persons so elected; on which the senate shall proceed, by ballot, to elect one, who shall be declared governor.

Art. IV. The governor shall authority, from time to time, at his discretion, to assemble and call together the councillors of this commonwealth for the time being; and the governor, with the said councillors, or five of them at least, shall and may, from time to time, hold and keep a council, for the ordering and directing the affairs of the commonwealth, agreeably to the constitution and the laws of the land.

Art. V. The governor, with advice of council, shall have full power and authority, during the session of the general court, to adjourn or prorogue the same at any time the two houses shall desire; and to dissolve the same on the day next preceding the last Wednesday in May; and, in the recess of the said court, to prorogue the same from time to time, not exceeding ninety days in any one recess; and to call it together sooner than the time to which it may be adjourned or prorogued, if the welfare of the commonwealth shall require the same; and in case of any infectious distemper prevailing in the place where the said court is next at any time to convene, or any other cause happening, whereby danger may arise to the health or lives of the members from their attendance, he may direct the session to be held at some other the most convenient place within the State.

And the governor shall dissolve the said general court on the day next preceding the last Wednesday in May.

Art. VI. In cases of disagreement between the two houses, with regard to the necessity, expediency, or time of adjournment or prorogation, the governor, with advice of the council, shall have a right to adjourn or prorogue the general court, not exceeding ninety days, as he shall determine the public good shall require.

Art. VII. The governor of this commonwealth, for the time being, shall be the commander-in-chief of the army and navy, and of all the military forces of the State, by sea and land; and shall have full power, by himself or by any commander, or other officer or officers, from time to time, to train, instruct, exercise, and govern the militia and navy; and, for the special defence and safety of the commonwealth, to assemble in martial array, and put in warlike posture, the inhabitants thereof, and to lead and conduct them, and with them to encounter, repel, resist, expel, and pursue, by force of arms, as by sea as by land, within or within the limits of this commonwealth; and also to kill, slay, and destroy, if necessary, and conquer, by all fitting ways, enterprises, and means whatsoever, all and every such person and persons as shall, at any time hereafter, in a hostile manner, attempt or enterprise the destruction, invasion, detriment, or annoyance of this commonwealth; and to use and exercise over the army and navy, and over the militia in actual service, the law-martial, in time of war or invasion, and also in time of rebellion, declared by the legislature to exist, as occasion shall necessarily require; and to take and surprise, by all ways and means whatsoever, all and every such person or persons, with their ships, arms, and ammunition, and other goods, as shall, in a hostile manner, invade, or attempt the invading, conquering, or annoying this commonwealth; and that the governor be intrusted with all these and other powers incident to the offices of captain-general and commander-in-chief, and admiral, to be exercised agreeably to the rules and regulations of the constitution and the laws of the land, and not otherwise.

Provided, That the said governor shall not, at any time hereafter, by virtue of any power by this constitution granted, or hereafter to be granted to him by the legislature, transport any of the inhabitants of this commonwealth, or oblige them to march out of the limits of the same, without their free and voluntary consent, or the consent of the general court; except so far as may be necessary to march or transport them by land or water for the defence of such part of the State to which they cannot otherwise conveniently have access.

Art. VIII. The power of pardoning offences, except such as persons may be convicted of before the senate, by an impeachment of the house, shall be in the governor, by and with the advice of council; but no charter or pardon, granted by the governor, with the advice of the council, before conviction, shall avail the party pleading the same, notwithstanding any general or particular expressions contained therein, descriptive of the offence or offences intended to be pardoned.

Art. IX. All judicial officers, the attorney-general, the solicitor-general, all sheriffs, coroners, and registers of probate, shall be nominated and appointed by the governor, by and with the advice and consent of the council; and every such nomination shall be made by the governor, and made at least seven days prior to such appointment.

Art. X. The captains and subalterns of the militia shall be elected by the written votes of the train-band and alarm-list of their respective companies, of twenty years of age and upwards; the field-officers of regiments shall be elected by the written votes of the captains and subalterns of their respective regiments; the brigadiers shall be elected, in like manner, by the field-officers of their respective brigades; and such officers, so elected, shall be commissioned by the governor, who shall determine their rank.

The legislature shall, by standing laws, direct the time and manner of convening the electors, and of collecting votes, and of certifying to the governer the officers elected.

The major-generals shall be appointed by the senate and house of representatives, each having a negative upon the other; and be commissioned by the governor.

And if the electors of brigadiers, field-officers, captains, or subalterns shall neglect or refuse to make such elections, after being duly notified, according to the laws for the time being, then the governor, with the advice of council, shall appoint suitable persons to fill such offices.

And no officer, duly commissioned to command in the militia, shall be removed from his office, but by the address of both houses to the governor, or by fair trial in court-martial, pursuant to the laws of the commonwealth for the time being.

The commanding officers of regiments shall appoint their adjutants and quartermasters; the brigadiers, their brigade-majors; and the major-generals, their aids; and the governor shall appoint the adjutant-general.

The governor, with the advice of council, shall appoint all officers of the Continental Army, whom, by the Confederation of the United States, it is provided that this commonwealth shall appoint, as also all officers of forts and garrisons.

The divisions of the militia into brigades, regiments, and companies, made in pursuance of the militia-laws now in force, shall be considered as the proper divisions of the militia in this commonwealth, until the same shall be altered in pursuance of some future law.

Art. XI. No moneys shall be issued out of the treasury of this commonwealth and disposed of, except such sums as may be appropriated for the redemption of bills of credit or treasurer's notes, or for the payment of interest arising thereon, but by warrant under the hand of the governor for the time being, with the advice and consent of the council for the necessary defence and support of the commonwealth, and for the protection and preservation of the inhabitants thereof, agreeably to the acts and resolves of the general court.

Art. XII. All public boards, the commissary-general, all superintending officers of public magazines and stores, belonging to this commonwealth, and all commanding officers of forts and garrisons within the same, shall, once in every three months, officially and without requisition, and at other times, when required by the governor, deliver to him an account of all goods, stores, provisions, ammunition, cannon, with their appendages, and small-arms with their accoutrements, and of all other public property whatever under their care, respectively; distinguishing the quantity, number, quality, and kind of each, as particularly as may be; together with the condition of such forts and garrisons; and the said commanding officer shall exhibit to the governor, when required by him, true and exact plans of such forts, and of the land and sea, or harbor or harbors, adjacent.

And the said boards, and all public officers, shall communicate to the governor, as soon as may be after receiving the same, all letters, dispatches, and intelligences of a public nature, which shall be directed to them respectively.

Art. XIII. As the public good requires that the governor should not be under the undue influence of any of the members of the general court, by a dependence on them for his support; that he should, in all cases, act with freedom for the benefit of the public; that he should not have his attention necessarily diverted from that object to his private concerns; and that he should maintain the dignity of the commonwealth in the character of its chief magistrate, it is necessary that he should have an honorable stated salary, of a fixed and permanent value, amply sufficient for those purposes, and established by standing laws; and it shall be among the first acts of the general court, after the commencement of this constitution, to establish such salary by law accordingly.

Permanent and honorable salaries shall also be established by law for the justices of the supreme judicial court.

And if it shall be found that any of the salaries aforesaid, so established, are insufficient, they shall, from time to time, be enlarged, as the general court shall judge proper.

CHAPTER II.

Section 2.— Lieutenant-Governor

Article I. There shall be annually elected a lieutenant-governor of the commonwealth of Massachusetts, whose title shall be "His Honor;" and who shall be qualified, in point of religion, property, and residence in the commonwealth, in the same manner with the governor; and the day and manner of his election, and the qualification of the electors, shall be the same as are required in the election of a governor. The return of the votes for this officer, and the declaration of his election, shall be in the same manner; and if no one person shall be found to have a majority of all the votes returned, the vacancy shall be filled by the senate and house of representatives, in the same manner as the governor is to be elected, in case no one person shall have a majority of the votes of the people to be governor.

Art. II. The governor, and in his absence the lieutenant-governor, shall be president of the council; but shall have no voice in council; and the lieutenant-governor shall always be a member of the council, except when the chair of the governor shall be vacant.

Art. III. Whenever the chair of the governor shall be vacant, by reason of his death, or absence from the commonwealth, or otherwise, the lieutenant-governor, for the time being, shall, during such vacancy perform all the duties incumbent upon the governor, and shall have and exercise all the powers and authorities which, by this constitution, the governor is vested with, when personally present.

CHAPTER II.

Section 3.— Council, and the Manner of Settling Elections by the Legislature

Article I. There shall be a council, for advising the governor in the executive part of the government, to consist of nine persons besides the lieutenant-governor, whom the governor, for the time being, shall have full power and authority, from time to time, at this discretion, to assemble and call together; and the governor, with the said councillors, or five of them at least, shall and may, from time to time, hold and keep a council, for the ordering and directing the affairs of the commonwealth, according to the laws of the land.

Art. II. Nine councillors shall be annually chosen from among the persons returned for councillors and senators, on the last Wednesday in May, by the joint ballot of the senators and representatives assembled in one room; and in case there shall not be found, upon the first choice, the whole number of nine persons who will accept a seat in the council, the deficiency shall be made up by the electors aforesaid from among the people at large; and the number of senators left shall constitute the senate for the year. The seats of the persons thus elected from the senate, and accepting the trust, shall be vacated in the senate.

Art. III. The councillors, in the civil arrangements of the commonwealth, shall have rank next after the lieutenant-governor.

Art. IV. Not more than two councillors shall be chosen out of any one district in this commonwealth.

Art. V. The resolutions and advice of the council shall be recorded in a register and signed by the members present; and this record may be called for, at any time, by either house of the legislature; and any member of the council may insert his opinion, contrary to the resolution of the majority.

Art. VI. Whenever the office of the governor and lieutenant-governor shall be vacant by reason of death, absence, or otherwise, then the council, or the major part of them, shall, during such vacancy, have full power and authority to do and execute all and every such acts, matters, and things, as the governor or the lieutenant-governor might or could, by virtue of this constitu-

tion, do or execute, if they, or either of them, were personally present.

Art. VII. And whereas the elections appointed to be made by this constitution on the last Wednesday in May annually, by the two houses of the legislature, may not be completed on that day, the said elections may be adjourned from day to day, until the same shall be completed. And the order of elections shall be as follows: The vacancies in the senate, if any, shall first be filled up; the governor and lieutenant-governor shall then be elected, provided there should be no choice of them by the people; and afterwards the two houses shall proceed to the election of the council.

Chapter II.

Section 4. — Secretary, Treasurer, Commissary, etc.

Article I. The secretary, treasurer, and receiver-general, and the commissary-general, notaries public, and naval officers, shall be chosen annually, by joint ballot of the senators and representatives, in one room. And, that the citizens of this commonwealth may be assured, from time to time, that the moneys remaining in the public treasury, upon the settlement and liquidation of the public accounts, are their property, no man shall be eligible as treasurer and receiver-general more than five years successively.

Art. II. The records of the commonwealth shall be kept in the office of the secretary, who may appoint his deputies, for whose conduct he shall be accountable; and he shall attend the governor and council, the senate and house of representatives in person or by his deputies, as they shall respectively require.

Chapter III.

Judiciary Power.

Article I. The tenure that all commission officers shall by law have in their offices shall be expressed in their respective commissions. All judicial officers, duly appointed, commissioned, and sworn, shall hold their offices during good behavior, excepting such concerning whom there is different provision made in this constitution: *Provided, nevertheless*, The governor, with consent of the council, may remove them upon the address of both houses of the legislature.

Art. II. Each branch of the legislature, as well as the governor and council, shall have authority to require the opinions of the justices of the supreme judicial court upon important questions of law, and upon solemn occasions.

Art. III. In order that the people may not suffer from the long continuance in place of any justice of the peace, who shall fail of discharging the important duties of his office with ability or fidelity, all commissions of justices of the peace shall expire and become void in the term of seven years from their respective dates; and, upon the expiration of any commission, the same may, if necessary, be renewed, or another person appointed, as shall most conduce to the well-being of the commonwealth.

Art. IV. The judges of probate of wills, and for granting letters of administration, shall hold their courts at such place or places, on fixed days, as the convenience of the people shall require; and the legislature shall, from time to time, hereafter, appoint such times and places; until which appointments the said courts shall be holden at the times and places which the respective judges shall direct.

Art. V. All causes of marriage, divorce, and alimony, and all appeals from the judges of probate, shall be heard and determined by the governor and council until the legislature shall, by law, make other provision.

CHAPTER IV.

Delegates to Congress

The delegates of this commonwealth to the Congress of the United States shall, some time in the month of June, annually, be elected by the joint ballot of the senate and house of representatives assembled together in one room; to serve in Congress for one year, to commence on the first Monday in November, then next ensuing. They shall have commissions under the hand of the governor, and the great seal of the commonwealth; but may be recalled at any time within the year, and others chosen and commissioned, in the same manner, in their stead.

CHAPTER V. — THE UNIVERSITY AT CAMBRIDGE, AND ENCOURAGEMENT OF LITERATURE, ETC.

Section 1.—The University

Article I. Whereas our wise and pious ancestors, so early as the year [1636], laid the foundation of Harvard College, in which university many persons of great prominence have, by the blessing of God, been initiated in those arts and sciences which qualified them for the public employments, both in church and State; and whereas the encouragement of arts and sciences, and all good literature, tends to the honor of God, the advantage of the Christian religion, and the great benefit of this and the other United States of America, it is declared, that the president and fellows of Harvard College, in their corporate capacity, and their successors in that capacity, their officers and servants, shall have, hold, use, exercise, and enjoy all the powers, authorities, rights, liberties, privileges, immunities, and franchises which they now have, or are entitled to have, hold, use, exercise, and enjoy; and the same are hereby ratified and confirmed unto them, the said president and fellows of Harvard College, and to their successors, and to their officers and servants, respectively, forever.

Art. II. And whereas there have been, at sundry times, by divers persons, gifts, grants, devises of houses, lands, tenements, goods, chattels, legacies, and conveyances heretofore made, either to Harvard College in Cambridge, in New England, or to the president and fellows of Harvard College, or to the said college, by some other description, under several charters successively, it is declared, that all the said gifts, grants, devises, legacies, and conveyances are hereby forever confirmed unto the president and fellows of Harvard College, and to their successors, in the capacity aforesaid, according to the true intent and meaning of the donor or donors, grantor or grantors, devisor or devisors.

Art. III. And whereas by an act of the general court of the colony of Massachusetts Bay, passed in the year [1642], the governor and deputy governor for the time being, and all the magistrates of that jurisdiction, were, with the President, and a number of the clergy, is the said act described, constituted the overseers of Harvard College; and it being necessary, in this new constitution of government, to ascertain who shall be deemed successors to the said governor, deputy governor, and magistrates, it is declared that the governor, lieutenant-governor, council, and senate of this commonwealth are, and shall be deemed, their successors; who, with the president of Harvard College, for the time being, together with the ministers of the congregational churches in the towns of Cambridge, Watertown, Charlestown, Boston, Roxbury and Dorchester, mentioned in the said act, shall be, and hereby are, vested with all the powers and authority belonging, or in any way appertaining, to the overseers of Harvard College: *Provided*, that nothing herein shall be construed to prevent the legislature of this commonwealth from making such alterations in the government of the said university as shall be conducive to its advantage, and the interest of the republic of letters, in as full a manner as might have been done by the legislature of the late province of the Massachusetts Bay.

Chapter V.

Section 2.—The Encouragement of Literature, etc.

Wisdom and knowledge, as well as virtue, diffused generally among the body of the people, being necessary for the preservation of their rights and liberties; and as these depend on spreading the opportunities and advantages of education in the various parts of the country, and among the different orders of the people, it shall be the duty of legislatures and magistrates, in all future periods of this commonwealth, to cherish the interests of literature and the sciences, and all seminaries of them; especially the university at Cambridge, public schools, and grammar-schools in the towns; to encourage private societies and public institutions, rewards and immunities, for the promotion of agriculture, arts, sciences, commerce, trades, manufactures, and a natural history of the country; to countenance and inculcate the principles of humanity and general benevolence, public and private charity, industry and frugality, honesty and punctuality in their dealings; sincerity, and good humor, and all social affections and generous sentiments, among the people.

Chapter VI.

Oaths and Subscriptions; Incompatibility of and Exclusion from Offices; Pecuniary Qualifications; Commissions; Writs; Confirmation of Laws; Habeas Corpus; The Enacting Style; Continuance of Officers; Provision for a Future Revisal of the Constitution, etc.

Article I. Any person chosen governor, lieutenant-governor, councillor, senator, or representative, and accepting the trust, shall, before he proceed to execute the duties of his place or office, make and subscribe the following declaration, viz:

"I, A.B., do declare that I believe the Christian religion, and have a firm persuasion of its truth; and that I am seized and possessed, in my own right, of the property required by the constitution, as one qualification for the office or place to which I am elected."

And the governor, lieutenant-governor, and councillors shall make and subscribe the said declaration, in the presence of the two houses of assembly; and the senators and representatives, first elected under this constitution, before the president and five of the council of the former constitution; and forever afterwards, before the governor and council for the time being.

And every person chosen to either of the places or offices aforesaid, as also any persons appointed or commissioned to any judicial, executive, military, or other office under the government, shall, before he enters on the discharge of the business of his place or office, take and subscribe the following declaration and oaths or affirmations, viz:

"I, A.B., do truly and sincerely acknowledge, profess, testify, and declare that the commonwealth of Massachusetts is, and of right ought to be, a free, sovereign, and independent State, and I do swear that I will bear true faith and allegiance to the said commonwealth, and that I will defend the same against traitorous conspiracies and all hostile attempts whatsoever; and that I do renounce and abjure all allegiance, subjection, and obedience to the King, Queen, or government of Great Britain, (as the case may be,) and every other foreign power whatsoever; and that no foreign prince, person, prelate, state, or potentate hath, or ought to have, any jurisdiction, superiority, preeminence, authority, dispensing or other power, in any matter, civil, ecclesiastical, or spiritual, within this commonwealth; except the authority and power which is or may be vested by their constituents in the Congress of the United States; and I do further testify and declare that no man, or body of men, have, or can have, any right to absolve or discharge me from the obligation of this oath, declaration, or affirmation; and that I do make this

acknowledgment, profession, testimony, declaration, denial, renunciation, and abjuration heartily and truly, according to the common meaning and acceptation of the foregoing words, without any equivocation, mental evasion, or secret reservation whatsoever: So help me, God."

"I, A.B., do solemnly swear and affirm that I will faithfully and impartially discharge and perform all the duties incumbent on me as _____, according to the best of my abilities and understanding, agreeably to the rules and regulations of the constitution and the laws of the commonwealth: So help me, God."

Provided always, That when any person, chosen and appointed as aforesaid, shall be of the denomination of people called Quakers, and shall decline taking the said oaths, he shall make his affirmation in the foregoing form, and subscribe the same, omitting the words, "I do swear," "and abjure," "oath or," "and abjuration," in the first oath; and in the second oath, the words, "swear and," and in each of them the words, "So help me, God;" subjoining instead thereof, "This I do under the pains and penalties of perjury."

And the said oaths or affirmations shall be taken and subscribed by the governor, lieutenant-governor, and councillors, before the president of the senate, in the presence of the two houses of assembly; and by the senators and representatives first elected under this constitution, before the president and five of the council of the former constitution; and forever afterwards before the governor and council for the time being; and by the residue of the officers aforesaid, before such persons and in such manner as from time to time shall be prescribed by the legislature.

Art. II. No governor, lieutenant-governor, or judge of the supreme judicial court shall hold any other office or place, under the authority of this commonwealth, except such as by the constitution they are admitted to hold, saving that the judges of the said court may hold the office of the justices of the peace through the State; nor shall they hold any other place or office, or receive any pension or salary from any other State, or government, or power, whatever.

No person shall be capable of holding or exercising at the same time, within this State, more than one of the following offices, viz: judge of probate, sheriff, register of probate, or register of deeds; and never more than any two offices, which are to be held by appointment of the governor, or the governor and council, or the senate, or the house of representatives, or by the election of the people of the State at large, or of the people of any county, military offices, and the offices of justices of the peace excepted, shall be held by one person.

No person holding the office of judge of the supreme judicial court, secretary, attorney-general, solicitor-general, treasurer or receiver-general, judge of probate, commissary-general, president, professor, or instructor of Harvard College, sheriff, clerk of the house of representatives, register of probate, register of deeds, clerk of the supreme judicial court, clerk of the inferior court of common pleas, or officer of the customs, including in this description naval officers, shall at the same time have a seat in the senate or house of representatives; but their being chosen or appointed to, and accepting the same, shall operate as a resignation of their seat in the senate or house of representatives; and the place so vacated shall be filled up.

And the same rule shall take place in case any judge of the said supreme judicial court or judge of probate shall accept a seat in council, or any councillor shall accept of either of those offices or places.

And no person shall ever be admitted to hold a seat in the legislature, or any office of trust or importance under the government of this commonwealth, who shall in the due course of law have been convicted of bribery or corruption in obtaining an election or appointment.

Art. III. In all cases where sums or money are mentioned in this constitution, the value thereof shall be computed in silver, at six shillings and eight pence per ounce; and it shall in the power of the legislature, from time to time, to increase such qualifications, as to property, of the persons to be elected to offices as the circumstances of the commonwealth shall require.

Art. IV. All commissions shall be in the name of the commonwealth of Massachusetts, signed by the governor, and attested by the secretary or his deputy, and have the great seal of the commonwealth affixed thereto.

Art. V. All writs, issuing of the clerk's office in any of the courts of law, shall be in the name of the commonwealth of Massachusetts; they shall be under the seal of the court from when they issue; they shall bear test of the first justice of the court to which they shall be returned who is not a party, and be signed by the clerk of such court.

Art. VI. All the laws which have heretofore been adopted, used, and approved in the province, colony, or State of Massachusetts Bay, and usually practiced on in the courts of law, shall still remain and be in full force, until altered or repealed by the legislature, such parts only excepted as are repugnant to the rights and liberties contained in this constitution.

Art. VII. The privilege and benefit of the writ of *habeas corpus* shall be enjoyed in this commonwealth, in the most free, easy, cheap, expeditious, and ample manner, and shall not be suspended by the legislature, except upon the most urgent and pressing occasions, and for a limited time, not exceeding twelve months.

Art. VIII. The enacting style, in making and passing all acts, statutes, and laws, shall be, *"Be it enacted by the senate and house of representatives in general court assembled, and by authority of the same."*

Art. IX. To the end there may be no failure of justice or danger arise to the commonwealth from a change in the form of government, all officers, civil and military, holding commissions under the government and people of Massachusetts Bay, in New England, and all other officers of the said government and people, at the time this constitution shall take effect, shall have, hold, use, exercise, and enjoy all the powers and authority to them granted or committed until other persons shall be appointed in their stead; and all courts of law shall proceed in the execution of the business of their respective departments; and all the executive and legislative officers, bodies, and powers shall continue in full force, in the enjoyment and exercise of all their trusts, employments, and authority, until the general court, and the supreme and executive officers under this constitution, are designated and invested with their respective trusts, powers, and authority.

Art. X. In order the more effectually to adhere to the principles of the constitution, and to correct those violations which by any means may be made therein, as well as to form such alterations as from experience shall be found necessary, the general court which shall be in the year of our Lord [1795] shall issue precepts to the selectmen of the several towns, and to the assessors of the unincorporated plantations, directing them to convene the qualified voters of their respective towns and plantations, for the purpose of collecting their sentiments on the necessity or expediency of revising the constitution in order to amendments.

And if it shall appear, by the returns made, that two-thirds of the qualified voters throughout the State, who shall assemble and vote in consequence of the said precepts, are in favor of such revision or amendment, the general court shall issue precepts, or direct them to be issued from the secretary's office, to the several towns to elect or direct them to be issued from the secretary's office, to the several towns to elect delegates to meet in convention for the purpose aforesaid.

And said delegates to be chosen in the same manner and proportion as their representatives in the second branch of the legislature are by this constitution to be chosen.

Art. XI. This form of government shall be enrolled on parchment and deposited in the secretary's office, and be a part of the laws of the land, and printed copies thereof shall be prefixed to the book containing the laws of this commonwealth in all future editions of the said laws.

JAMES BOWDOIN, *President*
Samuel Barrett, *Secretary*

CHAPTER 12

Articles of Confederation (March 1, 1781)

Congress of the Confederation

The History*

Before the Constitution there was the Articles of Confederation — in effect, the first constitution of the United States. Drafted in 1777 by the same Continental Congress that passed the Declaration of Independence, the articles established a "firm league of friendship" between and among the 13 states.

Created during the throes of the Revolutionary War, the Articles reflect the wariness by the states of a strong central government. Afraid that their individual needs would be ignored by a national government with too much power, and the abuses that often result from such power, the Articles purposely established a "constitution" that vested the largest share of power to the individual states.

Under the Articles each of the states retained their "sovereignty, freedom, and independence." Instead of setting up executive and judicial branches of government, there was a committee of delegates composed of representatives from each state. These individuals comprised the Congress, a national legislature called for by the Articles.

The Congress was responsible for conducting foreign affairs, declaring war or peace, maintaining an army and navy and a variety of other lesser functions. But the Articles denied Congress the power to collect taxes, regulate interstate commerce and enforce laws.

Eventually, these shortcomings would lead to the adoption of the U.S. Constitution. But during those years in which the 13 states were struggling to achieve their independent status, the Articles of Confederation stood them in good stead.

Adopted by Congress on November 15, 1777, the Articles became operative on March 1, 1781 when the last of the 13 states signed on to the document.

The Document

Articles of Confederation

To all to whom these Presents shall come, we the undersigned Delegates of the States affixed to our Names send greeting.

Articles of Confederation and perpetual

---

*Originally published as "The Articles of Confederation and Perpetual Union," *Early America's Milestone Historic Documents*, Archiving Early America, Seattle, Washington, 2009. For additional information see "The First Constitution — The Articles of Confederation," *The Charters of Freedom*, U.S. National Archives and Records Administration, College Park, Maryland, 2004. This agency is listed in the *National Resource Directory* section of this volume.

Union between the states of New Hampshire, Massachusetts-bay Rhode Island and Providence Plantations, Connecticut, New York, New Jersey, Pennsylvania, Delaware, Maryland, Virginia, North Carolina, South Carolina and Georgia.

I. The Stile of this Confederacy shall be "The United States of America."

II. Each state retains its sovereignty, freedom, and independence, and every power, jurisdiction, and right, which is not by this Confederation expressly delegated to the United States, in Congress assembled.

III. The said States hereby severally enter into a firm league of friendship with each other, for their common defense, the security of their liberties, and their mutual and general welfare, binding themselves to assist each other, against all force offered to, or attacks made upon them, or any of them, on account of religion, sovereignty, trade, or any other pretense whatever.

IV. The better to secure and perpetuate mutual friendship and intercourse among the people of the different States in this Union, the free inhabitants of each of these States, paupers, vagabonds, and fugitives from justice excepted, shall be entitled to all privileges and immunities of free citizens in the several States; and the people of each State shall free ingress and regress to and from any other State, and shall enjoy therein all the privileges of trade and commerce, subject to the same duties, impositions, and restrictions as the inhabitants thereof respectively, provided that such restrictions shall not extend so far as to prevent the removal of property imported into any State, to any other State, of which the owner is an inhabitant; provided also that no imposition, duties or restriction shall be laid by any State, on the property of the United States, or either of them.

If any person guilty of, or charged with, treason, felony, or other high misdemeanor in any State, shall flee from justice, and be found in any of the United States, he shall, upon demand of the Governor or executive power of the State from which he fled, be delivered up and removed to the State having jurisdiction of his offense.

Full faith and credit shall be given in each of these States to the records, acts, and judicial proceedings of the courts and magistrates of every other State.

V. For the most convenient management of the general interests of the United States, delegates shall be annually appointed in such manner as the legislatures of each State shall direct, to meet in Congress on the first Monday in November, in every year, with a power reserved to each State to recall its delegates, or any of them, at any time within the year, and to send others in their stead for the remainder of the year.

No State shall be represented in Congress by less than two, nor more than seven members; and no person shall be capable of being a delegate for more than three years in any term of six years; nor shall any person, being a delegate, be capable of holding any office under the United States, for which he, or another for his benefit, receives any salary, fees or emolument of any kind.

Each State shall maintain its own delegates in a meeting of the States, and while they act as members of the committee of the States.

In determining questions in the United States in Congress assembled, each State shall have one vote.

Freedom of speech and debate in Congress shall not be impeached or questioned in any court or place out of Congress, and the members of Congress shall be protected in their persons from arrests or imprisonments, during the time of their going to and from, and attendence on Congress, except for treason, felony, or breach of the peace.

VI. No State, without the consent of the United States in Congress assembled, shall send any embassy to, or receive any embassy from, or enter into any conference, agreement, alliance or treaty with any King,

Prince or State; nor shall any person holding any office of profit or trust under the United States, or any of them, accept any present, emolument, office or title of any kind whatever from any King, Prince or foreign State; nor shall the United States in Congress assembled, or any of them, grant any title of nobility.

No two or more States shall enter into any treaty, confederation or alliance whatever between them, without the consent of the United States in Congress assembled, specifying accurately the purposes for which the same is to be entered into, and how long it shall continue.

No State shall lay any imposts or duties, which may interfere with any stipulations in treaties, entered into by the United States in Congress assembled, with any King, Prince or State, in pursuance of any treaties already proposed by Congress, to the courts of France and Spain.

No vessel of war shall be kept up in time of peace by any State, except such number only, as shall be deemed necessary by the United States in Congress assembled, for the defense of such State, or its trade; nor shall any body of forces be kept up by any State in time of peace, except such number only, as in the judgement of the United States in Congress assembled, shall be deemed requisite to garrison the forts necessary for the defense of such State; but every State shall always keep up a well-regulated and disciplined militia, sufficiently armed and accoutered, and shall provide and constantly have ready for use, in public stores, a due number of filed pieces and tents, and a proper quantity of arms, ammunition and camp equipage.

No State shall engage in any war without the consent of the United States in Congress assembled, unless such State be actually invaded by enemies, or shall have received certain advice of a resolution being formed by some nation of Indians to invade such State, and the danger is so imminent as not to admit of a delay till the United States in Congress assembled can be consulted; nor shall any State grant commissions to any ships or vessels of war, nor letters of marque or reprisal, except it be after a declaration of war by the United States in Congress assembled, and then only against the Kingdom or State and the subjects thereof, against which war has been so declared, and under such regulations as shall be established by the United States in Congress assembled, unless such State be infested by pirates, in which case vessels of war may be fitted out for that occasion, and kept so long as the danger shall continue, or until the United States in Congress assembled shall determine otherwise.

VII. When land forces are raised by any State for the common defense, all officers of or under the rank of colonel, shall be appointed by the legislature of each State respectively, by whom such forces shall be raised, or in such manner as such State shall direct, and all vacancies shall be filled up by the State which first made the appointment.

VIII. All charges of war, and all other expenses that shall be incurred for the common defense or general welfare, and allowed by the United States in Congress assembled, shall be defrayed out of a common treasury, which shall be supplied by the several States in proportion to the value of all land within each State, granted or surveyed for any person, as such land and the buildings and improvements thereon shall be estimated according to such mode as the United States in Congress assembled, shall from time to time direct and appoint.

The taxes for paying that proportion shall be laid and levied by the authority and direction of the legislatures of the several States within the time agreed upon by the United States in Congress assembled.

IX. The United States in Congress assembled, shall have the sole and exclusive right and power of determining on peace and war, except in the cases mentioned in the sixth article — of sending and receiving ambassadors — entering into treaties and alliances, provided that no treaty of commerce shall be made whereby the legislative power of the respective States shall be restrained from imposing such imposts and duties on foreigners, as their own people are subjected to, or from prohibiting the exportation or importation of any species of goods or commodities whatsoever — of establishing rules for deciding in all cases, what captures on land or water shall be legal, and in what manner prizes taken by land or naval forces in the service of the United States shall be divided or appropriated — of granting letters of marque and reprisal in times of peace — appointing courts for the trial of piracies and felonies commited on the high seas and establishing courts for receiving and determining finally appeals in all cases of captures, provided that no member of Congress shall be appointed a judge of any of the said courts.

The United States in Congress assembled shall also be the last resort on appeal in all disputes and differences now subsisting or that hereafter may arise between two or more States concerning boundary, jurisdiction or any other causes whatever; which authority shall always be exercised in the manner following. Whenever the legislative or executive authority or lawful agent of any State in controversy with another shall present a petition to Congress stating the matter in question and praying for a hearing, notice thereof shall be given by order of Congress to the legislative or executive authority of the other State in controversy, and a day assigned for the appearance of the parties by their lawful agents, who shall then be directed to appoint by joint consent, commissioners or judges to constitute a court for hearing and determining the matter in question: but if they cannot agree, Congress shall name three persons out of each of the United States, and from the list of such persons each party shall alternately strike out one, the petitioners beginning, until the number shall be reduced to thirteen; and from that number not less than seven, nor more than nine names as Congress

shall direct, shall in the presence of Congress be drawn out by lot, and the persons whose names shall be so drawn or any five of them, shall be commissioners or judges, to hear and finally determine the controversy, so always as a major part of the judges who shall hear the cause shall agree in the determination: and if either party shall neglect to attend at the day appointed, without showing reasons, which Congress shall judge sufficient, or being present shall refuse to strike, the Congress shall proceed to nominate three persons out of each State, and the secretary of Congress shall strike in behalf of such party absent or refusing; and the judgement and sentence of the court to be appointed, in the manner before prescribed, shall be final and conclusive; and if any of the parties shall refuse to submit to the authority of such court, or to appear or defend their claim or cause, the court shall nevertheless proceed to pronounce sentence, or judgement, which shall in like manner be final and decisive, the judgement or sentence and other proceedings being in either case transmitted to Congress, and lodged among the acts of Congress for the security of the parties concerned: provided that every commissioner, before he sits in judgement, shall take an oath to be administered by one of the judges of the supreme or superior court of the State, where the cause shall be tried, 'well and truly to hear and determine the matter in question, according to the best of his judgement, without favor, affection or hope of reward': provided also, that no State shall be deprived of territory for the benefit of the United States.

All controversies concerning the private right of soil claimed under different grants of two or more States, whose jurisdictions as they may respect such lands, and the States which passed such grants are adjusted, the said grants or either of them being at the same time claimed to have originated antecedent to such settlement of jurisdiction, shall on the petition of either party to the Congress of the United States, be finally determined as near as may be in the same manner as is before presecribed for deciding disputes respecting territorial jurisdiction between different States.

The United States in Congress assembled shall also have the sole and exclusive right and power of regulating the alloy and value of coin struck by their own authority, or by that of the respective States —fixing the standards of weights and measures throughout the United States — regulating the trade and managing all affairs with the Indians, not members of any of the States, provided that the legislative right of any State within its own limits be not infringed or violated — establishing or regulating post offices from one State to another, throughout all the United States, and exacting such postage on the papers passing through the same as may be requisite to defray the expenses of the said office — appointing all officers of the land forces, in the service of the United States, excepting regimental officers — appointing all the officers of the naval forces, and commissioning all officers whatever in the service of the United States — making rules for the government and regulation of the said land and naval forces, and directing their operations.

The United States in Congress assembled shall have authority to appoint a committee, to sit in the recess of Congress, to be denominated 'A Committee of the States,' and to consist of one delegate from each State; and to appoint such other committees and civil officers as may be necessary for managing the general affairs of the United States under their direction — to appoint one of their members to preside, provided that no person be allowed to serve in the office of president more than one year in any term of three years; to ascertain the necessary sums of money to be raised for the service of the United States, and to appropriate and apply the same for defraying the public expenses — to borrow money, or emit bills on the credit of the United States, transmitting every half-year to the respective States an account of the

sums of money so borrowed or emitted — to build and equip a navy — to agree upon the number of land forces, and to make requisitions from each State for its quota, in proportion to the number of white inhabitants in such State; which requisition shall be binding, and thereupon the legislature of each State shall appoint the regimental officers, raise the men and cloath, arm and equip them in a solid-like manner, at the expense of the United States; and the officers and men so cloathed, armed and equipped shall march to the place appointed, and within the time agreed on by the United States in Congress assembled. But if the United States in Congress assembled shall, on consideration of circumstances judge proper that any State should not raise men, or should raise a smaller number of men than the quota thereof, such extra number shall be raised, officered, cloathed, armed and equipped in the same manner as the quota of each State, unless the legislature of such State shall judge that such extra number cannot be safely spread out in the same, in which case they shall raise, officer, cloath, arm and equip as many of such extra number as they judge can be safely spared. And the officers and men so cloathed, armed, and equipped, shall march to the place appointed, and within the time agreed on by the United States in Congress assembled.

The United States in Congress assembled shall never engage in a war, nor grant letters of marque or reprisal in time of peace, nor enter into any treaties or alliances, nor coin money, nor regulate the value thereof, nor ascertain the sums and expenses necessary for the defense and welfare of the United States, or any of them, nor emit bills, nor borrow money on the credit of the United States, nor appropriate money, nor agree upon the number of vessels of war, to be built or purchased, or the number of land or sea forces to be raised, nor appoint a commander in chief of the army or navy, unless nine States assent to the same: nor shall a question on any other point, except for adjourning from day to day be determined, unless by the votes of the majority of the United States in Congress assembled.

The Congress of the United States shall have power to adjourn to any time within the year, and to any place within the United States, so that no period of adjournment be for a longer duration than the space of six months, and shall publish the journal of their proceedings monthly, except such parts thereof relating to treaties, alliances or military operations, as in their judgement require secrecy; and the yeas and nays of the delegates of each State on any question shall be entered on the journal, when it is desired by any delegates of a State, or any of them, at his or their request shall be furnished with a transcript of the said journal, except such parts as are above excepted, to lay before the legislatures of the several States.

X. The Committee of the States, or any nine of them, shall be authorized to execute, in the recess of Congress, such of the powers of Congress as the United States in Congress assembled, by the consent of the nine States, shall from time to time think expedient to vest them with; provided that no power be delegated to the said Committee, for the exercise of which, by the Articles of Confederation, the voice of nine States in the Congress of the United States assembled be requisite.

XI. Canada acceding to this confederation, and adjoining in the measures of the United States, shall be admitted into, and entitled to all the advantages of this Union; but no other colony shall be admitted into the same, unless such admission be agreed to by nine States.

XII. All bills of credit emitted, monies borrowed, and debts contracted by, or under the authority of Congress, before the assembling of the United States, in pursuance of the present confederation, shall be deemed and considered as a charge against the United States, for payment and satisfaction whereof the said United States, and the public faith are hereby solemnly pleged.

XIII. Every State shall abide by the determination of the United States in Congress assembled, on all questions which by this confederation are submitted to them. And the Articles of this Confederation shall be inviolably observed by every State, and the Union shall be perpetual; nor shall any alteration at any time hereafter be made in any of them; unless such alteration be agreed to in a Congress of the United States, and be afterwards confirmed by the legislatures of every State.

And whereas it hath pleased the Great Governor of the World to incline the hearts of the legislatures we respectively represent in Congress, to approve of, and to authorize us to ratify the said Articles of Confederation and perpetual Union. Know Ye that we the undersigned delegates, by virtue of the power and authority to us given for that purpose, do by these presents, in the name and in behalf of our respective constituents, fully and entirely ratify and confirm each and every of the said Articles of Confederation and perpetual Union, and all and singular the matters and things therein contained: And we do further solemnly plight and engage the faith of our respective constituents, that they shall abide by the determinations of the United States in Congress assembled, on all questions, which by the said Confederation are submitted to them. And that the Articles thereof shall be inviolably observed by the States we respectively represent, and that the Union shall be perpetual.

In Witness whereof we have hereunto set our hands in Congress. Done at Philadelphia in the State of Pennsylvania the ninth day of July in the Year of our Lord One Thousand Seven Hundred and Seventy-Eight, and in the Third Year of the independence of America.

Agreed to by Congress 15 November 1777. In force after ratification by Maryland, 1 March 1781.

CHAPTER 13

Constitution of the United States (September 17, 1787)

Congress of the Confederation

The History*

The Constitution of the United States of America is the supreme law of the United States. It is the foundation and source of the legal authority underlying the existence of the United States of America and the Federal Government of the United States. It provides the framework for the organization of the United States Government. The document defines the three main branches of the government: The legislative branch with a bicameral Congress, an executive branch led by the President, and a judicial branch headed by the Supreme Court. Besides providing for the organization of these branches, the Constitution outlines obligations of each office, as well as provides what powers each branch may exercise. It also reserves numerous rights for the individual states, thereby establishing the United States' federal system of government. It is the shortest and oldest written constitution of any major sovereign state.

The United States Constitution was adopted on September 17, 1787, by the Constitutional Convention (or Constitutional Congress) in Philadelphia, Pennsylvania, and later ratified by conventions in each U.S. state in the name of "The People"; it has since been amended twenty-seven times, the first ten amendments being known as the Bill of Rights. The Articles of Confederation and Perpetual Union was actually the first constitution of the United States of America. The U.S. Constitution replaced the Articles of Confederation as the governing document for the United States after being ratified by nine states. The Constitution has a central place in United States law and political culture. The handwritten, or "engrossed," original document penned by Jacob Shallus is on display at the National Archives and Records Administration in Washington, D.C.

In September 1786, commissioners from five states met in the Annapolis Convention to discuss adjustments to the Articles of Confederation that would improve commerce. They invited state representatives to convene in Philadelphia to discuss improvements to the federal government. After debate, the Congress of the Confederation endorsed the plan to revise the Articles of Confederation

---

*Originally published as "United States Constitution," *Wikipedia*, Wikimedia Foundation, Inc., San Francisco, California, November 2009. For additional information see "Constitution of the United States," *The Charters of Freedom*, U.S. National Archives and Records Administration, College Park, Maryland, 2004. This agency is listed in the *National Resource Directory* section of this volume.

on February 21, 1787. Twelve states, Rhode Island being the only exception, accepted this invitation and sent delegates to convene in May 1787. The resolution calling the Convention specified that its purpose was to propose amendments to the Articles, but through discussion and debate it became clear by mid–June that, rather than amend the existing Articles, the Convention decided to propose a rewritten Constitution.

The Philadelphia Convention voted to keep the debates secret, so that the delegates could speak freely. They also decided to draft a new fundamental government design. Despite Article 13 of the Articles of Confederation stating that the union created under the Articles was "perpetual" and that any alteration must be "agreed to in a Congress of the United States, and be afterwards confirmed by the legislatures of every State," Article VII of the proposed constitution stipulated that only nine of the thirteen states would have to ratify for the new government to go into effect (for the participating states). Current knowledge of the drafting and construction of the United States Constitution comes primarily from the diaries left by James Madison, who kept a complete record of the proceedings at the Constitutional Convention.

The Virginia Plan was the unofficial agenda for the Convention, and was drafted chiefly by James Madison, considered to be "The Father of the Constitution" for his major contributions. It was weighted toward the interests of the larger states, and proposed among other points:

- A powerful bicameral legislature with a House and a Senate
- An executive chosen by the legislature
- A judiciary, with life-terms of service and vague powers
- The national legislature would be able to veto state laws

An alternate proposal, William Paterson's New Jersey Plan, gave states equal weights and was supported by the smaller states. Roger Sherman of Connecticut brokered The Great Compromise whereby the House would represent the people, a Senate would represent the states, and a president would be elected by electors.

The contentious issue of slavery was too controversial to be resolved during the convention. As a result, the original Constitution contained four provisions tacitly allowing slavery to continue for the next 20 years. Section 9 of Article I allowed the continued "importation" of such persons, Section 2 of Article IV prohibited the provision of assistance to escaping persons and required their return if successful and Section 2 of Article I defined other persons as "three-fifths" of a person for calculations of each state's official population for representation for federal taxation. Article V prohibited any amendments or legislation changing the provision regarding slave importation until 1808, thereby giving the States then existing 20 years to resolve this issue. The failure to do so was a contributing factor to the Civil War.

Contrary to the process for "alteration" spelled out in Article 13 of the Articles, Congress submitted the proposal to the states and set the terms for representation.

On September 17, 1787, the Constitution was completed in Philadelphia at the Federal Convention, followed by a speech given by Benjamin Franklin who urged unanimity, although they decided only nine states were needed to ratify the constitution for it to go into effect. The Convention submitted the Constitution to the Congress of the Confederation, where it received approval according to Article 13 of the Articles of Confederation.

Once the Congress of the Confederation received word of New Hampshire's ratification, it set a timetable for the start of operations under the Constitution, and on March 4, 1789, the government under the Constitution began operations.

The Document*

Constitution of the United States

We the People of the United States, in Order to form a more perfect Union, establish Justice, insure domestic Tranquility, provide for the common defense, promote the general Welfare, and secure the Blessings of Liberty to ourselves and our Posterity, do ordain and establish this Constitution for the United States of America.

ARTICLE. I

Section. 1.

All legislative Powers herein granted shall be vested in a Congress of the United States, which shall consist of a Senate and House of Representatives.

Section. 2.

The House of Representatives shall be composed of Members chosen every second Year by the People of the several States, and the Electors in each State shall have the Qualifications requisite for Electors of the most numerous Branch of the State Legislature.

No Person shall be a Representative who shall not have attained to the Age of twenty five Years, and been seven Years a Citizen of the United States, and who shall not, when elected, be an Inhabitant of that State in which he shall be chosen.

Representatives and direct Taxes shall be apportioned among the several States which may be included within this Union, according to their respective Numbers, which shall be determined by adding to the whole Number of free Persons, including those bound to Service for a Term of Years, and excluding Indians not taxed, three fifths of all other Persons. The actual Enumeration shall be made within three Years after the first Meeting of the Congress of the United States, and within every subsequent Term of ten Years, in such Manner as they shall by Law direct. The Number of Representatives shall not exceed one for every thirty Thousand, but each State shall have at Least one Representative; and until such enumeration shall be made, the State of New Hampshire shall be entitled to chuse three, Massachusetts eight, Rhode-Island and Providence Plantations one, Connecticut five, New-York six, New Jersey four, Pennsylvania eight, Delaware one, Maryland six, Virginia ten, North Carolina five, South Carolina five, and Georgia three.

When vacancies happen in the Representation from any State, the Executive Authority thereof shall issue Writs of Election to fill such Vacancies.

The House of Representatives shall chuse their Speaker and other Officers; and shall have the sole Power of Impeachment.

Section. 3.

The Senate of the United States shall be composed of two Senators from each State, chosen by the Legislature thereof for six Years; and each Senator shall have one Vote.

Immediately after they shall be assembled in Consequence of the first Election, they shall be divided as equally as may be into three Classes. The Seats of the Senators of the first Class shall be vacated at the Expiration of the second Year, of the second Class at the Expiration of the fourth Year, and of the third Class at the Expiration of the sixth Year, so that one third may be chosen every second Year; and if Vacancies happen by Resignation, or otherwise, during the Recess of the Legislature of any State, the Executive thereof may make temporary Appointments until the next Meeting of the Legislature, which shall then fill such Vacancies.

No Person shall be a Senator who shall not have attained to the Age of thirty Years, and been nine Years a Citizen of the United

---

*The text following is a transcription of the U.S. Constitution in its original form. Items that are underlined have since been either amended or superseded.

States, and who shall not, when elected, be an Inhabitant of that State for which he shall be chosen.

The Vice President of the United States shall be President of the Senate, but shall have no Vote, unless they be equally divided.

The Senate shall chuse their other Officers, and also a President pro tempore, in the Absence of the Vice President, or when he shall exercise the Office of President of the United States.

The Senate shall have the sole Power to try all Impeachments. When sitting for that Purpose, they shall be on Oath or Affirmation. When the President of the United States is tried, the Chief Justice shall preside: And no Person shall be convicted without the Concurrence of two thirds of the Members present.

Judgment in Cases of Impeachment shall not extend further than to removal from Office, and disqualification to hold and enjoy any Office of honor, Trust or Profit under the United States: but the Party convicted shall nevertheless be liable and subject to Indictment, Trial, Judgment and Punishment, according to Law.

Section. 4.

The Times, Places and Manner of holding Elections for Senators and Representatives, shall be prescribed in each State by the Legislature thereof; but the Congress may at any time by Law make or alter such Regulations, except as to the Places of chusing Senators.

The Congress shall assemble at least once in every Year, and such Meeting shall <u>be on the first Monday in December,</u> unless they shall by Law appoint a different Day.

Section. 5.

Each House shall be the Judge of the Elections, Returns and Qualifications of its own Members, and a Majority of each shall constitute a Quorum to do Business; but a smaller Number may adjourn from day to day, and may be authorized to compel the Attendance of absent Members, in such Manner, and under such Penalties as each House may provide.

Each House may determine the Rules of its Proceedings, punish its Members for disorderly Behaviour, and, with the Concurrence of two thirds, expel a Member.

Each House shall keep a Journal of its Proceedings, and from time to time publish the same, excepting such Parts as may in their Judgment require Secrecy; and the Yeas and Nays of the Members of either House on any question shall, at the Desire of one fifth of those Present, be entered on the Journal.

Neither House, during the Session of Congress, shall, without the Consent of the other, adjourn for more than three days, nor to any other Place than that in which the two Houses shall be sitting.

Section. 6.

The Senators and Representatives shall receive a Compensation for their Services, to be ascertained by Law, and paid out of the Treasury of the United States. They shall in all Cases, except Treason, Felony and Breach of the Peace, be privileged from Arrest during their Attendance at the Session of their respective Houses, and in going to and returning from the same; and for any Speech or Debate in either House, they shall not be questioned in any other Place.

No Senator or Representative shall, during the Time for which he was elected, be appointed to any civil Office under the Authority of the United States, which shall have been created, or the Emoluments whereof shall have been encreased during such time; and no Person holding any Office under the United States, shall be a Member of either House during his Continuance in Office.

Section. 7.

All Bills for raising Revenue shall originate in the House of Representatives; but the Senate may propose or concur with Amendments as on other Bills.

Every Bill which shall have passed the House of Representatives and the Senate, shall, before it become a Law, be presented to the President of the United States: If he approves he shall sign it, but if not he shall return it, with his Objections to that House in which it shall have originated, who shall enter the Objections at large on their Journal, and proceed to reconsider it. If after such Reconsideration two thirds of that House shall agree to pass the Bill, it shall be sent, together with the Objections, to the other House, by which it shall likewise be reconsidered, and if approved by two thirds of that House, it shall become a Law. But in all such Cases the Votes of both Houses shall be determined by yeas and Nays, and the Names of the Persons voting for and against the Bill shall be entered on the Journal of each House respectively. If any Bill shall not be returned by the President within ten Days (Sundays excepted) after it shall have been presented to him, the Same shall be a Law, in like Manner as if he had signed it, unless the Congress by their Adjournment prevent its Return, in which Case it shall not be a Law.

Every Order, Resolution, or Vote to which the Concurrence of the Senate and House of Representatives may be necessary (except on a question of Adjournment) shall be presented to the President of the United States; and before the Same shall take Effect, shall be approved by him, or being disapproved by him, shall be repassed by two thirds of the Senate and House of Representatives, according to the Rules and Limitations prescribed in the Case of a Bill.

Section. 8.

The Congress shall have Power To lay and collect Taxes, Duties, Imposts and Excises, to pay the Debts and provide for the common Defence and general Welfare of the United States; but all Duties, Imposts and Excises shall be uniform throughout the United States;

To borrow Money on the credit of the United States;

To regulate Commerce with foreign Nations, and among the several States, and with the Indian Tribes;

To establish an uniform Rule of Naturalization, and uniform Laws on the subject of Bankruptcies throughout the United States;

To coin Money, regulate the Value thereof, and of foreign Coin, and fix the Standard of Weights and Measures;

To provide for the Punishment of counterfeiting the Securities and current Coin of the United States;

To establish Post Offices and post Roads;

To promote the Progress of Science and useful Arts, by securing for limited Times to Authors and Inventors the exclusive Right to their respective Writings and Discoveries;

To constitute Tribunals inferior to the supreme Court;

To define and punish Piracies and Felonies committed on the high Seas, and Offences against the Law of Nations;

To declare War, grant Letters of Marque and Reprisal, and make Rules concerning Captures on Land and Water;

To raise and support Armies, but no Appropriation of Money to that Use shall be for a longer Term than two Years;

To provide and maintain a Navy;

To make Rules for the Government and Regulation of the land and naval Forces;

To provide for calling forth the Militia to execute the Laws of the Union, suppress Insurrections and repel Invasions;

To provide for organizing, arming, and disciplining, the Militia, and for governing such Part of them as may be employed in the Service of the United States, reserving to the States respectively, the Appointment of the Officers, and the Authority of training the Militia according to the discipline prescribed by Congress;

To exercise exclusive Legislation in all Cases whatsoever, over such District (not exceeding ten Miles square) as may, by Cession of particular States, and the Acceptance of Congress, become the Seat of the Government of the United States, and to exercise like Authority over all Places purchased by the Consent of the Legislature of the State in which the Same shall be, for the Erection of Forts, Magazines, Arsenals, dock-Yards, and other needful Buildings;— And

To make all Laws which shall be necessary and proper for carrying into Execution the foregoing Powers, and all other Powers vested by this Constitution in the Government of the United States, or in any Department or Officer thereof.

Section. 9.

The Migration or Importation of such Persons as any of the States now existing shall think proper to admit, shall not be prohibited by the Congress prior to the Year one thousand eight hundred and eight, but a Tax or duty may be imposed on such Importation, not exceeding ten dollars for each Person.

The Privilege of the Writ of Habeas Corpus shall not be suspended, unless when in Cases of Rebellion or Invasion the public Safety may require it.

No Bill of Attainder or ex post facto Law shall be passed.

No Capitation, or other direct, Tax shall be laid, <u>unless in Proportion to the Census or enumeration herein before directed to be taken.</u>

No Tax or Duty shall be laid on Articles exported from any State.

No Preference shall be given by any Regulation of Commerce or Revenue to the Ports of one State over those of another; nor shall Vessels bound to, or from, one State, be obliged to enter, clear, or pay Duties in a other.

No Money shall be drawn from the Treasury, but in Consequence of Appropriations made by Law; and a regular Statement and Account of the Receipts and Expenditures of all public Money shall be published from time to time.

No Title of Nobility shall be granted by the United States: And no Person holding any Office of Profit or Trust under them,

shall, without the Consent of the Congress, accept of any present, Emolument, Office, or Title, of any kind whatever, from any King, Prince, or foreign State.

Section. 10.

No State shall enter into any Treaty, Alliance, or Confederation; grant Letters of Marque and Reprisal; coin Money; emit Bills of Credit; make any Thing but gold and silver Coin a Tender in Payment of Debts; pass any Bill of Attainder, ex post facto Law, or Law impairing the Obligation of Contracts, or grant any Title of Nobility.

No State shall, without the Consent of the Congress, lay any Imposts or Duties on Imports or Exports, except what may be absolutely necessary for executing it's inspection Laws: and the net Produce of all Duties and Imposts, laid by any State on Imports or Exports, shall be for the Use of the Treasury of the United States; and all such Laws shall be subject to the Revision and Controul of the Congress.

No State shall, without the Consent of Congress, lay any Duty of Tonnage, keep Troops, or Ships of War in time of Peace, enter into any Agreement or Compact with another State, or with a foreign Power, or engage in War, unless actually invaded, or in such imminent Danger as will not admit of delay.

Article. II

Section. 1.

The executive Power shall be vested in a President of the United States of America. He shall hold his Office during the Term of four Years, and, together with the Vice President, chosen for the same Term, be elected, as follows:

Each State shall appoint, in such Manner as the Legislature thereof may direct, a Number of Electors, equal to the whole Number of Senators and Representatives to which the State may be entitled in the Congress: but no Senator or Representative, or

Person holding an Office of Trust or Profit under the United States, shall be appointed an Elector.

The Electors shall meet in their respective States, and vote by Ballot for two Persons, of whom one at least shall not be an Inhabitant of the same State with themselves. And they shall make a List of all the Persons voted for, and of the Number of Votes for each; which List they shall sign and certify, and transmit sealed to the Seat of the Government of the United States, directed to the President of the Senate. The President of the Senate shall, in the Presence of the Senate and House of Representatives, open all the Certificates, and the Votes shall then be counted. The Person having the greatest Number of Votes shall be the President, if such Number be a Majority of the whole Number of Electors appointed; and if there be more than one who have such Majority, and have an equal Number of Votes, then the House of Representatives shall immediately chuse by Ballot one of them for President; and if no Person have a Majority, then from the five highest on the List the said House shall in like Manner chuse the President. But in chusing the President, the Votes shall be taken by States, the Representation from each State having one Vote; A quorum for this purpose shall consist of a Member or Members from two thirds of the States, and a Majority of all the States shall be necessary to a Choice. In every Case, after the Choice of the President, the Person having the greatest Number of Votes of the Electors shall be the Vice President. But if there should remain two or more who have equal Votes, the Senate shall chuse from them by Ballot the Vice President.

The Congress may determine the Time of chusing the Electors, and the Day on which they shall give their Votes; which Day shall be the same throughout the United States.

No Person except a natural born Citizen, or a Citizen of the United States, at the time of the Adoption of this Constitution, shall be eligible to the Office of President; neither shall any Person be eligible to that Office who shall not have attained to the Age of thirty five Years, and been fourteen Years a Resident within the United States.

In Case of the Removal of the President from Office, or of his Death, Resignation, or Inability to discharge the Powers and Duties of the said Office, the Same shall devolve on the Vice President, and the Congress may by Law provide for the Case of Removal, Death, Resignation or Inability, both of the President and Vice President, declaring what Officer shall then act as President, and such Officer shall act accordingly, until the Disability be removed, or a President shall be elected.

The President shall, at stated Times, receive for his Services, a Compensation, which shall neither be increased nor diminished during the Period for which he shall have been elected, and he shall not receive within that Period any other Emolument from the United States, or any of them.

Before he enter on the Execution of his Office, he shall take the following Oath or Affirmation:—"I do solemnly swear (or affirm) that I will faithfully execute the Office of President of the United States, and will to the best of my Ability, preserve, protect and defend the Constitution of the United States."

Section. 2.

The President shall be Commander in Chief of the Army and Navy of the United States, and of the Militia of the several States, when called into the actual Service of the United States; he may require the Opinion, in writing, of the principal Officer in each of the executive Departments, upon any Subject relating to the Duties of their respective Offices, and he shall have Power to grant Reprieves and Pardons for Offences against the United States, except in Cases of Impeachment.

He shall have Power, by and with the

Advice and Consent of the Senate, to make Treaties, provided two thirds of the Senators present concur; and he shall nominate, and by and with the Advice and Consent of the Senate, shall appoint Ambassadors, other public Ministers and Consuls, Judges of the supreme Court, and all other Officers of the United States, whose Appointments are not herein otherwise provided for, and which shall be established by Law: but the Congress may by Law vest the Appointment of such inferior Officers, as they think proper, in the President alone, in the Courts of Law, or in the Heads of Departments.

The President shall have Power to fill up all Vacancies that may happen during the Recess of the Senate, by granting Commissions which shall expire at the End of their next Session.

Section. 3.

He shall from time to time give to the Congress Information of the State of the Union, and recommend to their Consideration such Measures as he shall judge necessary and expedient; he may, on extraordinary Occasions, convene both Houses, or either of them, and in Case of Disagreement between them, with Respect to the Time of Adjournment, he may adjourn them to such Time as he shall think proper; he shall receive Ambassadors and other public Ministers; he shall take Care that the Laws be faithfully executed, and shall Commission all the Officers of the United States.

Section. 4.

The President, Vice President and all civil Officers of the United States, shall be removed from Office on Impeachment for, and Conviction of, Treason, Bribery, or other high Crimes and Misdemeanors.

ARTICLE. III

Section. 1.

The judicial Power of the United States shall be vested in one supreme Court, and in such inferior Courts as the Congress may from time to time ordain and establish. The Judges, both of the supreme and inferior Courts, shall hold their Offices during good Behaviour, and shall, at stated Times, receive for their Services a Compensation, which shall not be diminished during their Continuance in Office.

Section. 2.

The judicial Power shall extend to all Cases, in Law and Equity, arising under this Constitution, the Laws of the United States, and Treaties made, or which shall be made, under their Authority;— to all Cases affecting Ambassadors, other public Ministers and Consuls;— to all Cases of admiralty and maritime Jurisdiction;— to Controversies to which the United States shall be a Party;— to Controversies between two or more States;—between a State and Citizens of another State,—between Citizens of different States,— between Citizens of the same State claiming Lands under Grants of different States, and between a State, or the Citizens thereof, and foreign States, Citizens or Subjects.

In all Cases affecting Ambassadors, other public Ministers and Consuls, and those in which a State shall be Party, the supreme Court shall have original Jurisdiction. In all the other Cases before mentioned, the supreme Court shall have appellate Jurisdiction, both as to Law and Fact, with such Exceptions, and under such Regulations as the Congress shall make.

The Trial of all Crimes, except in Cases of Impeachment, shall be by Jury; and such Trial shall be held in the State where the said Crimes shall have been committed; but when not committed within any State, the Trial shall be at such Place or Places as the Congress may by Law have directed.

Section. 3.

Treason against the United States, shall consist only in levying War against them, or in adhering to their Enemies, giving them

Aid and Comfort. No Person shall be convicted of Treason unless on the Testimony of two Witnesses to the same overt Act, or on Confession in open Court.

The Congress shall have Power to declare the Punishment of Treason, but no Attainder of Treason shall work Corruption of Blood, or Forfeiture except during the Life of the Person attainted.

Article. IV

Section. 1.

Full Faith and Credit shall be given in each State to the public Acts, Records, and judicial Proceedings of every other State. And the Congress may by general Laws prescribe the Manner in which such Acts, Records and Proceedings shall be proved, and the Effect thereof.

Section. 2.

The Citizens of each State shall be entitled to all Privileges and Immunities of Citizens in the several States.

A Person charged in any State with Treason, Felony, or other Crime, who shall flee from Justice, and be found in another State, shall on Demand of the executive Authority of the State from which he fled, be delivered up, to be removed to the State having Jurisdiction of the Crime.

No Person held to Service or Labour in one State, under the Laws thereof, escaping into another, shall, in Consequence of any Law or Regulation therein, be discharged from such Service or Labour, but shall be delivered up on Claim of the Party to whom such Service or Labour may be due.

Section. 3.

New States may be admitted by the Congress into this Union; but no new State shall be formed or erected within the Jurisdiction of any other State; nor any State be formed by the Junction of two or more States, or Parts of States, without the Consent of the Legislatures of the States concerned as well as of the Congress.

The Congress shall have Power to dispose of and make all needful Rules and Regulations respecting the Territory or other Property belonging to the United States; and nothing in this Constitution shall be so construed as to Prejudice any Claims of the United States, or of any particular State.

Section. 4.

The United States shall guarantee to every State in this Union a Republican Form of Government, and shall protect each of them against Invasion; and on Application of the Legislature, or of the Executive (when the Legislature cannot be convened), against domestic Violence.

Article. V

The Congress, whenever two thirds of both Houses shall deem it necessary, shall propose Amendments to this Constitution, or, on the Application of the Legislatures of two thirds of the several States, shall call a Convention for proposing Amendments, which, in either Case, shall be valid to all Intents and Purposes, as Part of this Constitution, when ratified by the Legislatures of three fourths of the several States, or by Conventions in three fourths thereof, as the one or the other Mode of Ratification may be proposed by the Congress; Provided that no Amendment which may be made prior to the Year One thousand eight hundred and eight shall in any Manner affect the first and fourth Clauses in the Ninth Section of the first Article; and that no State, without its Consent, shall be deprived of its equal Suffrage in the Senate.

Article. VI

All Debts contracted and Engagements entered into, before the Adoption of this Constitution, shall be as valid against the United States under this Constitution, as under the Confederation.

This Constitution, and the Laws of the United States which shall be made in Pursuance thereof; and all Treaties made, or which shall be made, under the Authority of the United States, shall be the supreme Law of the Land; and the Judges in every State shall be bound thereby, any Thing in the Constitution or Laws of any State to the Contrary notwithstanding.

The Senators and Representatives before mentioned, and the Members of the several State Legislatures, and all executive and judicial Officers, both of the United States and of the several States, shall be bound by Oath or Affirmation, to support this Constitution; but no religious Test shall ever be required as a Qualification to any Office or public Trust under the United States.

ARTICLE. VII

The Ratification of the Conventions of nine States, shall be sufficient for the Establishment of this Constitution between the States so ratifying the Same.

The Word, "the," being interlined between the seventh and eighth Lines of the first Page, the Word "Thirty" being partly written on an Erazure in the fifteenth Line of the first Page, The Words "is tried" being interlined between the thirty second and thirty third Lines of the first Page and the Word "the" being interlined between the forty third and forty fourth Lines of the second Page. Attest William Jackson Secretary

Done in Convention by the Unanimous Consent of the States present the Seventeenth Day of September in the Year of our Lord one thousand seven hundred and Eighty seven and of the Independence of the United States of America the Twelfth In witness whereof We have hereunto subscribed our Names,

G°. Washington
Presidt and deputy from Virginia

CHAPTER 14

Bill of Rights
(December 15, 1791)

United States Congress

The History*

In the United States, the Bill of Rights is the name by which the first ten amendments to the United States Constitution are known. They were introduced by James Madison to the First United States Congress in 1789 as a series of articles, and came into effect on December 15, 1791, when they had been ratified by three-fourths of the States. Thomas Jefferson was a proponent of the Bill of Rights.

The Bill of Rights prohibits Congress from making any law respecting an establishment of religion or prohibiting the free exercise thereof, forbids infringement of "...the right of the people to keep and bear Arms...," and prohibits the federal government from depriving any person of life, liberty, or property, without due process of law. In federal criminal cases, it requires indictment by grand jury for any capital or "infamous crime," guarantees a speedy public trial with an impartial jury composed of members of the state or judicial district in which the crime occurred, and prohibits double jeopardy. In addition, the Bill of Rights states that "the enumeration in the Constitution, of certain rights, shall not be construed to deny or disparage others retained by the people," and reserves all powers not granted to the federal government to the citizenry or States. Most of these restrictions were later applied to the states by a series of decisions applying the due process clause of the Fourteenth Amendment, which was ratified in 1868, after the American Civil War.

Madison proposed the Bill of Rights while ideological conflict between Federalists and anti–Federalists, dating from the 1787 Philadelphia Convention, threatened the overall ratification of the new national Constitution. It largely responded to the Constitution's influential opponents, including prominent Founding Fathers, who argued that the Constitution should not be ratified because it failed to protect the basic principles of human liberty. The Bill was influenced by George Mason's 1776 Virginia Declaration of Rights, the 1689 English Bill of Rights, works of the Age of Enlightenment pertaining to natural rights, and earlier

*Originally published as "United States Bill of Rights," *Wikipedia*, Wikimedia Foundation, Inc., San Francisco, California, November 2009. For additional information see "Bill of Rights," *The Charters of Freedom*, U.S. National Archives and Records Administration, College Park, Maryland, 2004. This agency is listed in the *National Resource Directory* section of this volume.

English political documents such as Magna Carta (1215).

Two additional articles were proposed to the States; only the final ten articles were ratified quickly and correspond to the First through Tenth Amendments to the Constitution. The first Article, dealing with the number and apportionment of U.S. Representatives, never became part of the Constitution. The second Article, limiting the ability of Congress to increase the salaries of its members, was ratified two centuries later as the 27th Amendment. Though they are incorporated into the document known as the "Bill of Rights," neither article establishes a right as that term is used today. For that reason, and also because the term had been applied to the first ten amendments long before the 27th Amendment was ratified, the term "Bill of Rights" in modern U.S. usage means only the ten amendments ratified in 1791.

The Bill of Rights plays a central role in American law and government, and remains a fundamental symbol of the freedoms and culture of the nation. One of the original fourteen copies of the Bill of Rights is on public display at the National Archives in Washington, D.C.

The Document

Bill of Rights

The Preamble to The Bill of Rights

Congress of the United States begun and held at the City of New York, on Wednesday the fourth of March, one thousand seven hundred and eighty nine.

THE Conventions of a number of the States, having at the time of their adopting the Constitution, expressed a desire, in order to prevent misconstruction or abuse of its powers, that further declaratory and restrictive clauses should be added. And as extending the ground of public confidence in the Government, will best ensure the beneficent ends of its institution.

RESOLVED by the Senate and House of Representatives of the United States of America, in Congress assembled, two thirds of both Houses concurring, that the following Articles be proposed to the Legislatures of the several States, as amendments to the Constitution of the United States, all, or any of which Articles, when ratified by three fourths of the said Legislatures, to be valid to all intents and purposes, as part of the said Constitution; viz.

ARTICLES in addition to, and Amendment of the Constitution of the United States of America, proposed by Congress, and ratified by the Legislatures of the several States, pursuant to the fifth Article of the original Constitution.

AMENDMENT I

Congress shall make no law respecting an establishment of religion, or prohibiting the free exercise thereof; or abridging the freedom of speech, or of the press; or the right of the people peaceably to assemble, and to petition the Government for a redress of grievances.

AMENDMENT II

A well-regulated militia, being necessary to the security of a free State, the right of the people to keep and bear arms, shall not be infringed.

AMENDMENT III

No soldier shall, in time of peace be quartered in any house, without the consent of the owner, nor in time of war, but in a manner to be prescribed by law.

AMENDMENT IV

The right of the people to be secure in their persons, houses, papers, and effects, against unreasonable searches and seizures, shall not be violated, and no warrants shall issue, but upon probable cause, supported by oath or affirmation, and particularly describing the place to be searched, and the persons or things to be seized.

Amendment V

No person shall be held to answer for a capital, or otherwise infamous crime, unless on a presentment or indictment of a Grand Jury, except in cases arising in the land or naval forces, or in the militia, when in actual service in time of war or public danger; nor shall any person be subject for the same offense to be twice put in jeopardy of life or limb; nor shall be compelled in any criminal case to be a witness against himself, nor be deprived of life, liberty, or property, without due process of law; nor shall private property be taken for public use without just compensation.

Amendment VI

In all criminal prosecutions, the accused shall enjoy the right to a speedy and public trial, by an impartial jury of the State and district wherein the crime shall have been committed, which district shall have been previously ascertained by law, and to be informed of the nature and cause of the accusation; to be confronted with the witnesses against him; to have compulsory process for obtaining witnesses in his favor, and to have the assistance of counsel for his defense.

Amendment VII

In suits at common law, where the value in controversy shall exceed twenty dollars, the right of trial by jury shall be preserved, and no fact tried by a jury shall be otherwise reexamined in any court of the United States, than according to the rules of the common law.

Amendment VIII

Excessive bail shall not be required, nor excessive fines imposed, nor cruel and unusual punishments inflicted.

Amendment IX

The enumeration in the Constitution, of certain rights, shall not be construed to deny or disparage others retained by the people.

Amendment X

The powers not delegated to the United States by the Constitution, nor prohibited by it to the States, are reserved to the States respectively, or to the people.

Note

The capitalization and punctuation in this version is from the enrolled original of the Joint Resolution of Congress proposing the Bill of Rights, which is on permanent display in the Rotunda of the National Archives Building, Washington, D.C. The above text is a transcription of the first ten amendments to the Constitution in their original form.

CHAPTER 15

Other Amendments to the Constitution of the United States (February 7, 1795, to May 7, 1992)

United States Congress

The History*

The authority to amend the Constitution of the United States is derived from Article V of the Constitution. After Congress proposes an amendment, the Archivist of the United States, who heads the National Archives and Records Administration (NARA), is charged with responsibility for administering the ratification process under the provisions of the United States Code (USC).

The Archivist has delegated many of the ministerial duties associated with this function to the Director of the Federal Register. Neither Article V of the Constitution nor section 106b describe the ratification process in detail. The Archivist and the Director of the Federal Register follow procedures and customs established by the Secretary of State, who performed these duties until 1950, and the Administrator of General Services, who served in this capacity until NARA assumed responsibility as an independent agency in 1985.

The Constitution provides that an amendment may be proposed either by the Congress with a two-thirds majority vote in both the House of Representatives and the Senate or by a constitutional convention called for by two-thirds of the State legislatures. None of the 27 amendments of the Constitution have been proposed by constitutional convention. The Congress proposes an amendment in the form of a joint resolution. Since the President does not have a constitutional role in the amendment process, the joint resolution does not go to the White House for signature or approval. The original document is forwarded directly to NARA's Office of the Federal Register (OFR) for processing and publication. The OFR adds legislative history notes to the joint resolution and publishes it in slip law format. The OFR also assembles an information package for the States which includes formal "red-line" copies of the joint resolution, copies of the joint resolution in slip law format, and the statutory procedure for ratification under 1 U.S.C. 106b.

*Originally published as "The Constitutional Amendment Process," *The Federal Register*, The National Archives, U.S. National Archives and Records Administration, College Park, Maryland, 2008. For additional information see "The Constitutional Amendment Process, *The Federal Register*, U.S. National Archives and Records Administration, College Park, Maryland, 2008. This agency is listed in the *National Resource Directory* section of this volume.

The Archivist submits the proposed amendment to the Senate for their consideration by sending a letter of notification to each Governor along with the informational material prepared by the OFR. The Governors then formally submit the amendment to their State legislatures. In the past, some State legislatures have not waited to receive official notice before taking action on a proposed amendment. When a State ratifies a proposed amendment, it sends the Archivist an original or certified copy of the State action, which is immediately conveyed to the Director of the Federal Register. The OFR examines ratification documents for facial legal sufficiency and an authenticating signature. If the documents are found to be in good order, the Director acknowledges receipt and maintains custody of them. The OFR retains these documents until an amendment is adopted or fails, and then transfers the records to the National Archives for preservation.

A proposed amendment becomes part of the Constitution as soon as it is ratified by three-fourths of the States (38 of 50 States). When the OFR verifies that it has received the required number of authenticated ratification documents, it drafts a formal proclamation for the Archivist to certify that the amendment is valid and has become part of the Constitution. This certification is published in the Federal Register and U.S. Statutes at Large and serves as official notice to the Congress and to the Nation that the amendment process has been completed.

In a few instances, States have sent official documents to NARA to record the rejection of an amendment or the rescission of a prior ratification. The Archivist does not make any substantive determinations as to the validity of State ratification actions, but it has been established that the Archivist's certification of the facial legal sufficiency of ratification documents is final and conclusive.

In recent history, the signing of the certification has become a ceremonial function attended by various dignitaries, which may include the President. President Johnson signed the certifications for the 24th and 25th Amendments as a witness, and President Nixon similarly witnessed the certification of the 26th Amendment along with three young scholars. On May 18, 1992, the Archivist performed the duties of the certifying official for the first time to recognize the ratification of the 27th Amendment, and the Director of the Federal Register signed the certification as a witness.

The Document

Other Amendments of the Constitution of the United States (Amendments XI to XXVII)

Constitutional Amendments 1–10 make up what is known as The Bill of Rights. Amendments 11–27 are given below.

AMENDMENT XI

Note: Article III, section 2, of the Constitution was modified by the 11th amendment. *Passed by Congress March 4, 1794. Ratified February 7, 1795.*

The Judicial power of the United States shall not be construed to extend to any suit in law or equity, commenced or prosecuted against one of the United States by citizens of another State, or by Citizens or Subjects of any Foreign State.

AMENDMENT XII

Note: A portion of Article II, section 1 of the Constitution was superseded by the 12th amendment. *Passed by Congress December 9, 1803. Ratified July 27, 1804.*

The Electors shall meet in their respective States and vote by ballot for President and Vice-President, one of whom, at least, shall not be an inhabitant of the same state with themselves; they shall name in their ballots the person voted for as President, and in distinct ballots the person voted for as Vice-President, and of the number of votes for each, which lists they shall sign and certify, and transmit sealed to the seat of the Government of the United States, directed to the President of the Senate; the President of the Senate shall, in the presence of the Senate and House of Representatives, open all the certificates and the votes shall then be counted;— The person having the greatest number of votes for President, shall be the President, if such number be a majority of the whole number of Electors appointed; and if no person have such majority, then from the persons having the highest numbers not exceeding three on the list of those voted for as President, the House of Representatives shall choose immediately, by ballot, the President. But in choosing the President, the votes shall be taken by States, the representation from each State having one vote; a quorum for this purpose shall consist of a member or members from two-thirds of the States, and a majority of all the States shall be necessary to a choice. [And if the House of Representatives shall not choose a President whenever the right of choice shall devolve upon them, before the fourth day of March next following, then the Vice-President shall act as President, as in case of the death or other constitutional disability of the President.—]* The person having the greatest number of votes as Vice-President, shall be the Vice-President, if such numbers be a majority of the whole number of electors appointed, and if no person have a majority, then from the two highest numbers on the list, the Senate shall choose the Vice-President; a quorum for the purpose shall consist of two-thirds of the whole number of Senators, and a majority of the whole number shall be necessary to a choice. But no person constitutionally ineligible to the office of President shall be eligible to that of Vice-President of the United States.

*Superseded by section 3 of the 20th amendment.

AMENDMENT XIII

Note: A portion of Article IV, section 2, of the Constitution was superseded by the 13th Amendment.
Passed by Congress January 31, 1865. Ratified December 6, 1865.

Section 1.

Neither slavery nor involuntary servitude, except as a punishment for crime whereof the party shall have been duly convicted, shall exist within the United States, or any place subject to their jurisdiction.

Section 2.

Congress shall have power to enforce this article by appropriate legislation.

AMENDMENT XIV

Note: Article I, section 2, of the Constitution was modified by section 2 of the 14th amendment.
Passed by Congress June 13, 1866. Ratified July 9, 1868.

Section 1.

All persons born or naturalized in the United States, and subject to the jurisdiction thereof, are citizens of the United States and of the State wherein they reside. No State shall make or enforce any law which shall abridge the privileges or immunities of citizens of the United States; nor shall any State deprive any person of life, liberty, or property, without due process of law; nor to deny to any person within its jurisdiction the equal protection of the laws.

Section 2.

Representatives shall be apportioned among the several States according to their respective numbers, counting the whole number of persons in each State, excluding Indians not taxed. But when the right to vote at any election for the choice of Electors for President and Vice-President of the United States, Representatives in Congress, the executive and judicial officers of a State, or the members of the legislature thereof, is denied to any of the male inhabitants of such State, being twenty-one years of age,* and citizens of the United States, or in any way abridged, except for participation in rebellion, or other crime, the basis of representation therein shall be reduced in the proportion which the number of such male citizens shall bear to the whole number of male citizens twenty-one years of age in such State.

Section 3.

No person shall be a Senator or Representative in Congress, or Elector of President and Vice-President, or hold any office, civil or military, under the United States, or under any State, who, having previously taken an oath, as a member of Congress, or as an officer of the United States, or as a member of any State Legislature, or as an executive or judicial officer of any State, to support the Constitution of the United States, shall have engaged in insurrection or rebellion against the same, or given aid or comfort to the enemies thereof. But Congress may by a vote of two-thirds of each House, remove such disability.

Section 4.

The validity of the public debt of the United States, authorized by law, including debts incurred for payment of pensions and bounties for services in suppressing insurrection or rebellion, shall not be questioned. But neither the United States nor any State shall assume or pay any debt or obligation incurred in aid of insurrection or rebellion against the United States, or any claim for the loss or emancipation of any slave; but all such debts, obligations and claims shall be held illegal and void.

Section 5.

The Congress shall have the power to enforce, by appropriate legislation, the provisions of this article.

*Changed by section 1 of the 26th amendment.

Amendment XV

Passed by Congress February 26, 1869. Ratified February 3, 1870.

Section 1.

The right of citizens of the United States to vote shall not be denied or abridged by the United States or by any State on account of race, color, or previous condition of servitude.

Section 2.

The Congress shall have the power to enforce this article by appropriate legislation.

Amendment XVI

Note: Article I, section 3, of the Constitution was modified by the 17th amendment. *Passed by Congress July 2, 1909. Ratified February 3, 1913.*

The Congress shall have power to lay and collect taxes on incomes, from whatever sources derived, without apportionment among the several States, and without regard to any census or enumeration.

Amendment XVII

Note: Article I, section 3, of the Constitution was modified by the 17th amendment. *Passed by Congress May 13, 1912. Ratified April 8, 1913.*

The Senate of the United States shall be composed of two Senators from each State, elected by the people thereof, for six years; and each Senator shall have one vote. The electors in each State shall have the qualifications requisite for electors of the most numerous branch of the State Legislatures.

When vacancies happen in the representation of any State in the Senate, the executive authority of such State shall issue writs of election to fill such vacancies: Provided, That the Legislature of any State may empower the Executive thereof to make temporary appointments until the people fill the vacancies by election as the Legislature may direct.

This amendment shall not be so construed as to affect the election or term of any Senator chosen before it becomes valid as part of the Constitution.

AMENDMENT XVIII

Passed by Congress December 18, 1917. Ratified January 16, 1919. Repealed by amendment 21.

Section 1.

After one year from the ratification of this article the manufacture, sale, or transportation of intoxicating liquors within, the importation thereof into, or the exportation thereof from the United States and all territory subject to the jurisdiction thereof for beverage purposes is hereby prohibited.

Section 2.

The Congress and the several States shall have concurrent power to enforce this article by appropriate legislation.

Section 3.

This article shall be inoperative unless it shall have been ratified as an amendment to the Constitution by the Legislatures of the several States, as provided in the Constitution, within seven years from the date of the submission hereof to the States by the Congress.

AMENDMENT XIX

Passed by Congress June 4, 1919. Ratified August 18, 1920.

The right of citizens of the United States to vote shall not be denied or abridged by the United States or by any State on account of sex.

Congress shall have power to enforce this article by appropriate legislation.

AMENDMENT XX

Note: Article I, section 4, of the Constitution was modified by section 2 of this amendment. In addition, a portion of the 12th amendment was superseded by section 3.

Passed by Congress March 2, 1932. Ratified January 23, 1933.

Section 1.

The terms of the President and the Vice-President shall end at noon on the 20th day of January, and the terms of Senators and Representatives at noon on the 3rd day of January, of the years in which such terms would have ended if this article had not been ratified; and the terms of their successors shall then begin.

Section 2.

The Congress shall assemble at least once in every year, and such meeting shall begin at noon on the 3rd day of January, unless they shall by law appoint a different day.

Section 3.

If, at the time fixed for the beginning of the term of the President, the President elect shall have died, the Vice-President elect shall become President. If a President shall not have been chosen before the time fixed for the beginning of his term, or if the President elect shall have failed to qualify, then the Vice-President elect shall act as President until a President shall have qualified; and the Congress may by law provide for the case wherein neither a President elect nor a Vice-President shall have qualified, declaring who shall then act as President, or the manner in which one who is to act shall be selected, and such person shall act accordingly until a President or Vice-President shall have qualified.

Section 4.

The Congress may by law provide for the case of the death of any of the persons from whom the House of representatives may choose a President whenever the right of choice shall have devolved upon them, and for the case of the death of any of the persons from whom the Senate may choose a Vice-President whenever the right of choice shall have devolved upon them.

Section 5.

Sections 1 and 2 shall take effect on the 15th day of October following the ratification of this article (October 1933).

Section 6.

This article shall be inoperative unless it shall have been ratified as an amendment to the Constitution by the Legislatures of three-fourths of the several States within seven years from the date of its submission.

Amendment XXI

Passed by Congress February 20, 1933. Ratified December 5, 1933.

Section 1.

The Eighteenth article of amendment to the Constitution of the United States is hereby repealed.

Section 2.

The transportation or importation into any State, Territory, or Possession of the United States for delivery or use therein of intoxicating liquors, in violation of the laws thereof, is hereby prohibited.

Section 3.

This article shall be inoperative unless it shall have been ratified as an amendment to the Constitution by conventions in the several States, as provided in the Constitution, within seven years from the date of the submission hereof to the States by the Congress.

Amendment XXII

Passed by Congress March 21, 1947. Ratified February 27, 1951.

Section 1.

No person shall be elected to the office of the President more than twice, and no person who has held the office of President, or acted as President, for more that two years of a term to which some other person was elected President shall be elected to the office of President more than once.

Section 2.

This article shall be inoperative unless it shall have been ratified as an amendment to the Constitution by the Legislatures of three-fourths of the several States within seven years from the date of its submission to the States by the Congress.

Amendment XXIII

Passed by Congress June 16, 1960. Ratified March 29, 1961.

Section 1.

The District constituting the seat of Government of the United States shall appoint in such manner as Congress may direct:

A number of electors of President and Vice President equal to the whole number of Senators and Representatives in Congress to which the District would be entitled if it were a State, but in no event more than the least populous State; they shall be in addition to those appointed by the States, but they shall be considered, for the purposes of the election of President and Vice President, to be electors appointed by a State; and they shall meet in the District and perform such duties as provided by the twelfth article of amendment.

Section 2.

The Congress shall have power to enforce this article by appropriate legislation.

Amendment XXIV

Passed by Congress August 27, 1962. Ratified January 23, 1964.

Section 1.

The right of citizens of the United States to vote in any primary or other election for President or Vice President, for electors for President or Vice President, or for Senator or Representative in Congress, shall not be denied or abridged by the United States or any State by reason of failure to pay poll tax or any other tax.

Section 2.

Congress shall have power to enforce this article by appropriate legislation.

AMENDMENT XXV

Note: Article II, section 1, of the Constitution was affected by the 25th amendment. *Passed by Congress July 6, 1965. Ratified February 10, 1967.*

Section 1.

In case of the removal of the President from office or of his death or resignation, the Vice President shall become President.

Section 2.

Whenever there is a vacancy in the office of the Vice President, the President shall nominate a Vice President who shall take the office upon confirmation by a majority vote of both houses of Congress.

Section 3.

Whenever the President transmits to the President Pro tempore of the Senate and the Speaker of the House of Representatives his written declaration that he is unable to discharge the powers and duties of his office, and until he transmits to them a written declaration to the contrary, such powers and duties shall be discharged by the Vice President as Acting President.

Section 4.

Whenever the Vice President and a majority of either the principal officers of the executive departments or of such other body as Congress may by law provide, transmits to the President Pro tempore of the Senate and the Speaker of the House of Representatives their written declaration that the President is unable to discharge the powers and duties of his office, the Vice President shall immediately assume the powers and duties of the office as Acting President.

Thereafter, when the President transmits to the President Pro tempore of the Senate and the Speaker of the House of Representatives his written declaration that no inability exists, he shall resume the powers and duties of his office unless the Vice President and a majority of either the principal officers of the executive departments or of such other body as Congress may by law provide, transmits within four days to the President Pro tempore of the Senate and the Speaker of the House of Representatives their written declaration that the President is unable to discharge the powers and duties of his office. Thereupon Congress shall decide the issue, assembling within forty-eight hours for that purpose if not in session. If the Congress, within twenty-one days after receipt of the latter written declaration, or, if Congress is not in session within twenty-one days after Congress is required to assemble, determines by two-thirds vote of both houses that the President is unable to discharge the powers and duties of his office, the Vice President shall continue to discharge the same as Acting President; otherwise, the President shall resume the powers and duties of his office.

AMENDMENT XXVI

Note: Amendment 14, section 2, of the Constitution was modified by section 1 of the 26th amendment.
Passed by Congress March 23, 1971. Ratified June 30, 1971.

Section 1.

The right of citizens of the United States, who are 18 years of age or older, to vote shall not be denied or abridged by the United States or any state on account of age.

Section 2.

The Congress shall have power to enforce this article by appropriate legislation.

AMENDMENT XXVII

Originally proposed September 25, 1789. Ratified May 7, 1992.

No law, varying the compensation for services of the Senators and Representatives, shall take effect, until an election of Representatives shall have intervened.

CHAPTER 16

Civil Rights Act (July 2, 1964)

United States Congress

The History*

In the 1960s, Americans who knew only the potential of "equal protection of the laws" expected by the president, the Congress, and the courts to fulfill the promise of the 14th Amendment. In response, all three branches of the federal government — as well as the public at large — debated a fundamental constitutional question: Does the Constitution's prohibition of denying equal protection always ban the use of racial, ethnic, or gender criteria in an attempt to bring social justice and social benefits?

In 1964 Congress passed Public Law 82-352 (78 Stat. 241). The provisions of this civil rights act forbade discrimination on the basis of sex as well as race in hiring, promoting, and firing. The word "sex" was added at the last moment. According to the *West Encyclopedia of American Law*, Representative Howard W. Smith (D-VA) added the word. His critics argued that Smith, a conservative Southern opponent of federal civil rights, did so to kill the entire bill. Smith, however, ar-

gued that he had amended the bill in keeping with his support of Alice Paul and the National Women's Party with whom he had been working. Martha W. Griffiths (D-MI) led the effort to keep the word "sex" in the bill.

In the final legislation, Section 703 (a) made it unlawful for an employer to "fail or refuse to hire or to discharge any individual, or otherwise to discriminate against any individual with respect to his compensation, terms, conditions or privileges or employment, because of such individual's race, color, religion, sex, or national origin." The final bill also allowed sex to be a consideration when sex is a bona fide occupational qualification for the job. Title VII of the act created the Equal Employment Opportunity Commission (EEOC) to implement the law.

Subsequent legislation expanded the role of the EEOC. Today, according to the *U.S. Government Manual of 1998–99*, the EEOC enforces laws that prohibit discrimination based on race, color, religion, sex, na-

*Originally published as "Teaching With Documents: The Civil Rights Act of 1964 and the Equal Opportunity Employment Commission," *Educators and Students Report*, The National Archives, U.S. National Archives and Records Administration, College Park, Maryland, 2008. For additional information see "Teaching with Documents: The Civil Rights Act of 1964 and the Equal Employment Opportunity Commission," *Educators and Students Report*, U.S. National Archives and Records Administration, College Park, Maryland, 2008. This agency is listed in the *National Resource Directory* section of this volume.

tional origin, disability, or age in hiring, promoting, firing, setting wages, testing, training, apprenticeship, and all other terms and conditions of employment. Race, color, sex, creed, and age are not protected classes. The proposal to add each group to protected-class status unleashed furious debate. But no words stimulate the passion of the debate more than "affirmative action."

As West defines the term, affirmative action "refers to both mandatory and voluntary programs intended to affirm the civil rights of designated classes of individuals by taking positive action to protect them" from discrimination. The issue for most Americans is fairness: Should the equal protection clause of the 14th Amendment be used to advance the liberty of one class of individuals for good reasons when that action may infringe on the liberty of another?

The EEOC, as an independent regulatory body, plays a major role in dealing with this issue. Since its creation in 1964, Congress has gradually extended EEOC powers to include investigatory authority, creating conciliation programs, filing lawsuits, and conducting voluntary assistance programs. While the Civil Rights Act of 1964 did not mention the words affirmative action, it did authorize the bureaucracy to make rules to help end discrimination. The EEOC has done so.

Today the regulatory authority of the EEOC includes enforcing a range of federal statutes prohibiting employment discrimination. According to the EEOC's own Web site, these include Title VII of the Civil Rights Act of 1964 that prohibits employment discrimination on the basis of race, color, religion, sex, or national origin; the Age Discrimination in Employment Act of 1967, and its amendments, that prohibits employment discrimination against individuals 40 years of age or older; the Equal Pay Act of 1963 that prohibits discrimination on the basis of gender in compensation for substantially similar work under similar conditions; Title I of the Americans with Disabilities Act

of 1990 that prohibits employment discrimination on the basis of disability in both the public and private sector, excluding the federal government; the Civil Rights Act of 1991 that provides for monetary damages in case of intentional discrimination; and Section 501 of the Rehabilitation Act of 1973, as amended, that prohibits employment discrimination against federal employees with disabilities. Title IX of the Education Act of 1972 forbade gender discrimination in education programs, including athletics, that received federal dollars. In the late 1970s Congress passed the Pregnancy Discrimination Act. This made it illegal for employers to exclude pregnancy and childbirth from their sick leave and health benefits plans.

Presidents also weighed in, employing a series of executive orders. President Lyndon B. Johnson ordered all executive agencies to require federal contractors to "take affirmative action to ensure that applicants are employed and that employees are treated during employment without regard to race, color, religion, sex, or national origin." This marked the first use of the phrase "affirmative action." In 1969 an executive order required that every level of federal service offer equal opportunities for women and established a program to implement that action. President Richard Nixon's Department of Labor adopted a plan requiring federal contractors to assess their employees to identify gender and race and to set goals to end any under-representation of women and minorities. By the 1990s Democratic and Republican administrations had taken a variety of actions that resulted in 160 different affirmative action federal programs. State and local governments were following suit.

The courts also addressed affirmative action. In addition to dealing with race, color, creed, and age, from the 1970s forward, the court dealt with gender questions. It voided arbitrary weight and height requirements (*Dothard v. Rawlinson*), erased mandatory pregnancy leaves (*Cleveland Board of Educa-*

tion v. LaFleur), allowed public employers to use carefully constructed affirmative action plans to remedy specific past discrimination that resulted in women and minorities being under-represented in the workplace (*Johnson v. Transportation Agency, Santa Clara County*), and upheld state and local laws prohibiting gender discrimination.

By the late 1970s all branches of the federal government and most state governments had taken at least some action to fulfill the promise of equal protection under the law. The EEOC served as the agent of implementation and complaint. Its activism divided liberals and conservatives, illuminating their differing views about the proper scope of government. In general, the political liberals embraced the creation of the EEOC as the birth of a federal regulatory authority that could promote the goal of equality by designing policies to help the historically disadvantaged, including women and minorities. In contrast, political conservatives saw the EEOC as a violation of their belief in fewer government regulations and fewer federal policies. To them, creating a strong economy, free from government intervention, would produce gains that would benefit the historically disadvantaged. Even the nonideological segment of the American population asked: What should government do, if anything, to ensure equal protection under the law?

In fiscal year 1997, the EEOC collected $111 million dollars in financial benefits for people who filed claims of discrimination. Its recent successful efforts include a $34 million settlement in a sexual harassment case with Mitsubishi Motor Manufacturing of America, resulting in the company's adoption of changes to its sexual harassment prevention policy. Working with state and local programs, the EEOC processes 48,000 claims annually.

The Document

Civil Rights Act

To enforce the constitutional right to vote, to confer jurisdiction upon the district courts of the United States to provide injunctive relief against discrimination in public accommodations, to authorize the Attorney General to institute suits to protect constitutional rights in public facilities and public education, to extend the Commission on Civil Rights, to prevent discrimination in federally assisted programs, to establish a Commission on Equal Employment Opportunity, and for other purposes.

Be it enacted by the Senate and House of Representatives of the United States of America in Congress assembled, That this Act may be cited as the "Civil Rights Act of 1964."

TITLE I—VOTING RIGHTS

SEC. 101. Section 2004 of the Revised Statutes (42 U.S.C. 1971), as amended by section 131 of the Civil Rights Act of 1957 (71 Stat. 637), and as further amended by section 601 of the Civil Rights Act of 1960 (74 Stat. 90), is further amended as follows:

(a) Insert "1" after "(a)" in subsection (a) and add at the end of subsection (a) the following new paragraphs:

"(2) No person acting under color of law shall—

"(A) in determining whether any individual is qualified under State law or laws to vote in any Federal election, apply any standard, practice, or procedure different from the standards, practices, or procedures applied under such law or laws to other individuals within the same county, parish, or similar political subdivision who have been found by State officials to be qualified to vote;

"(B) deny the right of any individual to vote in any Federal election because of an error or omission on any record or paper relating to any application, registration, or other act requisite to voting, if such error or omission is not material in determining whether such individual is qualified under State law to vote in such election; or

"(C) employ any literacy test as a qualification for voting in any Federal election unless (i) such test is administered to each individual and is conducted wholly in writing, and (ii) a certified copy of the test and of the answers given by the individual is furnished to him within twenty-five days of the submission of his request made within the period of time during which records and papers are required to be retained and preserved pursuant to title III of the Civil Rights Act of 1960 (42 U.S.C. 1974 — 74e; 74 Stat. 88): Provided, however, That the Attorney General may enter into agreements with appropriate State or local authorities that preparation, conduct, and maintenance of such tests in accordance with the provisions of applicable State or local law, including such special provisions as are necessary in the preparation, conduct, and maintenance of such tests for persons who are blind or otherwise physically handicapped, meet the purposes of this subparagraph and constitute compliance therewith.

"(3) For purposes of this subsection —

"(A) the term 'vote' shall have the same meaning as in subsection (e) of this section;

"(B) the phrase 'literacy test' includes any test of the ability to read, write, understand, or interpret any matter."

(b) Insert immediately following the period at the end of the first sentence of subsection (c) the following new sentence: "If in any such proceeding literacy is a relevant fact there shall be a rebuttable presumption that any person who has not been adjudged an incompetent and who has completed the sixth grade in a public school in, or a private school accredited by, any State or territory, the District of Columbia, or the Commonwealth of Puerto Rico where instruction is carried on predominantly in the English lan-guage, possesses sufficient literacy, comprehension, and intelligence to vote in any Federal election."

(c) Add the following subsection "(f)" and designate the present subsection "(f)" as subsection "(g)": "(f) When used in subsection (a) or (c) of this section, the words 'Federal election' shall mean any general, special, or primary election held solely or in part for the purpose of electing or selecting any candidate for the office of President, Vice President, presidential elector, Member of the Senate, or Member of the House of Representatives."

(d) Add the following subsection "(h)":

"(h) In any proceeding instituted by the United States in any district court of the United States under this section in which the Attorney General requests a finding of a pattern or practice of discrimination pursuant to subsection (e) of this section the Attorney General, at the time he files the complaint, or any defendant in the proceeding, within twenty days after service upon him of the complaint, may file with the clerk of such court a request that a court of three judges be convened to hear and determine the entire case. A copy of the request for a three-judge court shall be immediately furnished by such clerk to the chief judge of the circuit (or in his absence, the presiding circuit judge of the circuit) in which the case is pending. Upon receipt of the copy of such request it shall be the duty of the chief justice of the circuit or the presiding circuit judge, as the case may be, to designate immediately three judges in such circuit, of whom at least one shall be a circuit judge and another of whom shall be a district judge of the court in which the proceeding was instituted, to hear and determine such case, and it shall be the duty of the judges so designated to assign the case for hearing at the earliest practicable date, to participate in the hearing and determination thereof, and to cause the case to be in every way expedited.

An appeal from the final judgment of such court will lie to the Supreme Court.

"In any proceeding brought under subsection (c) of this section to enforce subsection (b) of this section, or in the event neither the Attorney General nor any defendant files a request for a three-judge court in any proceeding authorized by this subsection, it shall be the duty of the chief judge of the district (or in his absence, the acting chief judge) in which the case is pending immediately to designate a judge in such district to hear and determine the case. In the event that no judge in the district is available to hear and determine the case, the chief judge of the district, or the acting chief judge, as the case may be, shall certify this fact to the chief judge of the circuit (or, in his absence, the acting chief judge) who shall then designate a district or circuit judge of the circuit to hear and determine the case.

"It shall be the duty of the judge designated pursuant to this section to assign the case for hearing at the earliest practicable date and to cause the case to be in every way expedited."

TITLE II—INJUNCTIVE RELIEF AGAINST DISCRIMINATION IN PLACES OF PUBLIC ACCOMMODATION

SEC. 201. (a) All persons shall be entitled to the full and equal enjoyment of the goods, services, facilities, and privileges, advantages, and accommodations of any place of public accommodation, as defined in this section, without discrimination or segregation on the ground of race, color, religion, or national origin.

(b) Each of the following establishments which serves the public is a place of public accommodation within the meaning of this title if its operations affect commerce, or if discrimination or segregation by it is supported by State action:

(1) any inn, hotel, motel, or other establishment which provides lodging to transient guests, other than an establishment located within a building which contains not more than five rooms for rent or hire and which is actually occupied by the proprietor of such establishment as his residence;

(2) any restaurant, cafeteria, lunchroom, lunch counter, soda fountain, or other facility principally engaged in selling food for consumption on the premises, including, but not limited to, any such facility located on the premises of any retail establishment; or any gasoline station;

(3) any motion picture house, theater, concert hall, sports arena, stadium or other place of exhibition or entertainment; and

(4) any establishment (A)(i) which is physically located within the premises of any establishment otherwise covered by this subsection, or (ii) within the premises of which is physically located any such covered establishment, and (B) which holds itself out as serving patrons of such covered establishment.

(c) The operations of an establishment affect commerce within the meaning of this title if (1) it is one of the establishments described in paragraph (1) of subsection (b); (2) in the case of an establishment described in paragraph (2) of subsection (b), it serves or offers to serve interstate travelers or a substantial portion of the food which it serves, or gasoline or other products which it sells, has moved in commerce; (3) in the case of an establishment described in paragraph (3) of subsection (b), it customarily presents films, performances, athletic teams, exhibitions, or other sources of entertainment which move in commerce; and (4) in the case of an establishment described in paragraph (4) of subsection (b), it is physically located within the premises of, or there is physically located within its premises, an establishment the operations of which affect commerce within the meaning of this subsection. For purposes of this section, "commerce" means travel, trade, traffic, commerce, transportation, or communication among the several States, or between the District of Columbia and any State, or between any foreign country or any territory or possession and any State or the

District of Columbia, or between points in the same State but through any other State or the District of Columbia or a foreign country.

(d) Discrimination or segregation by an establishment is supported by State action within the meaning of this title if such discrimination or segregation (1) is carried on under color of any law, statute, ordinance, or regulation; or (2) is carried on under color of any custom or usage required or enforced by officials of the State or political subdivision thereof; or (3) is required by action of the State or political subdivision thereof.

(e) The provisions of this title shall not apply to a private club or other establishment not in fact open to the public, except to the extent that the facilities of such establishment are made available to the customers or patrons of an establishment within the scope of subsection (b).

SEC. 202. All persons shall be entitled to be free, at any establishment or place, from discrimination or segregation of any kind on the ground of race, color, religion, or national origin, if such discrimination or segregation is or purports to be required by any law, statute, ordinance, regulation, rule, or order of a State or any agency or political subdivision thereof.

SEC. 203. No person shall (a) withhold, deny, or attempt to withhold or deny, or deprive or attempt to deprive, any person of any right or privilege secured by section 201 or 202, or (b) intimidate, threaten, or coerce, or attempt to intimidate, threaten, or coerce any person with the purpose of interfering with any right or privilege secured by section 201 or 202, or (c) punish or attempt to punish any person for exercising or attempting to exercise any right or privilege secured by section 201 or 202.

SEC. 204. (a) Whenever any person has engaged or there are reasonable grounds to believe that any person is about to engage in any act or practice prohibited by section 203, a civil action for preventive relief, including an application for a permanent or temporary injunction, restraining order, or other order, may be instituted by the person aggrieved and, upon timely application, the court may, in its discretion, permit the Attorney General to intervene in such civil action if he certifies that the case is of general public importance. Upon application by the complainant and in such circumstances as the court may deem just, the court may appoint an attorney for such complainant and may authorize the commencement of the civil action without the payment of fees, costs, or security.

(b) In any action commenced pursuant to this title, the court, in its discretion, may allow the prevailing party, other than the United States, a reasonable attorney's fee as part of the costs, and the United States shall be liable for costs the same as a private person.

(c) In the case of an alleged act or practice prohibited by this title which occurs in a State, or political subdivision of a State, which has a State or local law prohibiting such act or practice and establishing or authorizing a State or local authority to grant or seek relief from such practice or to institute criminal proceedings with respect thereto upon receiving notice thereof, no civil action may be brought under subsection (a) before the expiration of thirty days after written notice of such alleged act or practice has been given to the appropriate State or local authority by registered mail or in person, provided that the court may stay proceedings in such civil action pending the termination of State or local enforcement proceedings.

(d) In the case of an alleged act or practice prohibited by this title which occurs in a State, or political subdivision of a State, which has no State or local law prohibiting such act or practice, a civil action may be brought under subsection (a): Provided, That the court may refer the matter to the Community Relations Service established by title X of this Act for as long as the court believes there is a reasonable possibility of obtaining voluntary compliance, but for not more than sixty days: Provided further, That upon expiration of such sixty-day period, the court may extend such period for an additional period, not to exceed a cumulative total of one hundred and twenty days, if it believes there then exists a reasonable possibility of securing voluntary compliance.

SEC. 205. The Service is authorized to make a full investigation of any complaint referred to it by the court under section 204(d) and may hold such hearings with respect thereto as may be necessary. The Service shall conduct any hearings with respect to any such complaint in executive session, and shall not release any testimony given therein except by agreement of all parties involved in the complaint with the permission of the court, and the Service shall endeavor to bring about a voluntary settlement between the parties.

SEC. 206. (a) Whenever the Attorney General has reasonable cause to believe that any person or group of persons is engaged in a pattern or practice of resistance to the full enjoyment of any of the rights secured by this title, and that the pattern or practice is of such a nature and is intended to deny the full exercise of the rights herein described, the Attorney General may bring a civil action in the appropriate district court of the United States by filing with it a complaint (1) signed by him (or in his absence the Acting Attorney General), (2) setting forth facts pertaining to such pattern or practice, and (3) requesting such preventive relief, including an application for a permanent or temporary injunction, restraining order or other order against the person or persons responsible for such pattern or practice, as he deems necessary to insure the full enjoyment of the rights herein described.

(b) In any such proceeding the Attorney General may file with the clerk of such court a request that a court of three judges be convened to hear and determine the case.

Such request by the Attorney General shall be accompanied by a certificate that, in his opinion, the case is of general public importance. A copy of the certificate and request for a three-judge court shall be immediately furnished by such clerk to the chief judge of the circuit (or in his absence, the presiding circuit judge of the circuit) in which the case is pending. Upon receipt of the copy of such request it shall be the duty of the chief judge of the circuit or the presiding circuit judge, as the case may be, to designate immediately three judges in such circuit, of whom at least one shall be a circuit judge and another of whom shall be a district judge of the court in which the proceeding was instituted, to hear and determine such case, and it shall be the duty of the judges so designated to assign the case for hearing at the earliest practicable date, to participate in the hearing and determination thereof, and to cause the case to be in every way expedited. An appeal from the final judgment of such court will lie to the Supreme Court.

In the event the Attorney General fails to file such a request in any such proceeding, it shall be the duty of the chief judge of the district (or in his absence, the acting chief judge) in which the case is pending immediately to designate a judge in such district to hear and determine the case. In the event that no judge in the district is available to hear and determine the case, the chief judge of the district, or the acting chief judge, as the case may be, shall certify this fact to the chief judge of the circuit (or in his absence, the acting chief judge) who shall then designate a district or circuit judge of the circuit to hear and determine the case.

It shall be the duty of the judge designated pursuant to this section to assign the case for hearing at the earliest practicable date and to cause the case to be in every way expedited.

SEC. 207. (a) The district courts of the United States shall have jurisdiction of proceedings instituted pursuant to this title and shall exercise the same without regard to whether the aggrieved party shall have exhausted any administrative or other remedies that may be provided by law.

(b) The remedies provided in this title shall be the exclusive means of enforcing the rights based on this title, but nothing in this title shall preclude any individual or any State or local agency from asserting any right based on any other Federal or State law not inconsistent with this title, including any statute or ordinance requiring nondiscrimination in public establishments or accommodations, or from pursuing any remedy, civil or criminal, which may be available for the vindication or enforcement of such right.

TITLE III—DESEGREGATION OF PUBLIC FACILITIES

SEC. 301. (a) Whenever the Attorney General receives a complaint in writing signed by an individual to the effect that he is being deprived of or threatened with the loss of his right to the equal protection of the laws, on account of his race, color, religion, or national origin, by being denied equal utilization of any public facility which is owned, operated, or managed by or on behalf of any State or subdivision thereof, other than a public school or public college as defined in section 401 of title IV hereof, and the Attorney General believes the complaint is meritorious and certifies that the signer or signers of such complaint are unable, in his judgment, to initiate and maintain appropriate legal proceedings for relief and that the institution of an action will materially further the orderly progress of desegregation in public facilities, the Attorney General is authorized to institute for or in the name of the United States a civil action in any appropriate district court of the United States against such parties and for such relief as may be appropriate, and such court shall have and shall exercise jurisdiction of proceedings instituted pursuant to this section. The Attorney General may implead as defendants such additional parties as are or become necessary to the grant of effective relief hereunder.

(b) The Attorney General may deem a person or persons unable to initiate and maintain appropriate legal proceedings within the meaning of subsection

(a) of this section when such person or persons are unable, either directly or through other interested persons or organizations, to bear the expense of the litigation or to obtain effective legal representation; or whenever he is satisfied that the institution of such litigation would jeopardize the personal safety, employment, or economic standing of such person or persons, their families, or their property.

SEC. 302. In any action or proceeding under this title the United States shall be liable for costs, including a reasonable attorney's fee, the same as a private person.

SEC. 303. Nothing in this title shall affect adversely the right of any person to sue for or obtain relief in any court against discrimination in any facility covered by this title.

SEC. 304. A complaint as used in this title is a writing or document within the meaning of section 1001, title 18, United States Code.

TITLE IV—DESEGREGATION OF PUBLIC EDUCATION

Definitions

SEC. 401. As used in this title—

(a) "Commissioner" means the Commissioner of Education.

(b) "Desegregation" means the assignment of students to public schools and within such schools without regard to their race, color, religion, or national origin, but "desegregation" shall not mean the assignment of students to public schools in order to overcome racial imbalance.

(c) "Public school" means any elementary or secondary educational institution, and "public college" means any institution of higher education or any technical or vocational school above the secondary school level, provided that such public school or public college is operated by a State, subdivision of a State, or governmental agency within a State, or operated wholly or predominantly from or through the use of governmental funds or property, or funds or property derived from a governmental source.

(d) "School board" means any agency or agencies which administer a system of one or more public schools and any other agency which is responsible for the assignment of students to or within such system.

SURVEY AND REPORT OF EDUCATIONAL OPPORTUNITIES

SEC. 402. The Commissioner shall conduct a survey and make a report to the President and the Congress, within two years of the enactment of this title, concerning the lack of availability of equal educational opportunities for individuals by reason of race, color, religion, or national origin in public educational institutions at all levels in the United States, its territories and possessions, and the District of Columbia.

TECHNICAL ASSISTANCE

SEC. 403. The Commissioner is authorized, upon the application of any school board, State, municipality, school district, or other governmental unit legally responsible for operating a public school or schools, to render technical assistance to such applicant in the preparation, adoption, and implementation of plans for the desegregation of public schools. Such technical assistance may, among other activities, include making available to such agencies information regarding effective methods of coping with special educational problems occasioned by desegregation, and making available to such agencies personnel of the Office of Education or other persons specially equipped to advise and assist them in coping with such problems.

TRAINING INSTITUTES

SEC. 404. The Commissioner is authorized to arrange, through grants or con-

tracts, with institutions of higher education for the operation of short-term or regular session institutes for special training designed to improve the ability of teachers, supervisors, counselors, and other elementary or secondary school personnel to deal effectively with special educational problems occasioned by desegregation. Individuals who attend such an institute on a full-time basis may be paid stipends for the period of their attendance at such institute in amounts specified by the Commissioner in regulations, including allowances for travel to attend such institute.

Grants

SEC. 405. (a) The Commissioner is authorized, upon application of a school board, to make grants to such board to pay, in whole or in part, the cost of—

(1) giving to teachers and other school personnel inservice training in dealing with problems incident to desegregation, and

(2) employing specialists to advise in problems incident to desegregation.

(b) In determining whether to make a grant, and in fixing the amount thereof and the terms and conditions on which it will be made, the Commissioner shall take into consideration the amount available for grants under this section and the other applications which are pending before him; the financial condition of the applicant and the other resources available to it; the nature, extent, and gravity of its problems incident to desegregation; and such other factors as he finds relevant.

Payments

SEC. 406. Payments pursuant to a grant or contract under this title may be made (after necessary adjustments on account of previously made overpayments or underpayments) in advance or by way of reimbursement, and in such installments, as the Commissioner may determine.

Suits by the Attorney General

SEC. 407. (a) Whenever the Attorney General receives a complaint in writing—

(1) signed by a parent or group of parents to the effect that his or their minor children, as members of a class of persons similarly situated, are being deprived by a school board of the equal protection of the laws, or

(2) signed by an individual, or his parent, to the effect that he has been denied admission to or not permitted to continue in attendance at a public college by reason of race, color, religion, or national origin, and the Attorney General believes the complaint is meritorious and certifies that the signer or signers of such complaint are unable, in his judgment, to initiate and maintain appropriate legal proceedings for relief and that the institution of an action will materially further the orderly achievement of desegregation in public education, the Attorney General is authorized, after giving notice of such complaint to the appropriate school board or college authority and after certifying that he is satisfied that such board or authority has had a reasonable time to adjust the conditions alleged in such complaint, to institute for or in the name of the United States a civil action in any appropriate district court of the United States against such parties and for such relief as may be appropriate, and such court shall have and shall exercise jurisdiction of proceedings instituted pursuant to this section, provided that nothing herein shall empower any official or court of the United States to issue any order seeking to achieve a racial balance in any school by requiring the transportation of pupils or students from one school to another or one school district to another in order to achieve such racial balance, or otherwise enlarge the existing power of the court to insure compliance with constitutional standards. The Attorney General may implead as defendants such additional parties as are or become necessary to the grant of effective relief hereunder.

(b) The Attorney General may deem a person or persons unable to initiate and maintain appropriate legal proceedings within the meaning of subsection

(a) of this section when such person or persons are unable, either directly or through other interested persons or organizations, to bear the expense of the litigation or to obtain effective legal representation; or whenever he is satisfied that the institution of such litigation would jeopardize the personal safety, employment, or economic standing of such person or persons, their families, or their property.

(c) The term "parent" as used in this section includes any person standing in loco parentis. A "complaint" as used in this section is a writing or document within the meaning of section 1001, title 18, United States Code.

SEC. 408. In any action or proceeding under this title the United States shall be liable for costs the same as a private person.

SEC. 409. Nothing in this title shall affect adversely the right of any person to sue for or obtain relief in any court against discrimination in public education.

SEC. 410. Nothing in this title shall prohibit classification and assignment for reasons other than race, color, religion, or national origin.

TITLE V—COMMISSION ON CIVIL RIGHTS

SEC. 501. Section 102 of the Civil Rights Act of 1957 (42 U.S.C. 1975a; 71 Stat. 634) is amended to read as follows:

"Rules of Procedure of the Commission Hearings

"SEC. 102. (a) At least thirty days prior to the commencement of any hearing, the Commission shall cause to be published in the Federal Register notice of the date on which such hearing is to commence, the place at which it is to be held and the subject of the hearing. The Chairman, or one designated by him to act as Chairman at a hearing of the Commission, shall announce in an opening statement the subject of the hearing.

"(b) A copy of the Commission's rules shall be made available to any witness before the Commission, and a witness compelled to appear before the Commission or required to produce written or other matter shall be served with a copy of the Commission's rules at the time of service of the subpoena.

"(c) Any person compelled to appear in person before the Commission shall be accorded the right to be accompanied and advised by counsel, who shall have the right to subject his client to reasonable examination, and to make objections on the record and to argue briefly the basis for such objections. The Commission shall proceed with reasonable dispatch to conclude any hearing in which it is engaged. Due regard shall be had for the convenience and necessity of witnesses.

"(d) The Chairman or Acting Chairman may punish breaches of order and decorum by censure and exclusion from the hearings.

"(e) If the Commission determines that evidence or testimony at any hearing may tend to defame, degrade, or incriminate any person, it shall receive such evidence or testimony or summary of such evidence or testimony in executive session. The Commission shall afford any person defamed, degraded, or incriminated by such evidence or testimony an opportunity to appear and be heard in executive session, with a reasonable number of additional witnesses requested by him, before deciding to use such evidence or testimony. In the event the Commission determines to release or use such evidence or testimony in such manner as to reveal publicly the identity of the person defamed, degraded, or incriminated, such evidence or testimony, prior to such public release or use, shall be given at a public session, and the Commission shall afford such person an opportunity to appear as a voluntary witness or to file a sworn statement in his behalf and to submit brief and pertinent sworn statements of others. The Commission shall receive and dispose of requests from such person to subpoena additional witnesses.

"(f) Except as provided in sections 102 and 105 (f) of this Act, the Chairman shall receive and the Commission shall dispose of requests to subpoena additional witnesses.

"(g) No evidence or testimony or summary of evidence or testimony taken in executive session may be released or used in public sessions without the consent of the Commission. Whoever releases or uses in public without the consent of the Commission such evidence or testimony taken in executive session shall be fined not more than $1,000, or imprisoned for not more than one year.

"(h) In the discretion of the Commission, witnesses may submit brief and pertinent sworn statements in writing for inclusion in the record. The Commission shall determine the pertinency of testimony and evidence adduced at its hearings.

"(i) Every person who submits data or evidence shall be entitled to retain or, on payment of lawfully prescribed costs, procure a copy or transcript thereof, except that a witness in a hearing held in executive session may for good cause be limited to inspection of the official transcript of his testimony. Transcript copies of public sessions may be obtained by the public upon the payment of the cost thereof. An accurate transcript shall be made of the testimony of all witnesses at all hearings, either public or executive sessions, of the Commission or of any subcommittee thereof.

"(j) A witness attending any session of the Commission shall receive $6 for each day's attendance and for the time necessarily occupied in going to and returning from the same, and 10 cents per mile for going from and returning to his place of residence. Witnesses who attend at points so far removed from their respective residences as to prohibit return thereto from day to day shall be entitled to an additional allowance of $10 per day for expenses of subsistence including the time necessarily occupied in going to and returning from the place of attendance. Mileage payments shall be tendered to the witness upon service of a subpoena issued on behalf of the Commission or any subcommittee thereof.

"(k) The Commission shall not issue any subpoena for the attendance and testimony of witnesses or for the production of written or other matter which would require the presence of the party subpoenaed at a hearing to be held outside of the State wherein the witness is found or resides or is domiciled or transacts business, or has appointed an agent for receipt of service of process except that, in any event, the Commission may issue subpoenas for the attendance and testimony of witnesses and the production of written or other matter at a hearing held within fifty miles of the place where the witness is found or resides or is domiciled or transacts business or has appointed an agent for receipt of service of process.

"(l) The Commission shall separately state and currently publish in the Federal Register (1) descriptions of its central and field organization including the established places at which, and methods whereby, the public may secure information or make requests; (2) statements of the general course and method by which its functions are channeled and determined, and (3) rules adopted as authorized by law. No person shall in any manner be subject to or required to resort to rules, organization, or procedure not so published."

SEC. 502. Section 103(a) of the Civil Rights Act of 1957 (42 U.S.C. 1975b(a); 71 Stat. 634) is amended to read as follows:

"SEC. 103. (a) Each member of the Commission who is not otherwise in the service of the Government of the United States shall receive the sum of $75 per day for each day spent in the work of the Commission, shall be paid actual travel expenses, and per diem in lieu of subsistence expenses when

away from his usual place of residence, in accordance with section 5 of the Administrative Expenses Act of 1946, as amended (5 U.S.C 73b-2; 60 Stat. 808)."

SEC. 503. Section 103(b) of the Civil Rights Act of 1957 (42 U.S.C.

1975(b); 71 Stat. 634) is amended to read as follows:

"(b) Each member of the Commission who is otherwise in the service of the Government of the United States shall serve without compensation in addition to that received for such other service, but while engaged in the work of the Commission shall be paid actual travel expenses, and per diem in lieu of subsistence expenses when away from his usual place of residence, in accordance with the provisions of the Travel Expenses Act of 1949, as amended (5 U.S.C. 835 – 42; 63 Stat. 166)."

SEC. 504. (a) Section 104(a) of the Civil Rights Act of 1957 (42 U.S.C. 1975c(a); 71 Stat. 635), as amended, is further amended to read as follows:

"Duties of the Commission

"SEC. 104. (a) The Commission shall —

"(1) investigate allegations in writing under oath or affirmation that certain citizens of the United States are being deprived of their right to vote and have that vote counted by reason of their color, race, religion, or national origin; which writing, under oath or affirmation, shall set forth the facts upon which such belief or beliefs are based;

"(2) study and collect information concerning legal developments constituting a denial of equal protection of the laws under the Constitution because of race, color, religion or national origin or in the administration of justice;

"(3) appraise the laws and policies of the Federal Government with respect to denials of equal protection of the laws under the Constitution because of race, color, religion or national origin or in the administration of justice;

"(4) serve as a national clearinghouse for information in respect to denials of equal protection of the laws because of race, color, religion or national origin, including but not limited to the fields of voting, education, housing, employment, the use of public facilities, and transportation, or in the administration of justice;

"(5) investigate allegations, made in writing and under oath or affirmation, that citizens of the United States are unlawfully being accorded or denied the right to vote, or to have their votes properly counted, in any election of presidential electors, Members of the United States Senate, or of the House of Representatives, as a result of any patterns or practice of fraud or discrimination in the conduct of such election; and

"(6) Nothing in this or any other Act shall be construed as authorizing the Commission, its Advisory Committees, or any person under its supervision or control to inquire into or investigate any membership practices or internal operations of any fraternal organization, any college or university fraternity or sorority, any private club or any religious organization."

(b) Section 104(b) of the Civil Rights Act of 1957 (42 U.S.C. 1975c(b); 71 Stat. 635), as amended, is further amended by striking out the present subsection "(b)" and by substituting therefor:

"(b) The Commission shall submit interim reports to the President and to the Congress at such times as the Commission, the Congress or the President shall deem desirable, and shall submit to the President and to the Congress a final report of its activities, findings, and recommendations not later than January 31, 1968."

SEC. 505. Section 105(a) of the Civil Rights Act of 1957 (42 U.S.C. 1975d(a); 71 Stat. 636) is amended by striking out in the last sentence thereof "$50 per diem" and inserting in lieu thereof "$75 per diem."

SEC. 506. Section 105(f) and section 105(g) of the Civil Rights Act of 1957 (42 U.S.C. 1975d (f) and (g); 71 Stat. 636) are amended to read as follows:

"(f) The Commission, or on the authorization of the Commission any subcommittee of two or more members, at least one of whom shall be of each major political party, may, for the purpose of carrying out the provisions of this Act, hold such hearings and act at such times and places as the Commission or such authorized subcommittee may deem advisable. Subpoenas for the attendance and testimony of witnesses or the production of written or other matter may be issued in accordance with the rules of the Commission as contained in section 102 (j) and (k) of this Act, over the signature of the Chairman of the Commission or of such subcommittee, and may be served by any person designated by such Chairman. The holding of hearings by the Commission, or the appointment of a subcommittee to hold hearings pursuant to this subparagraph, must be approved by a majority of the Commission, or by a majority of the members present at a meeting at which at least a quorum of four members is present.

"(g) In case of contumacy or refusal to obey a subpoena, any district court of the United States or the United States court of any territory or possession, or the District Court of the United States for the District of Columbia, within the jurisdiction of which the inquiry is carried on or within the jurisdiction of which said person guilty of contumacy or refusal to obey is found or resides or is domiciled or transacts business, or has appointed an agent for receipt of service of process, upon application by the Attorney General of the United States shall have jurisdiction to issue to such person an order requiring such person to appear before the Commission or a subcommittee thereof, there to produce pertinent, relevant and non-privileged evidence if so ordered, or there to give testimony touching the matter under investigation; and any failure to obey such order of the court may be punished by said court as a contempt thereof."

SEC. 507. Section 105 of the Civil Rights Act of 1957 (42 U.S.C. 1975d; 71 Stat. 636), as amended by section 401 of the Civil Rights Act of 1960 (42 U.S.C. 1975d(h); 74 Stat. 89), is further amended by adding a new subsection at the end to read as follows:

"(i) The Commission shall have the power to make such rules and regulations as are necessary to carry out the purposes of this Act."

TITLE VI—NONDISCRIMINATION IN FEDERALLY ASSISTED PROGRAMS

SEC. 601. No person in the United States shall, on the ground of race, color, or national origin, be excluded from participation in, be denied the benefits of, or be subjected to discrimination under any program or activity receiving Federal financial assistance.

SEC. 602. Each Federal department and agency which is empowered to extend Federal financial assistance to any program or activity, by way of grant, loan, or contract other than a contract of insurance or guaranty, is authorized and directed to effectuate the provisions of section 601 with respect to such program or activity by issuing rules, regulations, or orders of general applicability which shall be consistent with achievement of the objectives of the statute authorizing the financial assistance in connection with which the action is taken. No such rule, regulation, or order shall become effective unless and until approved by the President. Compliance with any requirement adopted pursuant to this section may be effected (1) by the termination of or refusal to grant or to continue assistance under such program or activity to any recipient as to whom there has been an express finding on the record, after opportunity for hearing, of a failure to comply with such requirement, but such termination or refusal shall be limited to the particular political entity, or part thereof, or other recipient as to whom such a finding has been made and, shall be limited in its effect to the par-

ticular program, or part thereof, in which such non-compliance has been so found, or (2) by any other means authorized by law: Provided, however, That no such action shall be taken until the department or agency concerned has advised the appropriate person or persons of the failure to comply with the requirement and has determined that compliance cannot be secured by voluntary means. In the case of any action terminating, or refusing to grant or continue, assistance because of failure to comply with a requirement imposed pursuant to this section, the head of the federal department or agency shall file with the committees of the House and Senate having legislative jurisdiction over the program or activity involved a full written report of the circumstances and the grounds for such action. No such action shall become effective until thirty days have elapsed after the filing of such report.

SEC. 603. Any department or agency action taken pursuant to section 602 shall be subject to such judicial review as may otherwise be provided by law for similar action taken by such department or agency on other grounds. In the case of action, not otherwise subject to judicial review, terminating or refusing to grant or to continue financial assistance upon a finding of failure to comply with any requirement imposed pursuant to section 602, any person aggrieved (including any State or political subdivision thereof and any agency of either) may obtain judicial review of such action in accordance with section 10 of the Administrative Procedure Act, and such action shall not be deemed committed to unreviewable agency discretion within the meaning of that section.

SEC. 604. Nothing contained in this title shall be construed to authorize action under this title by any department or agency with respect to any employment practice of any employer, employment agency, or labor organization except where a primary objective of the Federal financial assistance is to provide employment.

SEC. 605. Nothing in this title shall add to or detract from any existing authority with respect to any program or activity under which Federal financial assistance is extended by way of a contract of insurance or guaranty.

Title VII—Equal Employment Opportunity

Definitions

SEC. 701. For the purposes of this title —

(a) The term "person" includes one or more individuals, labor unions, partnerships, associations, corporations, legal representatives, mutual companies, joint-stock companies, trusts, unincorporated organizations, trustees, trustees in bankruptcy, or receivers.

(b) The term "employer" means a person engaged in an industry affecting commerce who has twenty-five or more employees for each working day in each of twenty or more calendar weeks in the current or preceding calendar year, and any agent of such a person, but such term does not include (1) the United States, a corporation wholly owned by the Government of the United States, an Indian tribe, or a State or political subdivision thereof, (2) a bona fide private membership club (other than a labor organization) which is exempt from taxation under section 501(c) of the Internal Revenue Code of 1954: Provided, That during the first year after the effective date prescribed in subsection (a) of section 716, persons having fewer than one hundred employees (and their agents) shall not be considered employers, and, during the second year after such date, persons having fewer than seventy-five employees (and their agents) shall not be considered employers, and, during the third year after such date, persons having fewer than fifty employees (and their agents) shall not be considered employers: Provided further, That it shall be the policy of the United States to insure equal employment opportu-

nities for Federal employees without discrimination because of race, color, religion, sex or national origin and the President shall utilize his existing authority to effectuate this policy.

(c) The term "employment agency" means any person regularly undertaking with or without compensation to procure employees for an employer or to procure for employees opportunities to work for an employer and includes an agent of such a person; but shall not include an agency of the United States, or an agency of a State or political subdivision of a State, except that such term shall include the United States Employment Service and the system of State and local employment services receiving Federal assistance.

(d) The term "labor organization" means a labor organization engaged in an industry affecting commerce, and any agent of such an organization, and includes any organization of any kind, any agency, or employee representation committee, group, association, or plan so engaged in which employees participate and which exists for the purpose, in whole or in part, of dealing with employers concerning grievances, labor disputes, wages, rates of pay, hours, or other terms or conditions of employment, and any conference, general committee, joint or system board, or joint council so engaged which is subordinate to a national or international labor organization.

(e) A labor organization shall be deemed to be engaged in an industry affecting commerce if (1) it maintains or operates a hiring hall or hiring office which procures employees for an employer or procures for employees opportunities to work for an employer, or (2) the number of its members (or, where it is a labor organization composed of other labor organizations or their representatives, if the aggregate number of the members of such other labor organization) is (A) one hundred or more during the first year after the effective date prescribed in subsection (a) of section 716, (B) seventy-five or more during the second year after such date or fifty or more during the third year, or (C) twenty-five or more thereafter, and such labor organization —

(1) is the certified representative of employees under the provisions of the National Labor Relations Act, as amended, or the Railway Labor Act, as amended;

(2) although not certified, is a national or international labor organization or a local labor organization recognized or acting as the representative of employees of an employer or employers engaged in an industry affecting commerce; or

(3) has chartered a local labor organization or subsidiary body which is representing or actively seeking to represent employees of employers within the meaning of paragraph (1) or (2); or

(4) has been chartered by a labor organization representing or actively seeking to represent employees within the meaning of paragraph (1) or (2) as the local or subordinate body through which such employees may enjoy membership or become affiliated with such labor organization; or

(5) is a conference, general committee, joint or system board, or joint council subordinate to a national or international labor organization, which includes a labor organization engaged in an industry affecting commerce within the meaning of any of the preceding paragraphs of this subsection.

(f) The term "employee" means an individual employed by an employer.

(g) The term "commerce" means trade, traffic, commerce, transportation, transmission, or communication among the several States; or between a State and any place outside thereof; or within the District of Columbia, or a possession of the United States; or between points in the same State but through a point outside thereof.

(h) The term "industry affecting commerce" means any activity, business, or industry in commerce or in which a labor dis-

pute would hinder or obstruct commerce or the free flow of commerce and includes any activity or industry "affecting commerce" within the meaning of the Labor-Management Reporting and Disclosure Act of 1959.

(i) The term "State" includes a State of the United States, the District of Columbia, Puerto Rico, the Virgin Islands, American Samoa, Guam, Wake Island, The Canal Zone, and Outer Continental Shelf Lands defined in the Outer Continental Shelf Lands Act.

Exemption

SEC. 702. This title shall not apply to an employer with respect to the employment of aliens outside any State, or to a religious corporation, association, or society with respect to the employment of individuals of a particular religion to perform work connected with the carrying on by such corporation, association, or society of its religious activities or to an educational institution with respect to the employment of individuals to perform work connected with the educational activities of such institution.

Discrimination Because of Race, Color, Religion, Sex, or National Origin

SEC. 703. (a) It shall be an unlawful employment practice for an employer —

(1) to fail or refuse to hire or to discharge any individual, or otherwise to discriminate against any individual with respect to his compensation, terms, conditions, or privileges of employment, because of such individual's race, color, religion, sex, or national origin; or

(2) to limit, segregate, or classify his employees in any way which would deprive or tend to deprive any individual of employment opportunities or otherwise adversely affect his status as an employee, because of such individual's race, color, religion, sex, or national origin.

(b) It shall be an unlawful employment practice for an employment agency to fail or refuse to refer for employment, or otherwise to discriminate against, any individual because of his race, color, religion, sex, or national origin, or to classify or refer for employment any individual on the basis of his race, color, religion, sex, or national origin.

(c) It shall be an unlawful employment practice for a labor organization —

(1) to exclude or to expel from its membership, or otherwise to discriminate against, any individual because of his race, color, religion, sex, or national origin;

(2) to limit, segregate, or classify its membership, or to classify or fail or refuse to refer for employment any individual, in any way which would deprive or tend to deprive any individual of employment opportunities, or would limit such employment opportunities or otherwise adversely affect his status as an employee or as an applicant for employment, because of such individual's race, color, religion, sex, or national origin; or

(3) to cause or attempt to cause an employer to discriminate against an individual in violation of this section.

(d) It shall be an unlawful employment practice for any employer, labor organization, or joint labor-management committee controlling apprenticeship or other training or retraining, including on-the-job training programs to discriminate against any individual because of his race, color, religion, sex, or national origin in admission to, or employment in, any program established to provide apprenticeship or other training.

(e) Notwithstanding any other provision of this title, (1) it shall not be an unlawful employment practice for an employer to hire and employ employees, for an employment agency to classify, or refer for employment any individual, for a labor organization to classify its membership or to classify or refer for employment any individual, or for an employer, labor organization, or joint labor-management committee controlling apprenticeship or other training or retraining programs to admit or employ any individual in any such program, on the basis of his re-

ligion, sex, or national origin in those certain instances where religion, sex, or national origin is a bona fide occupational qualification reasonably necessary to the normal operation of that particular business or enterprise, and (2) it shall not be an unlawful employment practice for a school, college, university, or other educational institution or institution of learning to hire and employ employees of a particular religion if such school, college, university, or other educational institution or institution of learning is, in whole or in substantial part, owned, supported, controlled, or managed by a particular religion or by a particular religious corporation, association, or society, or if the curriculum of such school, college, university, or other educational institution or institution of learning is directed toward the propagation of a particular religion.

(f) As used in this title, the phrase "unlawful employment practice" shall not be deemed to include any action or measure taken by an employer, labor organization, joint labor-management committee, or employment agency with respect to an individual who is a member of the Communist Party of the United States or of any other organization required to register as a Communist-action or Communist-front organization by final order of the Subversive Activities Control Board pursuant to the Subversive Activities Control Act of 1950.

(g) Notwithstanding any other provision of this title, it shall not be an unlawful employment practice for an employer to fail or refuse to hire and employ any individual for any position, for an employer to discharge any individual from any position, or for an employment agency to fail or refuse to refer any individual for employment in any position, or for a labor organization to fail or refuse to refer any individual for employment in any position, if—

(1) the occupancy of such position, or access to the premises in or upon which any part of the duties of such position is per-

formed or is to be performed, is subject to any requirement imposed in the interest of the national security of the United States under any security program in effect pursuant to or administered under any statute of the United States or any Executive order of the President; and

(2) such individual has not fulfilled or has ceased to fulfill that requirement.

(h) Notwithstanding any other provision of this title, it shall not be an unlawful employment practice for an employer to apply different standards of compensation, or different terms, conditions, or privileges of employment pursuant to a bona fide seniority or merit system, or a system which measures earnings by quantity or quality of production or to employees who work in different locations, provided that such differences are not the result of an intention to discriminate because of race, color, religion, sex, or national origin, nor shall it be an unlawful employment practice for an employer to give and to act upon the results of any professionally developed ability test provided that such test, its administration or action upon the results is not designed, intended or used to discriminate because of race, color, religion, sex or national origin. It shall not be an unlawful employment practice under this title for any employer to differentiate upon the basis of sex in determining the amount of the wages or compensation paid or to be paid to employees of such employer if such differentiation is authorized by the provisions of section 6(d) of the Fair Labor Standards Act of 1938, as amended (29 U.S.C. 206(d)).

(i) Nothing contained in this title shall apply to any business or enterprise on or near an Indian reservation with respect to any publicly announced employment practice of such business or enterprise under which a preferential treatment is given to any individual because he is an Indian living on or near a reservation.

(j) Nothing contained in this title shall be interpreted to require any employer, employment agency, labor organization, or joint labor-management committee subject to this title to grant preferential treatment to any individual or to any group because of the race, color, religion, sex, or national origin of such individual or group on account of an imbalance which may exist with respect to the total number or percentage of persons of any race, color, religion, sex, or national origin employed by any employer, referred or classified for employment by any employment agency or labor organization, admitted to membership or classified by any labor organization, or admitted to, or employed in, any apprenticeship or other training program, in comparison with the total number or percentage of persons of such race, color, religion, sex, or national origin in any community, State, section, or other area, or in the available work force in any community, State, section, or other area.

Other Unlawful Employment Practices

SEC. 704. (a) It shall be an unlawful employment practice for an employer to discriminate against any of his employees or applicants for employment, for an employment agency to discriminate against any individual, or for a labor organization to discriminate against any member thereof or applicant for membership, because he has opposed, any practice made an unlawful employment practice by this title, or because he has made a charge, testified, assisted, or participated in any manner in an investigation, proceeding, or hearing under this title.

(b) It shall be an unlawful employment practice for an employer, labor organization, or employment agency to print or publish or cause to be printed or published any notice or advertisement relating to employment by such an employer or membership in or any classification or referral for employment by such a labor organization, or relating to any classification or referral for employment by such an employment agency, indicating any preference, limitation, specification, or discrimination, based on race, color, religion, sex, or national origin, except that such a notice or advertisement may indicate a preference, limitation, specification, or discrimination based on religion, sex, or national origin when religion, sex, or national origin is a bona fide occupational qualification for employment.

Equal Employment Opportunity Commission

SEC. 705. (a) There is hereby created a Commission to be known as the Equal Employment Opportunity Commission, which shall be composed of five members, not more than three of whom shall be members of the same political party, who shall be appointed by the President by and with the advice and consent of the Senate. One of the original members shall be appointed for a term of one year, one for a term of two years, one for a term of three years, one for a term of four years, and one for a term of five years, beginning from the date of enactment of this title, but their successors shall be appointed for terms of five years each, except that any individual chosen to fill a vacancy shall be appointed only for the unexpired term of the member whom he shall succeed. The President shall designate one member to serve as Chairman of the Commission, and one member to serve as Vice Chairman. The Chairman shall be responsible on behalf of the Commission for the administrative operations of the Commission, and shall appoint, in accordance with the civil service laws, such officers, agents, attorneys, and employees as it deems necessary to assist it in the performance of its functions and to fix their compensation in accordance with the Classification Act of 1949, as amended. The Vice Chairman shall act as Chairman in the absence or disability of the Chairman or in the event of a vacancy in that office.

(b) A vacancy in the Commission shall not impair the right of the remaining members to exercise all the powers of the Commission and three members thereof shall constitute a quorum.

(c) The Commission shall have an official seal which shall be judicially noticed.

(d) The Commission shall at the close of each fiscal year report to the Congress and to the President concerning the action it has taken; the names, salaries, and duties of all individuals in its employ and the moneys it has disbursed; and shall make such further reports on the cause of and means of eliminating discrimination and such recommendations for further legislation as may appear desirable.

(e) The Federal Executive Pay Act of 1956, as amended (5 U.S.C. 2201–2209), is further amended —

(1) by adding to section 105 thereof (5 U.S.C. 2204) the following clause:

"(32) Chairman, Equal Employment Opportunity Commission"; and

(2) by adding to clause (45) of section 106(a) thereof (5 U.S.C. 2205(a)) the following: "Equal Employment Opportunity Commission (4)."

(f) The principal office of the Commission shall be in or near the District of Columbia, but it may meet or exercise any or all its powers at any other place. The Commission may establish such regional or State offices as it deems necessary to accomplish the purpose of this title.

(g) The Commission shall have power —

(1) to cooperate with and, with their consent, utilize regional, State, local, and other agencies, both public and private, and individuals;

(2) to pay to witnesses whose depositions are taken or who are summoned before the Commission or any of its agents the same witness and mileage fees as are paid to witnesses in the courts of the United States;

(3) to furnish to persons subject to this title such technical assistance as they may request to further their compliance with this title or an order issued thereunder;

(4) upon the request of (i) any employer, whose employees or some of them, or (ii) any labor organization, whose members or some of them, refuse or threaten to refuse to cooperate in effectuating the provisions of this title, to assist in such effectuation by conciliation or such other remedial action as is provided by this title;

(5) to make such technical studies as are appropriate to effectuate the purposes and policies of this title and to make the results of such studies available to the public;

(6) to refer matters to the Attorney General with recommendations for intervention in a civil action brought by an aggrieved party under section 706, or for the institution of a civil action by the Attorney General under section 707, and to advise, consult, and assist the Attorney General on such matters.

(h) Attorneys appointed under this section may, at the direction of the Commission, appear for and represent the Commission in any case in court.

(i) The Commission shall, in any of its educational or promotional activities, cooperate with other departments and agencies in the performance of such educational and promotional activities.

(j) All officers, agents, attorneys, and employees of the Commission shall be subject to the provisions of section 9 of the Act of August 2, 1939, as amended (the Hatch Act), notwithstanding any exemption contained in such section.

Prevention of Unlawful Employment Practices

SEC. 706. (a) Whenever it is charged in writing under oath by a person claiming to be aggrieved, or a written charge has been filed by a member of the Commission where he has reasonable cause to believe a violation of this title has occurred (and such charge sets forth the facts upon which it is based) that an employer, employment agency, or labor organization has engaged in an unlaw-ful employment practice, the Commission shall furnish such employer, employment agency, or labor organization (hereinafter referred to as the "respondent") with a copy of such charge and shall make an investigation of such charge, provided that such charge shall not be made public by the Commission. If the Commission shall determine, after such investigation, that there is reasonable cause to believe that the charge is true, the Commission shall endeavor to eliminate any such alleged unlawful employment practice by informal methods of conference, conciliation, and persuasion. Nothing said or done during and as a part of such endeavors may be made public by the Commission without the written consent of the parties, or used as evidence in a subsequent proceeding. Any officer or employee of the Commission, who shall make public in any manner whatever any information in violation of this subsection shall be deemed guilty of a misdemeanor and upon conviction thereof shall be fined not more than $1,000 or imprisoned not more than one year.

(b) In the case of an alleged unlawful employment practice occurring in a State, or political subdivision of a State, which has a State or local law prohibiting the unlawful employment practice alleged and establishing or authorizing a State or local authority to grant or seek relief from such practice or to institute criminal proceedings with respect thereto upon receiving notice thereof, no charge may be filed under subsection (a) by the person aggrieved before the expiration of sixty days after proceedings have been commenced under the State or local law, unless such proceedings have been earlier terminated, provided that such sixty-day period shall be extended to one hundred and twenty days during the first year after the effective date of such State or local law. If any requirement for the commencement of such proceedings is imposed by a State or local authority other than a requirement of the filing of a written and signed statement of the facts upon which the proceeding is based, the proceeding shall be deemed to have been commenced for the purposes of this subsection at the time such statement is sent by registered mail to the appropriate State or local authority.

(c) In the case of any charge filed by a member of the Commission alleging an unlawful employment practice occurring in a State or political subdivision of a State, which has a State or local law prohibiting the practice alleged and establishing or authorizing a State or local authority to grant or seek relief from such practice or to institute criminal proceedings with respect thereto upon receiving notice thereof, the Commission shall, before taking any action with respect to such charge, notify the appropriate State or local officials and, upon request, afford them a reasonable time, but not less than sixty days (provided that such sixty-day period shall be extended to one hundred and twenty days during the first year after the effective day of such State or local law), unless a shorter period is requested, to act under such State or local law to remedy the practice alleged.

(d) A charge under subsection (a) shall be filed within ninety days after the alleged unlawful employment practice occurred, except that in the case of an unlawful employment practice with respect to which the person aggrieved has followed the procedure set out in subsection (b), such charge shall be filed by the person aggrieved within two hundred and ten days after the alleged unlawful employment practice occurred, or within thirty days after receiving notice that the State or local agency has terminated the proceedings under the State or local law, whichever is earlier, and a copy of such charge shall be filed by the Commission with the State or local agency.

(e) If within thirty days after a charge is filed with the Commission or within thirty days after expiration of any period of reference under subsection (c) (except that in either case such period may be extended to not more than sixty days upon a determination by the Commission that further efforts to secure voluntary compliance are warranted), the Commission has been unable to obtain voluntary compliance with this title, the Commission shall so notify the person aggrieved and a civil action may, within thirty days thereafter, be brought against the respondent named in the charge (1) by the person claiming to be aggrieved, or (2) if such charge was filed by a member of the Commission, by any person whom the charge alleges was aggrieved by the alleged unlawful employment practice. Upon application by the complainant and in such circumstances as the court may deem just, the court may appoint an attorney for such complainant and may authorize the commencement of the action without the payment of fees, costs, or security. Upon timely application, the court may, in its discretion, permit the Attorney General to intervene in such civil action if he certifies that the case is of general public importance. Upon request, the court may, in its discretion, stay further proceedings for not more than sixty days pending the termination of State or local proceedings described in subsection (b) or the efforts of the Commission to obtain voluntary compliance.

(f) Each United States district court and each United States court of a place subject to the jurisdiction of the United States shall have jurisdiction of actions brought under this title. Such an action may be brought in any judicial district in the State in which the unlawful employment practice is alleged to have been committed, in the judicial district in which the employment records relevant to such practice are maintained and administered, or in the judicial district in which the plaintiff would have worked but for the alleged unlawful employment practice, but if the respondent is not found within any such district, such an action may be brought within the judicial district in which the respondent has his principal office. For purposes of sections 1404 and 1406 of title 28 of the United States Code, the judicial district in which the respondent has his principal office shall in all cases be considered a district in which the action might have been brought.

(g) If the court finds that the respondent has intentionally engaged in or is intentionally engaging in an unlawful employment practice charged in the complaint, the court may enjoin the respondent from engaging in such unlawful employment practice, and order such affirmative action as may be appropriate, which may include reinstatement or hiring of employees, with or without back pay (payable by the employer, employment agency, or labor organization, as the case may be, responsible for the unlawful employment practice). Interim earnings or amounts earnable with reasonable diligence by the person or persons discriminated against shall operate to reduce the back pay otherwise allowable. No order of the court shall require the admission or reinstatement of an individual as a member of a union or the hiring, reinstatement, or promotion of an individual as an employee, or the payment to him of any back pay, if such individual was refused admission, suspended, or expelled or was refused employment or advancement or was suspended or discharged for any reason other than discrimination on account of race, color, religion, sex or national origin or in violation of section 704(a).

(h) The provisions of the Act entitled "An Act to amend the Judicial Code and to define and limit the jurisdiction of courts sitting in equity, and for other purposes," approved March 23, 1932 (29 U.S.C. 101–115), shall not apply with respect to civil actions brought under this section.

(i) In any case in which an employer, employment agency, or labor organization fails to comply with an order of a court issued in a civil action brought under subsection (e), the Commission may commence proceedings to compel compliance with such order.

(j) Any civil action brought under subsection (e) and any proceedings brought under subsection (i) shall be subject to appeal as provided in sections 1291 and 1292, title 28, United States Code.

(k) In any action or proceeding under this title the court, in its discretion, may allow the prevailing party, other than the Commission or the United States, a reasonable attorney's fee as part of the costs, and the Commission and the United States shall be liable for costs the same as a private person.

SEC. 707. (a) Whenever the Attorney General has reasonable cause to believe that any person or group of persons is engaged in a pattern or practice of resistance to the full enjoyment of any of the rights secured by this title, and that the pattern or practice is of such a nature and is intended to deny the full exercise of the rights herein described, the Attorney General may bring a civil action in the appropriate district court of the United States by filing with it a complaint (1) signed by him (or in his absence the Acting Attorney General), (2) setting forth facts pertaining to such pattern or practice, and (3) requesting such relief, including an application for a permanent or temporary injunction, restraining order or other order against the person or persons responsible for such pattern or practice, as he deems necessary to insure the full enjoyment of the rights herein described.

(b) The district courts of the United States shall have and shall exercise jurisdiction of proceedings instituted pursuant to this section, and in any such proceeding the Attorney General may file with the clerk of such court a request that a court of three judges be convened to hear and determine the case. Such request by the Attorney General shall be accompanied by a certificate that, in his opinion, the case is of general public importance. A copy of the certificate and request for a three-judge court shall be immediately furnished by such clerk to the chief judge of the circuit (or in his absence, the presiding circuit judge of the circuit) in which the case is pending. Upon receipt of such request it shall be the duty of the chief judge of the circuit or the presiding circuit judge, as the case may be, to designate immediately three judges in such circuit, of whom at least one shall be a circuit judge and another of whom shall be a district judge of the court in which the proceeding was instituted, to hear and determine such case, and it shall be the duty of the judges so designated to assign the case for hearing at the earliest practicable date, to participate in the hearing and determination thereof, and to cause the case to be in every way expedited. An appeal from the final judgment of such court will lie to the Supreme Court.

In the event the Attorney General fails to file such a request in any such proceeding, it shall be the duty of the chief judge of the district (or in his absence, the acting chief judge) in which the case is pending immediately to designate a judge in such district to hear and determine the case. In the event that no judge in the district is available to hear and determine the case, the chief judge of the district, or the acting chief judge, as the case may be, shall certify this fact to the chief judge of the circuit (or in his absence, the acting chief judge) who shall then designate a district or circuit judge of the circuit to hear and determine the case.

It shall be the duty of the judge designated pursuant to this section to assign the case for hearing at the earliest practicable date and to cause the case to be in every way expedited.

Effect on State Laws

SEC. 708. Nothing in this title shall be deemed to exempt or relieve any person from any liability, duty, penalty, or punishment provided by any present or future law of any State or political subdivision of a State, other than any such law which purports to require or permit the doing of any act which would be an unlawful employment practice under this title.

Investigation, Inspections, Records, State Agencies

SEC. 709. (a) In connection with any investigation of a charge filed under section 706, the Commission or its designated representative shall at all reasonable times have access to, for the purposes of examination, and the right to copy any evidence of any person being investigated or proceeded against that relates to unlawful employment practices covered by this title and is relevant to the charge under investigation.

(b) The Commission may cooperate with State and local agencies charged with the administration of State fair employment practices laws and, with the consent of such agencies, may for the purpose of carrying out its functions and duties under this title and within the limitation of funds appropriated specifically for such purpose, utilize the services of such agencies and their employees and, notwithstanding any other provision of law, may reimburse such agencies and their employees for services rendered to assist the Commission in carrying out this title. In furtherance of such cooperative efforts, the Commission may enter into written agreements with such State or local agencies and such agreements may include provisions under which the Commission shall refrain from processing a charge in any cases or class of cases specified in such agreements and under which no person may bring a civil action under section 706 in any cases or class of cases so specified, or under which the Commission shall relieve any person or class of persons in such State or locality from requirements imposed under this section. The Commission shall rescind any such agreement whenever it determines that the agreement no longer serves the interest of effective enforcement of this title.

(c) Except as provided in subsection (d), every employer, employment agency, and labor organization subject to this title shall (1) make and keep such records relevant to the determinations of whether unlawful employment practices have been or are being committed, (2) preserve such records for such periods, and (3) make such reports therefrom, as the Commission shall prescribe by regulation or order, after public hearing, as reasonable, necessary, or appropriate for the enforcement of this title or the regulations or orders thereunder. The Commission shall, by regulation, require each employer, labor organization, and joint labor-management committee subject to this title which controls an apprenticeship or other training program to maintain such records as are reasonably necessary to carry out the purpose of this title, including, but not limited to, a list of applicants who wish to participate in such program, including the chronological order in which such applications were received, and shall furnish to the Commission, upon request, a detailed description of the manner in which persons are selected to participate in the apprenticeship or other training program. Any employer, employment agency, labor organization, or joint labor-management committee which believes that the application to it of any regulation or order issued under this section would result in undue hardship may (1) apply to the Commission for an exemption from the application of such regulation or order, or (2) bring a civil action in the United States district court for the district where such records are kept. If the Commission or the court, as the case may be, finds that the application of the regulation or order to the employer, employment agency, or labor organization in question would impose an undue hardship, the Commission or the court, as the case may be, may grant appropriate relief.

(d) The provisions of subsection (c) shall not apply to any employer, employment agency, labor organization, or joint labor-management committee with respect to matters occurring in any State or political subdivision thereof which has a fair employment practice law during any period in which such employer, employment agency, labor organ-

ization, or joint labor-management committee is subject to such law, except that the Commission may require such notations on records which such employer, employment agency, labor organization, or joint labor-management committee keeps or is required to keep as are necessary because of differences in coverage or methods of enforcement between the State or local law and the provisions of this title. Where an employer is required by Executive Order 10925, issued March 6, 1961, or by any other Executive order prescribing fair employment practices for Government contractors and subcontractors, or by rules or regulations issued thereunder, to file reports relating to his employment practices with any Federal agency or committee, and he is substantially in compliance with such requirements, the Commission shall not require him to file additional reports pursuant to subsection (c) of this section.

(e) It shall be unlawful for any officer or employee of the Commission to make public in any manner whatever any information obtained by the Commission pursuant to its authority under this section prior to the institution of any proceeding under this title involving such information. Any officer or employee of the Commission who shall make public in any manner whatever any information in violation of this subsection shall be guilty of a misdemeanor and, upon conviction thereof, shall be fined not more than $1,000, or imprisoned not more than one year.

Investigatory Powers

SEC. 710. (a) For the purposes of any investigation of a charge filed under the authority contained in section 706, the Commission shall have authority to examine witnesses under oath and to require the production of documentary evidence relevant or material to the charge under investigation.

(b) If the respondent named in a charge

filed under section 706 fails or refuses to comply with a demand of the Commission for permission to examine or to copy evidence in conformity with the provisions of section 709(a), or if any person required to comply with the provisions of section 709 (c) or (d) fails or refuses to do so, or if any person fails or refuses to comply with a demand by the Commission to give testimony under oath, the United States district court for the district in which such person is found, resides, or transacts business, shall, upon application of the Commission, have jurisdiction to issue to such person an order requiring him to comply with the provisions of section 709 (c) or (d) or to comply with the demand of the Commission, but the attendance of a witness may not be required outside the State where he is found, resides, or transacts business and the production of evidence may not be required outside the State where such evidence is kept.

(c) Within twenty days after the service upon any person charged under section 706 of a demand by the Commission for the production of documentary evidence or for permission to examine or to copy evidence in conformity with the provisions of section 709(a), such person may file in the district court of the United States for the judicial district in which he resides, is found, or transacts business, and serve upon the Commission a petition for an order of such court modifying or setting aside such demand. The time allowed for compliance with the demand in whole or in part as deemed proper and ordered by the court shall not run during the pendency of such petition in the court. Such petition shall specify each ground upon which the petitioner relies in seeking such relief, and may be based upon any failure of such demand to comply with the provisions of this title or with the limitations generally applicable to compulsory process or upon any constitutional or other legal right or privilege of such person. No objection which is not raised by such a petition

may be urged in the defense to a proceeding initiated by the Commission under subsection (b) for enforcement of such a demand unless such proceeding is commenced by the Commission prior to the expiration of the twenty-day period, or unless the court determines that the defendant could not reasonably have been aware of the availability of such ground of objection.

(d) In any proceeding brought by the Commission under subsection (b), except as provided in subsection (c) of this section, the defendant may petition the court for an order modifying or setting aside the demand of the Commission.

SEC. 711. (a) Every employer, employment agency, and labor organization, as the case may be, shall post and keep posted in conspicuous places upon its premises where notices to employees, applicants for employment, and members are customarily posted a notice to be prepared or approved by the Commission setting forth excerpts from, or summaries of, the pertinent provisions of this title and information pertinent to the filing of a complaint.

(b) A willful violation of this section shall be punishable by a fine of not more than $100 for each separate offense.

Veterans' Preference

SEC. 712. Nothing contained in this title shall be construed to repeal or modify any Federal, State, territorial, or local law creating special rights or preference for veterans.

Rules and Regulations

SEC. 713. (a) The Commission shall have authority from time to time to issue, amend, or rescind suitable procedural regulations to carry out the provisions of this title. Regulations issued under this section shall be in conformity with the standards and limitations of the Administrative Procedure Act.

(b) In any action or proceeding based on any alleged unlawful employment practice, no person shall be subject to any liability or punishment for or on account of (1) the commission by such person of an unlawful employment practice if he pleads and proves that the act or omission complained of was in good faith, in conformity with, and in reliance on any written interpretation or opinion of the Commission, or (2) the failure of such person to publish and file any information required by any provision of this title if he pleads and proves that he failed to publish and file such information in good faith, in conformity with the instructions of the Commission issued under this title regarding the filing of such information. Such a defense, if established, shall be a bar to the action or proceeding, notwithstanding that (A) after such act or omission, such interpretation or opinion is modified or rescinded or is determined by judicial authority to be invalid or of no legal effect, or (B) after publishing or filing the description and annual reports, such publication or filing is determined by judicial authority not to be in conformity with the requirements of this title.

Forcibly Resisting the Commission or its Representatives

SEC. 714. The provisions of section 111, title 18, United States Code, shall apply to officers, agents, and employees of the Commission in the performance of their official duties.

Special Study by Secretary of Labor

SEC. 715. The Secretary of Labor shall make a full and complete study of the factors which might tend to result in discrimination in employment because of age and of the consequences of such discrimination on the economy and individuals affected. The Secretary of Labor shall make a report to the Congress not later than June 30, 1965, containing the results of such study and shall include in such report such recommendations for legislation to prevent arbitrary discrimination in employment because of age as he determines advisable.

Effective Date

SEC. 716. (a) This title shall become effective one year after the date of its enactment.

(b) Notwithstanding subsection (a), sections of this title other than sections 703, 704, 706, and 707 shall become effective immediately.

(c) The President shall, as soon as feasible after the enactment of this title, convene one or more conferences for the purpose of enabling the leaders of groups whose members will be affected by this title to become familiar with the rights afforded and obligations imposed by its provisions, and for the purpose of making plans which will result in the fair and effective administration of this title when all of its provisions become effective. The President shall invite the participation in such conference or conferences of (1) the members of the President's Committee on Equal Employment Opportunity, (2) the members of the Commission on Civil Rights, (3) representatives of State and local agencies engaged in furthering equal employment opportunity, (4) representatives of private agencies engaged in furthering equal employment opportunity, and (5) representatives of employers, labor organizations, and employment agencies who will be subject to this title.

TITLE VIII—REGISTRATION AND VOTING STATISTICS

SEC. 801. The Secretary of Commerce shall promptly conduct a survey to compile registration and voting statistics in such geographic areas as may be recommended by the Commission on Civil Rights. Such a survey and compilation shall, to the extent recommended by the Commission on Civil Rights, only include a count of persons of voting age by race, color, and national origin, and determination of the extent to which such persons are registered to vote, and have voted in any statewide primary or general election in which the Members of the United

States House of Representatives are nominated or elected, since January 1, 1960. Such information shall also be collected and compiled in connection with the Nineteenth Decennial Census, and at such other times as the Congress may prescribe. The provisions of section 9 and chapter 7 of title 13, United States Code, shall apply to any survey, collection, or compilation of registration and voting statistics carried out under this title: Provided, however, That no person shall be compelled to disclose his race, color, national origin, or questioned about his political party affiliation, how he voted, or the reasons therefore, nor shall any penalty be imposed for his failure or refusal to make such disclosure. Every person interrogated orally, by written survey or questionnaire or by any other means with respect to such information shall be fully advised with respect to his right to fail or refuse to furnish such information.

TITLE IX—INTERVENTION AND PROCEDURE AFTER REMOVAL IN CIVIL RIGHTS CASES

SEC. 901. Title 28 of the United States Code, section 1447(d), is amended to read as follows:

"An order remanding a case to the State court from which it was removed is not reviewable on appeal or otherwise, except that an order remanding a case to the State court from which it was removed pursuant to section 1443 of this title shall be reviewable by appeal or otherwise."

SEC. 902. Whenever an action has been commenced in any court of the United States seeking relief from the denial of equal protection of the laws under the fourteenth amendment to the Constitution on account of race, color, religion, or national origin, the Attorney General for or in the name of the United States may intervene in such action upon timely application if the Attorney General certifies that the case is of general public importance. In such action the United

States shall be entitled to the same relief as if it had instituted the action.

TITLE X—ESTABLISHMENT OF COMMUNITY RELATIONS SERVICE

SEC. 1001. (a) There is hereby established in and as a part of the Department of Commerce a Community Relations Service (hereinafter referred to as the "Service"), which shall be headed by a Director who shall be appointed by the President with the advice and consent of the Senate for a term of four years. The Director is authorized to appoint, subject to the civil service laws and regulations, such other personnel as may be necessary to enable the Service to carry out its functions and duties, and to fix their compensation in accordance with the Classification Act of 1949, as amended. The Director is further authorized to procure services as authorized by section 15 of the Act of August 2, 1946 (60 Stat. 810; 5 U.S.C. 55(a)), but at rates for individuals not in excess of $75 per diem.

(b) Section 106(a) of the Federal Executive Pay Act of 1956, as amended (5 U.S.C. 2205(a)), is further amended by adding the following clause thereto:

"(52) Director, Community Relations Service."

SEC. 1002. It shall be the function of the Service to provide assistance to communities and persons therein in resolving disputes, disagreements, or difficulties relating to discriminatory practices based on race, color, or national origin which impair the rights of persons in such communities under the Constitution or laws of the United States or which affect or may affect interstate commerce. The Service may offer its services in cases of such disputes, disagreements, or difficulties whenever, in its judgment, peaceful relations among the citizens of the community involved are threatened thereby, and it may offer its services either upon its own motion or upon the request of an appropriate State or local official or other interested person.

SEC. 1003. (a) The Service shall, whenever possible, in performing its functions, seek and utilize the cooperation of appropriate State or local, public, or private agencies.

(b) The activities of all officers and employees of the Service in providing conciliation assistance shall be conducted in confidence and without publicity, and the Service shall hold confidential any information acquired in the regular performance of its duties upon the understanding that it would be so held. No officer or employee of the Service shall engage in the performance of investigative or prosecuting functions of any department or agency in any litigation arising out of a dispute in which he acted on behalf of the Service. Any officer or other employee of the Service, who shall make public in any manner whatever any information in violation of this subsection, shall be deemed guilty of a misdemeanor and, upon conviction thereof, shall be fined not more than $1,000 or imprisoned not more than one year.

SEC. 1004. Subject to the provisions of sections 205 and 1003(b), the Director shall, on or before January 31 of each year, submit to the Congress a report of the activities of the Service during the preceding fiscal year.

TITLE XI—MISCELLANEOUS

SEC. 1101. In any proceeding for criminal contempt arising under title II, III, IV, V, VI, or VII of this Act, the accused, upon demand therefor, shall be entitled to a trial by jury, which shall conform as near as may be to the practice in criminal cases. Upon conviction, the accused shall not be fined more than $1,000 or imprisoned for more than six months.

This section shall not apply to contempts committed in the presence of the court, or so near thereto as to obstruct the administration of justice, nor to the misbehavior, misconduct, or disobedience of any officer of the court in respect to writs, orders, or process of the court. No person shall be convicted of criminal contempt hereunder unless the act or omission constituting such contempt shall have been intentional, as required in other cases of criminal contempt.

Nor shall anything herein be construed to deprive courts of their power, by civil contempt proceedings, without a jury, to secure compliance with or to prevent obstruction of, as distinguished from punishment for violations of, any lawful writ, process, order, rule, decree, or command of the court in accordance with the prevailing usages of law and equity, including the power of detention.

SEC. 1102. No person should be put twice in jeopardy under the laws of the United States for the same act or omission. For this reason, an acquittal or conviction in a prosecution for a specific crime under the laws of the United States shall bar a proceeding for criminal contempt, which is based upon the same act or omission and which arises under the provisions of this Act; and an acquittal or conviction in a proceeding for criminal contempt, which arises under the provisions of this Act, shall bar a prosecution for a specific crime under the laws of the United States based upon the same act or omission.

SEC. 1103. Nothing in this Act shall be construed to deny, impair, or otherwise affect any right or authority of the Attorney General or of the United States or any agency or officer thereof under existing law to institute or intervene in any action or proceeding.

SEC. 1104. Nothing contained in any title of this Act shall be construed as indicating an intent on the part of Congress to occupy the field in which any such title operates to the exclusion of State laws on the same subject matter, nor shall any provision of this Act be construed as invalidating any provision of State law unless such provision is inconsistent with any of the purposes of this Act, or any provision thereof.

SEC. 1105. There are hereby authorized

to be appropriated such sums as are necessary to carry out the provisions of this Act.

SEC. 1106. If any provision of this Act or the application thereof to any person or circumstances is held invalid, the remainder of the Act and the application of the provision to other persons not similarly situated or to other circumstances shall not be affected thereby.

Approved July 2, 1964.

CHAPTER 17

Voting Rights Act (August 6, 1965)

United States Congress

The History*

This "act to enforce the fifteenth amendment to the Constitution" was signed into law 95 years after the amendment was ratified. In those years, African Americans in the South faced tremendous obstacles to voting, including poll taxes, literacy tests, and other bureaucratic restrictions to deny them the right to vote. They also risked harassment, intimidation, economic reprisals, and physical violence when they tried to register or vote. As a result, very few African Americans were registered voters, and they had very little, if any, political power, either locally or nationally.

In 1964, numerous demonstrations were held, and the considerable violence that erupted brought renewed attention to the issue of voting rights. The murder of voting-rights activists in Mississippi and the attack by state troopers on peaceful marchers in Selma, Alabama, gained national attention and persuaded President Johnson and Congress to initiate meaningful and effective national voting rights legislation. The combination of public revulsion to the violence and

Johnson's political skills stimulated Congress to pass the voting rights bill on August 5, 1965.

The legislation, which President Johnson signed into law the next day, outlawed literacy tests and provided for the appointment of Federal examiners (with the power to register qualified citizens to vote) in those jurisdictions that were "covered" according to a formula provided in the statute. In addition, Section 5 of the act required covered jurisdictions to obtain "preclearance" from either the District Court for the District of Columbia or the U.S. Attorney General for any new voting practices and procedures. Section 2, which closely followed the language of the 15th amendment, applied a nationwide prohibition of the denial or abridgment of the right to vote on account of race or color. The use of poll taxes in national elections had been abolished by the 24th amendment (1964) to the Constitution; the Voting Rights Act directed the Attorney General to challenge the use of poll taxes in state and local elections. In *Harper v. Virginia State Board of Elections*, 383 U.S. 663 (1966), the Supreme Court held Virginia's poll tax to be unconstitutional under the 14th amendment.

---

*Originally published as "Voting Rights Act (1965)," *America's Historical Documents*, The National Archives, U.S. National Archives and Records Administration, College Park, Maryland, 2008. For additional information see "Voting Rights Act (1965)," *America's Historical Documents*, U.S. National Archives and Records Administration, College Park, Maryland, 2008. This agency is listed in the *National Resource Directory* section of this volume.

Because the Voting Rights Act of 1965 was the most significant statutory change in the relationship between the Federal and state governments in the area of voting since the Reconstruction period following the Civil War, it was immediately challenged in the courts. Between 1965 and 1969, the Supreme Court issued several key decisions upholding the constitutionality of Section 5 and affirming the broad range of voting practices for which preclearance was required. [See *South Carolina v. Katzenbach*, 383 U.S. 301, 327–28 (1966) and *Allen v. State Board of Elections*, 393 U.S. 544 (1969)].

The law had an immediate impact. By the end of 1965, a quarter of a million new black voters had been registered, one-third by Federal examiners. By the end of 1966, only 4 out of the 13 southern states had fewer than 50 percent of African Americans registered to vote. The Voting Rights Act of 1965 was readopted and strengthened in 1970, 1975, and 1982.

The Document

Voting Rights Act

AN ACT To enforce the fifteenth amendment to the Constitution of the United States, and for other purposes.

Be it enacted by the Senate and House of Representatives of the United States of America in Congress [p*338] assembled, That this Act shall be known as the "Voting Rights Act of 1965."

SEC. 2. No voting qualification or prerequisite to voting, or standard, practice, or procedure shall be imposed or applied by any State or political subdivision to deny or abridge the right of any citizen of the United States to vote on account of race or color.

SEC. 3.

(a) Whenever the Attorney General institutes a proceeding under any statute to enforce the guarantees of the fifteenth amendment in any State or political subdivision the court shall authorize the appointment of Federal examiners by the United States Civil Service Commission in accordance with section 6 to serve for such period of time and for such political subdivisions as the court shall determine is appropriate to enforce the guarantees of the fifteenth amendment (1) as part of any interlocutory order if the court determines that the appointment of such examiners is necessary to enforce such guarantees or (2) as part of any final judgment if the court finds that violations of the fifteenth amendment justifying equitable relief have occurred in such State or subdivision: Provided, That the court need not authorize the appointment of examiners if any incidents of denial or abridgement of the right to vote on account of race or color (1) have been few in number and have been promptly and effectively corrected by State or local action, (2) the continuing effect of such incidents has been eliminated, and (3) there is no reasonable probability of their recurrence in the future. (b) If in a proceeding instituted by the Attorney General under any statute to enforce the guarantees of the fifteenth amendment in any State or political subdivision the court finds that a test or device has been used for the purpose or with the effect of denying or abridging the right of any citizen of the United States to vote on account of race or color, it shall suspend the use of [p*339] tests and devices in such State or political subdivisions as the court shall determine is appropriate and for such period as it deems necessary.

(c) If in any proceeding instituted by the Attorney General under any statute to enforce the guarantees of the fifteenth amendment in any State or political subdivision the court finds that violations of the fifteenth amendment justifying equitable relief have occurred within the territory of such State or political subdivision, the court, in addition to such relief as it may grant, shall retain jurisdiction for such period as it may deem appropriate and during such period no voting qualification or prerequisite to voting, or standard, practice, or procedure with respect to voting different from that in force or effect at the time the proceeding was commenced shall be enforced unless and until the court finds that such qualification, prerequisite, standard, practice, or procedure does not have the purpose and will not have the effect of denying or abridging the right to vote on account of race or color: Provided, That such qualification, prerequisite, standard, practice, or procedure may be enforced if the qualification, prerequisite, standard, practice, or procedure has been submitted by the chief legal officer or other appropriate official of such State or subdivision to the Attorney General and the Attorney General has not interposed an objection within sixty days after such submission, except that neither the court's finding nor the Attorney General's failure to object shall bar a subsequent action to enjoin enforcement of such qualification, prerequisite, standard, practice, or procedure.

SEC. 4. (a) To assure that the right of citizens of the United States to vote is not denied or abridged on account of race or color, no citizen shall be denied the right to vote in any Federal, State, or local election because of his failure to comply with any test or device in any State with respect to which the determinations have been [p*340] made under subsection (b) or in any political subdivision with respect to which such determinations have been made as a separate unit, unless the United States District Court for the District of Columbia in an action for a declaratory judgment brought by such State or subdivision against the United States has determined that no such test or device has been used during the five years preceding the filing of the action for the purpose or with the effect of denying or abridging the right to vote on account of race or color: Provided, That no such declaratory judgment shall issue with respect to any plaintiff for a period of five years after the entry of a final judgment of any court of the United States, other than the denial of a declaratory judgment under this section, whether entered prior to or after the enactment of this Act, determining that denials or abridgments of the right to vote on account of race or color through the use of such tests or devices have occurred anywhere in the territory of such plaintiff. An action pursuant to this subsection shall be heard and determined by a court of three judges in accordance with the provisions of section 2284 of title 28 of the United States Code and any appeal shall lie to the Supreme Court. The court shall retain jurisdiction of any action pursuant to this subsection for five years after judgment and shall reopen the action upon motion of the Attorney General alleging that a test or device has been used for the purpose or with the effect of denying or abridging the right to vote on account of race or color.

If the Attorney General determines that he has no reason to believe that any such test or device has been used during the five years preceding the filing of the action for the purpose or with the effect of denying or abridging the right to vote on account of race or color, he shall consent to the entry of such judgment.

(b) The provisions of subsection (a) shall apply in any State or in any political subdivision of a state which (1) the Attorney General determines maintained on November 1, 1964, any test or device, and with respect to which (2) the Director of the Census determines that less than 50 percentum of the persons of voting age residing therein were registered on November 1, 1964, or that less than 50 percentum of such persons voted in the presidential election of November 1964.

A determination or certification of the Attorney General or of the Director of the Census under this section or under section 6 or section 13 shall not be reviewable in any court and shall be effective upon publication in the Federal Register.

(c) The phrase "test or device" shall mean any requirement that a person as a prerequisite for voting or registration for voting (1) demonstrate the ability to read, write, understand, or interpret any matter, (2) demonstrate any educational achievement or his knowledge of any particular subject, (3) possess good moral character, or (4) prove his qualifications by the voucher of registered voters or members of any other class.

(d) For purposes of this section no State or political subdivision shall be determined to have engaged in the use of tests or devices for the purpose or with the effect of denying or abridging the right to vote on account of race or color if (1) incidents of such use have been few in number and have been promptly and effectively corrected by State or local action, (2) the continuing effect of such incidents has been eliminated, and (3) there is no reasonable probability of their recurrence in the future.

(e)(1) Congress hereby declares that to secure the rights under the fourteenth amendment of persons educated in American-flag schools in which the predominant [p*342] classroom language was other than English, it is necessary to prohibit the States from conditioning the right to vote of such persons on ability to read, write, understand, or interpret any matter in the English language. (2) No person who demonstrates that he has successfully completed the sixth primary grade in a public school in, or a private school accredited by, any State or territory, the District of Columbia, or the Commonwealth of Puerto Rico in which the predominant classroom language was other than English, shall be denied the right to vote in any Federal, State, or local election because of his inability to read, write, understand, or interpret any matter in the English language, except that, in States in which State law provides that a different level of education is presumptive of literacy, he shall demonstrate that he has successfully completed an equivalent level of education in a public school in,

or a private school accredited by, any State or territory, the District of Columbia, or the Commonwealth of Puerto Rico in which the predominant classroom language was other than English.

SEC. 5. Whenever a State or political subdivision with respect to which the prohibitions set forth in section 4(a) are in effect shall enact or seek to administer any voting qualification or prerequisite to voting, or standard, practice, or procedure with respect to voting different from that in force or effect on November 1, 1964, such State or subdivision may institute an action in the United States District Court for the District of Columbia for a declaratory judgment that such qualification, prerequisite, standard, practice, or procedure does not have the purpose and will not have the effect of denying or abridging the right to vote on account of race or color, and unless and until the court enters such judgment no person shall be denied the right to vote for failure to comply with such qualification, prerequisite, standard, practice, [p*343] or procedure: Provided, That such qualification, prerequisite, standard, practice, or procedure may be enforced without such proceeding if the qualification, prerequisite, standard, practice, or procedure has been submitted by the chief legal officer or other appropriate official of such State or subdivision to the Attorney General and the Attorney General has not interposed an objection within sixty days after such submission, except that neither the Attorney General's failure to object nor a declaratory judgment entered under this section shall bar a subsequent action to enjoin enforcement of such qualification, prerequisite, standard, practice, or procedure. Any action under this section shall be heard and determined by a court of three judges in accordance with the provisions of section 2284 of title 28 of the United States Code and any appeal shall lie to the Supreme Court.

SEC. 6. Whenever (a) a court has authorized the appointment of examiners pursuant to the provisions of section 3(a), or (b) unless a declaratory judgment has been rendered under section 4(a), the Attorney General certifies with respect to any political subdivision named in, or included within the scope of, determinations made under section 4(b) that (1) he has received complaints in writing from twenty or more residents of such political subdivision alleging that they have been denied the right to vote under color of law on account of race or color, and that he believes such complaints to be meritorious, or (2) that, in his judgment (considering, among other factors, whether the ratio of nonwhite persons to white persons registered to vote within such subdivision appears to him to be reasonably attributable to violations of the fifteenth amendment or whether substantial evidence exists that bona fide efforts are being made within such subdivision to comply with the fifteenth amendment), the appointment of examiners is otherwise necessary to [p*344] enforce the guarantees of the fifteenth amendment, the Civil Service Commission shall appoint as many examiners for such subdivision as it may deem appropriate to prepare and maintain lists of persons eligible to vote in Federal, State, and local elections. Such examiners, hearing officers provided for in section 9(a), and other persons deemed necessary by the Commission to carry out the provisions and purposes of this Act shall be appointed, compensated, and separated without regard to the provisions of any statute administered by the Civil Service Commission, and service under this Act shall not be considered employment for the purposes of any statute administered by the Civil Service Commission, except the provisions of section 9 of the Act of August 2, 1939, as amended (5 U.S.C. 118i), prohibiting partisan political activity: Provided, That the Commission is authorized, after consulting the head of the appropriate department or agency, to designate suitable persons in the official service of the United States, with their consent, to serve in these positions. Examiners and hearing officers shall have the power to administer oaths.

SEC. 7.

(a) The examiners for each political subdivision shall, at such places as the Civil Service Commission shall by regulation designate, examine applicants concerning their qualifications for voting. An application to an examiner shall be in such form as the Commission may require and shall contain allegations that the applicant is not otherwise registered to vote.

(b) Any person whom the examiner finds, in accordance with instructions received under section 9(b), to have the qualifications prescribed by State law not inconsistent with the Constitution and laws of the United States shall promptly be placed on a list of eligible voters. A challenge to such listing may be made in accordance with section 9(a) and shall not be the basis for a prosecution under section 12 of this Act. The examiner [p*345] shall certify and transmit such list, and any supplements as appropriate, at least once a month, to the offices of the appropriate election officials, with copies to the Attorney General and the attorney general of the State, and any such lists and supplements thereto transmitted during the month shall be available for public inspection on the last business day of the month and, in any event, not later than the forty-fifth day prior to any election. The appropriate State or local election official shall place such names on the official voting list. Any person whose name appears on the examiner's list shall be entitled and allowed to vote in the election district of his residence unless and until the appropriate election officials shall have been notified that such person has been removed from such list in accordance with subsection (d): Provided, That no person shall be entitled to vote in any election by virtue of this Act unless his name shall have been certified and transmitted on such a list to the offices of the appropriate election officials at least forty-five days prior to such election.

(c) The examiner shall issue to each person whose name appears on such a list a certificate evidencing his eligibility to vote.

(d) A person whose name appears on such a list shall be removed therefrom by an examiner if (1) such person has been successfully challenged in accordance with the procedure prescribed in section 9, or (2) he has been determined by an examiner to have lost his eligibility to vote under State law not inconsistent with the Constitution and the laws of the United States.

Sec. 8. Whenever an examiner is serving under this Act in any political subdivision, the Civil Service Commission may assign, at the request of the Attorney General, one or more persons, who may be officers of the United States, (1) to enter and attend at any place for holding an election in such subdivision for the purpose [p*346] of observing whether persons who are entitled to vote are being permitted to vote, and (2) to enter and attend at any place for tabulating the votes cast at any election held in such subdivision for the purpose of observing whether votes cast by persons entitled to vote are being properly tabulated. Such persons so assigned shall report to an examiner appointed for such political subdivision, to the Attorney General, and if the appointment of examiners has been authorized pursuant to section 3(a), to the court.

SEC. 9.

(a) Any challenge to a listing on an eligibility list prepared by an examiner shall be heard and determined by a hearing officer appointed by and responsible to the Civil Service Commission and under such rules as the Commission shall by regulation prescribe. Such challenge shall be entertained only if filed at such office within the State as the Civil Service Commission shall by regulation designate, and within ten days after the listing of the challenged person is made available for public inspection, and if supported by (1) the affidavits of at least two persons having personal knowledge of the facts constituting grounds for the challenge, and (2) a certification that a copy of the challenge and affidavits have been served by mail or in person upon the person challenged at his place of residence set out in the application. Such challenge shall be determined within fifteen days after it has been filed. A petition for review of the decision of the hearing officer may be filed in the United States court of appeals for the circuit in which the person challenged resides within fifteen days after service of such decision by mail on the person petitioning for review but no decision of a hearing officer shall be reversed unless clearly erroneous. Any person listed shall be entitled and allowed to vote pending final determination by the hearing officer and by the court [p*347].

(b) The times, places, procedures, and form for application and listing pursuant to this Act and removals from the eligibility lists shall be prescribed by regulations promulgated by the Civil Service Commission and the Commission shall, after consultation with the Attorney General, instruct examiners concerning applicable State law not inconsistent with the Constitution and laws of the United States with respect to (1) the qualifications required for listing, and (2) loss of eligibility to vote.

(c) Upon the request of the applicant or the challenger or on its own motion the Civil Service Commission shall have the power to require by subpoena the attendance and testimony of witnesses and the production of documentary evidence relating to any matter pending before it under the authority of this section. In case of contumacy or refusal to obey a subpoena, any district court of the United States or the United States court of any territory or possession, or the District Court of the United States for the District of Columbia, within the jurisdiction of which said person guilty of contumacy or refusal to obey is found or resides or is domiciled or transacts business, or has appointed an agent for receipt of service of process, upon application by the Attorney General of the United States shall have jurisdiction to issue to such person an order requiring such person to appear before the Commission or a hearing officer, there to produce pertinent, relevant, and nonprivileged documentary evidence if so ordered, or there to give testimony touching the matter under investigation, and any failure to obey such order of the court may be punished by said court as a contempt thereof.

SEC. 10. (a) The Congress finds that the requirement of the payment of a poll tax as a precondition to voting (i) precludes persons of limited means from voting or imposes unreasonable financial hardship upon such persons [p*348] as a precondition to their exercise of the franchise, (ii) does not bear a reasonable relationship to any legitimate State interest in the conduct of elections, and (iii) in some areas has the purpose or effect of denying persons the right to vote because of race or color. Upon the basis of these findings, Congress declares that the constitutional right of citizens to vote is denied or abridged in some areas by the requirement of the payment of a poll tax as a precondition to voting. (b) In the exercise of the powers of Congress under section 5 of the fourteenth amendment and section 2 of the fifteenth amendment, the Attorney General is authorized and directed to institute forthwith in the name of the United States such actions, including actions against States or political subdivisions, for declaratory judgment or injunctive relief against the enforcement of any requirement of the payment of a poll tax as a precondition to voting, or substitute therefor enacted after November 1, 1964, as will be necessary to implement the declaration of subsection (a) and the purposes of this section.

(c) The district courts of the United States shall have jurisdiction of such actions which shall be heard and determined by a court of three judges in accordance with the provisions of section 2284 of title 28 of the United States Code and any appeal shall lie to the Supreme Court. It shall be the duty of the judges designated to hear the case to assign the case for hearing at the earliest practicable date, to participate in the hearing and determination thereof, and to cause the case to be in every way expedited.

(d) During the pendency of such actions, and thereafter if the courts, notwithstanding this action by the Congress, should declare the requirement of the payment of a poll tax to be constitutional, no citizen of the United States who is a resident of a State or political [p*349] subdivision with respect to which determinations have been made under subsection 4(b) and a declaratory judgment has not been entered under subsection 4(a), during the first year he becomes otherwise entitled to vote by reason of registration by State or local officials or listing by an examiner, shall be denied the right to vote for failure to pay a poll tax if he tenders payment of such tax for the current year to an examiner or to the appropriate State or local official at least forty-five days prior to election, whether or not such tender would be timely or adequate under State law. An examiner shall have authority to accept such payment from any person authorized by this Act to make an application for listing, and shall issue a receipt for such payment. The examiner shall transmit promptly any such poll tax payment to the office of the State or local official authorized to receive such payment under State law, together with the name and address of the applicant.

SEC. 11. (a) No person acting under color of law shall fail or refuse to permit any person to vote who is entitled to vote under any provision of this Act or is otherwise qualified to vote, or willfully fail or refuse to tabulate, count, and report such person's vote. (b) No person, whether acting under color of law or otherwise, shall intimidate, threaten, or coerce, or attempt to intimidate, threaten, or coerce any person for voting or attempting to vote, or intimidate, threaten, or coerce, or attempt to intimidate, threaten, or coerce any person for urging or aiding any person to vote or attempt to vote, or intimidate, threaten, or coerce any person for exercising any powers or duties under section 3(a), 6, 8, 9, 10, or 12(e).

(c) Whoever knowingly or willfully gives false information as to his name, address, or period of residence in the voting district for the purpose of establishing his eligibility to register or vote, or conspires with another [p*350] individual for the purpose of encouraging his false registration to vote or illegal voting, or pays or offers to pay or accepts payment either for registration to vote or for voting shall be fined not more than $10,000 or imprisoned not more than five years, or both: Provided, however, That this provision shall be applicable only to general, special, or primary elections held solely or in part for the purpose of selecting or electing any candidate for the office of President, Vice President, presidential elector, Member of the United States Senate, Member of the United States House of Representatives, or Delegates or Commissioners from the territories or possessions, or Resident Commissioner of the Commonwealth of Puerto Rico.

(d) Whoever, in any matter within the jurisdiction of an examiner or hearing officer knowingly and willfully falsifies or conceals a material fact, or makes any false, fictitious, or fraudulent statements or representations, or makes or uses any false writing or document knowing the same to contain any false, fictitious, or fraudulent statement or entry, shall be fined not more than $10,000 or imprisoned not more than five years, or both.

SEC. 12. (a) Whoever shall deprive or attempt to deprive any person of any right secured by section 2, 3, 4, 5, 7, or 10 or shall violate section 11(a) or (b), shall be fined not more than $5,000, or imprisoned not more than five years, or both. (b) Whoever, within a year following an election in a political subdivision in which an examiner has been appointed (1) destroys, defaces, mutilates, or otherwise alters the marking of a paper ballot which has been cast in such election, or (2) alters any official record of voting in such election tabulated from a voting machine or otherwise, shall be fined not more than $5,000, or imprisoned not more than five years, or both [p*351].

(c) Whoever conspires to violate the provisions of subsection (a) or (b) of this section, or interferes with any right secured by section 2, 3 4, 5, 7, 10, or 11(a) or (b) shall be fined not more than $5,000, or imprisoned not more than five years, or both.

(d) Whenever any person has engaged or there are reasonable grounds to believe that any person is about to engage in any act or practice prohibited by section 2, 3, 4, 5, 7, 10, 11, or subsection (b) of this section, the Attorney General may institute for the United States, or in the name of the United States, an action for preventive relief, including an application for a temporary or permanent injunction, restraining order, or other order, and including an order directed to the State and State or local election officials to require them (1) to permit persons listed under this Act to vote and (2) to count such votes.

(e) Whenever in any political subdivision in which there are examiners appointed pursuant to this Act any persons allege to such an examiner within forty-eight hours after the closing of the polls that notwithstanding (1) their listing under this Act or registration by an appropriate election official and (2) their eligibility to vote, they have not been permitted to vote in such election, the examiner shall forthwith notify the Attorney General if such allegations in his opinion appear to be well founded. Upon receipt of such notification, the Attorney General may forthwith file with the district court an application for an order providing for the marking, casting, and counting of the ballots of such persons and requiring the inclusion of their votes in the total vote before the results of such election shall be deemed final and any force or effect given thereto. The district court shall hear and determine such matters immediately after the filing of such application. The remedy provided [p*352] in this subsection shall not preclude any remedy available under State or Federal law.

(f) The district courts of the United States shall have jurisdiction of proceedings instituted pursuant to this section and shall exercise the same without regard to whether a person asserting rights under the provisions of this Act shall have exhausted any administrative or other remedies that may be provided by law.

SEC. 13. Listing procedures shall be terminated in any political subdivision of any State (a) with respect to examiners appointed pursuant to clause (b) of section 6 whenever the Attorney General notifies the Civil Service Commission, or whenever the District Court for the District of Columbia determines in an action for declaratory judgment brought by any political subdivision with respect to which the Director of the Census has determined that more than 50 percentum of the nonwhite persons of voting age residing therein are registered to vote, (1) that all persons listed by an examiner for such subdivision have been placed on the appropriate voting registration roll, and (2) that there is no longer reasonable cause to believe that persons will be deprived of or denied the right to vote on account of race or color in such subdivision, and (b), with respect to examiners appointed pursuant to section 3(a), upon order of the authorizing court. A political subdivision may petition the Attorney General for the termination of listing procedures under clause (a) of this section, and may petition the Attorney General to request the Director of the Census to take such survey or census as may be appropriate for the making of the determination provided for in this section. The District Court for the District of Columbia shall have jurisdiction to require such survey or census to be made by the Director of the Census and it shall require him to do so if it deems the Attorney [p*353] General's refusal to request such survey or census to be arbitrary or unreasonable. SEC. 14.

(a) All cases of criminal contempt arising under the provisions of this Act shall be governed by section 151 of the Civil Rights Act of 1957 (42 U.S.C. 1995). (b) No court other than the District Court for the District of Columbia or a court of appeals in any proceeding under section 9 shall have jurisdiction to issue any declaratory judgment pursuant to section 4 or section 5 or any restraining order or temporary or permanent injunction against the execution or enforcement of any provision of this Act or any action of any Federal officer or employee pursuant hereto.

(c)(1) The terms "vote" or "voting" shall include all action necessary to make a vote effective in any primary, special, or general election, including, but not limited to, registration, listing pursuant to this Act, or other action required by law prerequisite to voting, casting a ballot, and having such ballot counted properly and included in the appropriate totals of votes cast with respect to candidates for public or party office and propositions for which votes are received in an election. (2) The term "political subdivision" shall mean any county or parish, except that, where registration for voting is not conducted under the supervision of a county or parish, the term shall include any other subdivision of a State which conducts registration for voting.

(d) In any action for a declaratory judgment brought pursuant to section 4 or section 5 of this Act, subpoenas for witnesses who are required to attend the District Court for the District of Columbia may be served in any judicial district of the United States: Provided, That no writ of subpoena shall issue for witnesses without the District of Columbia at a greater distance than one hundred [p*354] miles from the place of holding court without the permission of the District Court for the District of Columbia being first had upon proper application and cause shown.

SEC. 15. Section 2004 of the Revised Statutes (42 U.S.C. 1971), as amended by section 131 of the Civil Rights Act of 1957 (71 Stat. 637), and amended by section 601 of the Civil Rights Act of 1960 (74 Stat. 90), and as further amended by section 101 of the Civil Rights Act of 1964 (78 Stat. 241), is further amended as follows:

(a) Delete the word "Federal" wherever it appears in subsections (a) and (c); (b) Repeal subsection (f) and designate the present subsections (g) and (h) as (f) and (g), respectively.

SEC. 16. The Attorney General and the Secretary of Defense, jointly, shall make a full and complete study to determine whether, under the laws or practices of any State or States, there are preconditions to voting, which might tend to result in discrimination against citizens serving in the Armed Forces of the United States seeking to vote. Such officials shall, jointly, make a report to the Congress not later than June 30, 1966, containing the results of such study, together with a list of any States in which such preconditions exist, and shall include in such report such recommendations for legislation as they deem advisable to prevent discrimination in voting against citizens serving in the Armed Forces of the United States.

SEC. 17. Nothing in this Act shall be construed to deny, impair, or otherwise adversely affect the right to vote of any person registered to vote under the law of any State or political subdivision.

SEC. 18. There are hereby authorized to be appropriated such sums as are necessary to carry out the provisions of this Act [p*355].

SEC 19. If any provision of this Act or the application thereof to any person or circumstances is held invalid, the remainder of the Act and the application of the provision to other persons not similarly situated or to other circumstances shall not be affected thereby.

Approved August 6, 1965.

CHAPTER 18

Treaty of Paris (September 3, 1783)

Congress of the Confederation

The History*

The American War for Independence (1775–83) was actually a world conflict, involving not only the United States and Great Britain but also France, Spain, and the Netherlands. The peace process brought a vaguely formed, newly born United States into the arena of international diplomacy, playing against the largest, most sophisticated, and most established powers on earth.

The three American negotiators, John Adams, Benjamin Franklin, and John Jay, proved themselves to be masters of the game, outmaneuvering their counterparts and clinging fiercely to the points of national interest that guaranteed a future for the United States. Two crucial provisions of the treaty were British recognition of U.S. independence and the delineation of boundaries that would allow for American western expansion.

The Treaty of Paris of 1783 ended the War of Independence and granted the thirteen colonies political freedom. A preliminary treaty between Great Britain and the United States had been signed in 1782, but the final agreement was not signed until September 3, 1783.

In the final agreement, the British recognized the independence of the United States. The treaty established generous boundaries for the United States; U.S. territory now extended from the Atlantic Ocean to the Mississippi River in the west, and from the Great Lakes and Canada in the north to the 31st parallel in the south. The U.S. fishing fleet was guaranteed access to the fisheries off the coast of Newfoundland with their plentiful supply of cod.

Navigation of the Mississippi River was to be open to both the United States and Great Britain. Creditors of both countries were not to be impeded from collecting their debts, and Congress was to recommend to the states that loyalists to the British cause during the war should be treated fairly and their rights and confiscated property restored.

The treaty is named for the city in which it was negotiated and signed. The last page bears the signatures of David Hartley, who represented Great Britain, and the three American negotiators, who signed their names in alphabetical order.

*Originally published as "Treaty of Paris (1783)," *100 Milestone Documents*, The National Archives, U.S. National Archives and Records Administration, College Park, Maryland, 2009. For additional information see "Treaty of Paris," *Primary Documents in American History*, Library of Congress, Washington, DC, 2009. This agency is listed in the *National Resource Directory* section of this volume.

Many treaty documents, however, can be considered as originals. In this case, for example, the U.S. and British representatives signed at least three originals, two of which are in the holdings of the National Archives. On one of the signed originals the signatures and wax seals are arranged horizontally; on the other they are arranged vertically. In addition, handwritten certified copies were made for the use of Congress. Some online transcriptions of the treaty omit Delaware from the list of the former colonies, but the original text does list Delaware.

The Document

Treaty of Paris

In the name of the most holy and undivided Trinity.

It having pleased the Divine Providence to dispose the hearts of the most serene and most potent Prince George the Third, by the grace of God, king of Great Britain, France, and Ireland, defender of the faith, duke of Brunswick and Lunebourg, arch-treasurer and prince elector of the Holy Roman Empire etc., and of the United States of America, to forget all past misunderstandings and differences that have unhappily interrupted the good correspondence and friendship which they mutually wish to restore, and to establish such a beneficial and satisfactory intercourse, between the two countries upon the ground of reciprocal advantages and mutual convenience as may promote and secure to both perpetual peace and harmony; and having for this desirable end already laid the foundation of peace and reconciliation by the Provisional Articles signed at Paris on the 30th of November 1782, by the commissioners empowered on each part, which articles were agreed to be inserted in and constitute the Treaty of Peace proposed to be concluded between the Crown of Great Britain and the said United States, but which treaty was not

to be concluded until terms of peace should be agreed upon between Great Britain and France and his Britannic Majesty should be ready to conclude such treaty accordingly; and the treaty between Great Britain and France having since been concluded, his Britannic Majesty and the United States of America, in order to carry into full effect the Provisional Articles above mentioned, according to the tenor thereof, have constituted and appointed, that is to say his Britannic Majesty on his part, David Hartley, Esqr., member of the Parliament of Great Britain, and the said United States on their part, John Adams, Esqr., late a commissioner of the United States of America at the court of Versailles, late delegate in Congress from the state of Massachusetts, and chief justice of the said state, and minister plenipotentiary of the said United States to their high mightinesses the States General of the United Netherlands; Benjamin Franklin, Esqr., late delegate in Congress from the state of Pennsylvania, president of the convention of the said state, and minister plenipotentiary from the United States of America at the court of Versailles; John Jay, Esqr., late president of Congress and chief justice of the state of New York, and minister plenipotentiary from the said United States at the court of Madrid; to be plenipotentiaries for the concluding and signing the present definitive treaty; who after having reciprocally communicated their respective full powers have agreed upon and confirmed the following articles.

Article 1:

His Britannic Majesty acknowledges the said United States, viz., New Hampshire, Massachusetts Bay, Rhode Island and Providence Plantations, Connecticut, New York, New Jersey, Pennsylvania, Delaware, Maryland, Virginia, North Carolina, South Carolina and Georgia, to be free sovereign and independent states, that he treats with them as such, and for himself, his heirs, and successors, relinquishes all claims to the government, propriety, and territorial rights of the same and every part thereof.

ARTICLE 2:

And that all disputes which might arise in future on the subject of the boundaries of the said United States may be prevented, it is hereby agreed and declared, that the following are and shall be their boundaries, viz.; from the northwest angle of Nova Scotia, viz., that angle which is formed by a line drawn due north from the source of St. Croix River to the highlands; along the said highlands which divide those rivers that empty themselves into the river St. Lawrence, from those which fall into the Atlantic Ocean, to the northwesternmost head of Connecticut River; thence down along the middle of that river to the forty-fifth degree of north latitude; from thence by a line due west on said latitude until it strikes the river Iroquois or Cataraquy; thence along the middle of said river into Lake Ontario; through the middle of said lake until it strikes the communication by water between that lake and Lake Erie; thence along the middle of said communication into Lake Erie, through the middle of said lake until it arrives at the water communication between that lake and Lake Huron; thence along the middle of said water communication into Lake Huron, thence through the middle of said lake to the water communication between that lake and Lake Superior; thence through Lake Superior northward of the Isles Royal and Phelipeaux to the Long Lake; thence through the middle of said Long Lake and the water communication between it and the Lake of the Woods, to the said Lake of the Woods; thence through the said lake to the most northwesternmost point thereof, and from thence on a due west course to the river Mississippi; thence by a line to be drawn along the middle of the said river Mississippi until it shall intersect the northernmost part of the thirty-first degree of north latitude, South, by a line to be drawn due east from the de-

termination of the line last mentioned in the latitude of thirty-one degrees of the equator, to the middle of the river Apalachicola or Catahouche; thence along the middle thereof to its junction with the Flint River, thence straight to the head of Saint Mary's River; and thence down along the middle of Saint Mary's River to the Atlantic Ocean; east, by a line to be drawn along the middle of the river Saint Croix, from its mouth in the Bay of Fundy to its source, and from its source directly north to the aforesaid highlands which divide the rivers that fall into the Atlantic Ocean from those which fall into the river Saint Lawrence; comprehending all islands within twenty leagues of any part of the shores of the United States, and lying between lines to be drawn due east from the points where the aforesaid boundaries between Nova Scotia on the one part and East Florida on the other shall, respectively, touch the Bay of Fundy and the Atlantic Ocean, excepting such islands as now are or heretofore have been within the limits of the said province of Nova Scotia.

ARTICLE 3:

It is agreed that the people of the United States shall continue to enjoy unmolested the right to take fish of every kind on the Grand Bank and on all the other banks of Newfoundland, also in the Gulf of Saint Lawrence and at all other places in the sea, where the inhabitants of both countries used at any time heretofore to fish. And also that the inhabitants of the United States shall have liberty to take fish of every kind on such part of the coast of Newfoundland as British fishermen shall use, (but not to dry or cure the same on that island) and also on the coasts, bays and creeks of all other of his Britannic Majesty's dominions in America; and that the American fishermen shall have liberty to dry and cure fish in any of the unsettled bays, harbors, and creeks of Nova Scotia, Magdalen Islands, and Labrador, so long as the same shall remain unsettled, but so soon as the same or either of them shall be settled, it shall not be lawful for the said fishermen to dry or cure fish at such settlement without a previous agreement for that purpose with the inhabitants, proprietors, or possessors of the ground.

ARTICLE 4:

It is agreed that creditors on either side shall meet with no lawful impediment to the recovery of the full value in sterling money of all bona fide debts heretofore contracted.

ARTICLE 5:

It is agreed that Congress shall earnestly recommend it to the legislatures of the respective states to provide for the restitution of all estates, rights, and properties, which have been confiscated belonging to real British subjects; and also of the estates, rights, and properties of persons resident in districts in the possession on his Majesty's arms and who have not borne arms against the said United States. And that persons of any other description shall have free liberty to go to any part or parts of any of the thirteen United States and therein to remain twelve months unmolested in their endeavors to obtain the restitution of such of their estates, rights, and properties as may have been confiscated; and that Congress shall also earnestly recommend to the several states a reconsideration and revision of all acts or laws regarding the premises, so as to render the said laws or acts perfectly consistent not only with justice and equity but with that spirit of conciliation which on the return of the blessings of peace should universally prevail. And that Congress shall also earnestly recommend to the several states that the estates, rights, and properties, of such last mentioned persons shall be restored to them, they refunding to any persons who may be now in possession the bona fide price (where any has been given) which such persons may have paid on purchasing any of the said lands, rights, or properties since the confiscation.

And it is agreed that all persons who have any interest in confiscated lands, either by debts, marriage settlements, or otherwise, shall meet with no lawful impediment in the prosecution of their just rights.

ARTICLE 6:

That there shall be no future confiscations made nor any prosecutions commenced against any person or persons for, or by reason of, the part which he or they may have taken in the present war, and that no person shall on that account suffer any future loss or damage, either in his person, liberty, or property; and that those who may be in confinement on such charges at the time of the ratification of the treaty in America shall be immediately set at liberty, and the prosecutions so commenced be discontinued.

ARTICLE 7:

There shall be a firm and perpetual peace between his Britannic Majesty and the said states, and between the subjects of the one and the citizens of the other, wherefore all hostilities both by sea and land shall from henceforth cease. All prisoners on both sides shall be set at liberty, and his Britannic Majesty shall with all convenient speed, and without causing any destruction, or carrying away any Negroes or other property of the American inhabitants, withdraw all his armies, garrisons, and fleets from the said United States, and from every post, place, and harbor within the same; leaving in all fortifications, the American artilery that may be therein; and shall also order and cause all archives, records, deeds, and papers belonging to any of the said states, or their citizens, which in the course of the war may have fallen into the hands of his officers, to be forthwith restored and delivered to the proper states and persons to whom they belong.

ARTICLE 8:

The navigation of the river Mississippi, from its source to the ocean, shall forever remain free and open to the subjects of Great Britain and the citizens of the United States.

ARTICLE 9:

In case it should so happen that any place or territory belonging to Great Britain or to the United States should have been conquered by the arms of either from the other before the arrival of the said *Provisional Articles* in America, it is agreed that the same shall be restored without difficulty and without requiring any compensation.

ARTICLE 10:

The solemn ratifications of the present treaty expedited in good and due form shall be exchanged between the contracting parties in the space of six months or sooner, if possible, to be computed from the day of the signatures of the present treaty. In witness whereof we the undersigned, their ministers plenipotentiary, have in their name and in virtue of our full powers, signed with our hands the present definitive treaty and caused the seals of our arms to be affixed thereto.

Done at Paris, this third day of September in the year of our Lord, one thousand seven hundred and eighty-three.

D. HARTLEY (SEAL)
JOHN ADAMS (SEAL)
B. FRANKLIN (SEAL)
JOHN JAY (SEAL)

CHAPTER 19

Land Ordinance
(May 20, 1785)

Congress of the Confederation

The History*

The Land Ordinance of 1785 was adopted by the United States Congress on May 20, 1785. Under the Articles of Confederation, Congress did not have the power to raise revenue by direct taxation of the inhabitants of the United States. Therefore, the immediate goal of the ordinance was to raise money through the sale of land in the largely unmapped territory west of the original colonies acquired from Britain at the end of the Revolutionary War.

In addition, the act provided for the political organization of these territories. The earlier Ordinance of 1784 called for the land west of the Appalachian Mountains, north of the Ohio River and east of the Mississippi River to be divided into ten separate states. However, it did not define the mechanism by which the land would become states, or how the territories would be governed or settled before they became states. The Ordinance of 1785, along with the Northwest Ordinance of 1787, were intended to address these political needs.

The 1785 ordinance laid the foundations of land policy in the United States of America until passage of the Homestead Act of 1862. The Land Ordinance established the basis for the Public Land Survey System. The initial surveying was performed by Thomas Hutchins. After he died in 1789, responsibility for surveying was transferred to the Surveyor General. Land was to be systematically surveyed into square "townships," six miles (9.656 km) on a side. Each of these townships were subdivided into thirty-six "sections" of one square mile (2.59 km²) or 640 acres. These sections could then be further subdivided for sale to settlers and land speculators.

The ordinance was also significant for establishing a mechanism for funding public education. Section 16 in each township was reserved for the maintenance of public schools. Many schools today are still located in section sixteen of their respective townships, although a great many of the school sections were sold to raise money for public education. In theory, the federal government also reserved sections 8, 11, 26 and 29 to com-

---

*Originally published as "Land Ordinance of 1785," *Wikipedia*, Wikimedia Foundation, Inc., San Francisco, California, November 2009. For additional information see "The New Nation, 1783–1815: Policies and Problems of the Confederated Government," *American Memory Timeline*, Library of Congress, Washington, DC, 2007. This agency is listed in the *National Resource Directory* section of this volume.

pensate veterans of the Revolutionary War, but examination of property abstracts in Ohio indicates that this was not uniformly practiced. The Point of Beginning for the 1785 survey was where Ohio (as the easternmost part of the Northwest Territory), Pennsylvania and Virginia (now West Virginia) met, on the north shore of the Ohio River near East Liverpool, Ohio. There is a historical marker just north of the site, at the state line where Ohio Route 39 becomes Pennsylvania Route 68.

The Document

Land Ordinance

An Ordinance for ascertaining the mode of disposing of Lands in the Western Territory.

Be it ordained by the United States in Congress assembled, that the territory ceded by individual States to the United States, which has been purchased of the Indian inhabitants, shall be disposed of in the following manner:

A surveyor from each state shall be appointed by Congress, or a committee of the States, who shall take an Oath for the faithful discharge of his duty, before the Geographer of the United States, who is hereby empowered and directed to administer the same; and the like oath shall be administered to each chain carrier, by the surveyor under whom he acts.

The Geographer, under whose direction the surveyors shall act, shall occasionally form such regulations for their conduct, as he shall deem necessary; and shall have authority to suspend them for misconduct in Office, and shall make report of the same to Congress or to the Committee of the States; and he shall make report in case of sickness, death, or resignation of any surveyor.

The Surveyors, as they are respectively qualified, shall proceed to divide the said territory into townships of six miles square, by lines running due north and south, and others crossing these at right angles, as near as may be, unless where the boundaries of the late Indian purchases may render the same impracticable, and then they shall depart from this rule no farther than such particular circumstances may require; and each surveyor shall be allowed and paid at the rate of two dollars for every mile, in length, he shall run, including the wages of chain carriers, markers, and every other expense attending the same.

The first line, running north and south as aforesaid, shall begin on the river Ohio, at a point that shall be found to be due north from the western termination of a line, which has been run as the southern boundary of the state of Pennsylvania; and the first line, running east and west, shall begin at the same point, and shall extend throughout the whole territory. Provided, that nothing herein shall be construed, as fixing the western boundary of the state of Pennsylvania. The geographer shall designate the townships, or fractional parts of townships, by numbers progressively from south to north; always beginning each range with number one; and the ranges shall be distinguished by their progressive numbers to the westward. The first range, extending from the Ohio to the lake Erie, being marked number one. The geographer shall personally attend to the running of the first east and west line; and shall take the latitude of the extremes of the first north and south line, and of the mouths of the principal rivers.

The lines shall be measured with a chain; shall be plainly marked by chaps on the trees and exactly described on a plat; whereon shall be noted by the surveyor, at their proper distances, all mines, salt springs, salt licks and mill seats, that shall come to his knowledge, and all water courses, mountains and other remarkable and permanent things, over and near which such lines shall pass, and also the quality of the lands.

The plats of the townships respectively, shall be marked by subdivisions into lots of one mile square, or 640 acres, in the same direction as the external lines, and numbered from 1 to 36; always beginning the succeeding range of the lots with the number next to that with which the preceding one concluded. And where, from the causes before mentioned, only a fractional part of a township shall be surveyed, the lots protracted thereon, shall bear the same numbers as if the township had been entire. And the surveyors, in running the external lines of the townships, shall, at the interval of every mile, mark corners for the lots which are adjacent, always designating the same in a different manner from those of the townships.

The geographer and surveyors shall pay the utmost attention to the variation of the magnetic needle; and shall run and note all lines by the true meridian, certifying, with every plat, what was the variation at the times of running the lines thereon noted.

As soon as seven ranges of townships, and fractional parts of townships, in the direction from south to north, shall have been surveyed, the geographer shall transmit plats thereof to the board of treasury, who shall record the same with the report, in well bound books to be kept for that purpose. And the geographer shall make similar returns, from time to time, of every seven ranges as they may be surveyed. The Secretary at War shall have recourse thereto, and shall take by lot therefrom, a number of townships, and fractional parts of townships, as well from those to be sold entire as from those to be sold in lots, as will be equal to one seventh part of the whole of such seven ranges, as nearly as may be, for the use of the late continental army; and he shall make a similar draught, from time to time, until a sufficient quantity is drawn to satisfy the same, to be applied in manner hereinafter directed. The board of treasury shall, from time to time, cause the remaining numbers, as well those to be sold entire, as those to be sold in

lots, to be drawn for, in the name of the thirteen states respectively, according to the quotas in the last preceding requisition on all the states; provided, that in case more land than its proportion is allotted for sale, in any state, at any distribution, a deduction be made therefore at the next.

The board of treasury shall transmit a copy of the original plats, previously noting thereon, the townships, and fractional parts of townships, which shall have fallen to the several states, by the distribution aforesaid, to the Commissioners of the loan office of the several states, who, after giving notice of not less than two nor more than six months by causing advertisements to be posted up at the court houses, or other noted places in every county, and to be inserted in one newspaper, published in the states of their residence respectively, shall proceed to sell the townships, or fractional parts of townships, at public vendue, in the following manner, viz.: The township, or fractional part of a township, N 1, in the first range, shall be sold entire; and N 2, in the same range, by lots; and thus in alternate order through the whole of the first range. The township, or fractional part of a township, N 1, in the second range, shall be sold by lots; and N 2, in the same range, entire; and so in alternate order through the whole of the second range; and the third range shall be sold in the same manner as the first, and the fourth in the same manner as the second, and thus alternately throughout all the ranges; provided, that none of the lands, within the said territory, be sold under the price of one dollar the acre, to be paid in specie, or loan office certificates, reduced to specie value, by the scale of depreciation, or certificates of liquidated debts of the United States, including interest, besides the expense of the survey and other charges thereon, which are hereby rated at thirty six dollars the township, in specie or certificates as aforesaid, and so in the same proportion for a fractional part of a township, or of a lot, to be paid at the time of sales; on failure of which payment, the said lands shall again be offered for sale.

There shall be reserved for the United States out of every township, the four lots, being numbered 8, 11, 26, 29, and out of every fractional part of a township, so many lots of the same numbers as shall be found thereon, for future sale. There shall be reserved the lot N 16, of every township, for the maintenance of public schools, within the said township; also one third part of all gold, silver, lead and copper mines, to be sold, or otherwise disposed of as Congress shall hereafter direct.

When any township, or fractional part of a township, shall have been sold as aforesaid, and the money or certificates received therefore, the loan officer shall deliver a deed in the following terms:

The United States of America to all to whom these presents shall come, greeting:

Know ye, That for the consideration of _____ dollars we have granted, and hereby do grant and confirm _____ unto the township, (or fractional part of a township, as the case may be) numbered _____ in the range _____ excepting therefrom, and reserving one third part of all gold, silver, lead and copper mines within the same; and the lots Ns 8, 11, 26, and 29, for future sale or disposition, and the lot N 16, for the maintenance of public schools. To have to the said _____ his heirs and assigns for ever; (or if more than one purchaser to the said _____ their heirs and assigns for ever as tenants in Common.) In witness whereof, (A.B.) Commissioner of the loan office, in the State of _____ hath, in conformity to the Ordinance passed by the United States in Congress assembled, the twentieth day of May, in the year of our Lord one thousand seven hundred and eighty five, hereunto set his hand and affixed his seal this _____ day of _____ in the year of our Lord _____ and of the independence of the United States of America.

And when any township, or fractional part of a township, shall be sold by lots as aforesaid, the Commissioner of the loan office shall deliver a deed therefore in the following form:

The United States of America to all to whom these presents shall come, greeting:

Know ye, That for the consideration of _____ dollars, we have granted, and hereby do grant and confirm unto _____ the lot (or lots, as the case may be, in the township or fractional part of the township, as the case may be) numbered _____ in the range _____ excepting and reserving one third part of all gold, silver, lead and copper mines within the same, for future sale or disposition. To have to the said _____ his heirs and assigns for ever; (or if more than one purchaser, to the said _____ their heirs and assigns for ever as tenants in common). In witness whereof, (A.B.) Commissioner of the continental loan office in the state of _____ hath, in conformity to the Ordinance passed by the United States in Congress assembled, the twentieth day of May, in the year of our Lord 1785, hereunto set his hand and affixed his seal, this _____ day of _____ in the year of our Lord _____ and of the independence of the United States of America.

Which deeds shall be recorded in proper books by the commissioner of the loan office and shall be certified to have been recorded, previous to their being delivered to the purchaser, and shall be good and valid to convey the lands in the same described.

The commissioners of the loan offices respectively, shall transmit to the board of treasury every three months, an account of the townships, fractional parts of townships, and lots committed to their charge; specifying therein the names of the persons to whom sold, and the sums of money or certificates received for the same; and shall cause all certificates by them received, to be struck through with a circular punch; and they shall be duly charged in the books of the treasury, with the amount of the moneys or certificates, distinguishing the same, by them received as aforesaid.

If any township, or fractional part of a township or lot, remains unsold for eighteen months after the plat shall have been received, by the commissioners of the loan office, the same shall be returned to the board of treasury, and shall be sold in such manner as Congress may hereafter direct.

And whereas Congress by their resolutions of September 16 and 18 in the year 1776, and the 12th of August, 1780, stipulated grants of land to certain officers and soldiers of the late continental army, and by the resolution of the 22d September, 1780, stipulated grants of land to certain officers in the hospital department of the late continental army; for complying therefore with such engagements, Be it ordained, That the secretary at war, from the returns in his office, or such other evidence as the nature of the case may admit, determine who are the objects of the above resolutions and engagements, and the quantity of land to which such persons or their representatives are respectively entitled, and cause the townships, or fractional parts of townships, hereinbefore reserved for the use of the late continental army, to be drawn for in such manner as he shall deem expedient, to answer the purpose of an impartial distribution. He shall, from time to time, transmit certificates to the commissioners of the loan offices of the different states, to the lines of which the military claimants have respectively belonged, specifying the name and rank of the party, the terms of his engagement and time of his service, and the division, brigade, regiment or company to which he belonged, the quantity of land he is entitled to, and the township, or fractional part of a township, and range out of which his portion is to be taken.

The commissioners of the loan offices shall execute deeds for such undivided proportions in manner and form herein beforementioned, varying only in such a degree as to make the same conformable to the certificate from the Secretary at War.

Where any military claimants of bounty in land shall not have belonged to the line of any particular state, similar certificates shall be sent to the board of treasury, who shall execute deeds to the parties for the same.

The Secretary at War, from the proper returns, shall transmit to the board of treasury, a certificate specifying the name and rank of the several claimants of the hospital department of the late continental army, together with the quantity of land each claimant is entitled to, and the township, or fractional part of a township, and range out of which his portion is to be taken; and thereupon the board of treasury shall proceed to execute deeds to such claimants.

The board of treasury, and the commissioners of the loan offices in the states, shall, within 18 months, return receipts to the secretary at war, for all deeds which have been delivered, as also all the original deeds which remain in their hands for want of applicants, having been first recorded; which deeds so returned, shall be preserved in the office, until the parties or their representatives require the same.

And be it further Ordained, That three townships adjacent to lake Erie be reserved, to be hereafter disposed of by Congress, for the use of the officers, men and others, refugees from Canada, and the refugees from Nova Scotia, who are or may be entitled to grants of land under resolutions of Congress now existing, or which may hereafter be made respecting them, and for such other purposes as Congress may hereafter direct. And be it further Ordained, That the towns of Gnadenhutten, Schoenbrun and Salem, on the Muskingum, and so much of the lands adjoining to the said towns, with the buildings and improvements thereon, shall be reserved for the sole use of the Christian Indians, who were formerly settled there, or the remains of that society, as may, in the judgment of the geographer, be sufficient for them to cultivate.

Saving and reserving always, to all officers and soldiers entitled to lands on the northwest side of the Ohio, by donation or bounty from the commonwealth of Virginia, and to all persons claiming under them, all rights to which they are so entitled, under the deed of cession executed by the delegates for the state of Virginia, on the first day of March, 1784, and the act of Congress accepting the same: and to the end that the said rights may be fully and effectually secured, according to the true intent and meaning of the said deed of cession and act aforesaid, Be it Ordained, that no part of the land included between the rivers called little Miami and Sciota, on the northwest side of the river Ohio, be sold, or in any manner alienated, until there shall first have been laid off and appropriated for the said Officers and Soldiers, and persons claiming under them, the lands they are entitled to, agreeably to the said deed of cession and act of Congress accepting the same.

Done by the United States in Congress assembled, the 20th day of May, in the year of our Lord 1785, and of our sovereignty and independence the ninth.

Charles Thomson, *Secretary*
Richard H. Lee, *President*

CHAPTER 20

Northwest Ordinance (July 13, 1787)

Congress of the Confederation

The History*

The Northwest Ordinance (formally An Ordinance for the Government of the Territory of the United States, North-West of the River Ohio, and also known as the Freedom Ordinance) was an act of the Congress of the Confederation of the United States. The Ordinance unanimously passed on July 13, 1787. The primary effect of the ordinance was the creation of the Northwest Territory as the first organized territory of the United States out of the region south of the Great Lakes, north and west of the Ohio River, and east of the Mississippi River. On August 7, 1789, the U.S. Congress affirmed the Ordinance with slight modifications under the Constitution.

Arguably the single most important piece of legislation passed by members of the earlier Continental Congresses other than the Declaration of Independence, it established the precedent by which the United States would expand westward across North America by the admission of new states, rather than by the expansion of existing states.

The act also through the most empowered recognition of the importance of education and its encouragement provided for the concept of a sponsored higher education. The Morrill Act of 1862 and the Morrill Act of 1890 would follow and forever change the relationship of higher education and government. Higher education would become a tool for a good government and through the Hatch Act of 1887, an equal partner in supporting the growing needs of the expanding agrarian society.

Further, the banning of slavery in the territory had the effect of establishing the Ohio River as the boundary between free and slave territory in the region between the Appalachian Mountains and the Mississippi River. This division helped set the stage for the balancing act between free and slave states that was the basis of a critical political question in American politics in the 19th century until the Civil War.

The passage of the ordinance followed the relinquishing of all claims by the states over the territory, which was to be administered directly by Congress, with the intent of

*Originally published as "Northwest Ordinance," *Wikipedia*, Wikimedia Foundation, Inc., San Francisco, California, November 2009. For additional information see "Northwest Ordinance (1787)," *100 Milestone Documents*, U.S. National Archives and Records Administration, College Park, Maryland, 2008. This agency is listed in the *National Resource Directory* section of this volume.

eventual admission of newly created states from the territory. The legislation was revolutionary in that it established the precedent for lands to be administered by the central government, albeit temporarily, rather than underneath the jurisdiction of particular states.

The most significant intended purpose of the legislation was its mandate for the creation of new states from the region, once a population of 60,000 had been achieved within a particular territory. The actual legal mechanism of the admission of new states was established in the Enabling Act of 1802. The first state created from the territory was Ohio, in 1803.

The Northwest Ordinance, along with the Land Ordinance of 1785, laid the legal and cultural groundwork for Midwestern (and subsequently, western) development. Significantly, the free state legal philosophies of both Abraham Lincoln and Salmon P. Chase (Chief Justice, Senator, and early Ohio law author) were derived from the Northwest Ordinance.

The Document

Northwest Ordinance

An Ordinance for the government of the Territory of the United States northwest of the River Ohio.

Section 1. Be it ordained by the United States in Congress assembled, That the said territory, for the purposes of temporary government, be one district, subject, however, to be divided into two districts, as future circumstances may, in the opinion of Congress, make it expedient.

Sec. 2. Be it ordained by the authority aforesaid, That the estates, both of resident and nonresident proprietors in the said territory, dying intestate, shall descent to, and be distributed among their children, and the descendants of a deceased child, in equal parts; the descendants of a deceased child or grandchild to take the share of their deceased parent in equal parts among them: And where there shall be no children or descendants, then in equal parts to the next of kin in equal degree; and among collaterals, the children of a deceased brother or sister of the intestate shall have, in equal parts among them, their deceased parents' share; and there shall in no case be a distinction between kindred of the whole and half blood; saving, in all cases, to the widow of the intestate her third part of the real estate for life, and one third part of the personal estate; and this law relative to descents and dower, shall remain in full force until altered by the legislature of the district. And until the governor and judges shall adopt laws as hereinafter mentioned, estates in the said territory may be devised or bequeathed by wills in writing, signed and sealed by him or her in whom the estate may be (being of full age), and attested by three witnesses; and real estates may be conveyed by lease and release, or bargain and sale, signed, sealed and delivered by the person being of full age, in whom the estate may be, and attested by two witnesses, provided such wills be duly proved, and such conveyances be acknowledged, or the execution thereof duly proved, and be recorded within one year after proper magistrates, courts, and registers shall be appointed for that purpose; and personal property may be transferred by delivery; saving, however to the French and Canadian inhabitants, and other settlers of the Kaskaskies, St. Vincents and the neighboring villages who have heretofore professed themselves citizens of Virginia, their laws and customs now in force among them, relative to the descent and conveyance, of property.

Sec. 3. Be it ordained by the authority aforesaid, That there shall be appointed from time to time by Congress, a governor, whose commission shall continue in force for the term of three years, unless sooner revoked by Congress; he shall reside in the district, and have a freehold estate therein in 1,000 acres of land, while in the exercise of his office.

Sec. 4. There shall be appointed from time to time by Congress, a secretary, whose commission shall continue in force for four years unless sooner revoked; he shall reside in the district, and have a freehold estate therein in 500 acres of land, while in the exercise of his office. It shall be his duty to keep and preserve the acts and laws passed by the legislature, and the public records of the district, and the proceedings of the governor in his executive department, and transmit authentic copies of such acts and proceedings, every six months, to the Secretary of Congress: There shall also be appointed a court to consist of three judges, any two of whom to form a court, who shall have a common law jurisdiction, and reside in the district, and have each therein a freehold estate in 500 acres of land while in the exercise of their offices; and their commissions shall continue in force during good behavior.

Sec. 5. The governor and judges, or a majority of them, shall adopt and publish in the district such laws of the original States, criminal and civil, as may be necessary and best suited to the circumstances of the district, and report them to Congress from time to time: which laws shall be in force in the district until the organization of the General Assembly therein, unless disapproved of by Congress; but afterwards the Legislature shall have authority to alter them as they shall think fit.

Sec. 6. The governor, for the time being, shall be commander in chief of the militia, appoint and commission all officers in the same below the rank of general officers; all general officers shall be appointed and commissioned by Congress.

Sec. 7. Previous to the organization of the general assembly, the governor shall appoint such magistrates and other civil officers in each county or township, as he shall find necessary for the preservation of the peace and good order in the same: After the general assembly shall be organized, the powers and duties of the magistrates and other civil officers shall be regulated and defined by the said assembly; but all magistrates and other civil officers not herein otherwise directed, shall during the continuance of this temporary government, be appointed by the governor.

Sec. 8. For the prevention of crimes and injuries, the laws to be adopted or made shall have force in all parts of the district, and for the execution of process, criminal and civil, the governor shall make proper divisions thereof; and he shall proceed from time to time as circumstances may require, to lay out the parts of the district in which the Indian titles shall have been extinguished, into counties and townships, subject, however, to such alterations as may thereafter be made by the legislature.

Sec. 9. So soon as there shall be five thousand free male inhabitants of full age in the district, upon giving proof thereof to the governor, they shall receive authority, with time and place, to elect a representative from their counties or townships to represent them in the general assembly: Provided, That, for every five hundred free male inhabitants, there shall be one representative, and so on progressively with the number of free male inhabitants shall the right of representation increase, until the number of representatives shall amount to twenty five; after which, the number and proportion of representatives shall be regulated by the legislature: Provided, That no person be eligible or qualified to act as a representative unless he shall have been a citizen of one of the United States three years, and be a resident in the district, or unless he shall have resided in the district three years; and, in either case, shall likewise hold in his own right, in fee simple, two hundred acres of land within the same; Provided, also, That a freehold in fifty acres of land in the district, having been a citizen of one of the states, and being resident in the district, or the like freehold and two years residence in the district, shall be necessary to qualify a man as an elector of a representative.

Sec. 10. The representatives thus elected, shall serve for the term of two years; and, in case of the death of a representative, or removal from office, the governor shall issue a writ to the county or township for which he was a member, to elect another in his stead, to serve for the residue of the term.

Sec. 11. The general assembly or legislature shall consist of the governor, legislative council, and a house of representatives. The Legislative Council shall consist of five members, to continue in office five years, unless sooner removed by Congress; any three of whom to be a quorum: and the members of the Council shall be nominated and appointed in the following manner, to wit: As soon as representatives shall be elected, the Governor shall appoint a time and place for them to meet together; and, when met, they shall nominate ten persons, residents in the district, and each possessed of a freehold in five hundred acres of land, and return their names to Congress; five of whom Congress shall appoint and commission to serve as aforesaid; and, whenever a vacancy shall happen in the council, by death or removal from office, the house of representatives shall nominate two persons, qualified as aforesaid, for each vacancy, and return their names to Congress; one of whom congress shall appoint and commission for the residue of the term. And every five years, four months at least before the expiration of the time of service of the members of council, the said house shall nominate ten persons, qualified as aforesaid, and return their names to Congress; five of whom Congress shall appoint and commission to serve as members of the council five years, unless sooner removed. And the governor, legislative council, and house of representatives, shall have authority to make laws in all cases, for the good government of the district, not repugnant to the principles and articles in this ordinance established and declared. And all bills, having passed by a majority in the house, and by a majority in the council, shall be referred to the governor for his assent; but no bill, or legislative act whatever, shall be of any force without his assent. The governor shall have power to convene, prorogue, and dissolve the general assembly, when, in his opinion, it shall be expedient.

Sec. 12. The governor, judges, legislative council, secretary, and such other officers as Congress shall appoint in the district, shall take an oath or affirmation of fidelity and of office; the governor before the president of congress, and all other officers before the Governor. As soon as a legislature shall be formed in the district, the council and house assembled in one room, shall have authority, by joint ballot, to elect a delegate to Congress, who shall have a seat in Congress, with a right of debating but not voting during this temporary government.

Sec. 13. And, for extending the fundamental principles of civil and religious liberty, which form the basis whereon these republics, their laws and constitutions are erected; to fix and establish those principles as the basis of all laws, constitutions, and governments, which forever hereafter shall be formed in the said territory: to provide also for the establishment of States, and permanent government therein, and for their admission to a share in the federal councils on an equal footing with the original States, at as early periods as may be consistent with the general interest:

Sec. 14. It is hereby ordained and declared by the authority aforesaid, That the following articles shall be considered as articles of compact between the original States and the people and States in the said territory and forever remain unalterable, unless by common consent, to wit:

Art. 1. No person, demeaning himself in a peaceable and orderly manner, shall ever be molested on account of his mode of worship or religious sentiments, in the said territory.

Art. 2. The inhabitants of the said territory shall always be entitled to the benefits of the writ of habeas corpus, and of the trial by jury; of a proportionate representation of the people in the legislature; and of judicial proceedings according to the course of the common law. All persons shall be bailable, unless for capital offenses, where the proof shall be evident or the presumption great. All fines shall be moderate; and no cruel or unusual punishments shall be inflicted. No man shall be deprived of his liberty or property, but by the judgment of his peers or the law of the land; and, should the public exigencies make it necessary, for the common preservation, to take any person's property, or to demand his particular services, full compensation shall be made for the same. And, in the just preservation of rights and property, it is understood and declared, that no law ought ever to be made, or have force in the said territory, that shall, in any manner whatever, interfere with or affect private contracts or engagements, *bona fide*, and without fraud, previously formed.

Art. 3. Religion, morality, and knowledge, being necessary to good government and the happiness of mankind, schools and the means of education shall forever be encouraged. The utmost good faith shall always be observed towards the Indians; their lands and property shall never be taken from them without their consent; and, in their property, rights, and liberty, they shall never be invaded or disturbed, unless in just and lawful wars authorized by Congress; but laws founded in justice and humanity, shall from time to time be made for preventing wrongs being done to them, and for preserving peace and friendship with them.

Art. 4. The said territory, and the States which may be formed therein, shall forever remain a part of this Confederacy of the United States of America, subject to the Articles of Confederation, and to such alterations therein as shall be constitutionally made; and to all the acts and ordinances of the United States in Congress assembled, conformable thereto. The inhabitants and settlers in the said territory shall be subject to pay a part of the federal debts contracted or to be contracted, and a proportional part of the expenses of government, to be apportioned on them by Congress according to the same common rule and measure by which apportionments thereof shall be made on the other States; and the taxes for paying their proportion shall be laid and levied by the authority and direction of the legislatures of the district or districts, or new States, as in the original States, within the time agreed upon by the United States in Congress assembled. The legislatures of those districts or new States, shall never interfere with the primary disposal of the soil by the United States in Congress assembled, nor with any regulations Congress may find necessary for securing the title in such soil to the bona fide purchasers. No tax shall be imposed on lands the property of the United States; and, in no case, shall nonresident proprietors be taxed higher than residents. The navigable waters leading into the Mississippi and St. Lawrence, and the carrying places between the same, shall be common highways and forever free, as well to the inhabitants of the said territory as to the citizens of the United States, and those of any other States that may be admitted into the confederacy, without any tax, impost, or duty therefor.

Art. 5. There shall be formed in the said territory, not less than three nor more than five States; and the boundaries of the States, as soon as Virginia shall alter her act of cession, and consent to the same, shall become fixed and established as follows, to wit: The western State in the said territory, shall be bounded by the Mississippi, the Ohio, and Wabash Rivers; a direct line drawn from the Wabash and Post Vincents, due North, to the territorial line between the United States and Canada; and, by the said territorial line, to the Lake of the Woods and Mississippi. The middle State shall be bounded by the said direct line, the Wabash from Post Vincents to the Ohio, by the Ohio, by a direct line, drawn due north from the mouth of the Great Miami, to the said territorial line, and by the said territorial line. The eastern State shall be bounded by the last mentioned direct line, the Ohio, Pennsylvania, and the said territorial line: *Provided, however*, and it is further understood and declared, that the boundaries of these three States shall be subject so far to be altered, that, if Congress shall hereafter find it expedient, they shall have authority to form one or two States in that part of the said territory which lies north of an east and west line drawn through the southerly bend or extreme of Lake Michigan. And, whenever any of the said States shall have sixty thousand free inhabitants therein, such State shall be admitted, by its delegates, into the Congress of the United States, on an equal footing with the original States in all respects whatever, and shall be at liberty to form a permanent constitution and State government: Provided, the constitution and government so to be formed, shall be republican, and in conformity to the principles contained in these articles; and, so far as it can be consistent with the general interest of the confederacy, such admission shall be allowed at an earlier period, and when there may be a less number of free inhabitants in the State than sixty thousand.

Art. 6. There shall be neither slavery nor involuntary servitude in the said territory, otherwise than in the punishment of crimes whereof the party shall have been duly convicted: Provided, always, That any person escaping into the same, from whom labor or service is lawfully claimed in any one of the original States, such fugitive may be lawfully reclaimed and conveyed to the person claiming his or her labor or service as aforesaid.

Be it ordained by the authority aforesaid, That the resolutions of the 23rd of April, 1784, relative to the subject of this ordinance, be, and the same are hereby repealed and declared null and void.

Done by the United States, in Congress assembled, the 13th day of July, in the year of our Lord 1787, and of their sovereignty and independence the twelfth.

CHAPTER 21

Louisiana Purchase Treaty (April 30, 1803)

United States Congress

The History*

The story of the way in which the United States acquired Louisiana is complicated, involving power, politics, intrigue, and suspicion. It also reveals the foresight of Thomas Jefferson, who considered the purchase as one of his greatest achievements.

At the end of the French and Indian Wars in 1763, France lost all of its possessions in North America, dashing hopes of a colonial empire. This empire was centered on the Caribbean island of Santo Domingo and its lucrative cash crop of sugar. The French territory called Louisiana, extending from New Orleans up the Missouri River to modern-day Montana, was intended as a granary for this empire and produced flour, salt, lumber, and food for the sugar islands. By the terms of the 1763 Treaty of Fontainbleau, however, Louisiana west of the Mississippi was ceded to Spain, while the victorious British received the eastern portion of the huge colony.

When the United States won its independence from Great Britain in 1783, one of its major concerns was having a European power on its western boundary, and the need for unrestricted access to the Mississippi River. As American settlers pushed west, they found that the Appalachian Mountains provided a barrier to shipping goods eastward. The easiest way to ship produce was to build a flatboat and float down the Ohio and Mississippi Rivers to the port of New Orleans, from which goods could be put on ocean-going vessels. The problem with this route was that the Spanish owned both sides of the Mississippi below Natchez.

In 1795 the United States negotiated the Pinckney Treaty with Spain, which provided the right of navigation on the river and the right of deposit of U.S. goods at the port of New Orleans. The treaty was to remain in effect for three years, with the possibility of renewal. By 1802, U.S. farmers, businessmen, trappers and lumbermen were bringing over $1 million worth of produce through New Orleans each year. Spanish officials were becoming concerned, as U.S. settlement moved closer to their territory. Spain was eager to divest itself of Louisiana, which was a drain on

*Originally published as "The United States Takes Possession of the Louisiana Territory," *The Lewis and Clark Journey of Discovery,* National Park Service, U.S. Department of the Interior, Washington, DC, May 2007. For additional information see "Louisiana Purchase," *The Lewis and Clark Journey of Discovery,* National Park Service, U.S. Department of the Interior, Washington, DC, 2008. This agency is listed in the *National Resource Directory* section of this volume.

its financial resources. On October 1, 1800, Napoleon Bonaparte, First Consul of France, concluded the Treaty of San Ildefonso with Spain, which returned Louisiana to French ownership in exchange for a Spanish kingdom in Italy. Napoleon's ambitions in Louisiana involved the creation of a new empire centered on the Caribbean sugar trade. By terms of the Treaty of Ameins of 1800, Great Britain returned ownership of the islands of Martinique and Guadaloupe to the French. Napoleon looked upon Louisiana as a depot for these sugar islands, and as a buffer to U.S. settlement. In October of 1801 he sent a large military force to retake the important island of Santa Domingo, lost in a slave revolt in the 1790s.

Thomas Jefferson, third President of the United States, was disturbed by Napoleon's plans to re-establish French colonies in America. With the possession of New Orleans, Napoleon could close the Mississippi to U.S. commerce at any time. Jefferson authorized Robert R. Livingston, U.S. Minister to France, to negotiate for the purchase for up to $2 million of the City of New Orleans, portions of the east bank of the Mississippi, and free navigation of the river for U.S. commerce.

An official transfer of Louisiana to French ownership had not yet taken place, and Napoleon's deal with the Spanish was a poorly kept secret of the frontier. On October 18, 1802, however, a strange thing happened. Juan Ventura Moralis, Acting Intendant of Louisiana, made public the intention of Spain to revoke the right of deposit at New Orleans for all cargo from the United States. The closure of this vital port to the United States caused anger and consternation, and commerce in the west was virtually blockaded. Historians believe that the revocation of the right of deposit was prompted by abuses of the Americans, particularly smuggling, and not by French intrigues as was believed at the time. President Jefferson ignored public pressure for war with France, and appointed James Monroe special envoy to Napoleon, to assist in obtaining New Orleans for the United States. Jefferson boosted the authorized expenditure of funds to $10 million.

Meanwhile, Napoleon's plans in the Caribbean were being frustrated by Toussaint L'Ouverture, his army of former slaves, and yellow fever. During ten months of fierce fighting on Santo Domingo, France lost more than 40,000 soldiers. Without Santo Domingo Napoleon's colonial ambitions for a French empire were foiled in North America. Louisiana would be useless as a granary without sugar islanders to feed. Napoleon also considered the temper of the United States, where sentiment was growing against France and strong ties with Great Britain were being considered. Spain's refusal to sell Florida was the last straw, and Napoleon turned his attention once more to Europe; the sale of the now-useless Louisiana would supply needed funds to wage war there. Napoleon directed his ministers, Talleyrand and Barbé-Marbois, to offer the entire Louisiana territory to the United States — and quickly.

On April 11, 1803, Talleyrand asked Robert Livingston how much the United States was prepared to pay for Louisiana. Livingston was confused, as his instructions only covered the purchase of New Orleans and the immediate area, not the entire Louisiana territory. James Monroe agreed with Livingston that Napoleon might withdraw this offer at any time. To wait for approval from President Jefferson might take months, so Livingston and Monroe decided to open negotiations immediately. By April 30, they closed a deal for the purchase of the entire 828,000 square mile Louisiana territory for 60 million Francs (approximately $15 million). Part of this sum was used to forgive debts owed by France to the United States. The payment was made in United States bonds, which Napoleon sold at face value to the Dutch firm of Hope and Company, and the British banking house of Baring, at a discount of 87½ per each $100 unit. As a result, Napoleon received only $8,831,250 in cash for Louisiana. Dutiful banker Alexander Baring conferred with Marbois in Paris, shuttled to the United States to pick up the bonds, took them to Britain, and returned to France with the money — and Napoleon used these funds to wage war against Baring's own country!

When news of the purchase reached the United States, President Jefferson was surprised. He had authorized the expenditure of $10 million for a port city, and instead received treaties committing the government to spend $15 million on a land package which would double the size of the country. Jefferson's political opponents in the Federalist Party argued that the Louisiana purchase was a worthless desert, and that the Constitution did not provide for the acquisition of new land or negotiating treaties without the consent of the Senate. What really worried the opposition was the new states which would inevitably be carved from the Louisiana territory, strengthening Western and Southern interests in Congress, and further reducing the influence of New England Federalists in national affairs. President Jefferson was an enthusiastic supporter of westward expansion, and held firm in his support for the treaty. Despite Federalist objections, the U.S. Senate ratified the Louisiana treaty in the autumn of 1803.

A transfer ceremony was held in New Orleans on November 29, 1803. Since the Louisiana territory had never officially been turned over to the French, the Spanish took down their flag, and the French raised theirs. The following day, General James Wilkinson accepted possession of New Orleans for the United States. A similar ceremony was held in St. Louis on March 9, 1804, when a French tricolor was raised near the river, replacing the Spanish national flag. The following day, Captain Amos Stoddard of the First U.S. Artillery marched his troops into town and ran the stars and stripes up the fort's flagpole. The Louisiana territory was officially trans-ferred to the United States government, represented by Meriwether Lewis.

The Louisiana Territory, purchased for less than 5 cents an acre, was one of Thomas Jefferson's greatest contributions to his country. Louisiana doubled the size of the United States literally overnight, without a war or the loss of a single American life, and set a precedent for the purchase of territory. It opened the way for the eventual expansion of the United States across the continent to the Pacific, and its consequent rise to the status of world power. International affairs in the Caribbean and Napoleon's hunger for cash to support his war efforts were the background for a glorious achievement of Thomas Jefferson's presidency, new lands, and new opportunities for the nation.

The Document

Louisiana Purchase Treaty

TREATY BETWEEN THE UNITED STATES OF AMERICA AND THE FRENCH REPUBLIC

The President of the United States of America and the First Consul of the French Republic in the name of the French People desiring to remove all Source of misunderstanding relative to objects of discussion mentioned in the Second and fifth articles of the Convention of the 8th Vendémiaire on 9/30 September 1800 relative to the rights claimed by the United States in virtue of the Treaty concluded at Madrid the 27 of October 1795, between His Catholic Majesty & the Said United States, & willing to Strengthen the union and friendship which at the time of the Said Convention was happily reestablished between the two nations have respectively named their Plenipotentiaries to wit The President of the United States, by and with the advice and consent of the Senate of the Said States; Robert R. Livingston Minister Plenipotentiary of the United States and James Monroe Minister Plenipotentiary and Envoy extraordinary of the Said States near the Government of the French Republic; And the First Consul in the name of the French people, Citizen Francis Barbé Marbois Minister of the public treasury who after having respectively exchanged their full powers have agreed to the following Articles.

Article I

Whereas by the Article the third of the Treaty concluded at St. Ildefonso the 9th Vendémiaire on 1st October 1800 between the First Consul of the French Republic and his Catholic Majesty it was agreed as follows.

"His Catholic Majesty promises and engages on his part to cede to the French Republic six months after the full and entire execution of the conditions and Stipulations herein relative to his Royal Highness the Duke of Parma, the Colony or Province of Louisiana with the Same extent that it now has in the hand of Spain, & that it had when France possessed it; and Such as it Should be after the Treaties subsequently entered into between Spain and other States."

And whereas in pursuance of the Treaty and particularly of the third article the French Republic has an incontestible title to the domain and to the possession of the said Territory — The First Consul of the French Republic desiring to give to the United States a strong proof of his friendship doth hereby cede to the United States in the name of the French Republic for ever and in full Sovereignty the said territory with all its rights and appurtenances as fully and in the Same manner as they have been acquired by the French Republic in virtue of the above mentioned Treaty concluded with his Catholic Majesty.

Art: II

In the cession made by the preceeding article are included the adjacent Islands belonging to Louisiana all public lots and Squares, vacant lands and all public buildings, fortifications, barracks and other edifices which are not private property.— The Archives, papers & documents relative to the domain and Sovereignty of Louisiana and its dependances will be left in the possession of the Commissaries of the United States, and copies will be afterwards given in due form to the Magistrates and Municipal officers of such of the said papers and documents as may be necessary to them.

Art: III

The inhabitants of the ceded territory shall be incorporated in the Union of the United States and admitted as soon as possible according to the principles of the federal Constitution to the enjoyment of all these rights, advantages and immunities of citizens of the United States, and in the mean time they shall be maintained and protected in the free enjoyment of their liberty, property and the Religion which they profess.

Art: IV

There Shall be Sent by the Government of France a Commissary to Louisiana to the end that he do every act necessary as well to receive from the Officers of his Catholic Majesty the Said country and its dependances in the name of the French Republic if it has not been already done as to transmit it in the name of the French Republic to the Commissary or agent of the United States.

Art: V

Immediately after the ratification of the present Treaty by the President of the United States and in case that of the first Consul's shall have been previously obtained, the commissary of the French Republic shall remit all military posts of New Orleans and other parts of the ceded territory to the Commissary or Commissaries named by the President to take possession — the troops whether of France or Spain who may be there shall cease to occupy any military post from the time of taking possession and shall be embarked as soon as possible in the course of three months after the ratification of this treaty.

Art: VI

The United States promise to execute Such treaties and articles as may have been agreed between Spain and the tribes and nations of Indians until by mutual consent of the United States and the said tribes or nations other Suitable articles Shall have been agreed upon.

Art: VII

As it is reciprocally advantageous to the commerce of France and the United States to encourage the communication of both nations for a limited time in the country ceded by the present treaty until general arrangements relative to commerce of both nations may be agreed on; it has been agreed between the contracting parties that the French Ships coming directly from France or any of her colonies loaded only with the produce and manufactures of France or her Said Colonies; and the Ships of Spain coming directly from Spain or any of her colonies loaded only with the produce or manufactures of Spain or her Colonies shall be admitted during the Space of twelve years in the Port of New-Orleans and in all other legal ports-of-entry within the ceded territory in the Same manner as the Ships of the United States coming directly from France or Spain or any of their Colonies without being Subject to any other or greater duty on merchandize or other or greater tonnage than that paid by the citizens of the United States.

During that Space of time above mentioned no other nation Shall have a right to the Same privileges in the Ports of the ceded territory — the twelve years Shall commence three months after the exchange of ratifications if it Shall take place in France or three months after it Shall have been notified at Paris to the French Government if it Shall take place in the United States; It is however well understood that the object of the above article is to favour the manufactures, Commerce, freight and navigation of France and of Spain So far as relates to the importations that the French and Spanish Shall make into the Said Ports of the United States without in any Sort affecting the regulations that the United States may make concerning the exportation of the produce and merchandize of the United States, or any right they may have to make Such regulations.

Art: VIII

In future and for ever after the expiration of the twelve years, the Ships of France shall be treated upon the footing of the most favoured nations in the ports above mentioned.

Art: IX

The particular Convention Signed this day by the respective Ministers, having for its object to provide for the payment of debts due to the Citizens of the United States by the French Republic prior to the 30th Sept. 1800 (8th Vendémiaire an 9) is approved and to have its execution in the Same manner as if it had been inserted in this present treaty, and it Shall be ratified in the same form and in the Same time So that the one Shall not be ratified distinct from the other.

Another particular Convention Signed at the Same date as the present treaty relative to a definitive rule between the contracting parties is in the like manner approved and will be ratified in the Same form, and in the Same time and jointly.

Art: X

The present treaty Shall be ratified in good and due form and the ratifications Shall be exchanged in the Space of Six months after the date of the Signature by the Ministers Plenipotentiary or Sooner if possible.

In faith whereof the respective Plenipotentiaries have Signed these articles in the French and English languages; declaring nevertheless that the present Treaty was originally agreed to in the French language; and have thereunto affixed their Seals.

Done at Paris the tenth day of Floreal in

the eleventh year of the French Republic; and the 30th of April 1803.

> Robt R Livingston [seal]
> Jas. Monroe [seal]
> Barbé Marbois [seal]

The *Louisiana Purchase Treaty* of April 30, 1803, between the United States of America and the French Republic (as outlined above), was accompanied by two (2) convention agreements to pay for this historical land acquisition. The first convention agreement was for the payment of 60 million francs ($11,250,000), and the other was made for claims that American citizens had made against France in the amount of 20 million francs ($3,750,000).

While the primary land acquisition treaty is outlined above, the two (2) convention agreements necessary to implement this treaty are transcribed below. Both of these other agreements, also dated April 30, 1803, were essential to the implementation of the Louisiana Purchase Treaty.

A CONVENTION BETWEEN THE UNITED STATES OF AMERICA AND THE FRENCH REPUBLIC

The President of the United States of America and the First Consul of the French Republic in the name of the French people, in consequence of the treaty of cession of Louisiana which has been Signed this day; wishing to regulate definitively every thing which has relation to the Said cession have authorized to this effect the Plenipotentiaries, that is to say the President of the United States has, by and with the advice and consent of the Senate of the Said States, nominated for their Plenipotentiaries, Robert R. Livingston, Minister Plenipotentiary of the United States, and James Monroe, Minister Plenipotentiary and Envoy-Extraordinary of the Said United States, near the Government of the French Republic; and the First Consul of the French Republic, in the name of the French people, has named as Pleniopo-

tentiary of the Said Republic the citizen Francis Barbé Marbois who, in virtue of their full powers, which have been exchanged this day, have agreed to the followings articles:

Art: 1

The Government of the United States engages to pay to the French government in the manner Specified in the following article the sum of Sixty millions of francs independant of the Sum which Shall be fixed by another Convention for the payment of the debts due by France to citizens of the United States.

Art: 2

For the payment of the Sum of Sixty millions of francs mentioned in the preeeding article the United States shall create a Stock of eleven millions, two hundred and fifty thousand Dollars bearing an interest of Six per cent: per annum payable half yearly in London Amsterdam or Paris amounting by the half year to three hundred and thirty Seven thousand five hundred Dollars, according to the proportions which Shall be determined by the french Govenment to be paid at either place: The principal of the Said Stock to be reimbursed at the treasury of the United States in annual payments of not less than three millions of Dollars each; of which the first payment Shall commence fifteen years after the date of the exchange of ratifications:— this Stock Shall be transferred to the government of France or to Such person or persons as Shall be authorized to receive it in three months at most after the exchange of ratifications of this treaty and after Louisiana Shall be taken possession of the name of the Government of the United States.

It is further agreed that if the french Government Should be desirous of disposing of the Said Stock to receive the capital in Europe at Shorter terms that its measures for that purpose Shall be taken So as to favour in the greatest degree possible the credit of the United States, and to raise to the highest price the Said Stock.

Art: 3

It is agreed that the Dollar of the United States Specified in the present Convention shall be fixed at five francs 3333/100000 or five livres eight Sous tournois.

The present Convention Shall be ratified in good and due form, and the ratifications Shall be exchanged the Space of Six months to date from this day or Sooner it possible.

In faith of which the respective Plenipotentiaries have Signed the above articles both in the french and english languages, declaring nevertheless that the present treaty has been originally agreed on and written in the french language; to which they have hereunto affixed their Seals.

Done at Paris the tenth of Floreal eleventh year of the french Republic.

30th April 1803.

   Robt R Livingston [seal]
   Jas. Monroe [seal]
   Barbé Marbois [seal]

Convention between the United States of America and the French Republic

The President of the United States of America and the First Consul of the French Republic in the name of the French People having by a Treaty of this date terminated all difficulties relative to Louisiana, and established on a Solid foundation the friendship which unites the two nations and being desirous in complyance with the Second and fifth Articles of the Convention of the 8th Vendémiaire ninth year of the French Republic (30th September 1800) to Secure the payment of the Sums due by France to the citizens of the United States have respectively nominated as Plenipotentiaries that is to Say The President of the United States of America by and with the advise and consent of their Senate Robert R. Livingston Minister Plenipotentiary and James Monroe Minister Plenipotentiary and Envoy Extraordinary of the Said States near the Government of the French Republic: and the First Consul in the name of the French People the Citizen Francis Barbé Marbois Minister of the public treasury; who after having exchanged their full powers have agreed to the following articles.

Art: 1

The debts due by France to citizens of the United States contracted before the 8th Vendémiaire ninth year of the French Republic (30th September 1800) shall be paid according to the following regulations with interest at Six per Cent; to commence from the period when the accounts and vouchers were presented to the French Government.

Art: 2

The debts provided for by the preceeding Article are those whose result is comprised in the conjectural note annexed to the present Convention and which, with the interest cannot exceed the Sum of twenty millions of Francs. The claims comprised in the Said note which fall within the exceptions of the following articles, Shall not be admitted to the benefit of this provision.

Art: 3

The principal and interests of the Said debts Shall be discharged by the United States, by orders drawn by their Minister Plenipotentiary on their treasury, these orders Shall be payable Sixty days after the exchange of ratifications of the Treaty and the Conventions Signed this day, and after possession Shall be given of Louisiana by the Commissaries of France to those of the United States.

Art: 4

It is expressly agreed that the preceding articles Shall comprehend no debts but Such as are due to citizens of the United States who have been and are yet creditors of France for Supplies for embargoes and prizes made at Sea, in which the appeal has been properly lodged within the time mentioned in the Said

Convention 8th Vendémiaire ninth year, (30th Sept 1800).

Art: 5

The preceding Articles Shall apply only, First: to captures of which the council of prizes Shall have ordered restitution, it being well understood that the claimant cannot have recourse to the United States otherwise than he might have had to the Government of the French republic, and only in case of insufficiency of the captors — 2d the debts mentioned in the Said fifth Article of the Convention contracted before the 8th Vendémiaire an 9/30th September 1800 the payment of which has been heretofore claimed of the actual Government of France and for which the creditors have a right to the protection of the United States; — the Said 5th Article does not comprehend prizes whose condemnation has been or Shall be confirmed: it is the express intention of the contracting parties not to extend the benefit of the present Convention to reclamations of American citizens who Shall have established houses of Commerce in France, England or other countries than the United States in partnership with foreigners, and who by that reason and the nature of their commerce ought to be regarded as domiciliated in the places where Such house exist. — All agreements and bargains concerning merchandize, which Shall not be the property of American citizens, are equally excepted from the benefit of the said Conventions, Saving however to Such persons their claims in like manner as if this Treaty had not been made.

Art: 6

And that the different questions which may arise under the preceding article may be fairly investigated, the Ministers Plenipotentiary of the United States Shall name three persons, who Shall act from the present and provisionally, and who shall have full power to examine, without removing the documents, all the accounts of the different claims already liquidated by the Bureaus established for this purpose by the French Republic, and to ascertain whether they belong to the classes designated by the present Convention and the principles established in it or if they are not in one of its exceptions and on their Certificate, declaring that the debt is due to an American Citizen or his representative and that it existed before the 8th Vendémiaire 9th year/30 September 1800 the debtor shall be entitled to an order on the Treasury of the United States in the manner prescribed by the 3d Article.

Art: 7

The Same agents Shall likewise have power, without removing the documents, to examine the claims which are prepared for verification, and to certify those which ought to be admitted by uniting the necessary qualifications, and not being comprised in the exceptions contained in the present Convention.

Art: 8

The Same agents shall likewise examine the claims which are not prepared for liquidation, and certify in writing those which in their judgement ought to be admitted to liquidation.

Art: 9

In proportion as the debts mentioned in these articles Shall be admitted they Shall be discharged with interest at Six per Cent: by the Treasury of the United States.

Art: 10

And that no debt shall not have the qualifications above mentioned and that no unjust or exorbitant demand may be admitted, the Commercial agent of the United States at Paris or such other agent as the Minister Plenipotentiary or the United States Shall think proper to nominate shall assist at the operations of the Bureaus and cooperate in the examinations of the claims; and if this agent Shall be of the opinion that any debt is not completely proved, or if he shall judge that it is not comprised in the principles of the fifth article above mentioned, and if notwithstanding his opinion the Bureaus established by the french Government should think that it ought to be liquidated, he shall transmit his observations to the board established by the United States, who, without removing documents, shall make a complete examination of the debt and vouchers which Support it, and report the result to the Minister of the United States.— The Minister of the United States Shall transmit his observations in all Such cases to the Minister of the treasury of the French Republic, on whose report the French Government Shall decide definitively in every case.

The rejection of any claim Shall have no other effect than to exempt the United States from the payment of it, the French Government reserving to itself, the right to decide definitively on Such claim So far as it concerns itself.

Art: 11

Every necessary decision Shall be made in the course of a year to commence from the exchange of ratifications, and no reclamation Shall be admitted afterwards.

Art: 12

In case of claims for debts contracted by the Government of France with citizens of the United States Since the 8th Vendémiaire 9th year/30 September 1800 not being comprised in this Convention may be pursued, and the payment demanded in the Same manner as if it had not been made.

Art: 13

The present convention Shall be ratified in good and due form and the ratifications Shall be exchanged in Six months from the date of the Signature of the Ministers Plenipotentiary, or Sooner if possible.

In faith of which, the respective Ministers Plenipotentiary have signed the above Articles both in the french and english languages, declaring nevertheless that the present treaty has been originally agreed on and written in the french language, to which they have hereunto affixed their Seals.

Done at Paris, the tenth of Floreal, eleventh year of the French Republic.

30th April 1803.

Robt R Livingston [seal]
Jas. Monroe [seal]
Barbé Marbois [seal]

CHAPTER 22

Transcontinental Treaty (February 22, 1819)

United States Congress

The History*

The colonies of East Florida and West Florida remained loyal to the British during the war for American Independence, but by the Treaty of Paris in 1783 they returned to Spanish control. After 1783, American immigrants moved into West Florida. In 1810, these American settlers in West Florida rebelled, declaring independence from Spain. President James Madison and Congress used the incident to claim the region, knowing full well that the Spanish government was seriously weakened by Napoleon's invasion of Spain.

The United States asserted that the portion of West Florida from the Mississippi to the Peridido rivers was part of the Louisiana Purchase of 1803. Negotiations over Florida began in earnest with the mission of Don Luis de Onís to Washington in 1815 to meet Secretary of State James Monroe. The issue was not resolved until Monroe was president and John Quincy Adams his Secretary of State.

Although U.S.–Spanish relations were strained over suspicions of American support for the independence struggles of Spanish-American colonies, the situation became critical when General Andrew Jackson seized the Spanish forts at Pensacola and St. Marks in his 1818 authorized raid against Seminoles and escaped slaves who were viewed as a threat to Georgia. Jackson executed two British citizens on charges of inciting the Indians and runaways.

Monroe's government seriously considered denouncing Jackson's actions, but Adams defended Jackson citing the necessity to restrain the Indians and escaped slaves since the Spanish failed to do so. Adams also sensed that Jackson's Seminole campaign was popular with Americans and it strengthened his diplomatic hand with Spain.

Adam used Jackson's military action to present Spain with a demand to either control the inhabitants of East Florida or cede it to the United States. Minister Onís and Secretary Adams reached an agreement whereby Spain ceded East Florida to the

*Originally published as "Acquisition of Florida: Treaty of Adams-Onis (1819) and Transcontinental Treaty (1821)," *Timeline of U.S. Diplomatic History (1801–1829)*, Office of the Historian, Bureau of Public Affairs, U.S. Department of State, Washington, DC, 2000. For additional information see "Acquisition of Florida: Treaty of Adams-Onis (1819) and Transcontinental Treaty (1821)," *Timeline of U.S. Diplomatic History (1801–1829)*, Office of the Historian, Bureau of Public Affairs, U.S. Department of State, Washington, DC, 2004. This agency is listed in the *National Resource Directory* section of this volume.

United States and renounced all claim to West Florida. Spain received no compensation, but the United States agreed to assume liability for $5 million in damage done by American citizens who rebelled against Spain.

Under the Onís-Adams Treaty of 1819 (also called the Transcontinental Treaty and ratified in 1821) the United States and Spain defined the western limits of the Louisiana Purchase and Spain surrendered its claims to the Pacific Northwest. In return, the United States recognized Spanish sovereignty over Texas.

The Document

Transcontinental Treaty

The United States of America and His Catholic Majesty, desiring to consolidate, on a permanent basis, the friendship and good correspondence which happily prevails between the two parties, have determined to settle and terminate all their differences and pretensions, by a treaty, which shall designate, with precision, the limits of their respective bordering territories in North America.

With this intention the President of the United States has furnished with their full powers John Quincy Adams, Secretary of State of the said United States; and His Catholic Majesty has appointed the Most Excellent Lord Don Luis De Onís, Gonzales, Lopez y Vara, Lord of the Town of Rayaces, Perpetual Regidor of the Corporation of the city of Salamanca, Knight Grand Cross of the Royal American Order of Isabella the Catholic, decorated with the Lys of La Vendee, Knight Pensioner of the Royal and Distinguished Spanish Order of Charles the Third, Member of the Supreme Assembly of the said Royal Order; of the Council of His Catholic Majesty; his Secretary, with Exercise of Decrees, and His Envoy Extraordinary and Minister Plenipotentiary near the United States of America.

And the said Plenipotentiaries, after having exchanged their powers, have agreed upon and concluded the following articles:

ARTICLE I

There shall be a firm and inviolable peace and sincere friendship between the United States and their citizens and His Catholic Majesty, his successors and subjects, without exception of persons or places.

ARTICLE II

His Catholic Majesty cedes to the United States, in full property and sovereignty, all the territories which belong to him, situated to the eastward of the Mississippi, known by the name of East and West Florida. The adjacent islands dependent on said provinces, all public lots and squares, vacant lands, public edifices, fortifications, barracks, and other buildings, which are not private property, archives and documents, which relate directly to the property and sovereignty of said provinces, are included in this article. The said archives and documents shall be left in possession of the commissaries or officers of the United States, duly authorized to receive them.

ARTICLE III

The boundary-line between the two countries, west of the Mississippi, shall begin on the Gulph of Mexico, at the mouth of the river Sabine, in the sea, continuing north, along the western bank of that river, to the 32d degree of latitude; thence, by a line due north, to the degree of latitude where it strikes the Rio Roxo of Nachitoches, or Red River; then following the course of the Rio Roxo westward, to the degree of longitude 100 west from London and 23 from Washington; then, crossing the said Red River, and running thence, by a line due north, to the river Arkansas; thence, following the course of the southern bank of the Arkansas, to its source, in latitude 42 north; and thence, by that parallel of latitude, to the

South Sea. The whole being as laid down in Melish's map of the United States, published at Philadelphia, improved to the first of January, 1818. But if the source of the Arkansas River shall be found to fall north or south of latitude 42, then the line shall run from the said source due south or north, as the case may be, till it meets the said parallel of latitude 42, and thence, along the said parallel, to the South Sea: All the islands in the Sabine, and the said Red and Arkansas Rivers, throughout the course thus described. to belong to the United States; but the use of the waters, and the navigation of the Sabine to the sea, and of the said rivers Roxo and Arkansas, throughout the extent of the said boundary, on their respective banks, shall be common to the respective inhabitants of both nations.

The two high contracting parties agree to cede and renounce all their rights, claims, and pretensions to the territories described by the said line, that is to say: The United States hereby cede to His Catholic Majesty, and renounce forever, all their rights, claims, and pretensions, to the territories lying west and south of the above-described line; and, in like manner, His Catholic Majesty cedes to the said United States all his rights, claims, and pretensions to any territories east and north of the said line, and for himself, his heirs, and successors, renounces all claim to the said territories forever.

Article IV

To fix this line with more precision, and to place the landmarks which shall designate exactly the limits of both nations, each of the contracting parties shall appoint a Commissioner and a surveyor, who shall meet before the termination of one year from the date of the ratification of this treaty at Nachitoches, on the Red River, and proceed to run and mark the said line, from the mouth of the Sabine to the Red River, and from the Red River to the river Arkansas, and to ascertain the latitude of the source of the said river

Arkansas, in conformity to what is above agreed upon and stipulated and the line of latitude 42, to the South Sea: they shall make out plans, and keep journals of their proceedings, and the result agreed upon by them shall be considered as part of this treaty, and shall have the same force as if it were inserted therein. The two Governments will amicably agree respecting the necessary articles to be furnished to those persons, and also as to their respective escorts, should such be deemed necessary.

Article V

The inhabitants of the ceded territories shall be secured in the free exercise of their religion, without any restriction; and all those who may desire to remove to the Spanish dominions shall be permitted to sell or export their effects, at any time whatever, without being subject, in either case, to duties.

Article VI

The inhabitants of the territories which His Catholic Majesty cedes to the United States, by this treaty, shall be incorporated in the Union of the United States as soon as may be consistent with the principles of the Federal Constitution, and admitted to the enjoyment of all the privileges, rights, and immunities of the citizens of the United States.

Article VII

The officers and troops of His Catholic Majesty, in the territories hereby ceded by him to the United States, shall be withdrawn, and possession of the places occupied by them shall be given within six months after the exchange of the ratifications of this treaty, or sooner if possible, by the officers of His Catholic Majesty to the commissioners or officers of the United States duly appointed to receive them; and the United States shall furnish the transports and escort necessary to convey the Spanish officers and troops and their baggage to the Havana.

ARTICLE VIII

All the grants of land made before the 24th of January, 1818, by His Catholic Majesty, or by his lawful authorities, in the said territories ceded by His Majesty to the United States, shall be ratified and confirmed to the persons in possession of the lands, to the same extent that the same grants would be valid if the territories had remained under the dominion of His Catholic Majesty. But the owners in possession of such lands, who, by reason of the recent circumstances of the Spanish nation, and the revolutions in Europe, have been prevented from fulfilling all the conditions of their grants, shall complete them within the terms limited in the same, respectively, from the date of this treaty; in default of which the said grants shall be null and void. All grants made since the said 24th of January, 1818, when the first proposal, on the part of His Catholic Majesty, for the cession of the Floridas was made, are hereby declared and agreed to be null and void.

ARTICLE IX

The two high contracting parties, animated with the most earnest desire of conciliation, and with the object of putting an end to all the differences which have existed between them, and of confirming the good understanding which they wish to be forever maintained between them, reciprocally renounce all claims for damages or injuries which they, themselves, as well as their respective citizens and subjects, may have suffered until the time of signing this treaty.

1. The renunciation of the United States will extend to all the injuries mentioned in the convention of the 11th of August, 1802.

2. To all claims on account of prizes made by French privateers, and condemned by French Consuls, within the territory and jurisdiction of Spain.

3. To all claims of indemnities on ac-count of the suspension of the right of deposit at New Orleans in 1802.

4. To all claims of citizens of the United States upon the Government of Spain, arising from the unlawful seizures at sea, and in the ports and territories of Spain, or the Spanish colonies.

5. To all claims of citizens of the United States upon the Spanish Government, statements of which, soliciting the interposition of the Government of the United States have been presented to the Department of State, or to the Minister of the United States in Spain, the date of the convention of 1802 and until the signature of this treaty.

The renunciation of His Catholic Majesty extends —

1. To all the injuries mentioned in the convention of the 11th of August, 1802.

2. To the sums which His Catholic Majesty advanced for the return of Captain Pike from the Provincias Internas.

3. To all injuries caused by the expedition of Miranda, that was fitted out and equipped at New York.

4. To all claims of Spanish subjects upon the Government of the United States arizing from unlawful seizures at sea, or within the ports and territorial Jurisdiction of the United States.

Finally, to all the claims of subjects of His Catholic Majesty upon the Government of the United States in which the interposition of his Catholic Majesty's Government has been solicited, before the date of this treaty and since the date of the convention of 1802, or which may have been made to the department of foreign affairs of His Majesty, or to his Minister of the United States.

And the high contracting parties, respectively, renounce all claim to indemnities for any of the recent events or transactions of their respective commanders and officers in the Floridas.

The United States will cause satisfaction to be made for the injuries, if any, which, by process of law, shall be established to have been suffered by the Spanish officers, and individual Spanish inhabitants, by the late operations of the American Army in Florida.

ARTICLE X

The convention entered into between the two Governments, on the 11th of August, 1802, the ratifications of which were exchanged the 21st December, 1818, is annulled.

ARTICLE XI

The United States, exonerating Spain from all demands in future, on account of the claims of their citizens to which the renunciations herein contained extend, and considering them entirely cancelled, undertake to make satisfaction for the same, to an amount not exceeding five millions of dollars. To ascertain the full amount and validity of those claims, a commission, to consist of three Commissioners, citizens of the United States, shall be appointed by the President, by and with the advice and consent of the Senate, which commission shall meet at the city of Washington, and, within the space of three years from the time of their first meeting, shall receive, examine, and decide upon the amount and validity of all the claims included within the descriptions above mentioned. The said Commissioners shall take an oath or affirmation, to be entered on the record of their proceedings, for the faithful and diligent discharge of their duties; and, in case of the death, sickness, or necessary absence of any such Commissioner, his place may be supplied by the appointment, as aforesaid, or by the President of the United States, during the recess of the Senate, of another Commissioner in his stead.

The said Commissioners shall be authorized to hear and examine, on oath, every question relative to the said claims, and to receive all suitable authentic testimony concerning the same. And the Spanish Government shall furnish all such documents and elucidations as may be in their possession, for the adjustment of the said claims, according to the principles of justice, the laws of nations, and the stipulations of the treaty between the two parties of 27th October, 1795; the said documents to be specified, when demanded, at the instance of the said Commissioners.

The payment of such claims as may be admitted and adjusted by the said Commissioners, or the major part of them, to an amount not exceeding five millions of dollars, shall be made by the United States, either immediately at their Treasury, or by the creation of stock, bearing an interest of six per cent. per annum, payable from the proceeds of sales of public lands within the territories hereby ceded to the United States, or in such other manner as the Congress of the United States may prescribe by law.

The records of the proceedings of the said Commissioners, together with the vouchers and documents produced before them, relative to the claims to be adjusted and decided upon by them, shall, after the close of their transactions, be deposited in the Department of State of the United States; and copies of them, or any part of them, shall be furnished to the Spanish Government, if required' at the demand of the Spanish Minister in the United States.

ARTICLE XII

The treaty of limits and navigation, of 1795, remains confirmed in all and each one of its articles excepting the 2, 3, 4, 21, and the second clause of the 22d article, which, having been altered by this treaty, or having received their entire execution, are no longer valid.

With respect to the 15th article of the same treaty of friendship, limits, and navigation of 1795, in which it is stipulated that the flag shall cover the property, the two high contracting parties agree that this shall be so understood with respect to those powers who recognize this principle; but if either of the two contracting parties shall be at war with a third party, and the other neutral, the flag of the neutral shall cover the property of enemies whose government acknowledge this principle, and not of others.

ARTICLE XIII

Both contracting parties, wishing to favor their mutual commerce, by affording in their ports every necessary assistance to their respective merchant-vessels, have agreed that the sailors who shall desert from their vessels in the ports of the other, shall be arrested and delivered up, at the instance of the consul, who shall prove, nevertheless, that the deserters belonged to the vessels that claimed them, exhibiting the document that is customary in their nation: that is to say, the American Consul in a Spanish port shall exhibit the document known lay the name of articles, and the Spanish Consul in American ports the roll of the vessel; and if the name of the deserter or deserters are claimed shall appear in the one or the other, they shall be arrested, held in custody, and delivered to the vessel to which they shall belong.

ARTICLE XIV

The United States hereby certify that they have not received any compensation from France for the injuries they suffered from her privateers, Consuls, and tribunals on the coasts and in the ports of Spain, for the satisfaction of which provision is made by this treaty; and they will present an authentic statement of the prizes made, and of their true value, that Spain may avail herself of the same in such manner as she may deem just and proper.

Article XV

The United States, to give to His Catholic Majesty a proof of their desire to ce-

ment the relations of amity subsisting between the two nations, and to favor the commerce of the subjects of His Catholic Majesty, agree that Spanish vessels, coming Onisladen only with productions of Spanish growth or manufactures, directly from the ports of Spain, or of her colonies, shall be admitted, for the term of twelve years, to the ports of Pensacola and St. Augustine, in the Floridas, without paying other or higher duties on their cargoes, or of tonnage, than will be paid by the vessels of the United States. During the said term no other nation shall enjoy the same privileges within the ceded territories. The twelve years shall commence three months after the exchange of the ratifications of this treaty.

ARTICLE XVI

The present treaty shall be ratified in due form, by the contracting parties, and the ratifications shall be exchanged in six months from this time, or sooner if possible.

In witness whereof we, the underwritten Plenipotentiaries of the United States of America and of His Catholic Majesty, have signed, by virtue of our powers, the present treaty of amity, settlement, and limits, and have thereunto affixed our seals, respectively.

Done at Washington this twenty-second day of February, one thousand eight hundred and nineteen.

JOHN QUINCY ADAMS. [L. S.]
LUIS DE ONIS. [L. S.]

NOTE

The Transcontinental Treaty was originally known as the Treaty of Adams-Onís until approved by the U.S. Congress in 1821.

CHAPTER 23

Resolution for the Annexation of Texas (March 1, 1845)

United States Congress

The History*

The Texas Annexation of 1845 was the voluntary annexation of the Republic of Texas to the United States of America, becoming the twenty-eighth state. Texas claimed but never controlled parts of present-day Colorado, Kansas, New Mexico, Oklahoma, and Wyoming, which became parts of other territories of the United States in the Compromise of 1850.

Anglo-American immigrants, primarily from the South, began immigrating to Mexican Texas in the early 1820s at the request of the Mexican government, which sought to populate the sparsely inhabited lands of its northern frontier. Anglo-Americans soon became a majority in Texas and eventually became disillusioned with Mexican rule. Coahuila y Texas, a Mexican state of which Texas was a constituent part after 1824, endorsed a plan for gradual emancipation in 1827, which angered many slaveholding settlers who had moved to Texas from the South. For this and other reasons, Texas declared independence from Mexico, resulting

in war with Mexico. In 1836, the fighting ended and Sam Houston became the first president of the Republic of Texas, elected on a platform that favored annexation to the United States.

In August 1837, James Freeman, the Texan ambassador to the United States, submitted an annexation proposal to the Van Buren administration. Believing that annexation would lead to war with Mexico, the administration declined Texas' proposal. After the election of Mirabeau B. Lamar, an opponent of annexation, as president of Texas in 1838 and the United States' apprehension regarding annexation, Texas withdrew its offer.

In 1843, President John Tyler came out in support of annexation, entering negotiations with the Republic of Texas for an annexation treaty, which he submitted to the Senate. On 8 June 1844, the treaty was defeated 35 to 16, well below the two-thirds majority necessary for ratification. Of the 29 Whig senators, 28 voted against the treaty with only one Whig, a southerner, supporting it. The Democratic senators were more divided on the issue with six northern De-

*Originally published as "Texas Annexation," *Wikipedia*, Wikimedia Foundation, Inc., San Francisco, California, November 2009. For additional information see "Diplomacy and Westward Expansion: The Annexation of Texas (1845)," *Timeline of U.S. Diplomatic History (1830–1860)*, Office of the Historian, Bureau of Public Affairs, U.S. Department of State, Washington, DC, 2004. This agency is listed in the *National Resource Directory* section of this volume.

mocrats and one southern Democrat opposing the treaty and five northern Democrats and ten southern Democrats supporting it.

James K. Polk, a Democrat and a strong supporter of territorial expansion, was elected president in November 1844 with a mandate to acquire both the Republic of Texas and Oregon Country. After the election, the Tyler administration realized that public opinion was in favor of annexation, consulted with President-elect Polk, and set out to accomplish annexation by means of a joint resolution. The resolution declared that Texas would be admitted as a state as long as it approved annexation by 1 January 1846, that it could split itself up into four additional states, and that possession of the Republic's public lands would shift to the state of Texas upon its admission. On 26 February 1845, six days before Polk took office, Congress passed the joint resolution. Not long afterwards, Andrew Jackson Donelson, the American chargé d'affaires in Texas and the nephew of former president Andrew Jackson, presented the American resolution to President Anson Jones of Texas. In July 1845, the Texan Congress endorsed the American annexation offer with only one dissenting vote and began writing a state constitution. The citizens of Texas approved the new constitution and the annexation ordinance in October 1845 and Polk signed the documents formally integrating Texas into the United States on 29 December 1845.

The joint resolution and ordinance of annexation contain language permitting the formation of up to four additional states out of the former territories of the Republic of Texas:

New States of convenient size not exceeding four in number, in addition to said State of Texas and having sufficient population, may, hereafter by the consent of said State, be formed out of the territory thereof, which shall be entitled to admission under the provisions of the Federal Constitution.

The joint resolution required that if any new states were formed out of Texas' lands, those north of the Missouri Compromise line would become free states and those south of the line could choose whether or not to permit slavery. Article Four of the Constitution prohibits the creation of new states out of existing ones without the consent of both the legislature of that state and of Congress, and the division of Texas into multiple states has never been attempted.

The joint resolution and ordinance of annexation have no language specifying the boundaries of Texas, but only refer in general terms to "the territory properly included within, and rightfully belonging to the Republic of Texas," and state that the new State of Texas is to be formed "subject to the adjustment by this [U.S.] government of all questions of boundary that may arise with other governments."

According to George Lockhart Rives, "That treaty had been expressly so framed as to leave the boundaries of Texas undefined, and the joint resolution of the following winter was drawn in the same manner. It was hoped that this might open the way to a negotiation, in the course of which the whole subject of the boundaries of Mexico, from the Gulf to the Pacific, might be reconsidered, but these hopes came to nothing."

There was an ongoing border dispute between the Republic of Texas and Mexico prior to annexation. Texas claimed the Rio Grande as its border, while Mexico maintained that it was the Nueces River and did not recognize Texas independence. President James K. Polk ordered General Zachary Taylor to garrison the southern border of Texas, as defined by the former Republic. Taylor moved into Texas, ignoring Mexican demands that he withdraw, and marched as far south as the Rio Grande, where he began to build a fort near the river's mouth on the Gulf of Mexico. The Mexican government regarded this action as a violation of its sovereignty.

The Republic of Texas never controlled what is now New Mexico. The failed Texas

Santa Fe Expedition of 1841 was its only attempt to take that territory. El Paso was only taken under Texas governance by Robert Neighbors in 1850, over four years after annexation; he was not welcomed in New Mexico. Texas continued to claim New Mexico as far as the Rio Grande, supported by the rest of the South, and opposed by the North and by New Mexico itself, until agreeing to today's boundary in the Compromise of 1850.

The original controversy about the legality of the annexation of Texas stems from the fact that Congress approved the annexation of Texas as a territory with a simple majority vote approval instead of annexing the land by Treaty, as was done with Native American lands. After the United States and the Republic of Texas were unable to reach a Treaty agreement, Congress passed a Joint Resolution for Annexing Texas to the United States. The Republic of Texas' Annexation Convention then submitted the Ordinance of Annexation to popular vote in October 1845 and the public approved the measure. This Ordinance of Annexation was submitted and approved by the House and Senate of the United States and signed by the President on December 29, 1845. While this was an awkward, if not unusual, treaty process it was fully accepted by all parties involved, and more importantly all parties performed on those agreements making them legally binding. In addition, the United States Supreme Court decided in the case of *DeLima v. Bidwell*, 182 U.S. 1 (1901), that annexation by joint resolution of Congress is legal.

The Document

Resolution for the Annexation of Texas

Resolved by the Senate and House of Representatives of the United States of America in Congress assembled, That Congress doth consent that the territory properly included within, and rightfully belonging to the Republic of Texas, may be erected into a new state, to be called the state of Texas, with a republican form of government, to be adopted by the people of said republic, by deputies in Convention assembled, with the consent of the existing government, in order that the same may be admitted as one of the states of this Union.

2. And be it further resolved, That the foregoing consent of Congress is given upon the following conditions, and with the following guarantees, to wit: First — said state to be formed, subject to the adjustment by this government of all questions of boundary that may arise with other governments; and the constitution thereof, with the proper evidence of its adoption by the people of said republic of Texas, shall be transmitted to the President of the United States, to be laid before Congress for its final action, on or before the first day of January, one thousand eight hundred and forty-six. Second — said state, when admitted into the Union, after ceding to the United States all public edifices, fortifications, barracks, ports and harbors, navy and navy-yards, docks, magazines, arms, armaments, and all other property and means pertaining to the public defence belonging to said republic of Texas, shall retain all the public funds, debts, taxes, and dues of every kind which may belong to or be due and owing said republic; and shall also retain all the vacant and unappropriated lands lying within its limits, to be applied to the payment of the debts and liabilities of said republic of Texas; and the residue of said lands, after discharging said debts and liabilities, to be disposed of as said state may direct; but in no event are said debts and liabilities to become a charge upon the government of the United States. Third — New states, of convenient size, not exceeding four in number, in addition to said state of Texas, and having

sufficient population, may hereafter, by the consent of said state, be formed out of the territory thereof, which shall be entitled to admission under the provisions of the federal constitution. And such states as may be formed out of that portion of said territory lying south of thirty-six degrees thirty minutes north latitude, commonly known as the Missouri Compromise line, shall be admitted into the Union with or without slavery, as the people of each state asking admission may desire. And in such state or states as shall be formed out of said territory north of said Missouri compromise line, slavery, or involuntary servitude, (except for crime,) shall be prohibited.

3. And be it further resolved, That if the President of the United States shall in his judgment and discretion deem it most advisable, instead of proceeding to submit the foregoing resolution to the Republic of Texas, as an overture on the part of the United States for admission, to negotiate with that Republic; then,

Be it resolved, that a state, to be formed out of the present Republic of Texas, with suitable extent and boundaries, and with two representatives in Congress, until the next apportionment of representation, shall be admitted into the Union, by virtue of this act, on an equal footing with the existing states, as soon as the terms and conditions of such admission, and the cession of the remaining Texan territory to the United States shall be agreed upon by the governments of Texas and the United States: And that the sum of one hundred thousand dollars be, and the same is hereby, appropriated to defray the expenses of missions and negotiations, to agree upon the terms of said admission and cession, either by treaty to be submitted to the Senate, or by articles to be submitted to the two Houses of Congress, as the President may direct.

Approved, March 1, 1845

Ordinance for the Annexation of Texas

AN ORDINANCE

Whereas,

the Congress of the United States of America has passed resolutions providing for the annexation of Texas to that Union, which resolutions were offered by the President of the United States on the first day of March, 1845; and

Whereas,

the President of the United States has submitted to Texas the first and second sections of said resolutions, as the basis upon which Texas may be admitted as one of the States of the said Union; and

Whereas,

the existing Government of the Republic of Texas, has assented to the proposals thus made,— the terms and conditions of which are as follows:

Joint Resolutions for annexing Texas to the United States

Resolved by the Senate and House of Representatives of the United States of America in Congress assembled, That Congress doth consent that the territory properly included within, and rightfully belonging to the Republic of Texas, may be erected into a new state, to be called the state of Texas, with a republican form of government, to be adopted by the people of said republic, by deputies in Convention assembled, with the consent of the existing government, in order that the same may be admitted as one of the States of this Union.

2nd. And be it further resolved, That the foregoing consent of Congress is given upon the following conditions, and with the following guarantees, to wit: First, said state to be formed, subject to the adjustment by this government of all questions of boundary that may arise with other governments; and the constitution thereof, with the proper evidence of its adoption by the people of said republic of Texas, shall be transmitted to the President of the United States, to be laid before Congress for its final action, on or before the first day of January, one thousand eight hundred and forty-six. Second, said state, when admitted into the Union, after ceding to the United States all public edifices, fortifications, barracks, ports and harbors, navy and navy-yards, docks, magazines, arms, armaments, and all other property and means pertaining to the public defence belonging to said republic of Texas, shall retain all the public funds, debts, taxes, and dues of every kind which may belong to or be due and owing said republic; and shall also retain all the vacant and unappropriated lands lying within its limits, to be applied to the payment of the debts and liabilities of said republic of Texas; and the residue of said lands, after discharging said debts and liabilities, to be disposed of as said state may direct; but in no event are said debts and liabilities to become a charge upon the government of the United States. Third — New states, of convenient size, not exceeding four in number, in addition to said state of Texas, and having sufficient population, may hereafter, by the consent of said state, be formed out of the territory thereof, which shall be entitled to admission under the provisions of the federal constitution. And such states as may be formed out of that portion of said territory lying south of thirty-six degrees thirty minutes north latitude, commonly known as the Missouri compromise line, shall be admitted into the Union with or without slavery, as the people of each state asking admission may desire. And in such state or states as shall be formed out of said territory north of said Missouri compromise line, slavery, or involuntary servitude, (except for crime,) shall be prohibited.

Now in order to manifest the assent of the people of this Republic, as required in the above recited portions of said resolutions, we the deputies of the people of Texas, in convention assembled, in their name and in their authority, do ordain and declare, that we assent to and accept the proposals, conditions and guarantees, contained in the first and second sections of the Resolution of the Congress of the United States aforesaid.

In testimony whereof, we have hereunto subscribed our names

Thomas J. Rusk
President

followed by 61 signatures

Attest
James H. Raymond
Secretary of the Convention

Approved on July 4, 1845

CHAPTER 24

Oregon Treaty
(June 15, 1846)

United States Congress

The History*

The Oregon Treaty is a treaty between the United Kingdom of Great Britain and Ireland and the United States that was signed on June 15, 1846, in Washington, D.C. The treaty brought an end to the Oregon boundary dispute by settling competing American and British claims to the Oregon Country, which had been jointly occupied by both Britain and the U.S. since the Treaty of 1818.

The Treaty of 1818 set the boundary between the United States and British North America along the 49th parallel of north latitude from Minnesota to the "Stony Mountains" (now know as the Rocky Mountains). West of those mountains was known to the Americans as the Oregon Country and to the British as the Columbia Department or Columbia District of the Hudson's Bay Company. (Also included in the region was the southern portion of another fur district, New Caledonia.) The treaty provided for joint control of that land for ten years. Both countries could claim land and both were guaranteed free navigation throughout.

Joint control steadily grew less tolerable for both sides. After a British minister rejected U.S. President James K. Polk's offer to settle the boundary at the 49th parallel north, Democratic expansionists called for the annexation of the entire region up to 54°40', the southern limit of Russian America as established by parallel treaties between the Russian Empire and the U.S. (1824) and Britain (1825). However, after the outbreak of the Mexican-American War diverted U.S. attention and resources, a compromise was reached.

The treaty was negotiated by U.S. Secretary of State James Buchanan, who later became president, and Richard Pakenham, British envoy to the United States and member of the Privy Council of the United Kingdom for Queen Victoria. The treaty was signed on June 15, 1846.

The Oregon Treaty set the U.S. and British North American border at the 49th parallel with the exception of Vancouver Island, which was retained in its entirety by the British. Vancouver Island, with all coastal islands, was constituted as the Colony of

*Originally published as "Oregon Treaty," *Wikipedia*, Wikimedia Foundation, Inc., San Francisco, California, November 2009. For additional information see "Diplomacy and Westward Expansion: The Oregon Territory (1846)," *Timeline of U.S. Diplomatic History (1830–1860)*, Office of the Historian, Bureau of Public Affairs, U.S. Department of State, Washington, DC, 2004. This agency is listed in the *National Resource Directory* section of this volume.

Vancouver Island in 1849. The U.S. portion of the region was organized as Oregon Territory on August 14, 1848, with Washington Territory being formed from it in 1853. The British portion remained unorganized until 1858 when the Colony of British Columbia was declared as a result of the Fraser Canyon Gold Rush and fears of reasserted American expansionist intentions. The two British colonies were amalgamated in 1866 as the Colony of British Columbia. When the Colony of British Columbia joined Canada in 1871, the 49th Parallel and marine boundaries established by the Oregon Treaty became the U.S.–Canadian border.

The treaty defined the border in the Strait of June de Fuca through the major channel. Unfortunately, the "major channel" was not defined.

- Navigation of "channel[s] and straits, south of the forty-ninth parallel of north latitude, remain free and open to both parties."
- The "Puget's Sound Agricultural Company" retains the right to their property north of the Columbia River, and shall be compensated for properties surrendered if required by the United States. (The Puget's Sound Agricultural Company was a subsidiary of the Hudson's Bay Company).
- The property rights of the Hudson's Bay Company and all British subjects south of the new boundary will be respected.

In 1859, an unclear description of the maritime border in the treaty led to the bloodless war known as the Pig War over the ownership of the San Juan Islands.

The Document

Oregon Treaty[1]

THE United States of America and her Majesty the Queen of the United Kingdom of Great Britain and Ireland, deeming it to be desirable for the future welfare of both countries that the state of doubt and uncertainty which has hitherto prevailed respecting the sovereignty and government of the territory on the northwest coast of America, lying westward of the Rocky or Stony Mountains, should be finally terminated by an amicable compromise of the rights mutually asserted by the two parties over the said territory, have respectively named plenipotentiaries to treat and agree concerning the terms of such settlement — that is to say: the President of the United States of America has, on his part, furnished with full powers James Buchanan, Secretary of State of the United States, and her Majesty the Queen of the United Kingdom of Great Britain and Ireland has, on her part, appointed the Right Honorable Richard Pakenham, a member of her Majesty's Most Honorable Privy Council, and her Majesty's Envoy Extraordinary and Minister Plenipotentiary to the United States; who, after having communicated to each other their respective full powers, found in good and due form, have agreed upon and concluded the following articles: —

ARTICLE I.

From the point on the forty-ninth parallel of north latitude, where the boundary laid down in existing treaties and conventions between the United States and Great Britain terminates, the line of boundary between the territories of the United States and those of her Britannic Majesty shall be continued westward along the said forty-ninth parallel of north latitude to the middle of the channel which separates the continent from Vancouver's Island, and thence southerly through the middle of the said channel, and of Fuca's Straits, to the Pacific Ocean: Provided, however, That the navigation of the whole of the said channel and straits, south of the forty-ninth parallel of north latitude, remain free and open to both parties.

ARTICLE II.

From the point at which the forty-ninth parallel of north latitude shall be found to intersect the great northern branch of the Columbia River, the navigation of the said branch shall be free and open to the Hudson's Bay Company, and to all British subjects trading with the same, to the point where the said branch meets the main stream of the Columbia, and thence down the said main stream to the ocean, with Fee access into and through the said river or rivers, it being understood that all the usual portages along the line thus described shall, in like manner, be free and open. In navigating the said river or rivers, British subjects, with their goods and produce, shall be treated on the same footing as citizens of the United States; it being, however, always understood that nothing in this article shall be construed as preventing, or intended to prevent, the government of the United States from making any regulations respecting the navigation of the said river or rivers not inconsistent with the present treaty.

ARTICLE III.

In the future appropriation of the territory south of the forty-ninth parallel of north latitude, as provided in the first article of this treaty, the possessory rights of the Hudson's Bay Company, and of all British subjects who may be already in the occupation of land or other property lawfully acquired within the said territory, shall be respected.

ARTICLE IV.

The farms, lands, and other property of every description, belonging to the Puget's Sound Agricultural Company, on the north side of the Columbia River, shall be confirmed to the said company. In case, however, the situation of those farms and lands should be considered by the United States to be of public and political importance, and the United States government should signify a desire to obtain possession of the whole, or of any part thereof, the property so required shall be transferred to the said government, at a proper valuation, to be agreed upon between the parties.

ARTICLE V.

The present treaty shall be ratified by the President of the United States, by and with the advice and consent of the Senate thereof, and by her Britannic Majesty; and the ratifications shall be exchanged at London, at the expiration of six months from the date hereof, or sooner, if possible.

In witness whereof, the respective Plenipotentiaries have signed the same, and have affixed thereto the seals of their arms.

Done at Washington, the fifteenth day of June, in the year of our Lord one thousand eight hundred and forty-six.

JAMES BUCHANAN [L S.]
RICHARD PAKENHAM [L. S.]

NOTE

1. Officially titled the *Treaty between Her Majesty and the United States of America, for the Settlement of the Oregon Boundary* and styled in the United States as the *Treaty with Great Britain, in Regard to Limits Westward of the Rocky Mountains*, and also known as the *Buchanan-Pakenham* (or *Packenham*) *Treaty* or (sharing the name with several other unrelated treaties) the *Treaty of Washington*.

CHAPTER 25

Treaty of Guadalupe Hidalgo (February 2, 1848)

United States Congress

The History*

The Treaty of Guadalupe Hidalgo which brought an official end to the Mexican-American War (1846–1848) was signed on February 2, 1848, at Guadalupe Hidalgo, a city north of the capital where the Mexican government had fled with the advance of U.S. forces.

With the defeat of its army and the fall of the capital, Mexico City, in September 1847 the Mexican government surrendered to the United States and entered into negotiations to end the way. The peace talks were negotiated by Nicholas Trist, chief clerk of the State Department, who had accompanied General Winfield Scott as a diplomat and President Polk's representative. Trist and General Scott, after two previous unsuccessful attempts to negotiate a treaty with Santa Anna, determined that the only way to deal with Mexico was as a conquered enemy. Nicholas Trist negotiated with a special commission representing the collapsed government led by Don Bernardo Couto, Don Miguel Atristain, and Don Luis Gonzaga Cuevas of Mexico.

Under the terms of the treaty negotiated by Trist, Mexico ceded to the United States Upper California and New Mexico. This was known as the Mexican Cession and included present-day Arizona and New Mexico and parts of Utah, Nevada, and Colorado (see Article V of the treaty). Mexico relinquished all claims to Texas and recognized the Rio Grande as the southern boundary with the United States (see Article V).

The United States paid Mexico $15,000,000 "in consideration of the extension acquired by the boundaries of the United States" (see Article XII of the treaty) and agreed to pay American citizens' debts owed to them by the Mexican government (see Article XV). Other provisions included protection of property and civil rights of Mexican nationals living within the new boundaries of the United States (see Articles VIII and IX), the promise of the United States to police its boundaries (see Article XI), and compulsory arbitration of future

*Originally published as "Teaching with Documents: The Treaty of Guadalupe Hidalgo," *Educators and Students Report*, The National Archives, U.S. National Archives and Records Administration, College Park, Maryland, 2009. For additional information see "Diplomacy and Westward Expansion: The Treaty of Guadalupe Hidalgo (1848), *Timeline of U.S. Diplomatic History (1830–1860)*, Office of the Historian, Bureau of Public Affairs, U.S. Department of State, Washington, DC, 2004. This agency is listed in the *National Resource Directory* section of this volume.

disputes between the two countries (see Article XXI).

Trist sent a copy to Washington by the fastest means available, forcing Polk to decide whether or not to repudiate the highly satisfactory handiwork of his discredited subordinate. Polk chose to forward the treaty to the Senate. When the Senate reluctantly ratified the treaty (by a vote of 34 to 14) on March 10, 1848, it deleted Article X guaranteeing the protection of Mexican land grants. Following the ratification, U.S. troops were removed from the Mexican capital.

To carry the treaty into effect, commissioner Colonel Jon Weller and surveyor Andrew Grey were appointed by the United States government and General Pedro Conde and Sr. Jose Illarregui were appointed by the Mexican government to survey and set the boundary. A subsequent treaty of December 30, 1853, altered the border from the initial one by adding 47 more boundary markers to the original six. Of the 53 markers, the majority were rude piles of stone; a few were of durable character with proper inscriptions.

Over time, markers were moved or destroyed, resulting in two subsequent conventions (1882 and 1889) between the two countries to more clearly define the boundaries. Photographers were brought in to document the location of the markers. These photographs are in Record Group 77, Records of the Office of the Chief Engineers, in the National Archives.

The Document

Treaty of Guadalupe Hidalgo

In the Name of Almighty God

The United States of America and the United Mexican States animated by a sincere desire to put an end to the calamities of the war which unhappily exists between the two Republics and to establish Upon a solid basis relations of peace and friendship, which shall confer reciprocal benefits upon the citizens of both, and assure the concord, harmony, and mutual confidence wherein the two people should live, as good neighbors have for that purpose appointed their respective plenipotentiaries, that is to say: The President of the United States has appointed Nicholas P. Trist, a citizen of the United States, and the President of the Mexican Republic has appointed Don Luis Gonzaga Cuevas, Don Bernardo Couto, and Don Miguel Atristain, citizens of the said Republic; Who, after a reciprocal communication of their respective full powers, have, under the protection of Almighty God, the author of peace, arranged, agreed upon, and signed the following: Treaty of Peace, Friendship, Limits, and Settlement between the United States of America and the Mexican Republic.

ARTICLE I

There shall be firm and universal peace between the United States of America and the Mexican Republic, and between their respective countries, territories, cities, towns, and people, without exception of places or persons.

ARTICLE II

Immediately upon the signature of this treaty, a convention shall be entered into between a commissioner or commissioners appointed by the General-in-chief of the forces of the United States, and such as may be appointed by the Mexican Government, to the end that a provisional suspension of hostilities shall take place, and that, in the places occupied by the said forces, constitutional order may be reestablished, as regards the political, administrative, and judicial branches, so far as this shall be permitted by the circumstances of military occupation.

ARTICLE III

Immediately upon the ratification of the present treaty by the Government of the United States, orders shall be transmitted to the commanders of their land and naval forces, requiring the latter (provided this treaty shall then have been ratified by the Government of the Mexican Republic, and the ratifications exchanged) immediately to desist from blockading any Mexican ports and requiring the former (under the same condition) to commence, at the earliest moment practicable, withdrawing all troops of the United States then in the interior of the Mexican Republic, to points that shall be selected by common agreement, at a distance from the seaports not exceeding thirty leagues; and such evacuation of the interior of the Republic shall be completed with the least possible delay; the Mexican Government hereby binding itself to afford every facility in its power for rendering the same convenient to the troops, on their march and in their new positions, and for promoting a good understanding between them and the inhabitants. In like manner orders shall be despatched to the persons in charge of the custom houses at all ports occupied by the forces of the United States, requiring them (under the same condition) immediately to deliver possession of the same to the persons authorized by the Mexican Government to receive it, together with all bonds and evidences of debt for duties on importations and on exportations, not yet fallen due. Moreover, a faithful and exact account shall be made out, showing the entire amount of all duties on imports and on exports, collected at such custom-houses, or elsewhere in Mexico, by authority of the United States, from and after the day of ratification of this treaty by the Government of the Mexican Republic; and also an account of the cost of collection; and such entire amount, deducting only the cost of collection, shall be delivered to the Mexican Government, at the city of Mexico, within three months after the exchange of ratifications.

The evacuation of the capital of the Mexican Republic by the troops of the United States, in virtue of the above stipulation, shall be completed in one month after

the orders there stipulated for shall have been received by the commander of said troops, or sooner if possible.

ARTICLE IV

Immediately after the exchange of ratifications of the present treaty all castles, forts, territories, places, and possessions, which have been taken or occupied by the forces of the United States during the present war, within the limits of the Mexican Republic, as about to be established by the following article, shall be definitely restored to the said Republic, together with all the artillery, arms, apparatus of war, munitions, and other public property, which were in the said castles and forts when captured, and which shall remain there at the time when this treaty shall be duly ratified by the Government of the Mexican Republic. To this end, immediately upon the signature of this treaty, orders shall be despatched to the American officers commanding such castles and forts, securing against the removal or destruction of any such artillery, arms, apparatus of war, munitions, or other public property. The city of Mexico, within the inner line of intrenchments surrounding the said city, is comprehended in the above stipulation, as regards the restoration of artillery, apparatus of war, & c.

The final evacuation of the territory of the Mexican Republic, by the forces of the United States, shall be completed in three months from the said exchange of ratifications, or sooner if possible; the Mexican Government hereby engaging, as in the foregoing article, to use all means in its power for facilitating such evacuation, and rendering it convenient to the troops, and for promoting a good understanding between them and the inhabitants.

If, however, the ratification of this treaty by both parties should not take place in time to allow the embarcation of the troops of the United States to be completed before the commencement of the sickly season, at the

Mexican ports on the Gulf of Mexico, in such case a friendly arrangement shall be entered into between the General-in-Chief of the said troops and the Mexican Government, whereby healthy and otherwise suitable places, at a distance from the ports not exceeding thirty leagues, shall be designated for the residence of such troops as may not yet have embarked, until the return of the healthy season. And the space of time here referred to as, comprehending the sickly season shall be understood to extend from the first day of May to the first day of November.

All prisoners of war taken on either side, on land or on sea, shall be restored as soon as practicable after the exchange of ratifications of this treaty. It is also agreed that if any Mexicans should now be held as captives by any savage tribe within the limits of the United States, as about to be established by the following article, the Government of the said United States will exact the release of such captives and cause them to be restored to their country.

ARTICLE V

The boundary line between the two Republics shall commence in the Gulf of Mexico, three leagues from land, opposite the mouth of the Rio Grande, otherwise called Rio Bravo del Norte, or Opposite the mouth of its deepest branch, if it should have more than one branch emptying directly into the sea; from thence up the middle of that river, following the deepest channel, where it has more than one, to the point where it strikes the southern boundary of New Mexico; thence, westwardly, along the whole southern boundary of New Mexico (which runs north of the town called Paso) to its western termination; thence, northward, along the western line of New Mexico, until it intersects the first branch of the river Gila; (or if it should not intersect any branch of that river, then to the point on the said line nearest to such branch, and thence in a direct line to the same); thence down the middle of the

said branch and of the said river, until it empties into the Rio Colorado; thence across the Rio Colorado, following the division line between Upper and Lower California, to the Pacific Ocean.

The southern and western limits of New Mexico, mentioned in the article, are those laid down in the map entitled "Map of the United Mexican States, as organized and defined by various acts of the Congress of said republic, and constructed according to the best authorities. Revised edition. Published at New York, in 1847, by J. Disturnell," of which map a copy is added to this treaty, bearing the signatures and seals of the undersigned Plenipotentiaries. And, in order to preclude all difficulty in tracing upon the ground the limit separating Upper from Lower California, it is agreed that the said limit shall consist of a straight line drawn from the middle of the Rio Gila, where it unites with the Colorado, to a point on the coast of the Pacific Ocean, distant one marine league due south of the southernmost point of the port of San Diego, according to the plan of said port made in the year 1782 by Don Juan Pantoja, second sailing-master of the Spanish fleet, and published at Madrid in the year 1802, in the atlas to the voyage of the schooners Sutil and Mexicana; of which plan a copy is hereunto added, signed and sealed by the respective Plenipotentiaries.

In order to designate the boundary line with due precision, upon authoritative maps, and to establish upon the ground land-marks which shall show the limits of both republics, as described in the present article, the two Governments shall each appoint a commissioner and a surveyor, who, before the expiration of one year from the date of the exchange of ratifications of this treaty, shall meet at the port of San Diego, and proceed to run and mark the said boundary in its whole course to the mouth of the Rio Bravo del Norte. They shall keep journals and make out plans of their operations; and the result agreed upon by them shall be deemed a part of this treaty, and shall have the same force as if it were inserted therein. The two Governments will amicably agree regarding what may be necessary to these persons, and also as to their respective escorts, should such be necessary.

The boundary line established by this article shall be religiously respected by each of the two republics, and no change shall ever be made therein, except by the express and free consent of both nations, lawfully given by the General Government of each, in conformity with its own constitution.

ARTICLE VI

The vessels and citizens of the United States shall, in all time, have a free and uninterrupted passage by the Gulf of California, and by the river Colorado below its confluence with the Gila, to and from their possessions situated north of the boundary line defined in the preceding article; it being understood that this passage is to be by navigating the Gulf of California and the river Colorado, and not by land, without the express consent of the Mexican Government.

If, by the examinations which may be made, it should be ascertained to be practicable and advantageous to construct a road, canal, or railway, which should in whole or in part run upon the river Gila, or upon its right or its left bank, within the space of one marine league from either margin of the river, the Governments of both republics will form an agreement regarding its construction, in order that it may serve equally for the use and advantage of both countries.

ARTICLE VII

The river Gila, and the part of the Rio Bravo del Norte lying below the southern boundary of New Mexico, being, agreeably to the fifth article, divided in the middle between the two republics, the navigation of the Gila and of the Bravo below said boundary shall be free and common to the vessels and citizens of both countries; and neither

shall, without the consent of the other, construct any work that may impede or interrupt, in whole or in part, the exercise of this right; not even for the purpose of favoring new methods of navigation. Nor shall any tax or contribution, under any denomination or title, be levied upon vessels or persons navigating the same or upon merchandise or effects transported thereon, except in the case of landing upon one of their shores. If, for the purpose of making the said rivers navigable, or for maintaining them in such state, it should be necessary or advantageous to establish any tax or contribution, this shall not be done without the consent of both Governments.

The stipulations contained in the present article shall not impair the territorial rights of either republic within its established limits.

ARTICLE VIII

Mexicans now established in territories previously belonging to Mexico, and which remain for the future within the limits of the United States, as defined by the present treaty, shall be free to continue where they now reside, or to remove at any time to the Mexican Republic, retaining the property which they possess in the said territories, or disposing thereof, and removing the proceeds wherever they please, without their being subjected, on this account, to any contribution, tax, or charge whatever.

Those who shall prefer to remain in the said territories may either retain the title and rights of Mexican citizens, or acquire those of citizens of the United States. But they shall be under the obligation to make their election within one year from the date of the exchange of ratifications of this treaty; and those who shall remain in the said territories after the expiration of that year, without having declared their intention to retain the character of Mexicans, shall be considered to have elected to become citizens of the United States.

In the said territories, property of every kind, now belonging to Mexicans not established there, shall be inviolably respected. The present owners, the heirs of these, and all Mexicans who may hereafter acquire said property by contract, shall enjoy with respect to it guarantees equally ample as if the same belonged to citizens of the United States.

ARTICLE IX

The Mexicans who, in the territories aforesaid, shall not preserve the character of citizens of the Mexican Republic, conformably with what is stipulated in the preceding article, shall be incorporated into the Union of the United States and be admitted at the proper time (to be judged of by the Congress of the United States) to the enjoyment of all the rights of citizens of the United States, according to the principles of the Constitution; and in the mean time, shall be maintained and protected in the free enjoyment of their liberty and property, and secured in the free exercise of their religion without restriction.

ARTICLE X

[Stricken out]

ARTICLE XI

Considering that a great part of the territories, which, by the present treaty, are to be comprehended for the future within the limits of the United States, is now occupied by savage tribes, who will hereafter be under the exclusive control of the Government of the United States, and whose incursions within the territory of Mexico would be prejudicial in the extreme, it is solemnly agreed that all such incursions shall be forcibly restrained by the Government of the United States whensoever this may be necessary; and that when they cannot be prevented, they shall be punished by the said Government, and satisfaction for the same shall be exacted all in the same way, and with equal diligence and energy, as if the same incursions were

meditated or committed within its own territory, against its own citizens.

It shall not be lawful, under any pretext whatever, for any inhabitant of the United States to purchase or acquire any Mexican, or any foreigner residing in Mexico, who may have been captured by Indians inhabiting the territory of either of the two republics; nor to purchase or acquire horses, mules, cattle, or property of any kind, stolen within Mexican territory by such Indians.

And in the event of any person or persons, captured within Mexican territory by Indians, being carried into the territory of the United States, the Government of the latter engages and binds itself, in the most solemn manner, so soon as it shall know of such captives being within its territory, and shall be able so to do, through the faithful exercise of its influence and power, to rescue them and return them to their country. or deliver them to the agent or representative of the Mexican Government. The Mexican authorities will, as far as practicable, give to the Government of the United States notice of such captures; and its agents shall pay the expenses incurred in the maintenance and transmission of the rescued captives; who, in the mean time, shall be treated with the utmost hospitality by the American authorities at the place where they may be. But if the Government of the United States, before receiving such notice from Mexico, should obtain intelligence, through any other channel, of the existence of Mexican captives within its territory, it will proceed forthwith to effect their release and delivery to the Mexican agent, as above stipulated.

For the purpose of giving to these stipulations the fullest possible efficacy, thereby affording the security and redress demanded by their true spirit and intent, the Government of the United States will now and hereafter pass, without unnecessary delay, and always vigilantly enforce, such laws as the nature of the subject may require. And, finally, the sacredness of this obligation shall never be lost sight of by the said Government, when providing for the removal of the Indians from any portion of the said territories, or for its being settled by citizens of the United States; but, on the contrary, special care shall then be taken not to place its Indian occupants under the necessity of seeking new homes, by committing those invasions which the United States have solemnly obliged themselves to restrain.

ARTICLE XII

In consideration of the extension acquired by the boundaries of the United States, as defined in the fifth article of the present treaty, the Government of the United States engages to pay to that of the Mexican Republic the sum of fifteen millions of dollars.

Immediately after the treaty shall have been duly ratified by the Government of the Mexican Republic, the sum of three millions of dollars shall be paid to the said Government by that of the United States, at the city of Mexico, in the gold or silver coin of Mexico. The remaining twelve millions of dollars shall be paid at the same place, and in the same coin, in annual installments of three millions of dollars each, together with interest on the same at the rate of six per centum per annum. This interest shall begin to run upon the whole sum of twelve millions from the day of the ratification of the present treaty by — the Mexican Government, and the first of the installments shall be paid — at the expiration of one year from the same day. Together with each annual installment, as it falls due, the whole interest accruing on such installment from the beginning shall also be paid.

ARTICLE XIII

The United States engage, moreover, to assume and pay to the claimants all the amounts now due them, and those hereafter to become due, by reason of the claims already liquidated and decided against the Mexican Republic, under the conventions between the two republics severally concluded on the eleventh day of April, eighteen hundred and thirty-nine, and on the thirtieth day of January, eighteen hundred and forty-three; so that the Mexican Republic shall be absolutely exempt, for the future, from all expense whatever on account of the said claims.

ARTICLE XIV

The United States do furthermore discharge the Mexican Republic from all claims of citizens of the United States, not heretofore decided against the Mexican Government, which may have arisen previously to the date of the signature of this treaty; which discharge shall be final and perpetual, whether the said claims be rejected or be allowed by the board of commissioners provided for in the following article, and whatever shall be the total amount of those allowed.

ARTICLE XV

The United States, exonerating Mexico from all demands on account of the claims of their citizens mentioned in the preceding article, and considering them entirely and forever canceled, whatever their amount may be, undertake to make satisfaction for the same, to an amount not exceeding three and one-quarter millions of dollars. To ascertain the validity and amount of those claims, a board of commissioners shall be established by the Government of the United States, whose awards shall be final and conclusive; provided that, in deciding upon the validity of each claim, the board shall be guided and governed by the principles and rules of decision prescribed by the first and fifth articles of the unratified convention, concluded at the city of Mexico on the twentieth day of November, one thousand eight hundred and forty-three; and in no case shall an award be made in favour of any claim not embraced by these principles and rules.

If, in the opinion of the said board of

commissioners or of the claimants, any books, records, or documents, in the possession or power of the Government of the Mexican Republic, shall be deemed necessary to the just decision of any claim, the commissioners, or the claimants through them, shall, within such period as Congress may designate, make an application in writing for the same, addressed to the Mexican Minister of Foreign Affairs, to be transmitted by the Secretary of State of the United States; and the Mexican Government engages, at the earliest possible moment after the receipt of such demand, to cause any of the books, records, or documents so specified, which shall be in their possession or power (or authenticated copies or extracts of the same), to be transmitted to the said Secretary of State, who shall immediately deliver them over to the said board of commissioners; provided that no such application shall be made by or at the instance of any claimant, until the facts which it is expected to prove by such books, records, or documents, shall have been stated under oath or affirmation.

Article XVI

Each of the contracting parties reserves to itself the entire right to fortify whatever point within its territory it may judge proper so to fortify for its security.

Article XVII

The treaty of amity, commerce, and navigation, concluded at the city of Mexico, on the fifth day of April, A. D. 1831, between the United States of America and the United Mexican States, except the additional article, and except so far as the stipulations of the said treaty may be incompatible with any stipulation contained in the present treaty, is hereby revived for the period of eight years from the day of the exchange of ratifications of this treaty, with the same force and virtue as if incorporated therein; it being understood that each of the contracting parties reserves to itself the right, at any time after the said period of eight years shall have expired, to terminate the same by giving one year's notice of such intention to the other party.

Article XVIII

All supplies whatever for troops of the United States in Mexico, arriving at ports in the occupation of such troops previous to the final evacuation thereof, although subsequently to the restoration of the custom-houses at such ports, shall be entirely exempt from duties and charges of any kind; the Government of the United States hereby engaging and pledging its faith to establish and vigilantly to enforce, all possible guards for securing the revenue of Mexico, by preventing the importation, under cover of this stipulation, of any articles other than such, both in kind and in quantity, as shall really be wanted for the use and consumption of the forces of the United States during the time they may remain in Mexico. To this end it shall be the duty of all officers and agents of the United States to denounce to the Mexican authorities at the respective ports any attempts at a fraudulent abuse of this stipulation, which they may know of, or may have reason to suspect, and to give to such authorities all the aid in their power with regard thereto; and every such attempt, when duly proved and established by sentence of a competent tribunal, They shall be punished by the confiscation of the property so attempted to be fraudulently introduced.

Article XIX

With respect to all merchandise, effects, and property whatsoever, imported into ports of Mexico, whilst in the occupation of the forces of the United States, whether by citizens of either republic, or by citizens or subjects of any neutral nation, the following rules shall be observed:

(1) All such merchandise, effects, and property, if imported previously to the restoration of the custom-houses to the Mexican authori-

ties, as stipulated for in the third article of this treaty, shall be exempt from confiscation, although the importation of the same be prohibited by the Mexican tariff.

(2) The same perfect exemption shall be enjoyed by all such merchandise, effects, and property, imported subsequently to the restoration of the custom-houses, and previously to the sixty days fixed in the following article for the coming into force of the Mexican tariff at such ports respectively; the said merchandise, effects, and property being, however, at the time of their importation, subject to the payment of duties, as provided for in the said following article.

(3) All merchandise, effects, and property described in the two rules foregoing shall, during their continuance at the place of importation, and upon their leaving such place for the interior, be exempt from all duty, tax, or imposts of every kind, under whatsoever title or denomination. Nor shall they be there subject to any charge whatsoever upon the sale thereof.

(4) All merchandise, effects, and property, described in the first and second rules, which shall have been removed to any place in the interior, whilst such place was in the occupation of the forces of the United States, shall, during their continuance therein, be exempt from all tax upon the sale or consumption thereof, and from every kind of impost or contribution, under whatsoever title or denomination.

(5) But if any merchandise, effects, or property, described in the first and second rules, shall be removed to any place not occupied at the time by the forces of the United States, they shall, upon their introduction into such place, or upon their sale or consumption there, be subject to the same duties which, under the Mexican laws, they would be required to pay in such cases if they had been imported in time of peace, through the maritime custom-houses, and had there paid the duties conformably with the Mexican tariff.

(6) The owners of all merchandise, effects, or property, described in the first and second rules, and existing in any port of Mexico, shall have the right to reship the same, exempt from all tax, impost, or contribution whatever.

With respect to the metals, or other property, exported from any Mexican port whilst in the occupation of the forces of the United States, and previously to the restora-tion of the custom-house at such port, no person shall be required by the Mexican authorities, whether general or state, to pay any tax, duty, or contribution upon any such exportation, or in any manner to account for the same to the said authorities.

ARTICLE XX

Through consideration for the interests of commerce generally, it is agreed, that if less than sixty days should elapse between the date of the signature of this treaty and the restoration of the custom houses, conformably with the stipulation in the third article, in such case all merchandise, effects and property whatsoever, arriving at the Mexican ports after the restoration of the said custom-houses, and previously to the expiration of sixty days after the day of signature of this treaty, shall be admitted to entry; and no other duties shall be levied thereon than the duties established by the tariff found in force at such custom-houses at the time of the restoration of the same. And to all such merchandise, effects, and property, the rules established by the preceding article shall apply.

ARTICLE XXI

If unhappily any disagreement should hereafter arise between the Governments of the two republics, whether with respect to the interpretation of any stipulation in this treaty, or with respect to any other particular concerning the political or commercial relations of the two nations, the said Governments, in the name of those nations, do promise to each other that they will endeavour, in the most sincere and earnest manner, to settle the differences so arising, and to preserve the state of peace and friendship in which the two countries are now placing themselves, using, for this end, mutual representations and pacific negotiations. And if, by these means, they should not be enabled to come to an agreement, a resort shall not, on this account, be had to reprisals, aggression, or hostility of any kind, by the one republic against the other, until the Government of that which deems itself aggrieved shall have maturely considered, in the spirit of peace and good neighbourship, whether it would not be better that such difference should be settled by the arbitration of commissioners appointed on each side, or by that of a friendly nation. And should such course be proposed by either party, it shall be acceded to by the other, unless deemed by it altogether incompatible with the nature of the difference, or the circumstances of the case.

ARTICLE XXII

If (which is not to be expected, and which God forbid) war should unhappily break out between the two republics, they do now, with a view to such calamity, solemnly pledge themselves to each other and to the world to observe the following rules; absolutely where the nature of the subject permits, and as closely as possible in all cases where such absolute observance shall be impossible:

(1). The merchants of either republic then residing in the other shall be allowed to remain twelve months (for those dwelling in the interior), and six months (for those dwelling at the seaports) to collect their debts and settle their affairs; during which periods they shall enjoy the same protection, and be on the same footing, in all respects, as the citizens or subjects of the most friendly nations; and, at the expiration thereof, or at any time before, they shall have full liberty to depart, carrying off all their effects without molestation or hindrance, conforming therein to the same laws which the citizens or subjects of the most friendly nations are required to conform to. Upon the entrance of the armies of either nation into the territories of the other, women and children, ecclesiastics, scholars of every faculty, cultivators of the earth, merchants, artisans, manufacturers, and fishermen, unarmed and inhabiting unfortified towns, villages, or places, and in general all persons whose occupations are for the common subsistence and benefit of mankind, shall be allowed to continue their respective employments, unmolested in their persons. Nor shall their houses or goods be burnt or otherwise destroyed, nor their cattle taken, nor their fields wasted, by the armed force into whose power, by the events of war, they may happen to fall; but if the necessity arise to take anything from them for the use of such armed force, the same shall be paid for at an equitable price. All churches, hospitals, schools, colleges, libraries, and other establishments for charitable and beneficent purposes, shall be respected, and all persons connected with the same protected in the discharge of their duties, and the pursuit of their vocations.

(2). In order that the fate of prisoners of war may be alleviated all such practices as those of sending them into distant, inclement or unwholesome districts, or crowding them into close and noxious places, shall be studiously avoided. They shall not be confined in dungeons, prison ships, or prisons; nor be put in irons, or bound or otherwise restrained in the use of their limbs. The officers shall enjoy liberty on their paroles, within convenient districts, and have comfortable quarters; and the common soldiers shall be disposed in cantonments, open and extensive enough for air and exercise and lodged in barracks as roomy and good as are provided by the party in whose power they are for its own troops. But if any officer shall break his parole by leaving the district so assigned him, or any other prisoner shall escape from the limits of his cantonment after they shall have been designated to him, such individual, officer, or other prisoner, shall forfeit so much of the benefit of this article as provides for his liberty on parole or in cantonment. And if any officer so breaking his parole or any common soldier so escaping from the limits assigned him, shall afterwards be found in arms previously to his being regularly exchanged, the person so offending shall be dealt with according to the established laws of war. The officers shall be daily furnished, by the party in whose power they are, with as many rations, and of the same articles, as are allowed either in kind or by commutation, to officers of equal rank in its own army; and all others shall be daily furnished with such ration as is allowed to a common soldier in its own service; the value of all which supplies shall, at the close of the war, or at periods to be agreed upon between the respective commanders, be paid by the other party, on a mutual adjustment of accounts for the subsistence of prisoners; and such accounts shall not be mingled with or set off against any others, nor the balance due on them withheld, as a compensation or reprisal for any cause whatever, real or pretended. Each party shall be allowed to keep a commissary of prisoners, appointed by itself, with every cantonment of prisoners, in possession of the other; which commissary shall see the prisoners as often as he pleases; shall be allowed to receive, exempt from all duties and taxes, and to distribute, whatever comforts may be sent to them by their friends; and shall be free to transmit his reports in open letters to the party by whom he is employed. And it is declared that neither the pretense that war dissolves all treaties, nor any other whatever, shall be considered as annulling or suspending the solemn covenant contained in this article. On the contrary, the state of war is precisely that for which it is provided; and, during which, its stipulations are to be as sacredly observed as the most acknowledged obligations under the law of nature or nations.

ARTICLE XXIII

This treaty shall be ratified by the President of the United States of America, by and with the advice and consent of the Senate thereof; and by the President of the Mexican Republic, with the previous approbation of its general Congress; and the ratifications shall be exchanged in the City of Washington, or at the seat of Government of Mexico, in four months from the date of the signature hereof, or sooner if practicable. In faith whereof we, the respective Plenipotentiaries, have signed this treaty of peace, friendship, limits, and settlement, and have hereunto affixed our seals respectively. Done in quintuplicate, at the city of Guadalupe Hidalgo, on the second day of February, in the year of our Lord one thousand eight hundred and forty-eight.

N. P. TRIST
LUIS P. CUEVAS
BERNARDO COUTO
MIGL. ATRISTAIN

CHAPTER 26

Gadsden Purchase Treaty (December 30, 1853)

United States Congress

The History*

The Gadsden Purchase, or Treaty, was an agreement between the United States and Mexico, finalized in 1854, in which the United States agreed to pay Mexico $10 million for a 29,670 square mile portion of Mexico that later became part of Arizona and New Mexico. Gadsden's Purchase provided the land necessary for a southern transcontinental railroad and attempted to resolve conflicts that lingered after the Mexican-American War.

While the Treaty of Guadalupe Hidalgo formally ended the Mexican-American War in February 1848, tensions between the Governments of Mexico and the United States continued to simmer over the next six years. The two countries each claimed the Mesilla Valley as part of their own country. The Mexican Government demanded monetary compensation for Native American attacks in the region because, under the Treaty, the United States had agreed to protect Mexico from such attacks; however, the United States refused to comply, insisting that while they had agreed to protect Mexico from Native American attacks, they had not agreed to financially compensate for attacks that did occur. The persistent efforts of private American citizens to enter Mexico illegally and incite rebellions in an effort to gain territory exacerbated tensions between the governments.

These continuing tensions between Mexico and the United States complicated U.S. efforts to find a southern route for a transcontinental railroad as the only viable routes passed through Mexican territory. In 1847, the United States attempted to buy the Isthmus of Tehuantepec, an isthmus on the southern edge of North America, as an alternative means of providing a southern connection between the Atlantic and Pacific oceans. Mexico, however, had already granted Mexican Don José de Garay the right to build colonies for Americans on the isthmus with capital from the New Orleans Company. Fearing the colonists would rebel as those in Texas had, Mexican President Juan Ceballos revoked the grant, angering U.S. investors.

*Originally published as "Diplomacy and Westward Expansion: Gadsden Purchase (1853–1854)," *Timeline of U.S. Diplomatic History (1830–1860)*, Office of the Historian, Bureau of Public Affairs, U.S. Department of State, Washington, DC, 2000. For additional information see "Diplomacy and Westward Expansion: Gadsden Purchase (1853–1854)," *Timeline of U.S. Diplomatic History (1830–1860)*, Office of the Historian, Bureau of Public Affairs, U.S. Department of State, Washington, DC, 2004. This agency is listed in the *National Resource Directory* section of this volume.

In 1853, Mexican officials evicted Americans from their property in the disputed Mesilla Valley. When the U.S. Government did not act, Governor William Lane of New Mexico declared the Mesilla Valley part of the U.S. territory of New Mexico. Mexican President Antonio de Santa Anna responded by sending troops into the valley. Attempting to defuse the situation, U.S. President Franklin Pierce sent James Gadsden, the new U.S. Minister to Mexico, to negotiate with Santa Anna. Secretary of State William Marcy instructed Gadsden to renegotiate a border that provided a route for a southern railroad, arrange for a release of U.S. financial obligations for Native American attacks, and settle the monetary claims between the countries related to the Garay project.

Gadsden met with Santa Anna on September 25, 1853. President Pierce sent verbal instructions for Gadsden through Christopher Ward, an agent for U.S. investors in the Garay project, giving Gadsden negotiating options ranging from $50 million for lower California and a large portion of northern Mexico to $15 million for a smaller land deal that would still provide for a southern railroad. Ward also lied to Gadsden, stating the President wanted the claims of the Garay party addressed in any treaty concluded with the Mexican Government; however, President Pierce never gave Ward these instructions because he did not believe in government involvement in affairs between private companies and foreign governments.

Santa Anna refused to sell a large portion of Mexico, but he needed money to fund an army to put down ongoing rebellions, so on December 30, 1853 he and Gadsden signed a treaty stipulating that the United States would pay $15 million for 45,000 square miles south of the New Mexico territory and assume private American claims, including those related to the Garay deal. The United States Government agreed to work toward preventing American raids along Mexico's border and Mexico voided U.S. responsibility for Native American attacks.

With a great deal of difficulty resulting from the increasing strife between the northern and southern states, the U.S. Senate ratified a revised treaty on April 25, 1854. The new treaty reduced the amount paid to Mexico to $10 million and the land purchased to 29,670 square miles, and removed any mention of Native American attacks and private claims. President Pierce signed the treaty and Gadsden presented the new treaty to Santa Anna, who signed it on June 8, 1854.

After Gadsden's Purchase a new border dispute caused tension over the United States' payment, and the treaty failed to resolve the issues surrounding financial claims and border attacks. However, it did create the southern border of the present-day United States, despite the beliefs of the vast majority of policymakers at the time who thought the United States would eventually expand further into Mexico.

The Document

Gadsden Purchase Treaty

WHEREAS a treaty between the United States of America and the Mexican Republic was concluded and signed at the City of Mexico on the thirtieth day of December, one thousand eight hundred and fifty-three; which treaty, as amended by the Senate of the United States, and being in the English and Spanish languages, is word for word as follows:

In the Name of Almighty God:

The Republic of Mexico and the United States of America desiring to remove every cause of disagreement which might interfere in any manner with the better friendship and intercourse between the two countries, and especially in respect to the true limits which should be established, when, notwithstanding what was covenanted in the treaty of

Guadalupe Hidalgo in the year 1848, opposite interpretations have been urged, which might give occasion to questions of serious moment: to avoid these, and to strengthen and more firmly maintain the peace which happily prevails between the two republics, the President of the United States has, for this purpose, appointed James Gadsden, Envoy Extraordinary and Minister Plenipotentiary of the same, near the Mexican government, and the President of Mexico has appointed as Plenipotentiary "ad hoc" his excellency Don Manuel Diez de Bonilla, cavalier grand cross of the national and distinguished order of Guadalupe, and Secretary of State, and of the office of Foreign Relations, and Don Jose Salazar Ylarregui and General Mariano Monterde as scientific commissioners, invested with full powers for this negotiation, who, having communicated their respective full powers, and finding them in due and proper form, have agreed upon the articles following:

ARTICLE I.

The Mexican Republic agrees to designate the following as her true limits with the United States for the future: retaining the same dividing line between the two Californias as already defined and established, according to the 5th article of the treaty of Guadalupe Hidalgo, the limits between the two republics shall be as follows: Beginning in the Gulf of Mexico, three leagues from land, opposite the mouth of the Rio Grande, as provided in the 5th article of the treaty of Guadalupe Hidalgo; thence, as defined in the said article, up the middle of that river to the point where the parallel of 31° 47' north latitude crosses the same; thence due west one hundred miles; thence south to the parallel of 31° 20' north latitude; thence along the said parallel of 31° 20' to the 111th meridian of longitude west of Greenwich; thence in a straight line to a point on the Colorado River twenty English miles below the junction of the Gila and Colorado rivers; thence up the

middle of the said river Colorado until it intersects the present line between the United States and Mexico.

For the performance of this portion of the treaty, each of the two governments shall nominate one commissioner, to the end that, by common consent the two thus nominated, having met in the city of Paso del Norte, three months after the exchange of the ratifications of this treaty, may proceed to survey and mark out upon the land the dividing line stipulated by this article, where it shall not have already been surveyed and established by the mixed commission, according to the treaty of Guadalupe, keeping a journal and making proper plans of their operations. For this purpose, if they should judge it necessary, the contracting parties shall be at liberty each to unite to its respective commissioner, scientific or other assistants, such as astronomers and surveyors, whose concurrence shall not be considered necessary for the settlement and of a true line of division between the two Republics; that line shall be alone established upon which the commissioners may fix, their consent in this particular being considered decisive and an integral part of this treaty, without necessity of ulterior ratification or approval, and without room for interpretation of any kind by either of the parties contracting.

The dividing line thus established shall, in all time, be faithfully respected by the two governments, without any variation therein, unless of the express and free consent of the two, given in conformity to the principles of the law of nations, and in accordance with the constitution of each country respectively.

In consequence, the stipulation in the 5th article of the treaty of Guadalupe Hidalgo upon the boundary line therein described is no longer of any force, wherein it may conflict with that here established, the said line being considered annulled and abolished wherever it may not coincide with the present, and in the same manner remaining in full force where in accordance with the same.

ARTICLE II.

The government of Mexico hereby releases the United States from all liability on account of the obligations contained in the eleventh article of the treaty of Guadalupe Hidalgo; and the said article and the thirty-third article of the treaty of amity, commerce, and navigation between the United States of America and the United Mexican States concluded at Mexico, on the fifth day of April, 1831, are hereby abrogated.

ARTICLE III.

In consideration of the foregoing stipulations, the Government of the United States agrees to pay to the government of Mexico, in the city of New York, the sum of ten millions of dollars, of which seven millions shall be paid immediately upon the exchange of the ratifications of this treaty, and the remaining three millions as soon as the boundary line shall be surveyed, marked, and established.

ARTICLE IV.

The provisions of the 6th and 7th articles of the treaty of Guadalupe Hidalgo having been rendered nugatory, for the most part, by the cession of territory granted in the first article of this treaty, the said articles are hereby abrogated and annulled, and the provisions as herein expressed substituted therefor. The vessels, and citizens of the United States shall, in all time, have free and uninterrupted passage through the Gulf of California, to and from their possessions situated north of the boundary line of the two countries. It being understood that this passage is to be by navigating the Gulf of California and the river Colorado, and not by land, without the express consent of the Mexican government; and precisely the same provisions, stipulations, and restrictions, in all respects, are hereby agreed upon and adopted, and shall be scrupulously observed and enforced by the two contracting governments in reference to the Rio Colorado, so far and for

such distance as the middle of that river is made their common boundary line by the first article of this treaty.

The several provisions, stipulations, and restrictions contained in the 7th article of the treaty of Guadalupe Hidalgo shall remain in force only so far as regards the Rio Bravo del Forte, below the initial of the said boundary provided in the first article of this treaty; that is to say, below the intersection of the 31° 47' 30" parallel of latitude, with the boundary line established by the late treaty dividing said river from its mouth upwards, according to the fifth article of the treaty of Guadalupe.

ARTICLE V.

All the provisions of the eighth and ninth, sixteenth and seventeenth articles of the treaty of Guadalupe Hidalgo, shall apply to the territory ceded by the Mexican Republic in the first article of the present treaty, and to all the rights of persons and property, both civil and ecclesiastical, within the same, as fully and as effectually as if the said articles were herein again recited and set forth.

ARTICLE VI.

No grants of land within the territory ceded by the first article of this treaty bearing date subsequent to the day — twenty-fifth of September — when the minister and subscriber to this treaty on the part of the United States, proposed to the Government of Mexico to terminate the question of boundary, will be considered valid or be recognized by the United States, or will any grants made previously be respected or be considered as obligatory which have not been located and duly recorded in the archives of Mexico.

ARTICLE VII.

Should there at any future period (which God forbid) occur any disagreement between the two nations which might lead to a rupture of their relations and reciprocal peace, they bind themselves in like manner to procure by every possible method the adjustment of every difference; and should they still in this manner not succeed, never will they proceed to a declaration of war, without having previously paid attention to what has been set forth in article twenty-one of the treaty of Guadalupe for similar cases; which article, as well as the twenty-second is here reaffirmed.

ARTICLE VIII.

The Mexican Government having on the 5th of February, 1853, authorized the early construction of a plank and railroad across the Isthmus of Tehuantepec, and, to secure the stable benefits of said transit way to the persons and merchandise of the citizens of Mexico and the United States, it is stipulated that neither government will interpose any obstacle to the transit of persons and merchandise of both nations; and at no time shall higher charges be made on the transit of persons and property of citizens of the United States, than may be made on the persons and property of other foreign nations, nor shall any interest in said transit way, nor in the proceeds thereof, be transferred to any foreign government.

The United States, by its agents, shall have the right to transport across the isthmus, in closed bags, the mails of the United States not intended for distribution along the line of communication; also the effects of the United States government and its citizens, which may be intended for transit, and not for distribution on the isthmus, free of custom-house or other charges by the Mexican government. Neither passports nor letters of security will be required of persons crossing the isthmus and not remaining in the country.

When the construction of the railroad shall be completed, the Mexican government agrees to open a port of entry in addition to the port of Vera Cruz, at or near the terminus of said road on the Gulf of Mexico.

The two governments will enter into arrangements for the prompt transit of troops and munitions of the United States, which that government may have occasion to send from one part of its territory to another, lying on opposite sides of the continent.

The Mexican government having agreed to protect with its whole power the prosecution, preservation, and security of the work, the United States may extend its protection as it shall judge wise to it when it may feel sanctioned and warranted by the public or international law.

ARTICLE IX.

This treaty shall be ratified, and the respective ratifications shall be exchanged at the city of Washington within the exact period of six months from the date of its signature, or sooner, if possible.

In testimony whereof, we, the plenipotentiaries of the contracting parties, have hereunto affixed our hands and seals at Mexico, the thirtieth (30th) day of December, in the year of our Lord one thousand eight hundred and fifty-three, in the thirty-third year of the independence of the Mexican republic, and the seventy-eighth of that of the United States.

JAMES GADSDEN,
MANUEL DIEZ DE BONILLA
JOSE SALAZAR YLARBEGUI
J. MARIANO MONTERDE,

And whereas the said treaty, as amended, has been duly ratified on both parts, and the respective ratifications of the same have this day been exchanged at Washington, by WILLIAM L. MARCY, Secretary of State of the United States, and SENOR GENERAL DON JUAN N. ALMONTE, Envoy Extraordinary and Minister Plenipotentiary of the Mexican Republic, on the part of their respective Governments:

Now, therefore, be it known that I, FRANKLIN PIERCE, President of the United States of America, have caused the said treaty to be made public, to the end that the same, and every clause and article thereof, may be observed and fulfilled with good faith by the United States and the citizens thereof

In witness whereof I have hereunto set my hand and caused the seal of the United States to be affixed.

Done at the city of Washington, this thirtieth day of June, in the year of our Lord one thousand eight hundred and fifty-four, and of the Independence of the United States the seventy-eighth.

BY THE PRESIDENT:
FRANKLIN PIERCE,
W. L. MARCY, Secretary of State.

CHAPTER 27

Alaska Treaty
(March 30, 1867)

United States Congress

The History*

In 1866 the Russian government offered to sell the territory of Alaska to the United States. Secretary of State William H. Seward, enthusiastic about the prospects of American expansion, negotiated the deal for the Americans. Edward de Stoeckl, Russian minister to the United States, negotiated for the Russians. On March 30, 1867, the two parties agreed that the United States would pay Russia $7.2 million for the territory of Alaska.

For less than 2 cents an acre, the United States acquired nearly 600,000 square miles. Opponents of the Alaska Purchase persisted in calling it "Seward's Folly" or "Seward's Icebox" until 1896, when the great Klondike Gold Strike convinced even the harshest critics that Alaska was a valuable addition to American territory.

The check for $7.2 million was made payable to the Russian Minister to the United States Edward de Stoeckl, who negotiated the deal for the Russians. Also shown here is the Treaty of Cession, signed by Tzar Alexander

II, which formally concluded the agreement for the purchase of Alaska from Russia.

Juneau officially replaced Sitka as capital in 1900, but it did not begin to function as such until 1906. In the same year Alaska was finally awarded a territorial representative in Congress. A new era began for Alaska when local government was established in 1912 and it became a U.S. territory. The building of the Alaska railroad from Seward to Fairbanks was commenced with government funds in 1915. Already, however, gold mining was dying out, and Alaska receded into one of its quiet periods. The fishing industry, which had gradually advanced during the gold era, became the major enterprise.

Alaska enjoyed an economic boom during World War II. The Alaska Highway was built, supplying a weak but much-needed link with the United States. After Japanese troops occupied the Aleutian islands of Attu and Kiska, U.S. forces prepared for a counterattack. Attu was retaken in May 1943, after intense fighting, and the Japanese evacuated Kiska in August after intensive U.S. bombardments. Dutch Harbor became a

*Originally published as "Check for the Purchase of Alaska (1868)," *100 Milestone Documents*, The National Archives, U.S. National Archives and Records Administration, College Park, Maryland, 2008. For additional information see "The Purchase of Alaska (1868)," *America's Historical Documents*, U.S. National Archives and Records Administration, College Park, Maryland, 2008. This agency is listed in the *National Resource Directory* section of this volume.

major key in the U.S. defense system. The growth of air travel after the war and the permanent military bases established in Alaska resulted in tremendous growth; between 1950 and 1960 the population nearly doubled.

In 1958, Alaskans approved statehood by a 5 to 1 vote, and on January 3, 1959, Alaska was officially admitted into the Union as a state, the first since Arizona in 1912. On March 27, 1964, the strongest earthquake ever recorded in North America occurred in Alaska, taking approximately 114 lives and causing extensive property damage. Some cities were almost totally destroyed, and the fishing industry was especially hard hit, with the loss of fleets, docks, and canneries from the resulting tsunami. Reconstruction, with large-scale federal aid, was rapid. The Alaska Native Claims Settlement Act (1971) gave roughly 44 million acres (17.8 million hectares; 10% of the state) and almost $1 billion to Alaskan native peoples in exchange for renunciation of all aboriginal claims to land in the state.

The Document

Alaska Purchase Treaty[1]

Whereas a treaty between the United States of America and his Majesty the Emperor of all the Russias was concluded and signed by their respective plenipotentiaries at the city of Washington, on the thirtieth day of March, last, which treaty, being in English and French languages, is, word for word as follows:

(The French version is omitted for brevity).

The United States of America and His Majesty the Emperor of all the Russias, being desirous of strengthening, if possible, the good understanding which exists between them, have, for that purpose, appointed as their Plenipotentiaries: the President of the

United States, William H. Seward, Secretary of State; and His Majesty the Emperor of all the Russias, the Privy Councillor Edward de Stoeckl, his Envoy Extraordinary and Minister Plenipotentiary to the United States.

And the said Plenipotentiaries, having exchanged their full powers, which were found to be in due form, have agreed upon and signed the following articles:

ARTICLE I.

His Majesty the Emperor of all the Russias agrees to cede to the United States, by this convention, immediately upon the exchange of the ratifications thereof, all the territory and dominion now possessed by his said Majesty on the continent of America and in the adjacent islands, the same being contained within the geographical limits herein set forth, to wit: The eastern limit is the line of demarcation between the Russian and the British possessions in North America, as established by the convention between Russia and Great Britain, of February 28–16, 1825, and described in Articles III and IV of said convention, in the following terms:

"Commencing from the southernmost point of the island called Prince of Wales Island, which point lies in the parallel of 54 degrees 40 minutes north latitude, and between the 131st and the 133d degree of west longitude, (meridian of Greenwich,) the said line shall ascend to the north along the channel called Portland channel, as far as the point of the continent where it strikes the 56th degree of north latitude; from this last-mentioned point, the line of demarcation shall follow the summit of the mountains situated parallel to the coast as far as the point of intersection of the 141st degree of west longitude, (of the same meridian;) and finally, from the said point of intersection, the said meridian line of the 141st degree, in its prolongation as far as the Frozen ocean. "IV. With reference to the line of demarcation laid down in the preceding article, it is understood —

"1st. That the island called Prince of Wales Island shall belong wholly to Russia," (now, by this cession, to the United States.)

"2d. That whenever the summit of the mountains which extend in a direction parallel to the coast from the 56th degree of north latitude to the point of intersection of the 141st degree of west longitude shall prove to be at the distance of more than ten marine leagues from the ocean, the limit between the British possessions and the line of coast which is to belong to Russia as above mentioned (that is to say, the limit to the possessions ceded by this convention) shall be formed by a line parallel to the winding of the coast, and which shall never exceed the distance of ten marine leagues therefrom."

The western limit within which the territories and dominion conveyed, are contained, passes through a point in Behring's straits on the parallel of sixty-five degrees thirty minutes north latitude, at its intersection by the meridian which passes midway between the islands of Krusenstern, or Ignalook, and the island of Ratmanoff, or Noonarbook, and proceeds due north, without limitation, into the same Frozen ocean. The same western limit, beginning at the same initial point, proceeds thence in a course nearly southwest through Behring's straits and Behring's sea, so as to pass midway between the northwest point of the island of St. Lawrence and the southeast point of Cape Choukotski, to the meridian of one hundred and seventy-two west longitude; thence, from the intersection of that meridian, in a south-westerly direction, so as to pass midway between the island of Attou and the Copper island of the Kormandorski couplet or group in the North Pacific ocean, to the meridian of one hundred and ninety-three degrees west longitude, so as to include in the territory conveyed the whole of the Aleutian islands east of that meridian.

ARTICLE II.

In the cession of territory and dominion made by the preceding article are included the right of property in all public lots and squares, vacant lands, and all public buildings, fortifications, barracks, and other edifices which are not private individual property. It is, however, understood and agreed, that the churches which have been built in the ceded territory by the Russian government, shall remain the property of such members of the Greek Oriental Church resident in the territory, as may choose to worship therein. Any government archives, papers, and documents relative to the territory and dominion aforesaid, which may be now existing there, will be left in the possession of the agent of the United States; but an authenticated copy of such of them as may be required, will be, at all times, given by the United States to the Russian government, or to such Russian officers or subjects as they may apply for.

ARTICLE III.

The inhabitants of the ceded territory, according to their choice, reserving their natural allegiance, may return to Russia within three years; but if they should prefer to remain in the ceded territory, they, with the exception of uncivilized native tribes, shall be admitted to the enjoyment of all the rights, advantages, and immunities of citizens of the United States, and shall be maintained and protected in the free enjoyment of their liberty, property, and religion. The uncivilized tribes will be subject to such laws and regulations as the United States may, from time to time, adopt in regard to aboriginal tribes of that country.

ARTICLE IV.

His Majesty the Emperor of all the Russias shall appoint, with convenient despatch, an agent or agents for the purpose of formally delivering to a similar agent or agents appointed on behalf of the United States, the territory, dominion, property, dependencies and appurtenances which are ceded as above, and for doing any other act which may be necessary in regard thereto. But the cession, with the right of immediate possession, is nevertheless to be deemed complete and absolute on the exchange of ratifications, without waiting for such formal delivery.

ARTICLE V.

Immediately after the exchange of the ratifications of this convention, any fortifications or military posts which may be in the ceded territory shall be delivered to the agent of the United States, and any Russian troops which may be in the territory shall be withdrawn as soon as may be reasonably and conveniently practicable.

ARTICLE VI.

In consideration of the cession aforesaid, the United States agree to pay at the treasury in Washington, within ten months after the exchange of the ratifications of this convention, to the diplomatic representative or other agent of his Majesty the Emperor of all the Russias, duly authorized to receive the same, seven million two hundred thousand dollars in gold. The cession of territory and dominion herein made is hereby declared to be free and unencumbered by any reservations, privileges, franchises, grants, or possessions, by any associated companies, whether corporate or incorporate, Russian or any other, or by any parties, except merely private individual property holders; and the cession hereby made, conveys all the rights, franchises, and privileges now belonging to Russia in the said territory or dominion, and appurtenances thereto.

ARTICLE VII.

When this convention shall have been duly ratified by the President of the United States, by and with the advice and consent of the Senate, on the one part, and on the other by his Majesty the Emperor of all the Russias, the ratifications shall be exchanged at Washington within three months from the date hereof, or sooner if possible.

In faith whereof, the respective plenipotentiaries have signed this convention, and thereto affixed the seals of their arms.

Done at Washington, the thirtieth day of March, in the year of our Lord one thousand eight hundred and sixty-seven.

[L. S.] WILLIAM H. SEWARD.
[L. S.] EDOUARD DE STOECKL.

And whereas the said Treaty has been duly ratified on both parts, and the respective ratifications of the same were exchanged at Washington on this twentieth day of June, by William H. Seward, Secretary of State of the United States, and the Privy Counsellor Edward de Stoeckl, the Envoy Extraordinary of His Majesty the Emperor of all the Russias, on the part of their respective governments, Now, therefore, be it known that I, Andrew Johnson, President of the United States of America, have caused the said Treaty to be made public, to the end that the same and every clause and article thereof may be observed and fulfilled with good faith by the United States and the citizens thereof.

In witness whereof, I have hereunto set my hand, and caused the seal of the United States to be affixed.

Done at the city of Washington, this twentieth day of June in the year of our Lord one thousand eight hundred and sixty-seven, and of the Independence of the United States the ninety-first.

[L.S.] ANDREW JOHNSON
By the President:
William H. Seward, Secretary of State

NOTE

1. *Treaty concerning the Cession of the Russian Possessions in North America by his Majesty the Emperor of all the Russias to the United States of America; Concluded March 30, 1867; Ratified by the United States May 28, 1867; Exchanged June 20, 1867; Proclaimed by the United States June 20, 1867.*

CHAPTER 28

Hawaii Resolution
(July 7, 1898)

United States Congress

The History[*]

When the Hawaiian islands were formally annexed by the United States in 1898, the event marked the end of a lengthy internal struggle between native Hawaiians and white American businessmen for control of the Hawaiian government. In 1893 the last monarch of Hawaii, Queen Lili'uokalani, was overthrown by party of businessmen, who then imposed a provisional government. Soon after, President Benjamin Harrison submitted a treaty to annex the Hawaiian islands to the U.S. Senate for ratification. In 1897, the treaty effort was blocked when the newly-formed Hawaiian Patriotic League, composed of native Hawaiians, successfully petitioned the U.S. Congress in opposition to the treaty. The League's lobbying efforts left only 46 Senators in favor of the resolution, less than the ⅔ majority needed for approval of a treaty. The League's victory was short-lived, however, as unfolding world events soon forced the annexation issue to the fore again. With the explosion of the U.S.S. *Maine* in February 1898 signaling the start of the Spanish-American War, establishing a mid–Pacific fueling station and naval base became a strategic imperative for the United States. The Hawaiian islands were the clear choice, and this time Congress moved to annex the Hawaiian islands by Joint Resolution, a process requiring only a simple majority in both houses of Congress. On July 12, 1898, the Joint Resolution passed and the Hawaiian islands were officially annexed by the United States.

The Hawaiian islands had a well-established culture and long history of self-governance when Captain James Cook, the first European explorer to set foot on Hawaii, landed in 1778. The influence of European and American settlers quickly began to alter traditional ways of life. Originally governed by individual chiefs or kings, the islands united under the rule of a single monarch, King Kamehameha, in 1795, less than two decades after Cook's arrival. Later the traditional Hawaiian monarchy was overthrown in favor of a constitutional monarchy. Eventually, the monarchy itself was abandoned in favor of a government elected by a small

*Originally published as "Teaching with Documents: The 1897 Petition Against the Annexation of Hawaii," *Educators and Students Report*, The National Archives, U.S. National Archives and Records Administration, College Park, Maryland, 2008. For additional information see "Joint Resolution to Provide for Annexing the Hawaiian Islands to the United States (1868)," *100 Milestone Documents*, U.S. National Archives and Records Administration, College Park, Maryland, 2008. This agency is listed in the *National Resource Directory* section of this volume.

group of enfranchised voters, although the Hawaiian monarch was retained as the ceremonial head of the government. Even elements of daily life felt the social and economic impact of the white planters, missionaries and businessmen. The landholding system changed, and many aspects of traditional culture were prohibited including teaching the Hawaiian language and performing the native Hula dance.

In 1887, the struggle for control of Hawaii was at its height as David Kalakaua was elected to the Hawaiian throne. King Kalakaua signed a reciprocity treaty with the United States making it possible for sugar to be sold to the U.S. market tax-free, but the *haole*— or "white"— businessmen were still distrustful of him. They criticized his ties to men they believed to be corrupt, his revival of Hawaiian traditions such as the historic Hula, and construction of the royal Iolani Palace. A scandal involving Kalakaua erupted in the very year he was crowned, and it united his opponents, a party of businessmen under the leadership of Lorrin Thurston. The opposition used the threat of violence to force Kalakaua to accept a new constitution that stripped the monarchy of executive powers and replaced the cabinet with members of the businessmen's party. The new constitution, which effectively disenfranchised most native Hawaiian voters, came to be known as the "Bayonet Constitution" because Kalakaua signed it under duress.

When King Kalakaua died in 1891, his sister Lili'uokalani succeeded him, and members of the native population persuaded the new queen to draft a new constitution in an attempt to restore native rights and powers. The move was countered by the Committee on Annexation, a small group of white businessmen and politicians who felt that annexation by the United States, the major importer of Hawaiian products, would be beneficial for the economy of Hawaii. Supported by John Stevens, the U.S. Minister to Hawaii, and a contingent of Marines from the warship, U.S.S. *Boston*, the Committee

on Annexation overthrew Queen Lili'uokalani in a bloodless coup on January 17, 1893 and established a revolutionary regime.

Without permission from the U.S. State Department, Minister Stevens then recognized the new government and proclaimed Hawaii a U.S. protectorate. The Committee immediately proclaimed itself to be the Provisional Government. President Benjamin Harrison signed a treaty of annexation with the new government, but before the Senate could ratify it, Grover Cleveland replaced Harrison as president and subsequently withdrew the treaty.

Shortly into his presidency, Cleveland appointed James Blount as a special investigator to investigate the events in the Hawaiian islands. Blount found that Minister Stevens had acted improperly and ordered that the American flag be lowered from Hawaiian government buildings. He also ordered that Queen Lili'uokalani be restored to power, but Sanford Dole, the president of the Provisional Government of Hawaii, refused to turn over power. Dole successfully argued that the United States had no right to interfere in the internal affairs of Hawaii. The Provisional Government then proclaimed Hawaii a republic in 1894, and soon the Republic of Hawaii was officially recognized by the United States.

The overthrow of Lili'uokalani and imposition of the Republic of Hawaii was contrary to the will of the native Hawaiians. Native Hawaiians staged mass protest rallies and formed two gender-designated groups to protest the overthrow and prevent annexation. One was the *Hui Hawaii Aloha Aina*, loosely translated as the Hawaiian Patriotic League, and the other was its female counterpart, the *Hui Hawaii Aloha Aina o Na Wahine*. On January 5, 1895, the protests took the form of an armed attempt to derail the annexation but the armed revolt was suppressed by the forces of the Republic. The leaders of the revolt were imprisoned along with Queen Lili'uokalani who was jailed for failing to put down the revolt.

In March 1897, William McKinley was inaugurated as President of the United States. McKinley was in favor of annexation, and the change in leadership was soon felt. On June 16, 1897, McKinley and three representatives of the government of the Republic of Hawaii — Lorrin Thurston, Francis Hatch, and William Kinney — signed a treaty of annexation. President McKinley then submitted the treaty to the U.S. Senate for ratification.

The *Hui Aloha Aina* for Women and the *Hui Aloha Aina* for Men now organized a mass petition drive. They hoped that if the U.S. government realized that the majority of native Hawaiian citizens opposed annexation, the move to annex Hawaii would be stopped. Between September 11 and October 2, 1897, the two groups collected petition signatures at public meetings held on each of the five principal islands of Hawaii. The petition, clearly marked "Petition Against Annexation" and written in both the Hawaiian and English languages, was signed by 21,269 native Hawaiian people, or more than half the 39,000 native Hawaiians and mixed-blood persons reported by the Hawaiian Commission census for the same year.

Four delegates, James Kaulia, David Kalauokalani, John Richardson, and William Auld, arrived in Washington, D.C. on December 6 with the 556-page petition in hand. That day, as they met with Queen Lili'uokalani, who was already in Washington lobbying against annexation, the second session of the 55th Congress opened. The delegates and Lili'uokalani planned a strategy to present the petition to the Senate.

The delegation and Lili'uokalani met Senator George Hoar, chairman of the Senate Committee on Foreign Relations on the following day, and on December 9, with the delegates present, Senator Hoar read the text of the petition to the Senate. It was formally accepted. The next day the delegates met with Secretary of State John Sherman and submitted a formal statement protesting the

annexation to him. In the following days, the delegates met with many senators, voicing opposition to the annexation. By the time the delegates left Washington on February 27, 1898, there were only 46 senators willing to vote for annexation. The treaty was defeated in the Senate.

Other events brought the subject of annexation up again immediately. On February 15, 1898, the U.S. Battleship *Maine* was blown up in Havana harbor in Cuba. The ensuing Spanish-American War, part of which was fought in the Philippine Islands, established the strategic value of the Hawaiian islands as a mid-Pacific fueling station and naval installation. The pro-annexation forces in Congress submitted a proposal to annex the Hawaiian islands by joint resolution, which required only a simple majority vote in both houses. This eliminated the ⅔ majority needed to ratify a treaty, and by result, the necessary support in place. House Joint Resolution 259, 55th Congress, 2nd session, known as the "Newlands Resolution," passed Congress and was signed into law by President McKinley on July 7, 1898.

Once annexed by the United States, the Hawaiian islands remained a U.S. territory until 1959, when they were admitted to statehood as the 50th state. The story of the annexation is a story of conflicting goals as the white businessmen struggled to obtain favorable trade conditions and native Hawaiians sought to protect their cultural heritage and maintain a national identity. The 1897 Petition by the Hawaiian Patriotic League stands as evidence that the native Hawaiian people objected to annexation, but because the interests of the businessmen won out, over the coming decades most historians who wrote the history of Hawaii emphasized events as told by the Provisional Government and largely neglected the struggle of the Native Hawaiians. Today, there is a growing movement on the Islands to revive interest in the native Hawaiian language and culture. Primary sources such as this petition bear witness that there is another side to the story.

The Document

Hawaii Resolution[1]

To Provide for Annexing the Hawaiian Islands to the United States.

Whereas the Government of the Republic of Hawaii having, in due form, signified its consent, in the manner provided by its constitution, to cede absolutely and without reserve to the United States of America all rights of sovereignty of whatsoever kind in and over the Hawaiian Islands and their dependencies, and also to cede and transfer to the United States the absolute fee and ownership of all public, Government, or Crown lands, public buildings or edifices, ports, harbors, military equipment, and all other public property of every kind and description belonging to the Government of the Hawaiian Islands, together with every right and appurtenance thereunto appertaining; Therefore

Resolved by the Senate and House of Representatives of the United States of America in Congress Assembled, That said cession is accepted, ratified, and confirmed, and that the said Hawaiian Islands and their dependencies be, and they are hereby, annexed as a part of the territory of the United States and are subject to the sovereign dominion thereof, and that all and singular the property and rights hereinbefore mentioned are vested in the United States of America.

The existing laws of the United States relative to public lands shall not apply to such lands in the Hawaiian Islands; but the Congress of the United States shall enact special laws for their management and disposition: *Provided,* That all revenue from or proceeds of the same, except as regards such part thereof as may be used or occupied for the civil, military, or naval purposes of the United States, or may be assigned for the use of the local government, shall be used solely for the benefit of the inhabitants of the Hawaiian Islands for educational and other public purposes.

Until Congress shall provide for the government of such islands all the civil, judicial, and military powers exercised by the officers of the existing government in said islands shall be vested in such person or persons and shall be exercised in such manner as the President of the United States shall direct; and the President shall have the power to remove said officers and fill the vacancies so occasioned.

The existing treaties of the Hawaiian Islands with foreign nations shall forthwith cease and determine, being replaced by such treaties as may exist, or as may be hereafter concluded, between the United States and such foreign nations. The municipal legislation of the Hawaiian Islands, not enacted for the fulfillment of the treaties so extinguished, and not inconsistent with this joint resolution nor contrary to the Constitution of the United States nor to any existing treaty of the United States, shall remain in force until the Congress of the United States shall otherwise determine.

Until legislation shall be enacted extending the United States customs laws and regulations to the Hawaiian Islands the existing customs relations of the Hawaiian Islands with the United States and other countries shall remain unchanged.

The public debt of the Republic of Hawaii, lawfully existing at the date of the passage of this joint resolution, including the amounts due to depositors in the Hawaiian Postal Savings Bank, is hereby assumed by the Government of the United States; but the liability of the United States in this regard shall in no case exceed four million dollars. So long, however, as the existing Government and the present commercial relations of the Hawaiian Islands are continued as hereinbefore provided said Government shall continue to pay the interest on said debt.

There shall be no further immigration of Chinese into the Hawaiian Islands, except upon such conditions as are now or may hereafter be allowed by the laws of the United States; no Chinese, by reason of anything herein contained, shall be allowed to enter the United States from the Hawaiian Islands.

The President shall appoint five commissioners, at least two of whom shall be residents of the Hawaiian Islands, who shall, as soon as reasonably practicable, recommend to Congress such legislation concerning the Hawaiian Islands as they shall deem necessary or proper.

SEC. 2. That the commissioners hereinbefore provided for shall be appointed by the President, by and with the advice and consent of the Senate.

SEC. 3. That the sum of one hundred thousand dollars, or so much thereof as may be necessary; is hereby appropriated, out of any money in the Treasury not otherwise appropriated, and to be immediately available, to be expended at the discretion of the President of the United States of America, for the purpose of carrying this joint resolution into effect.

SEREXO E. PAYNE,
Speaker of the House of Representatives
Pro Tempore.
GARRETT A. HOBART,
Vice-President of the United States and President of the Senate.

Approved July 7th, 1898.

WILLIAM McKINLEY.
President

NOTE

1. This is Resolution No. 55, known as the "Newlands Resolution," 2nd Session, 55TH Congress, July 7, 1898. During the period between annexation and the establishment of Territorial government, June 14, 1900, the relations between Hawaii and the United States remained practically unchanged. The laws of Hawaii continued in force, and the constitution and laws of the United States in general did not extend to Hawaii, except as otherwise provided by the resolution.

SECTION V: THE FUTURE

CHAPTER 29

The Future of Democracy

Robert M. Gates

Senator Warner is a special friend. He has introduced me to the United States Senate for confirmation four times. The first time was more than 20 years ago. And that dates us both. He is a great Virginian, a great American, and we will certainly all miss him when he brings his remarkable career in public service to a close next year.

I want to thank Justice Sandra Day O'Connor, one of the most distinguished jurists and public servants in America, for inviting me today. It was Justice O'Connor who administered my oath of office as Director of Central Intelligence in 1991. And last year we served together on the Baker-Hamilton Commission. Little did I know that my sojourn to Iraq a little over a year ago with the group would be only the first of many such visits for me.

Justice O'Connor and I share something else in common — a love of the College of William and Mary, where she is currently the chancellor. And of course, it was a special pleasure to see her four months ago when I had the honor of giving the commencement address at my alma mater. Attending college here in Williamsburg shaped my love of history and my belief that public service is a vital component of a working democracy — and of a meaningful life.

This setting is fitting for my topic today: a "realist's" view of promoting democracy abroad.

I had quite a reputation as a pessimist when I was in the intelligence business. A journalist once described me as the Eeyore of national security — able to find the darkest cloud in any silver lining. I used to joke that when an intelligence officer smelled the flowers, he'd look around for the coffin. Today, as one looks around the world — wars in Iraq and Afghanistan, an ambitious and fanatical theocracy in Iran, a nuclear North Korea, terrorism, and more — there would seem to be ample grounds to be gloomy.

But there is a different perspective if we step back and look at the world through a wider lens — a perspective that shows a dramatic growth in human freedom and democracy in just the time since this fall's college freshmen were born. Since 1989, hundreds of millions of people — from Eastern and Central Europe and the former Soviet Union, to South Africa, Afghanistan, Iraq, and elsewhere — have been liberated: they have left the darkness of despotism and walked into the bright sunshine of freedom.

Many have seized the opportunity, and freedom has prospered and strengthened; others liberated from the yoke of tyrannical

*This chapter is based on a speech given by Robert M. Gates at the *World Forum on the Future of Democracy* held in Williamsburg, VA, on September 17, 2007. The entire speech is available on the U.S. Department of Defense website (http://www.defenselink.mil/).

ideologies or dictators continue to struggle to fully realize the dream. At no time in history, though, has freedom come to so many in so short a time. And in every case, the United States, overtly or covertly, in large ways or small, played a role in their liberation.

Still, we Americans continue to wrestle with the appropriate role this country should play in advancing freedom and democracy in the world. It was a source of friction through the entire Cold War. In truth, it has been a persistent question for this country throughout our history: How should we incorporate America's democratic ideals and aspirations into our relations with the rest of the world? And in particular, when to, and whether to try to change the way other nations govern themselves? Should America's mission to make the world "safe for democracy," as Woodrow Wilson said, or, in the words of John Quincy Adams, should America be "the well-wisher of freedom and independence of all" but the "champion and indicator only of our own"?

During my time today, I'd like to put this question and its associated debates in some historical context — a context I hope might help inform the difficult policy choices our nation faces today.

Let me first speak to geography — this place we are in.

It is a strange quirk of history that a backwoods outpost in an unexplored corner of America would hold in it the seeds of a global movement toward liberty and self-governance — toward the democratic institutions that underpin the free nations of the world and give hope to countless people in many others.

So much of what defines America first took root here in Virginia along the banks of the James River. When you think about it, the initial impetus for these institutions owed as much to the struggle for survival as to anything else. The challenges were myriad: along with disease, hunger, and war, the settlers

faced no small number of divisions and discord. Four hundred years removed from those early days, it is all too easy to forget about these stormy beginnings.

The revolution that brought about this nation was similarly chaotic. As my distinguished William and Mary classmate, the historian Joe Ellis, wrote in his book, *Founding Brothers*, "No one present at the start knew how it would turn out in the end. What in retrospect has the look of a foreordained unfolding of God's will was in reality an improvisational affair in which sheer chance, pure luck — both good and bad — and specific decisions made in the crucible of specific military and political crises determined the outcome." Ellis further wrote "the real drama of the American Revolution ... was its inherent messiness. This ... exciting but terrifying sense that all the major players had at the time — namely, that they were making it up as they went along, improvising on the edge of catastrophe." We would do well to be mindful of the turbulence of our own early history as we contemplate the challenges facing contemporary fledgling democracies struggling to find their footing.

When I retired from government in 1993, it seemed that the success and spread of democracy was inexorable, a foregone conclusion — that with the collapse of the Soviet Union, the evolution of political systems had reached, in the words of one scholar at the time, the "end of history." But the relative calm in the immediate aftermath of the Cold War served only to mask new threats to the security of democratic nations: ethnic conflicts, new genocides, the proliferation of weapons of mass destruction — especially by rogue states and, above all, a new, more formidable, and more malignant form of terrorism embraced by Islamic extremists.

These new threats, and in particular, the conflicts in Iraq and Afghanistan, and the wider challenge of dealing with radical jihadist movements since September 11th, once again have people talking about the competing impulses in U.S. foreign policy: realism versus idealism, freedom versus security, values versus interests.

This is not a new debate. Not long after winning our own independence, the U.S. was faced with how to respond to the French Revolution — an issue that consumed the politics of the country during the 1790s. The issue was whether to support the revolutionary government and its war against an alliance of European monarchies led by Great Britain. To many, like Thomas Jefferson, the French Revolution, with its stated ideals of liberty, equality, and fraternity, seemed a natural successor to our own. Jefferson wrote that "this ball of liberty, I believe most piously, is now so well in motion that it will roll round the globe."

John Adams and the Federalists, however, were just as adamantly opposed. They were appalled by the revolution's excesses and feared the spread of violent French radicalism to our shores. In fact, they accused the Jeffersonians of being "pimps of France," who "represented cutthroats who walk in rags." The Federalists mocked Jefferson for his rhetorical defense of freedom and equality across the Atlantic while he continued to own slaves. Adams and Alexander Hamilton were, in turn, accused of being crypto-monarchists.

It was left to President George Washington to resolve the matter. He had said that: "My best wishes are irresistibly excited whensoever, in any country, I see an oppressed nation unfurl the banners of freedom." But the European wars and, in particular, our estrangement from the British, had begun to disrupt the lives of ordinary Americans by impeding trade and causing riots and refugees. Washington, understanding the fragility of America's position at the time, adopted a neutrality policy towards France and would go on to make a peace treaty with Great Britain — sparking massive protests and accusations of selling out the spirit of 1776.

Consider the great historic irony: The United States had recently broken free of the British monarchy only with the help of an absolutist French king. Yet when France itself turned in the direction of popular rule and was confronted by Europe's monarchies, the United States took a pass and made amends with our old British foe.

In short, from our earliest days, America's leaders have struggled with "realistic" versus "idealistic" approaches to the international challenges facing us. The most successful leaders, starting with Washington, have steadfastly encouraged the spread of liberty, democracy, and human rights. At the same time, however, they have fashioned policies blending different approaches with different emphases in different places and different times.

Over the last century, we have allied with tyrants to defeat other tyrants. We have sustained diplomatic relations with governments even as we supported those attempting their overthrow.

We have at times made human rights the centerpiece of our national strategy even as we did business with some of the worst violators of human rights. We have worked with authoritarian governments to advance our own security interests even while urging them to reform.

We have used our military to eliminate governments seen as a threat to our national security, to undo aggression, to end ethnic slaughter, and to prevent chaos. In recent times, we have done this in Grenada, Panama, Kuwait, the Balkans, Haiti, Afghanistan, and Iraq. In the process, we have brought the possibility of democracy and freedom to tens of millions more who had been oppressed or were suffering.

To win and protect our own freedom, the United States has made common cause with countries that were far from free — from Louis XVI, to one of history's true monsters, Joseph Stalin. Without the one there is no American independence. Without the other, no end to the Third Reich. It is neither hypocrisy nor cynicism to believe fervently in freedom while adopting different approaches to advancing freedom at different times along the way — including temporarily making common cause with despots to defeat greater or more urgent threats to our freedom or interests.

The consuming goal for most of my professional life was containing the threat of the Soviet Union and seeing a Europe made whole and free. For most of the Cold War, the ideal surely seemed distant, even unreachable. One prominent columnist wrote in *Time* magazine in 1982 that "it would be wishful thinking to predict that international Communism someday will either self-destruct or so exhaust itself."

During that struggle, as for most of our history, inspiring presidential rhetoric about freedom, along with many firm stands for human rights and self-determination, had to coexist with often grubby compromises and marriages of convenience that were necessary to stave off the Evil Empire.

But the Western democracies — joined as the Atlantic Alliance — came together to get the big things right. The democracies' shared belief in political and economic freedom and religious tolerance was the glue that held us fast despite the many quarrels along the way.

President Bush said in his second inaugural address, "[I]t is the policy of the United States to seek and support the growth of democratic movements and institutions in every nation and culture, with the ultimate goal of ending tyranny in our world."

When we discuss openly our desire for democratic values to take hold across the globe, we are describing a world that may be many years or decades off. Though achievement of the ideal may be limited by time, space, resources, or human nature, we must not allow ourselves to discard or disparage the ideal itself. It is vital that we speak out about what we believe and let the world know where we stand. It is vital that we give hope and aid to those who seek freedom.

I still remember working on the advance team for President Ford when he attended the Helsinki conference in 1975. Many critics were opposed to America's participation, since they believed that the accords did little but ratify the Soviet Union's takings in Eastern and Central Europe. The treaty's provisions on human rights were disparaged as little more than window dressing. However, the conference and treaty represent another of history's ironies. The Soviets demanded the conference for decades, finally got it, and it helped destroy them from the inside. We "realists" opposed holding the conference for decades, and attended grudgingly. We were wrong. For the meeting played a key role in our winning the Cold War.

Why? Because the human-rights provisions of the treaty made a moral statement whose significance was not lost on the dissidents behind the Iron Curtain. Helsinki became a spur for action, a rallying cry to fight tyranny from within and plant democracy in its place.

Vaclav Havel later said that the accords were a "shield, a chance to resist coercion and make it more difficult for the forces of coercion to retaliate." Lech Walesa called it a turning point "on the road to change in Gdansk."

President Carter's promotion of the spirit of Helsinki — his elevation of human rights — for the first time in the Cold War denied the Soviet Union the respect and the legitimacy it craved. Ronald Reagan's muscular words — labeling the U.S.S.R. the "Evil Empire" and demanding that Mr. Gorbachev tear down that wall — combined with his muscular defense policies hastened the implosion of the Soviet system.

Did these policies reflect hard-edged realism or lofty idealism? Both, actually. Were they implemented to defend our interests or to spread our democratic values? Again, both.

An underlying theme of American history is that we are compelled to defend our security and our interests in ways that, in the long run, lead to the spread of democratic values and institutions.

Since September 11th, these questions, contradictions, and dilemmas have taken on new urgency and presented new challenges for decision-makers, especially in an information age where every flaw and inconsistency — in words or deeds — is highlighted, magnified, and disseminated around the globe.

And, as with the Cold War, every action we take sends a signal about the depth of our strength and resolve. For our friends and allies, as well as our enemies and potential adversaries, our commitment to democratic values must be matched by actions.

Consider Afghanistan. The democracies of the West and our partners are united in the desire to see stability and decent government take hold in a land that was not only Al Queda's base of operation, but also home to one of the most oppressive governments in the world. And yet, though there is little doubt about the justness, necessity, and legitimacy of the Afghanistan mission, even though we agree that democracy is key to enduring stability there, many Allies are reluctant to provide the necessary resources and put their men and women in the line of fire.

Afghanistan is, in a very real sense, a litmus test of whether an alliance of advanced democracies can still make sacrifices and meet commitments to advance democracy. It would be a mark of shame on all of us if an alliance built on the foundation of democratic values were to falter at the very moment that it tries to lay that foundation for democracy elsewhere — especially in a mission that is crucial to our own security.

Likewise, for America to leave Iraq and the Middle East in chaos would betray and demoralize our allies there and in the region, while emboldening our most dangerous adversaries. To abandon an Iraq where just two years ago 12 million people quite literally

risked their lives to vote for a constitutional democracy would be an offense to our interests as well as our values, a setback for the cause of freedom as well as the goal of stability.

Americans have never been a patient people. Today, we look at Russia, China, Afghanistan, Iraq, and others — and wonder at their excruciatingly slow progress toward democratic institutions and the rule of law.

The eminent French historian Helene Carrere d'Encausse wrote in 1992: "Reforms, when they go against the political traditions of the centuries, cannot be imposed in a hurry merely by enshrining them in the law. It takes time, and generally they are accompanied by violence." She added: "Reforms that challenge centuries of social relations based on ... the exclusion of the majority of society from the political process, are too profound to be readily accepted by those who have to pay the price of reform, even if they are seen to be indispensable. Reforms need time to develop ... It is this time that reformers have often lacked."

For more than 60 years, from Germany and Japan to South Korea, the Balkans, Haiti, Afghanistan, and Iraq, we and our allies have provided reformers — those who seek a free and democratic society — with time for their efforts to take hold. We must be realists and recognize that the institutions that underpin an enduring free society can only take root over time.

It is our country's tragedy, and our glory, that the tender shoots of freedom around the world for so many decades have been so often nourished with American blood. The spread of liberty both manifests our ideals and protects our interests — in making the world "safe for democracy," we are also the "champion and vindicator" of our own. In reality, Wilson and Adams must coexist.

Throughout more than two centuries, the United States has made its share of mistakes. From time to time, we have strayed from our ideals and have been arrogant in dealing with others. Yet, what has brought us together with our democratic allies is a shared belief that the future of democracy and its spread is worth our enduring labors and sacrifices — reflecting both our interests and our ideals.

I would like to close by returning to this corner of Virginia. In September 1796, shortly before George Washington left office, he addressed in his farewell statement an American people who had passed through the dangerous fires of war and revolution to form a union that was far from "perfect," but was a historic accomplishment nonetheless. He told them: "You have, in common cause, fought and triumphed together; the independence and liberty you possess are the work of joint councils and joint efforts, of common dangers, sufferings, and successes."

In this historic place, among old friends and new, let us take time to reflect on the common causes in which we have fought and triumphed together — to protect our own liberty, and to extend its blessings to others. As we prepare for the challenges ahead, let us never forget that together we will face common dangers, sufferings, and successes — but with confidence that, together, we will continue to protect that tender shoot of liberty first planted in this place so long ago.

At the time this was written, Robert M. Gates was Secretary of Defense, Defense Department, U.S. Government, Washington, D.C. He was originally appointed by President Bush, and was asked to reman in this position by President Obama.

Appendices

Containing A. Original Thirteen Biritish Colonies; B. States and Their Dates of Admission to the Union; C. Presidents of the United States; D. Formal Declarations of War by the United States; E. Number of Governmental Units in the United States; F. United States Voting Rights History; G. Major Cases in Supreme Court History; H. Local Government Historical Document; I. Abbreviations and Acronyms; J. Glossary; K. State Library Resource Directory; L. National Resource Directory

A. Original Thirteen British Colonies

(listed by name of colony, year founded, and person or group who founded it)

Virginia	1607	Settlers from the Virginia Company, located in London, England.
Massachusetts	1620	Pilgrims and Puritans, for their own religious and personal freedom.
New Hampshire	1623	English colonists who had a land grant from England.
New York	1626	Dutch, for trading purposes; the English assumed control in 1664.
Maryland	1632	Lord Baltimore, as a safe place for people of the Catholic faith.
Rhode Island	1636	Roger Williams, who was banished from the Colony of Massachusetts for religious reasons.
Connecticut	1636	Thomas Hooker, who led a group from the Colony of Massachusetts.
Delaware	1638	Swedish, then Dutch; the English were given the land in 1664.
North Carolina	1653	Settlers from the Colony of Virginia, many of whom wanted more religious freedom.
South Carolina	1663	British and French for the purpose of religious freedom.
New Jersey	1674	Dutch, Swedish, and Englishmen were granted land by the Duke of York, who was given the land by the English government.
Pennsylvania	1681	William Penn, as a haven for Quakers, also known as the *Society of Friends* at the time.
Georgia	1732	James Oglethorpe was given the property by George II, the King of Great Britain, for whom the colony was named.

NOTE

For additional information concerning this subject, and related information, please refer to the *United Kingdom Parliamentary Archives* and the *U.S. National Archives and Records Administration*, which are listed in the *National Resource Directory* section of this volume.

B. States and Their Dates of Admission to the Union

(listed by rank of admittance, name of state, and date admitted)

1	Delaware	Dec. 7, 1787	26	Michigan	Jan. 26, 1837
2	Pennsylvania	Dec. 12, 1787	27	Florida	March 3, 1845
3	New Jersey	Dec. 18, 1787	28	Texas	Dec. 29, 1845
4	Georgia	Jan. 2, 1788	29	Iowa	Dec. 28, 1846
5	Connecticut	Jan. 9, 1788	30	Wisconsin	May 26, 1848
6	Massachusetts	Feb. 6, 1788	31	California	Sept. 9, 1850
7	Maryland	April 28, 1788	32	Minnesota	May 11, 1858
8	South Carolina	May 23, 1788	33	Oregon	Feb. 14, 1859
9	New Hampshire	June 21, 1788	34	Kansas	Jan. 29, 1861
10	Virginia	June 25, 1788	35	West Virginia	June 20, 1863
11	New York	July 26, 1788	36	Nevada	October 31, 1864
12	North Carolina	Nov. 21, 1789	37	Nebraska	March 1, 1867
13	Rhode Island	May 29, 1790	38	Colorado	Aug. 1, 1876
14	Vermont	March 4, 1791	39	North Dakota	Nov. 2, 1889
15	Kentucky	June 1, 1792	40	South Dakota	Nov. 2, 1889
16	Tennessee	June 1, 1796	41	Montana	Nov. 8, 1889
17	Ohio	March 1, 1803	42	Washington	Nov. 11, 1889
18	Louisiana	April 30, 1812	43	Idaho	July 3, 1890
19	Indiana	Dec. 11, 1816	44	Wyoming	July 10, 1890
20	Mississippi	Dec. 10, 1817	45	Utah	Jan. 4, 1896
21	Illinois	Dec. 3, 1818	46	Oklahoma	Nov. 16, 1907
22	Alabama	Dec. 14, 1819	47	New Mexico	Jan. 6, 1912
23	Maine	March 15, 1820	48	Arizona	Feb. 14, 1912
24	Missouri	Aug. 10, 1821	49	Alaska	Jan. 3, 1959
25	Arkansas	June 15, 1836	50	Hawaii	Aug. 21, 1959

C. Presidents of the United States

(listed by name of president, years served, and party affiliation)

George Washington, 1789–1797, Federalist
John Adams, 1797–1801, Federalist
Thomas Jefferson, 1801–1809, Dem.-Rep.
James Madison, 1809–1817, Dem.-Rep.
James Monroe, 1817–1825, Dem.-Rep.
John Quincy Adams, 1825–1829, Dem.-Rep.
Andrew Jackson, 1829–1837, Democratic
Martin Van Buren, 1837–1841, Democratic
William H. Harrison, 1841, Whig
John Tyler, 1841–1845, Whig
James K. Polk, 1845–1849, Democratic
Zachary Taylor, 1849–1850, Whig
Millard Fillmore, 1850–1853, Whig
Franklin Pierce, 1853–1857, Democratic
James Buchanan, 1857–1861, Democratic
Abraham Lincoln, 1861–1865, Republican
Andrew Johnson, 1865–1869, Dem. (Unionist)
Ulysses S. Grant, 1869–1877, Republican
Rutherford B. Hayes, 1877–1881, Republican

James A. Garfield, 1881, Republican
Chester A. Arthur, 1881–1885, Republican
Grover Cleveland, 1885–1889, Democratic
Benjamin Harrison, 1889–1893, Republican
Grover Cleveland, 1893–1897, Democratic
William McKinley, 1897–1901, Republican
Theodore Roosevelt, 1901–1909, Republican
William H. Taft, 1909–1913, Republican
Woodrow Wilson, 1913–1921, Democratic
Warren G. Harding, 1921–1923, Republican
Calvin Coolidge, 1923–1929, Republican
Herbert C. Hoover, 1929–1933, Republican
Franklin D. Roosevelt, 1933–1945, Democratic
Harry S Truman, 1945–1953, Democratic
Dwight D. Eisenhower, 1953–1961, Republican
John F. Kennedy, 1961–1963, Democratic
Lyndon B. Johnson, 1963–1969, Democratic
Richard M. Nixon, 1969–1974, Republican
Gerald R. Ford, 1974–1977, Republican

James Earl Carter, 1977–1981, Democratic
Ronald Reagan, 1981–1989, Republican
George H.W. Bush, 1989–1993, Republican

William J. Clinton, 1993–2001, Democratic
George W. Bush, 2001–2009, Republican
Barack Obama, 2009-present, Democratic

D. Formal Declarations of War by the United States

(listed by name of war, opponents, date authorized, president, and concluding document)

War of 1812	British Empire	June 18, 1812	Madison	Treaty of Ghent (Dec. 24, 1814)
Mexican-American War	Mexico	May 11, 1846	Polk	Treaty of Guadalupe Hildalgo (Feb. 2, 1848)
Spanish-American War	Spain	April 24, 1898	McKinley	Treaty of Paris (Dec. 10, 1898)
World War I	Germany	April 6, 1917	Wilson	Treaty of Berlin (Aug. 25, 1921)
	Austria-Hungary	Dec. 7, 1917		Treaty of Trianon (in part)
World War II	Japan	Dec. 8, 1941		Treaty of San Francisco (Sept. 8, 1951)
	Germany	Dec. 11, 1941	F. Roosevelt, Truman	Treaty on the Final Settlement with Respect to Germany (Sept. 12, 1990), Treaty of Vienna with Austria (May 15, 1955)
	Italy Bulgaria Hungary Romania	June 5, 1942		Paris Peace Treaty (Feb. 10, 1947)

NOTE

For additional information concerning this subject, and related information, please refer to the *U.S. National Archives and Records Administration*, which are listed in the *National Resource Directory* section of this volume.

E. Number of Governmental Units in the United States

Federal and State Governments

Type of Government	1962	2007	Increase/(Decrease)
U.S. Government	1	1	-0-
State Governments	50	50	-0-
Subtotal	*51*	*51*	*-0-*

Local Governments

	1962	2007	
County	3,043	3,033	(10)
Municipal	18,000	19,492	1,492
Township and Town	17,142	16,519	(623)
School District	34,678	13,051	(21,627)
Special District	18,323	37,381	19,058
Subtotal	*91,186*	*89,476*	*(1,710)*
Grand Total	***91,237***	***89,527***	***(1,710)***

NOTE

For additional information concerning this document, and related information, please refer to the *U.S. Bureau of the Census*, which is listed in the *National Resource Directory* section of this volume.

F. United States Voting Rights History

(Year, Legislation, Impact)

1776	*Declaration of Independence*	Right to vote during the Colonial and Revolutionary periods is restricted to property owners.
1787	*United States Constitution*	States are given the power to regulate their own voting rights.
1856	*State Legislation*	North Carolina is the last state to remove property ownership as a requirement for voting.
1868	*14th Amendment to the U.S. Constitution*	Citizenship is granted to all former slaves. Voters are still defined as male. Voting regulations are still a right of the states.
1870	*15th Amendment to the U.S. Constitution*	It is now law that the right to vote cannot be denied by the federal or state governments based on race.
1887	*Daws Act*	Citizenship is granted to Native Americans who give up their tribal affiliations.
1890	*State Constitution*	Wyoming is admitted to statehood and becomes the first state to legislate voting rights for women in its state constitution.
1913	*17th Amendment to the U.S. Constitution*	New law that allows citizens to vote for members of the U.S. Senate, instead of the past practice of having them elected by State Legislatures.
1915	*U.S. Supreme Court Decision*	The U.S. Supreme Court outlawed, in *Guinn v. United States* (Oklahoma), literacy tests for federal elections. The court ruled that this practice was in violation of the 15th Amendment to the U.S. Constitution.
1920	*19th Amendment to the U.S. Constitution*	Women were given the right to vote in both state and federal elections.
1924	*Indian Citizenship Act*	This law granted all Native Americans the rights of citizenship, including the right to vote in federal elections.
1944	*U.S. Supreme Court Decision*	The U.S. Supreme Court outlawed, in *Smith v. Allright* (Texas), "white primaries" in Texas and other States. The court ruled that this practice was in violation of the 15th Amendment to the U.S. Constitution.
1957	*Civil Rights Act*	The first law to implement the 15th Amendment to the U.S. Constitution is passed. This law established the Civil Rights Commission, which formally investigates complaints of voter discrimination made by citizens.
1960	*U.S. Supreme Court Decision*	The U.S. Supreme Court, in *Gomillion v. Lightfoot* (Alabama), outlawed the use of "gerrymandering" in election practices. This practice includes boundary determination (or redistricting) changes being made for electoral advantage.
1961	*23rd Amendment to the U.S. Constitution*	Citizens of Washington, DC, are given the right to vote in presidential elections.
1964	*24th Amendment to the U.S. Constitution*	The right for citizens to vote in federal elections cannot be denied for failure to pay a poll tax.

1965	*Voting Rights Act*	This law forbids states from imposing discriminatory restrictions on the voting rights of citizens, and provides mechanisms to the federal government for the enforcement of this law. This act was expanded and renewed in 1970, 1975, 1982, and 2006.
1966	*U.S. Supreme Court Decision*	The U.S. Supreme Court, in *Harper v. Virginia Board of Education* (Virginia), eliminated the poll tax as a qualification for voting in any election. This practice was found to be in violation of the 24th Amendment to the U.S. Constitution.
1966	*U.S. Supreme Court Decision*	The U.S. Supreme Court, in *South Carolina v. Katzenbach* (South Carolina), upheld the legality of the Voting Rights Act of 1965.
1970	*U.S. Supreme Court Decision*	The U.S. Supreme Court, in *Oregon v. Mitchell* (Oregon), upheld the ban on the use of literacy tests as a requirement for voting. This ban was made permanent in the 1975 amendment to the Voting Rights Act.
1971	*26th Amendment to the U.S. Constitution*	The national legal voting age is reduced from 21 years old to 18 years old.
1972	*U.S. Supreme Court Decision*	The U.S. Supreme Court, in *Dunn v. Blumstein* (Tennessee), ruled that lengthy residency requirements for voting in state and local elections are unconstitutional, and suggested a 30-day residency period as being adequate.
1975	*Amendments to the Voting Rights Act*	Mandated that certain voting materials must be printed in languages besides English so that people who do not read English can participate in the voting process.
1993	*National Voter Registration Act*	Attempts to increase the number of eligible citizens who register to vote by making registration available at each state's Department of Motor Vehicles, as well as public assistance and disability agencies.
2002	*Help America Vote Act*	Law requires that states comply with federal mandates for provisional ballots; disability access; centralized, computerized voting lists; electronic voting; and the requirement that first-time voters present identification before they can vote.
2003	*Federal Voting Standards and Procedures Act*	Requires all states to streamline their voter registration process, voting practices, and election procedures.

NOTE

For additional information concerning these documents, and related information, please refer to *the Federal Election Commission*, which is listed in the *National Resource Directory* section of this volume.

G. Major Cases in Supreme Court History

(listed by name of court case, year decided, and legal impact)

Marbury v. Madison, 1803

"A law repugnant to the Constitution is void."

With these words, Chief Justice John Marshall established the Supreme Court's role in the new government. Hereafter, the Court was recognized as having the power to review all acts of Congress where constitutionality was at issue, and judge whether they abide by the Constitution.

McCulloch v. Maryland, 1819

"Let the end be legitimate ... and all means which are ... consistent with the letter and spirit of the Constitution, are constitutional."

Chief Justice Marshall invoked this phrase to establish the right of Congress to pass laws that are "necessary and proper" to conduct the business of the U.S. government. Here, the court upheld Congress' power to create a national bank.

Gibbons v. Ogden, 1824

When a federal and state law are in conflict, the federal law is supreme.

Congress and New York had both passed laws regulating the steamboat industry. Gibbons had a federal permit for a steamboat business; Ogden had a state permit for the same waters. Siding with Gibbons, the Court said that, in matters of interstate commerce, the "Supremacy Clause" tilts the balance of power in favor of federal legislation.

Charles River Bridge, 1837

The responsibility of government is to "sacredly guard" the rights of property for the prosperity of the community.

The Charles River Bridge was erected in 1785 by Harvard College and some prominent Bostonians under a legal charter granted by the state of Massachusetts. The legislature granted a charter to the Warren Bridge Company in 1828 because a new bridge was badly needed. It was to be free of tolls once construction costs were covered. The proprietors of the Charles River Bridge were afraid that the new bridge would destroy the value of their stock and tried to block the construction of the Warren Bridge. The case involved a conflict between established rights on one side and the rights of the community on the other. The Court ruled that it had not entered into a bridge contract with the Charles River Bridge Company that would prohibit the building of a competitive bridge. Justice Roger B. Taney stated that the rights of property must be "sacredly guarded," the community also has rights, and the responsibility of all government is to promote the happiness and prosperity of the community.

Dred Scott v. Sandford, 1857

"The Constitution does not consider slaves to be U.S. citizens. Rather, they are constitutionally protected property of their masters."

Chief Justice Roger Taney authored this opinion — one of the most important and scorned in the nation's history. Dred Scott, a slave, had moved with his master to Illinois, a free state. He moved again to a slave state, Missouri, and filed suit to gain freedom, under that state's law of "Once free, always free." Taney held that Scott had never been free at all, and cited Constitutional grounds for placing the slavery decision in the hands of the states. In trying to put an end to the slavery controversy, Taney instead sped the nation toward civil war. The decision was later overturned by the Thirteenth Amendment.

Munn v. Illinois, 1877

Businesses that serve the public interest are subject to regulation by state government.

The Illinois state legislature passed a law that established the maximum rates that private companies could charge in storing or transporting agricultural products. In Chicago the company of Munn and Scott was found guilty of breaking the law and the verdict was upheld on appeal before the Supreme Court. The appeal was heard along with seven other railroad cases that dealt with the violation of the regulatory legislation passed by the state of Illinois. The Court ruled that any business that served the public interest was subject to regulation by the state government. If the rates were not satisfactory according to the owners of the companies, the complaints should be taken to the legislature and not to the courts.

Plessy v. Ferguson, 1896

Jim Crow laws are constitutional under the doctrine of "Separate but Equal."

Police arrested Homer Plessy for refusing to leave a railroad car that prohibited "colored" people. Under Louisiana law, Plessy was "colored" because he was one-eighth black. The court ruled that the race-based "Jim Crow" laws did not violate the Constitution as long as the states proffered separate but equal treatment.

"The Constitution is color blind, and neither knows nor tolerates classes among citizens."

— Justice John Marshall Harlan, from the lone dissenting opinion in Plessy v. Ferguson

Lochner v. New York, 1905

The Constitution bars a state from interfering with an employee's right to contract with an employer.

The above reasoning led to the "Lochner Era" — thirty-two years of wrangling between the court and legislatures. Lochner's bakery violated a New York labor law. The court struck down the law, saying that the 14th Amendment's Due Process Clause barred states from regulating commerce in this manner. This clause, the Court said, implied that individuals have a fundamental right to contract with employers, and states cannot interfere with that right.

Schenck v. United States, 1919

Speech that presents a "clear and present danger" to the security of the United States is in violation of the principle of free speech as protected by the First Amendment to the Constitution.

During World War I (1918), Charles Schenck was the general secretary of the Socialist Party, and was arrested for distributing literature discouraging young men from enlisting in the armed forces. The basis for his opposition to the draft or enlistment was the first clause of the Thirteenth Amendment which prohibited slavery or involuntary servitude. Schenck appealed his conviction and the case went to the Supreme Court. Justice Oliver Wendell Holmes stated that "the character of every act depends upon the circumstances in which it is done. The most stringent protection of free speech would not protect a man in falsely shouting fire in a theatre and causing a panic. [The] question in every case is whether the words used are used in such circumstances and are of such a nature as to create a clear and present danger that they will bring about the substantive evils that Congress has a right to protect." Distributing the literature during peace time would have been an entirely different matter, but in time of war Schenck's actions, according to the Court, presented a "clear and present danger" to the security of the United States.

Near v. Minnesota, 1931

"The liberty of the press ... is safeguarded from invasion by state action."

Although the First Amendment ensures a free press, until this case, it only protected the press from federal laws, not state laws. Minnesota shut down J. M. Near's Saturday Press for publishing vicious anti-Semitic and racist remarks. In what is regarded as the landmark free press decision, the Court ruled a state cannot engage in "prior restraint"; that is, with rare exceptions, it cannot stop a person from publishing or expressing a thought.

West Coast Hotel v. Parrish, 1937

"The switch in time that saved nine."

F.D.R. rallied against the Court's holdings in the Lochner era. The Court struck down New Deal Laws, designed to pull the country out of the Depression, on grounds that they interfered with a worker's "right to contract." F.D.R. pledged to expand the Court and pack it with pro "New

Deal" members. In this case, the Court rejected the Lochner era decisions and said the government could regulate commerce.

Brown v. Board of Education, 1954

"In the field of public education, the doctrine of 'separate but equal' has no place."

This unanimous decision marked the beginning of the end for the "Separate But Equal" era that started with Plessy, and the start of a new period of American race relations. With Brown, desegregation of public schools began — as did resistance to it. Ten contentious years later, the Civil Rights Act of 1964 made racial equality a matter of federal law.

Mapp v. Ohio, 1961

Evidence that is illegally obtained by the state may not be used against a defendant in court.

Until Mapp, only the federal government was barred from using illegally obtained evidence. So when local police entered Dolly Mapp's home without a search warrant and arrested her for possessing obscene books, her conviction initially stood. The Court overturned her conviction, however, and extended the constitutional rule to apply to the states and their subdivisions.
"I know it when I see it."

— Justice Potter Stewart's definition of obscenity in *Jacobellis v. Ohio*, 1964

Baker v. Carr, 1962

"One person, one vote."

The above phrase was not authored until a year after Baker, but it has its philosophical roots here. In this case, a group of Tennessee voters sued the state, claiming its voting districts diluted their political power. Until this point, the Court refused to decide this kind of case, leaving such "political questions" to the states. Baker, however, held that the states must meet a constitutional standard for appointment: districts cannot be drawn in such a way that they violate the Equal Protection clause of the 14th Amendment.

Engel v. Vitale, 1962

Public institutions (i.e., a school system) cannot require prayer.

Lawrence Roth, an avowed atheist, objected that the Long Island, New York, School System was forcing his two children to recite a 22-word prayer at the beginning of the day. There were actually four other parents involved in the suit against school board president William Vitale, Jr.

The Supreme Court ruled that although the prayer was non-sectarian and noncompulsory, "it is no part the business of government to compose official prayers." Because New York provided the prayer, it indirectly approved religion and that was unconstitutional.

Gideon v. Wainwright, 1963

Defendants in criminal cases have an absolute right to counsel.

Too poor to afford a lawyer, Clarence Earl Gideon was convicted for breaking into a pool-room — a felony crime in Florida. He appealed to the Supreme Court, which ruled that the government must provide free counsel to accused criminals who cannot pay for it themselves. At first, the ruling applied to felonies only. It was later extended to cover any cases where the penalty was six months imprisonment or longer.

New York Times Co. v. Sullivan, 1964

To win a libel case, public figures must prove "actual malice" on the part of the writer.

In 1964, the *Times* published an ad critical of an elected commissioner of an Alabama city. The commissioner sued for libel and won. The Supreme Court overturned that ruling, and said that, to ensure "uninhibited, robust and wide-open" debate about public figures, the law must protect writers from libel suits. Thus, unless the words are penned with "knowing falsity" or "reckless disregard for the truth," a writer cannot be successfully sued by a public figure for libel.

Griswold v. Connecticut, 1965

The Constitution implies a right to privacy in matters of contraception between married people.

Estelle Griswold, the director of a Planned Parenthood clinic, broke an 1879 Connecticut law banning contraception. The Court struck down the law, making it a landmark case in which the Court read the Constitution to protect individual privacy. This was to be the foundation of further privacy rulings, including the right to privacy in matters of abortion.

Miranda v. Arizona, 1966

"You have the right to remain silent..."

After police questioning, Ernesto Miranda confessed to kidnapping and raping a woman. The Court struck down the conviction, on grounds that he was not informed of his 5th Amendment right against self-incrimination. Hereafter, the Miranda warnings have been a standard feature of arrest procedures.

Tinker v. Des Moines, 1969

School dress codes are not in violation of the First Amendment's guarantee of the freedom of expression.

The Des Moines public school system made a rule stating that any student wearing an armband would be asked to remove it on the grounds that the wearing of such would cause a disturbance. If the student refused to comply, the consequence was suspension from school. Three public school students wore black armbands to express their opposition to the United States' involvement in the Vietnam War. They refused to remove the armbands and were suspended. The parents of the students argued that the students' actions were not interfering with the rights of the other students. The case was argued in 1968 and the ruling was handed down in 1969. The Court ruled that the wearing of armbands was "closely akin to 'pure speech,'" and thus was protected by the First Amendment to the Constitution. The rule banning armbands lacked the proper justification for enforcement. This ruling eventually had an effect on school dress codes in that the style of clothing one wears indicates an expression of that individual.

San Antonio Independent School District v. Rodrigues, 1973

The Constitution does not guarantee a fundamental right to education.

In 1968, a group of low-income parents sued San Antonio, claiming the city's wealthy precincts had better schools. The Court upheld the districting plan, saying the Constitution did not guarantee an education, and upholding this tenet: The Constitution does not compel government to provide services like education or welfare to the people. Rather, it places boundaries on government action.

Roe v. Wade, 1973

The Constitutionality implied right to privacy protects a woman's choice in matters of abortion.

Norma McCorvey sought an abortion in Texas, but was denied under state law. The Court struck down that law, on grounds that it is unconstitutionally restricting the woman's right to choose. The opinion set forth guidelines for state abortion regulations; states could restrict a woman's right to choose only in the later stages of the pregnancy. Later modified but not overruled, the decision stands as one of the Court's most controversial.

United States v. Nixon, 1974

"Neither separation of powers, nor the need for confidentiality can sustain unqualified Presidential immunity from the judicial process."

President Nixon sought precisely this type of immunity, rather than relinquishing the famous White House tapes during the Watergate scandal. The Court unanimously rejected his plea as an unconstitutional power play. The House began impeachment proceedings shortly thereafter, and two weeks after the ruling, Nixon resigned.

Texas v. Johnson, 1989

The Constitution protects desecration of the flag as a form of symbolic speech.

Johnson burned a flag in front of a Dallas building in 1984. He was convicted of violating a Texas law that made it a crime to intentionally desecrate a state or national flag. Justice Brennan wrote for a 5-to-4 majority that "Government may not prohibit the expression of an idea because society finds the idea itself offensive or disagreeable."

Cruzan v. Missouri Dept. of Health, 1990

While the Constitution protects a person's right to reject life-preserving medical treatment (their "right to die"), states can regulate that interest if the regulation is reasonable.

Nancy Cruzan lay in a permanent vegetative state as a result of injuries suffered in an auto accident. Her parents sought to withdraw life-sustaining treatment and allow her to die, claiming she'd said this would be her wish under such circumstances. The state refused, and the Supreme Court upheld the state's guidelines for the continuation of medical treatment, which allowed withdrawal of treatment only with clear and convincing evidence that this is what the patient would have wanted. The Court said that, given the need to protect against abuses of such situations, the state can continue life support as long as its standards for doing so are reasonable.

NOTE

For additional information concerning this subject, and related information, please refer to the *Constitution Facts* and the *Supreme Court Historical Society*, which are listed in the *National Resource Directory* section of this volume.

H. Local Government Historical Document

(Mecklenburg County was the first local government in America to declare its Independence from Great Britain)

The Mecklenburg Resolution[1]
(May 20, 1775)

I. *Resolved*: That whosoever directly or indirectly abets, or in any way, form, or manner countenances the unchartered and dangerous invasion of our rights, as claimed by Great Britain, is an enemy to this country — to America — and to the inherent and inalienable rights of man.

II. *Resolved*: That we do hereby declare ourselves a free and independent people; are, and of right ought to be a sovereign and self-governing association, under the control of no power, other than that of our God and the General Government of the Congress: To the maintenance of which Independence we solemnly pledge to each other our mutual co-operation, our Lives, our Fortunes, and our most Sacred Honor.

III. *Resolved*: That as we acknowledge the existence and control of no law or legal officer, civil or military, within this county, we do hereby ordain and adopt as a rule of life, all, each, and every one of our former laws, wherein, nevertheless, the Crown of Great Britain never can be considered as holding rights, privileges, or authorities therein.

IV. *Resolved*: That all, each, and every Military Officer in this country is hereby reinstated in his former command and authority, he acting to their regulations, and that every Member present of this Delegation, shall henceforth be a Civil Officer, viz: a Justice of the Peace, in the character of a Committee Man, to issue process, hear and determine all matters of controversy, according to said adopted laws, and to preserve Peace, Union, and Harmony in said county, to use every exertion to spread the

Love of Country and Fire of Freedom throughout America, until a more general and organized government be established in this Province.

ABRAHAM ALEXANDER, *Chairman.*
JOHN MCKNITT ALEXANDER, *Secretary.*

REFERENCE

1. This declaration of independence (with supplementary set of resolutions establishing a form of government) was adopted (as it is claimed) by a convention of delegates from different sections of Mecklenburg County, which assembled at Charlotte May 20, 1775.

SOURCE

The Avalon Project, which is listed in the *National Resource Directory* section of this volume.

I. Abbreviations and Acronyms

(listed in alphabetical order)

A	Bureau of Administration
AID	Agency for International Development
A/IM	Information Management
APEC	Asia Pacific Economic Cooperation Forum
ATA	Anti-terrorism Assistance
ATF	Bureau of Alcohol, Tobacco and Firearms
BIT	Bilateral Investment Treaty
CA	Bureau of Consular Affairs
CDC	Centers for Disease Control
CIA	Central Intelligence Agency
CPM	Civilian Personnel Management
DEA	Drug Enforcement Administration
DLEA	Drug Law Enforcement Agency
DOC	Department of Commerce
DOD	Department of Defense
DOE	Department of Energy
DOJ	Department of Justice
DRL	Bureau of Democracy, Human Rights and Labor
DS	Bureau of Diplomatic Security
DTS-PO	Diplomatic Telecommunications Service — Program Office
E/CBA	Office of Business Affairs
EB	Bureau of Economic and Business Affairs
EPA	Environmental Protection Agency
ESA	Emergency Security Appropriation
ESF	Economic Support Funds
EUR	Bureau of European and Eurasian Affairs
Ex-lm	Bank Export-Import Bank
FAA	Federal Aviation Administration
FBI	Federal Bureau of Investigation
FBO	Foreign Buildings Operations
FMP	Bureau of Finance and Management Policy (Now RM — Office of Resource Management
FSA	Freedom Support Act
FSC	Financial Service Center
FSI	Foreign Service Institute
G	Under Secretary for Global Affairs
GAO	General Accounting Office
GCC	Gulf Cooperation Council
GDP	Gross Domestic Product
H	Bureau of Legislative Affairs
HHS	Department of Health and Human Services
ICASS	International Cooperative Administrative Support Services
IDP	Individual Development Plan Internally Displaced Person
IEA	International Energy Agency
IFI	International Financial Institution
INL	Bureau of International Narcotics and Law Enforcement Affairs
INR	Bureau of Intelligence and Research
INS	Immigration and Naturalization Service
IO	Bureau of International Organization Affairs
IPMS	Integrated Personnel Management System
IT	Information Technology
L	Office of the Legal Adviser
LEA	Local Educational Agency
MAI	Multilateral Agreement on Investment
M/CIO	Chief Information Officer
M/FLO	Family Liaison Office

M/MED	Office of Medical Services
M/P	Office of Management Policy and Planning
NADR	Nonproliferation, Anti-terrorism, Demining, and Related Programs
NEC	National Economic Council
NIS	New Independent States
NGO	Nongovernmental Organization
NOAA	National Oceanic and Atmospheric Administration
NSC	National Security Council
OBO	Overseas Buildings Operations
OECD	Organization for Economic Cooperation and Development
OES	Bureau of Oceans, Environment, and Scientific Affairs
OIG	Office of The Inspector General
OMB	Office of Management and Budget
ONDCP	Office of National Drug Control Policy
OPIC	Overseas Private Investment Corporation
OSM	Overseas Staffing Model
PA	Bureau of Public Affairs
PER	Bureau of Personnel
PVO	Private Voluntary Organization
Prepcom	Preparatory Committee
Pol-Mil	Political and Military
PRM	Bureau of Population, Refugees and Migration
RM	Bureau of Resource Management

RSO	Regional Security Officer
S/CT	Coordinator for Counterterrorism
SEED	Southeast European Development
S/EEOCR	Office of Equal Employment Opportunity and Civil Rights
S/RPP	Secretary's Office of Resources, Plans, and Policy
S/S-O	Operations Center
T	Under Secretary for Arms Control and International Security
TDA	Trade and Development Agency
UN	United Nations
USAID	U.S. Agency for International Development
USDA	U.S. Department of Agriculture
USG	U.S. Government
USOECD	Mission to the Organization for Economic Cooperation and Development
USTR	United States Trade Representative
USUN	U.S. Mission to the United Nations
WHA	Bureau of Western Hemisphere Affairs
WMD	Weapons of Mass Destruction
WTO	World Trade Organization

NOTE

For additional information concerning this subject, and related information, please refer to the *U.S. Department of State*, which is listed in the *National Resource Directory* section of this volume.

J. Glossary

(listed in alphabetical order)

Agora— the administrative center of ancient Athens, Greece, with courts, temples, and similar buildings. As the central meeting place of ancient Athens, the agora has become associated in modern memory with the origins of democratic concepts and institutions.

Civic responsibility— In democracy, civic responsibility means taking active measures to be part of the community, to improve the community, to run for public office, to report crime and corruption and to help others achieve their potential.

Common law— The traditional body of British law dating from the Middle Ages that became increasingly codified in England and America in the 18th century and formed the basis of American constitutional government.

Constitutionalism— Pertaining to the fundamental law of a democracy, as codified in a constitution, Democratic constitutions spell out the fundamental structure of government, but usually leave elaboration to legislative bodies.

Corruption— Social or governmental behavior that illegally or immorally diverts resources to the self that properly belong to others or to society as a whole. Corruption saps the vitality of democracy. To participate actively in a democratic society, citizens need to be sure the fruits of their labor will go to legitimate goals and institutions, not corrupt individuals.

Demos— An ancient Greek word for the citizens of a Greek state. In liberal democracy, the concept of "demos" is all-important, for it is the fundamental rights of ordinary people that give legitimacy to the state.

Direct democracy— When people in a small group or geographic area assemble and regulate their community personally, without electing representatives, it is called "direct democracy." This is as opposed to "representative democracy," the most common arrangement, which involves voting for officials to represent a large group of citizens in a legislature.

Due process— Legal process that respects the rights of the accused, no matter how unpopular. Due process is the fundamental characteristic of democracy. In general due process guarantees rights to a fair hearing or trial before an impartial magistrate, and freedom from cruel or unusual punishment.

Fundamental rights— In democratic theory, fundamental rights generally include the right to liberty, freedom of thought and justice before the law, as well as basic social equality with other human beings.

Habeas corpus— A Latin phrase referring to one of the central concepts of due process, which is that people may not be arrested and held in detention without cause and without a legal warrant from a judge. In democracy, a citizen who feels he is unlawfully imprisoned may petition for a writ of *habeas corpus* and a hearing before a judge. If being held illegally by the state, he must be released. *Habeas corpus* may be suspended in wartime or emergency.

Independent judiciary— In democratic constitutional theory, the judiciary (the courts) must be independent in the sense of not being subservient to the executive (the leader) nor to the legislature. The judiciary must have sufficient prestige, power, and the popular respect in order to be able to define the structure of the constitution, enforce constitutional law, and restrain the other branches of government from lawless behavior.

Interest groups— In democracies, nongovernmental organizations that represent various segments of society with various goals or needs. Interest groups try to influence public opinion and public officials in order to gain recognition for their cause.

Liberal democracy— The modern form of democracy, which tends to stress individual rights and protections, as opposed to collective rights.

Minority rights— Most decisions in democracy are made by voting. While the majority that wins the vote achieves its objectives, it still must respect the rights of the minority that lost the vote. Minority rights mean that political losers are not oppressed, imprisoned or silenced, and may continue to represent their political interests in the hope of winning someday.

Natural rights— A concept that arose in the 18th century, from the concept of natural law. Natural rights means that all human beings have rights because they are human. The concept of natural rights is the basis of the democratic belief that all human beings are fundamentally similar, and have the same rights before government and the law.

Nongovernmental organizations (NGOs)— In democracy, organizations that are important or essential to the functioning of society, yet not part of government. They may include churches, unions, professional or business groups, or interest groups focusing on issues such as human rights or the environment. Some operate within national boundaries; increasingly, some of these groups operate on an international basis.

Pluralism— The recognition in democratic culture that individuals may retain their cultural and group traits while being part of a large democratic nation.

Representative democracy— As opposed to direct democracy, representative democracy occurs when the population becomes too large for direct democracy. Basically, it means that people vote for elected officials to run their government or governments.

Sovereignty— The right to rule a given nation. In democracy, the theory is that the people, taken as a whole, have sovereignty.

Transparency— The right of ordinary citizens in a democracy to know what is happening in their government, in leadership councils, in the legislature, in the courts and in administrative bodies. In recent decades, democratic governments have become more transparent, opening more meetings to the public and releasing more information to the press and to citizens. Even so, democratic government still has the right to protect essential or sensitive information.

NOTE

For additional information concerning these subjects, and related information, please refer to the *U.S. Department of State*, which is listed in the *National Resource Directory* section of this volume.

K. State Library Resource Directory

Most state libraries have copies of state laws, both proposed and adopted, in an online database. Many states also have copies of the various laws adopted in those cities and towns within their jurisdiction. They are an excellent resource. The contact information for the various state libraries is shown below.

Alabama
(http://www.apls.state.la.us/)

Alaska
(http://www.library.state.ak.us/)

Arizona
(http://www.lib.az.us/)

Arkansas
(http://www.asl.lib.ar.us/)

California
(http://www.library.ca.gov/)

Colorado
(http://www.cde.state.co.us/)

Connecticut
(http://www.cslib.org/)

Delaware
(http://www.state.lib.de.us/)

District of Columbia
(http://dclibrary.org/)

Florida
(http://dlis.dos.state.fl.us/)

Georgia
(http://www.georgialibraries.org/)

Hawaii
(http://www.librarieshawaii.org/)

Idaho
(http://www.lili.org/)

Illinois
(http://www.cyberdriveillinois.com/departments/library/)

Indiana
(http://www.statelib.lib.in.us/)

Iowa
(http://www.silo.lib.ia.us/)

Kansas
(http://www.skyways.org/KSL/)

Kentucky
(http://www.kdla.ky.gov/)

Louisiana
(http://www.state.lib.la.us/)

Maine
(http://www.state.me.us/msl/)

Maryland
(http://www.sailor.lib.md.us/)

Massachusetts
(http://mass.gov/mblc/)

Michigan
(http://www.michigan.gov/hal/)

Minnesota
(http://www.state.mn.us/libraries/)

Mississippi
(http://www.mlc.lib.ms.us/)

Missouri
(http://www.sos.mo.gov/library/)

Montana
(http://msl.state.mt.us/)

Nebraska
(http://www.nlc.state.ne.us/)

Nevada
(http://dmla.clan.lib.nv.us/)

New Hampshire
(http://www.state.nh.us/nhls/)

New Jersey
(http://www.njstatelib.org/)

New Mexico
(http://www.stlib.state.nm.us/)

New York
(http://www.nysl.nysed.gov/)

North Carolina
(http://statelibrary.dcr.state.nc.us/)

North Dakota
(http://ndsl.lib.state.nd.us/)

Ohio
(http://winslo.state.oh.us/)

Oklahoma
(http://www.odl.state.ok.us/)

Oregon
(http://oregon.gov/OSL/)

Pennsylvania
(http://www.statelibrary.state.pa.us/libraries/)

Rhode Island
(http://www.olis.ri.gov/)

South Carolina
(http://www.statelibrary.sc.gov/)

South Dakota
(http://www.sdstatelibrary.com/)

Tennessee
(http://www.tennessee.gov/tsla/)

Texas
(http://www.tsl.state.tx.us/)

Utah
(http://library.ut.gov/index.html/)

Vermont
(http://dol.state.vt.us/)

Virginia
(http://www.lva.lib.va.us/)

Washington
(http://www.secstate.was.gov/library/)

West Virginia
(http://librarycommission/lib.wv.us/)

Wisconsin
(http://www.dpi.state.wi.us/dltcl/pld/)

Wyoming
(http://www-wsl.state.wy.us/)

L. National Resource Directory

(organized by topics for the public, nonprofit, and educational sectors)

Civic Education

Ackerman Center for Democratic Citizenship
(http://www.edci.purdue.edu/ackerman/)

American Democracy Project
(http://www.aascu.org/programs/adp/)

Bill of Rights Institute
(http://www.billofrightsinstitute.org/)

Center for Civic Education
(http://www.civiced.org/)

Center for Youth Citizenship
(http://www.youthcitizenship.org/)

Civic Education Project
(http://www.civiceducationproject.org/)

Civnet
(http://civnet.org/)

Constitutional Rights Foundation
(http://www.crf-usa.org/)

Kellogg Foundation
(http://www.wkkf.org/)

National Commission on Civic Renewal
(http://www.pauf.umd.edu/Affiliates/)

National Endowment for Democracy
(http://www.ned.org/)

National Institute for Citizen Education and Law
(http://www.indiana.edu/~ssdc/nicel.html/)

Civil Rights and Civil Liberties

American Civil Liberties Union
(http://www.aclu.org/)

Citizens Commission on Civil Rights
(http://www.cccr.org/)

Constitution Society
(http://www.constitution.org/)

Freedom Forum
(http://www.freedomforum.org/)

Judicial Watch
(http://www.judicialwatch.org/)

League of Women Voters
(http://www.lwv.org/)

National Coalition Against Censorship
(http://www.ncac.org/)

Project Vote Smart
(http://www.vote-smart.org/)

Historical

Center for the Study of Federalism
(http://www.temple.edu/federalism/)

Center for the Study of the Presidency
(http://www.thepresidency.org/)

Constitutional Facts
(http://www.constitutionfacts.com/)

Freedom Foundation at Valley Forge
(http://www.ffvf.org/)

National Constitution Center
(http://www.constitutioncenter.org/)

Supreme Court Historical Society
(http://www.supremecourthistory.org/)

The Avalon Project
(http://avalon.law.yale.edu/)

White House Historical Association
(http://www.whitehousehistory.org/)

Political Parties

Democratic National Committee
(http://www.democrats.org/)

Green Party of North America
(http://www/greens.org/)

Libertarian Party
(http://www.lp.org/)

Natural Law Party
(http://www.natural-law.org/)

Reform Party
(http://www.reformparty.org/)

Republican National Committee
(http://www.rnc.org/)

Socialist Party
(http://www.socialist.org/)

Professional Associations

American Bar Association
(http://www.abanet.org/)

American Planning Association
(http://www.planning.org/)

American Political Science Association
(http://www.apsanet.org/)

American Society for Public Administration
(http://www.aspanet.org/)

Association for Metropolitan Planning
Organizations
(http://www.ampo.org/)

Public Policy

Association for Public Policy Analysis and
Management
(http://www.appam.org/)

Center for Policy Alternatives
(http://www.cfpa.org/)

Center for Public Integrity
(http://www.publicintegrity.org/)

Common Cause
(http://www.commoncause.org/)

National Center for Policy Analysis
(http://www.ncpa.org/)

National Center for Public Policy Research
(http://www.nationalcenter.org/)

National Legal Center for Public Interest
(http://www.nlcpi.org/)

Pew Research Center
(http://pewresearch.org/)

State and Local Government

Council of State Governments
(http://www.csg.org/)

International City/County Management
Association
(http://www.icma.org/)

Local Government Commission
(http://www.lgc.org/)

Meyner Center for the Study of State and
Local Government
(http://www.lafayette.edu/publius/)

National Association of Counties
(http://www.naco.org/)

National Association of Regional Councils
(http://www.narc.org/)

National Association of Towns and Townships
(http://www.natat.org/)

National Center for State Courts
(http://www.ncsconline.org/)

National Civic League
(http://www.ncl.org/)

National Conference of State Legislatures
(http://www.ncsl.org/)

National Governors Association
(http://www.nga.org/)

National League of Cities
(http://www.nlc.org/)

Secretary of State
State of Connecticut
(http://www.sots.ct.gov/)

U.S. Conference of Mayors
(http://www.usmayors.oeg/)

State Supreme Judicial Court
Commonwealth of Massachusetts
(http://www.mass.gov/courts/sjc/)

U.S. Government

Federal Communications Commission
(http://www.fcc.gov/)

Federal Elections Commission
(http://www.fec.gov/)

Federal Judicial Center
(http://www.fjc.gov/)

Federal Judiciary Homepage
(http://www.uscourts.gov/)

Library of Congress
(http://lcweb.loc.gov/)

National Endowment for the Humanities
(http://www.neh.fed.us/)

Thomas Legislative Information
(http://thomas.loc.gov/)

U.S. Census Bureau
(http://www.census.gov/)

U.S. Congress
(http://www.congresslink.org/)

U.S. Department of State
(http://www.state.gov/)

U.S. Department of the Interior
(http://www.doi.gov/)

U.S. House of Representatives
(http://www.house.gov/)

U.S. National Archives and Records
Administration
(http://www.archives.gov/)

U.S. Senate
(http://www.senate.gov/)

U.S. Supreme Court
(http://www.supremecourtus.gov/)

White House
(http://www.whitehouse.gov/)

Others

Brookings Institution
(http://www.Brookings.edu/)

Heritage Foundation
(http://www.heritage.org/)

National Humanities Institute
(http://www.nhinet.org/)

National Taxpayers Union
(http://www.ntu.org/)

National Urban League
(http://www.nul.org/)

Smithsonian Institution
(http://www.si.edu/)

Street Law, Inc.
(http://www.streetlaw.org/)

Supreme Court Decisions
(http://supct.law.cornell.edu/supct/)

The Future of American Democracy Foundation
(http://thefutureofamericandemocracyfounda
tion.org/)

United Kingdom Parliamentary Archives
(http://www.parliament.uk/archives/)

Urban Institute
(http://www.urban.org/)

Wikipedia Encyclopedia
(http://www.wikipedia.org/)

NOTE

Some professional associations are listed under headings that fit their primary mission. Those that don't fit into one of the general topics are listed above under "others."

Bibliography

Albert, Gail, ed. *Service Learning Reader: Reflections and Perspectives on Service* (Raleigh, NC: National Society for Experiential Education, 1994).

Almond, Gabriel A., and Sidney Verba. *The Civic Culture* (Boston: Little, Brown, 1966).

Amidei, Nancy. *So You Want to Make a Difference: Advocacy Is the Key* (Washington, DC: OMB Watch, 1991).

Anderson, James E. *Public Policymaking*, 3rd ed. (Boston: Houghton Mifflin, 1997).

Barber, Benjamin R. *An Aristocracy of Everyone: The Politics of Education and the Future of America* (New York: Oxford University Press, 1992).

Barber, James David. *The Book of Democracy* (Englewood Cliffs, NJ: Prentice Hall, 1995).

Bardach, Eugene. *The Implementation Game* (Cambridge, MA: MIT Press, 1979).

_____. *A Practical Guide for Policy Analysis: The Eightfold Path to More Effective Problem Solving* (Washington, DC: CQ Press, 2009).

Battistoni, Richard M., and William E. Hudson, eds. *Experiencing Citizenship: Concepts and Models for Service-Learning in Political Science* (Washington, DC: American Association of Higher Education, 1997).

Bellah, Robert N., Richard Madsen, William M. Sullivan, Ann Swidler, and Steven M. Tipton, *Habits of the Heart: Individualism and Commitment in American Life* (New York: Harper and Row, 1985).

Birkland, Thomas A. *An Introduction to the Policy Process: Theories, Concepts, and Models of Public Policy Making* (Armonk, NY: M.E. Sharpe, 2005).

Bluhm, William T., and Robert A. Heineman. *Ethics and Public Policy: Method and Cases* (Upper Saddle River, NJ: Pearson Education, 2007).

Brown, Richard D. *The Strength of a People: The Idea of an Informed Citizen in America, 1650–1870* (Chapel Hill: University of North Carolina Press, 1996).

Dahl, Robert A. *Pluralist Democracy in the United States* (Chicago: Rand McNally, 1966).

Dye, Thomas A. *Understanding Public Policy*, 12th ed. (Upper Saddle River, NJ: Pearson Education, 2008).

Ehrlich, Thomas, ed. *Civic Responsibility and Higher Education* (Phoenix, AZ: Oryx, 2000).

Eliasoph, Nina. *Avoiding Politics: How Americans Produce Apathy in Everyday Life* (Cambridge: Cambridge University Press, 1998).

Etzioni, Amitai. *The Spirit of Community: Rights, Responsibilities and the Communitarian Agenda* (New York: Crown, 1993).

The Federalist Papers: Alexander Hamilton, James Madison, John Jay, ed. Clinton Rossiter and Charles R. Resler (New York: Mentor Books, 1999).

Fisher, Louis. *The Politics of Shared Power* (Washington, DC: CQ Press, 1993).

Gerber, Elizabeth R., Arthur Lupia, Mathew D. McCubbins, and D. Roderick Kiewiet. *Stealing the Initiative: How State Government Responds to Direct Democracy* (Upper Saddle River, NJ: Prentice-Hall, 2001).

Gerston, Larry N. *American Federalism: A Concise Introduction* (Armonk, NY: M. E. Sharpe, 2007).

_____. *Public Policymaking in a Democratic Society: A Guide to Civic Engagement* (Armonk, NY: M. E. Sharpe, 2008).

_____. *Public Policymaking: Process and Principles* (Armonk, NY: M. E. Sharpe, 1997).

Goggin, Malcolm L., Ann O'M. Bowman, James P. Lester, and Lawrence J. O'Toole, Jr. *Implementation Theory and Practice* (New York: HarperCollins, 1990).

Goldwin, Robert A. *From Parchment to Power: How James Madison Used the Bill of Rights to Save the Constitution* (Washington, DC: AEA Press, 1997).

Gordon, Rick, et al., eds. *Problem Based Service Learning: A Fieldguide for Making a Difference in Higher Education* (Keene, NH: Antioch New England Graduate School, 2000).

Hofstadter, Richard. *The American Political Tradition* (New York: Knopf, 1948).

Hudson, William E. *American Democracy in Peril*, 5th ed. (Washington, DC: CQ Press, 2006).

Issues for Debate in American Public Policy, 2nd ed. (Washington, DC: Congressional Quarterly, 2000).

Jacoby, Barbara, and Associates. *Service-Learning in*

Higher Education: Concepts and Practices (San Francisco: Jossey-Bass, 1996).

Jones, Charles O. *An Introduction to the Study of Public Policy*, 3rd ed. (Belmont, CA: Brooks/Cole, 1984).

Kammen, Michael, ed. *The Origins of the American Constitution: A Documentary History* (New York: Penguin, 1986).

Kemp, Roger L. *Forms of Local Government: A Handbook on City, County, and Regional Options* (Jefferson, NC: McFarland, 2007).

_____. *How American Governments Work: A Handbook of City, County, Regional, State, and Federal Operations* (Jefferson, NC: McFarland, 2002).

_____. *Local Government Election Practices: A Handbook for Public Officials and Citizens* (Jefferson, NC: McFarland, 2006).

_____. *Model Government Charters: A City, County, Regional, State, and Federal Handbook* (Jefferson, NC: McFarland, 2007).

Kendall, Jane C,. ed. *Combining Service and Learning: A Resource Book for Community and Public Service* (Raleigh, NC: National Society for Experiential Education, 1990).

Kingdon, John W. *Agendas, Alternatives, and Public Policies*, 2nd ed. (New York: Longman, 1995).

Levy, Leonard W., and Kenneth L. Karst, eds. *Encyclopedia of the American Constitution*, 2nd ed., 6 vols. (New York: Macmillan Reference USA, 2000).

Lipsky, Michael. *Street-Level Bureaucracy: Dilemmas of the Individual in Public Services* (New York: Russell Sage Foundation, 1997).

Loeb, Paul Rogat. *Soul of a Citizen: Living with Conviction in a Cynical Time* (New York: St. Martin's, 1999).

Magleby David B., and Paul C. Light. *State and Local Politics: Government by the People* (Upper Saddle River, NJ: Pearson Education, Inc., 2010).

Meier, Kenneth J., and John Bohte. *Politics and the Bureaucracy: Policy Making in the Fourth Branch of Government*, 5th ed. (Belmont, CA: Thomson Wadsworth, 2007).

Nock, Steven L., and Paul W. Kingston. *The Sociology of Public Issues* (Belmont, CA: Wadsworth, 1989).

Peltason, J.W. *Corwin and Peltason's Understanding the Constitution*, 8th ed. (New York: Holt, Rinehart, and Winston, 1979).

Putnam, Robert D. *Bowling Alone: The Collapse and Revival of American Community* (New York: Simon and Schuster, 2000).

Rakove, Jack. *Original Meanings: Politics and Ideas in the Making of the Constitution* (New York: Vintage, 1996).

Rosenberg, Nathan. *Exploring the Black Box: Technology, Economics and History* (Cambridge: Cambridge University Press, 1994).

Rosenthal, Alan. *The Decline of Representative Democracy: Process, Participation, and Power in State Legislatures* (Washington, DC: CQ Press, 1998).

Sabatier, Paul A., ed. *Theories of the Political Process* (Boulder, CO: Westview, 1999).

_____, and Hank C. Jenkins-Smith, eds. *Policy Change and Learning: An Advocacy Approach* (Boulder, CO: Westview, 1993).

Schattschneider, E. E. *The Semi-Sovereign People* (New York: Holt, Rinehart, and Winston, 1960).

Scher, Richard, Jon L. Mills, and John J. Hotaling. *Voting Rights and Democracy* (Chicago: Nelson-Hall, 1997).

Sherman, Arnold K., and Aliza Kolker. *The Social Bases of Politics* (Belmont, CA: Wadsworth, 1989).

Shi, Fengan. *The Real Thing: Contemporary Documents in American Government* (New York: St. Martin's, 1997).

Skocpol, Theda, and Morris P. Fiorina, eds. *Civic Engagement in American Democracy* (Washington, DC: Brookings Institute, 1999).

Tocqueville, Alexis de. *Democracy in America*, 2 vols. (New York: Vintage Books, 1945, 1956).

Tussman, Joseph. *Obligation and the Body Politic* (New York: Oxford University Press, 1960).

Verba, Sidney, Kay Lehman Schlozman, and Henry Brady. *Voice and Equality: Civic Voluntarism in American Politics* (Cambridge, MA: Harvard University Press, 1995).

Volgy, Thomas J. *Politics in the Trenches: Citizens, Politicians, and the Fate of Democracy* (Tucson: University of Arizona Press, 2001).

Woshinsky, Oliver H. *Culture and Politics: An Introduction to Mass and Elite Political Behavior* (Englewood Cliffs, NJ: Prentice-Hall, 1995).

Periodicals

American Journal of Political Science
Midwest Political Science Association
(http://www.ajps.org/)

American City & County
Penton Media, Inc.
(http://www.americancityandcounty.com/)

Civil Rights Journal
U.S. Commission on Civil Rights
(http://www.usccr.gov/pubs/crj/)

Comparative Politics
The City University of New York
(http://web.gc.cuny.edu/jcp/)

Congressional Digest
The Congressional Digest Corporation
(http://www.congressionaldigest.com/)

CQ Weekly
Congressional Quarterly Inc.
(http://www.cq.com/)

Federal Election Commission Record
Federal Election Commission
(http://purl.access.gpo.gov/)

Governing
Congressional Quarterly Inc.
(http://www.governing.com/)

In These Times
Institute for Public Affairs
(http://www.inthesetimes.com/)

Journal of Political Economy
University of Chicago Press
(http://www.journals.uchicago.edu/jpe/)

Journal of Politics
Southern Political Science Association
(http://www.unc.edu/depts/politics/)

National Review
National Review, Inc.
(http://www.nationalreview.com/)

Perspectives on Political Science
Heldref Publications
(http://www.heldref.org/)

Policy Studies Journal
John Wiley & Sons, Inc.
(http://www.wiley.com/WileyCDA/)

Political Behavior
Plenum Publishing Corporation
(http://www.uky.edu/Journals/PolBeh/)

Political Research Quarterly
University of Utah
(http://prq.sagepub.com/)

Political Science Quarterly
The Academy of Political Science
(http://www.psqonline.org/)

Political Theory
Sage Publications, Inc.
(http://www.sagepub.com/)

Politics
Political World Communications, LLC
(http://www.PoliticsMagazine.com/)

Polity
Northeastern Political Science Association
(http://www.palgrave-journals.com/polity/)

Public Administration Review
American Society for Public Administration
(http://www.aspanet.org/)

Public Management
International City/County Management Association
(http://www.icma.org/)

Public Opinion Quarterly
University of Chicago Press
(http://poq.oxford.journals.org/)

Spectrum: The Journal of State Government
The Council of State Governments
(http://www.csg.org/)

State & Local Government Review
University of Georgia
(http://www.cviog.uga.edu/)

State Magazine
U.S. State Department
(http://www.state.gov/)

The American Interest
The American Interest, LLC
(http://www.the-american-interest.com/)

The American Political Science Review
American Political Science Association
(http://www.apsanet.org/)

The Journal of Federalism
Center for the Study of State & Local Government
(http://www.lafayette.edu/publius/)

The Nation
The Nation Company, LP
(http://www.TheNation.com/)

The Next American City
The Next American City Inc.
(http://www.americancity.org/)

Review of Politics
The University of Notre Dame
(http://www.nd.edu/~rop/)

Index

www.ingramcontent.com/pod-product-compliance
Lightning Source LLC
Chambersburg PA
CBHW080552270326

41929CB00019B/3269